Advance praise for the new edition

"With this new edition of *Strike!* Jeremy Brecher has brought the story of U.S. labor up to date. From the Great Upheaval of 1877 to the Teamsters' UPS strike of 1997, here is the story of mass working-class action and organization. For a new generation that is once again discovering the power of organized workers and a class-based social movement, Brecher presents an important and critical perspective on the labor movement and U.S. history. For anyone who wants to get behind the headlines on the 'resurgence of U.S. labor,' *Strike!* is essential reading."

—Elaine Bernard, Executive Director,
Harvard University Trade Union Program

"For the past twenty-five years, anyone getting turned on to American labor history has turned first to *Strike!* This new anniversary edition, which adds an in-depth examination of recent events and experiences, guarantees that this book will be the first source consulted by the next generation of workers and students who seek out the 'hidden history' of the American working class."

—Peter Rachleff, author, *Hard-Pressed in the Heartland*

"*Strike!* manifests the real roots of workers' struggle—battles that moved from the streets of Minneapolis in 1934, to the mass confrontations of the 1960s against the Vietnam War, poverty, and racism, to the war zone of the 1990s in Decatur, Illinois. Jeremy Brecher's underlying message is powerful: workers will be exploited and reviled unless we challenge those who appoint themselves as our masters."

—Dan Lane, activist and locked-out Staley worker

"Jeremy Brecher's *Strike!* is one of the most important books on labor history published since World War II. It is a much-needed history of recent labor struggles. But what makes it indispensable is its point of view, its spirit, which is that of rank-and-file resistance to both corporate power and trade union bureaucracy. Its emphasis on worker-community solidarity, across all boundaries, is exactly what is needed in our time."

—Howard Zinn, author, *A People's History of the United States*

"*Strike!* is the single most important book about the history of the American labor movement published in our time. And now Jeremy Brecher has brought the history up to date—just in time to make a new generation ready for this new era of labor struggle."

—Dick Flacks, University of California, Santa Barbara

"Jeremy Brecher's *Strike!*, a labor and left-wing classic, has educated tens of thousands of readers over the decades and now comes back again—better than ever."

—Paul Buhle, co-editor, *Encyclopedia of the American Left*

"When *Strike!* first appeared in 1972, it provided a healthy antidote to the narcotic of standard labor history. Rather than merely being the victims or at times allegedly the beneficiaries of government or corporate largess, workers, as Brecher shows in exciting, exhilarating strokes, not only have the power to change the world for the betterment of all humanity, but at their best moments, are capable of doing so in democratic, participatory fashion."

—Michael Goldfield, author, *The Color of Politics*

"Jeremy Brecher views the past quarter-century as a time of retrenchment and disorganization between periods of mass strikes. In a new last chapter, he tells the stories of Pittston, Staley, and other prefigurative struggles. This chapter will serve future historians as a definitive introduction to the emerging era of wider solidarity and more militant tactics."

—Staughton Lynd, editor, *We Are All Leaders*

Praise for the first edition

"An exciting history of American labor."

—*The New York Times Book Review* New and Recommended list

"Splendid ... clearly the best single-volume summary yet published of American general strikes."

—*The Washington Post*

"Brecher, a gifted young radical historian ... offers a graphic history of industrial strikes ... His research is thorough, his presentation lucid and often absorbing ... draws its strength from a coherent view."

—*Publishers Weekly*

"An objective, minimally tendentious study of the American experience ... a bracing draft of history ... brings to life the flashpoints of labor history."

—Richard Lingeman, *The New York Times*

"A magnificent book. I hope it will take its place as the standard history of American labor."

—Staughton Lynd, labor historian

"The best book I have seen on American labor as a social movement. An important contribution to sociology as well as history. By focusing on mass actions of workers, Brecher sheds new light on the role of trade unions and radical organizations in the labor movement. Well-written, well-researched and well-argued. I highly recommend it as a text for courses on social movements, political sociology, and American society."

—William Kornhauser, University of California, Berkeley

"*Strike!* will undoubtedly be a controversial book ... The case materials are well-researched ... what is original and useful is their collection in a highly readable form and their integration with a theory of mass behavior ... should become the basis for further critical research."

—*Labor History*

"An excellent and exciting book."

—*Fusion*

"A really impressive piece of work which deserves the widest possible circulation. It offers simultaneously a readable and largely accurate account of many of the major strikes of American workers since 1877 [and] an extremely useful and well-researched account of today's rank and file struggles."

—David Montgomery, labor historian

"Scholarly, genuinely stirring."

—*The New York Times Book Review*

South End Press Classics

Manning Marable, Series Editor

South End Press is pleased to announce the inauguration of the South End Press Classics Series, edited by Manning Marable, Professor of History and Director of the Institute for Research in African-American Studies at Columbia University. The aim of this series is to make available in new editions works that have been instrumental in shaping political consciousness and activism in the United States and which retain contemporary relevance to the project of radical social, cultural, and political change.

Volume 1

Strike! Revised and Updated Edition
Jeremy Brecher

Forthcoming Titles in the South End Press Classics Series

Detroit: I Do Mind Dying, revised edition
Dan Georgakas and Marvin Surkin

How Capitalism Underdeveloped Black America, revised edition
Manning Marable

Strike!

Revised and Updated Edition

Jeremy Brecher

South End Press
Boston, MA

South End Press Classics, Volume I. Series editor: Manning Marable.

Cover photograph: A mass rally of more than 100,000 demonstrates for the right to strike in Detroit's Cadillac Square on March 23, 1937. Photo credit: Archives of Labor and Urban Affairs, Wayne State University.
Cover design by Beth Fortune

Grateful acknowledgement is made for permission to quote the following material: Louis Adamic, *My America*, Harper & Row Publishers, Inc; Henry Kraus, *The Many and the Few*, Plantin Press; Ruth McKenney, *Industrial Valley*, Curtis Brown Limited; E.A. Ross, "The Trade Union as a Wage-Fixing Institution," *American Economic Review*; Charles Rumford Walker, *The American City*, Holt, Rinehart, and Winston, Inc.; and Bill Watson, "Counter-Planning on the Shop Floor," *Radical America*.

Text design and production by South End Press. Printed in the U.S.A.

Library of Congress Cataloging-in-Publication Data

Brecher, Jeremy.
Strike! / Jeremy Brecher. — Rev. ed.
    p.   cm. — (South End Press Classics ; v. 1)
Includes bibliographical references and index.
ISBN 0-89608-570-8 (cloth). — ISBN 0-89608-569-4 (paper)
1. Strikes and lockouts—United States—History. I. Title.
II. Series

HD5324.B7 1997
331.892'973—dc21   97-33289
                                                    CIP

South End Press, 116 Saint Botolph Street, Boston, MA 02115-4818

05 04 03 02 01 00 99 98 97   1 2 3 4 5 6 7 8 9

Union printed.

Table of Contents

About the Author

Jeremy Brecher is an independent author, researcher, and screenwriter. He has received three Emmy Awards, the Edgar Dale Screenwriting Award, and the National Bar Association's Silver Gavel Award for his work as a documentary screenwriter. In addition to *Strike!*, Brecher's books include:

History from Below: How to Uncover and Tell the Story of Your Community, Association, or Union, revised edition (West Cornwall, Connecticut: Commonwork/Advocate Press, 1996). "Jeremy Brecher's work is astonishing and refreshing and, God knows, necessary. In this work lies the way to help cure our national amnesia."—Studs Terkel

Global Village or Global Pillage: Economic Reconstruction from the Bottom Up, with Tim Costello (Boston: South End Press, 1994). "Penetrating analysis ... crisp and simple language ... as penetrating as it is succinct. An effective antidote to the mood of resignation before the omnipotence of transnational business institutions which pervades the political discourse of our times ... timely and important."—David Montgomery, *The Nation*

Global Visions: Beyond the New World Order, edited with John Brown Childs and Jill Cutler (Boston: South End Press, 1993).

Building Bridges: The Emerging Grassroots Alliance of Labor and Community, edited with Tim Costello (New York: Monthly Review Press, 1990). "A splendid collection of essays ... one of the best practical how-to organizing manuals around ... massively inspiring." —Dana Frank, *The Nation*.

Brass Valley: The Story of Working People's Lives and Struggles in an American Industrial Region, with Jerry Lombardi and Jan Stackhouse (Philadelphia: Temple University Press, 1982). "The most comprehensive social history of a city or region in twentieth century America yet to appear ... a great achievement in using oral history to explore work and community life in twentieth-century America."—Gary Gerstle, in *Technology and Culture*. Selected for inclusion in the "UAW's Labor Bookshelf."

Common Sense for Hard Times, with Tim Costello, second edition (Boston and New York: South End Press, with Two Continents Publishing Group, 1977).

Root and Branch: The Rise of the Workers' Movements, edited with the Root and Branch collective (Greenwich, Connecticut: Fawcett, 1975).

Acknowledgments

Even so personal a project as writing a book is only made possible by the help of many other people. I would like to thank here those who have been of the most immediate help. Almost all have disagreed at one point or another; responsibility for errors of fact or interpretation remains completely my own.

Much of the initial work on this book was done at the Institute for Policy Studies in Washington, D.C. The Fellows, students, staff, and hangers-on of the Institute contributed much to my education in the years I was preparing to write *Strike!* It was Marcus Raskin there who gave me the necessary encouragement to stop talking and start writing.

The collaborators who produced the magazine *Root and Branch* contributed much individually and together to my understanding of the matters dealt with herein.

Edward M. Brecher not only made available an ideal place to prepare the manuscript, but gave me the benefit of his writing experience by painstakingly blue-penciling the first draft.

Sharon Hammer, printer and artist, skillfully prepared the final manuscript. She was also the first to appreciate the humor of the book.

A grant from the Louis M. Rabinowitz Foundation helped finance my research.

James H. Williams, Catherine Roraback, and Joel and Jeanne Stein lent me materials which otherwise would have been difficult to obtain.

A number of others were extremely generous with their time in reading and commenting on the manuscript before final revision of the first edition. I would like to thank especially Stanley Aronowitz, William Earl Brecher, Fred Gardner, Dorothy Lee, Staughton Lynd, Paul Mattick, Jr., David Montgomery, Alan Rinzler, Steve Sapolsky, and Arthur Waskow.

I would like to thank Elaine Bernard, Tim Costello, Jill Cutler, Richard Flacks, Dana Frank, Becky Glass, Fred Glass, Mike Goldfield, Paul Kumar, Dan Lane, Staughton Lynd, Jeff MacGregor, Peter Rachleff, Jerry Tucker, Joe Uehlein, and John Yrchik for their comments on an earlier draft of "American Labor on the Eve of the Millennium," the new concluding chapter prepared for the twenty-fifth anniversary edition. The chapter also reflects what I have learned from my twenty-year collaboration with Tim Costello. I am grateful to Jill Cutler, who helped edit the revised manuscript and read proofs. Anthony Arnove, my editor at South End Press, labored long and hard to transform *Strike!* into a book for today. I'd like to thank South End Press for keeping *Strike!* out there doing its work.

Introduction

This book is the story of repeated, massive, and sometimes violent revolts by ordinary working people in America. The story includes virtually nationwide general strikes, the seizure of vast industrial establishments, non-violent direct action on a massive scale, and armed battles with artillery and tanks. It encompasses the repeated repression of workers' rebellions by company-sponsored violence, local police, state militias, and the U.S. Army and National Guard. It reveals a dimension of American history rarely found in the usual high school or college history course, let alone in the way that history is presented in the media.

The United States is often presumed to be a land of individual freedom. That view often leads people to try to meet their needs by individual effort. But from time to time people come up against another reality. Most of our society's resources have long been controlled by a few.[1] The rest have no way to make a living but to sell their ability to work.[2] Most Americans are—by no choice of their own—workers. The basic experience of being a worker—of not having sufficient economic resources to live except by going to work for someone else—shapes most people's daily lives, as well as the life of our society.

As workers, people experience a denial of freedom that is very different from the touted liberty of American life. "Opportunity" is reduced to the opportunity to sell your time and creative capacities to one employer or another—or to fall into poverty if you don't. The "freedom to choose" is replaced by the freedom to do what you are told.

Meanwhile, the wealth created by the labor of the many is owned by a tiny minority, primarily in the form of giant corporations that dominate the national and now increasingly global economy.[3] They control the labor of millions of people in the United States and worldwide. The wealth and power of corporations and those who own them is further parlayed into power over the media, the political process, the institutions that shape knowledge and opinion, and ultimately over the government. Workers are thereby rendered relatively powerless, as individuals, even in supposedly democratic societies.

But individuals are not alone in this condition. They share it with their co-workers and with the great majority of other people who are also workers. At times, therefore, people to a greater or lesser extent come to see themselves as having interests in common with other working people and in conflict with their employers. Then they may turn to collective rather than individual strategies for solving their problems. This process can be seen repeatedly in the lives of individuals, the experience of social groups, the history of the United States, and indeed worldwide.

When workers begin to pursue collective strategies, they discover they have far greater power together than they have alone. They are the great majority in any workplace, community, or country. All the functions of their employer, indeed of society, depend on their labor. By withdrawing their labor and by refusing to cooperate with established authorities in other ways, they can bring any workplace, community, or even country to a halt.

The extent to which people realize and act on their common interests and power as workers waxes and wanes. At times workers' action has primarily taken the form of semi-clandestine resistance to authority in workplaces and communities, presenting a surface appearance of "labor peace." Sometimes it has taken the form of orderly participation in institutionalized, government-regulated systems of collective bargaining by trade union representatives. But sometimes their struggle has been publicly visible, violent, and dramatic.

Strike! is a history of those times—the times of peak conflict that it describes, borrowing a term from Rosa Luxemburg, as periods of "mass strike."[4] These periods show a great diversity of activities, including strikes, general strikes, occupations, mass demonstrations, and sometimes even armed confrontations. But they are all marked by three characteristics: an expanding challenge to established authority in workplaces and beyond; a tendency for workers to take control of their own activity; and a widening solidarity and mutual support among different groups of working people.

The main actors in the story are ordinary working people. What happens when people go to work, make a home, shop, and try to make a life may seem at first glance far removed from making history. But in trying to solve the problems of their daily lives, people sometimes find they must act in ways that challenge the existing order—and thereby make history.

"Ordinary" workers are often portrayed in the news media and even in history texts as a passive mass, controlled and directed by unions and labor leaders. But in periods of mass strike we find ordinary working people thinking, planning, drawing lessons from their own experience, organizing themselves, and taking action in common. They may use unions and other established organizations as their means to do so; but in many cases they have had to organize themselves and act outside established channels.

Indeed, one of the most remarkable aspects of this history is how frequently workers have found the unions and labor officials who claim to represent them thwarting their action instead. Far from fomenting strikes and rebellions, unions and labor leaders have frequently tried to prevent or contain them, while the drive to extend these struggles has often come from a most undocile rank and file. In part this is because unions—no less than churches, governments, and other organizations—often become bureaucracies with professionalized leaders whose experiences and material interests diverge from those they represent. But it is also because of the accommodation that corporations and government, faced with continuing worker resistance and rebellion, gradually reached with organized labor. This "class compromise" gave unions the legal right to represent and bargain on behalf of their members, but also made them responsible for strictly limiting the means their members could use and the objectives they could pursue. Unions have often opposed the will of their own members to forestall devastating counterattack by employers and government. *Strike!* reveals repeated instances of this continuing tension between union structures and rank-and-file union members.

Strike! was originally published in 1972. In some ways, the great mass strikes of the past are even more relevant today than when it was first published. For a quarter of a century, American workers have faced declining wages, growing economic insecurity, and worsening conditions on the job. The system of institutionalized collective bargaining that was established in national law and practice in the late 1930s and early 1940s is now hardly more than a remnant, covering barely 15 percent of the workforce. Government protections for working people are being dismantled day by day. Corporations and those who own them have grown wealthier and more powerful—not only on a national but increasingly on a global scale. While individualistic "free-market" ideology has become increasingly prevalent, working people are less and less able to solve their problems through individual strategies.

Worldwide, workers, indeed whole populations, have been turning to mass strikes and other kinds of direct action in response to pressures from global corporations and their political allies. Just in the two years before this edition of *Strike!* was published, there were general strikes and other mass labor struggles in Argentina, Belgium, Brazil, Canada, Colombia, Ecuador, France, Haiti, Italy, South Korea, and Spain, among others. Far from being a thing of the past, the mass strike is proving to be a significant feature of the era of globalization.

•

Today is not the first time that American workers have faced job degradation, inadequate pay, economic insecurity, and powerlessness in the workplace. Yet—despite the great increase in scholarly research on labor and other non-elite history—schools and media still teach us little about the history of workers and how they have dealt with such problems in the past. This neglect of ordinary people's history is itself part of history. Half a century ago, two labor leaders described "the iron curtain" drawn "between the people and their past": "The generals, the diplomats, and the politicos learned long ago that history is more than a record of the past; it is, as well, a source from which may be drawn a sense of strength and direction for the future. At all costs, that sense of strength and direction must be denied to the millions of men and women who labor for their living. Hence, the record of their past achievements is deliberately obscured in order to dull their aspirations for the future."[5] The purpose of this book is to help lift that iron curtain.

As working people begin to seek collective strategies, a knowledge of the past can be empowering. Consider the workers at the Pittston coal company who in 1989, like so many people in the past few years, were told they would have to accept cuts in their health care and pensions, give up work-rule protections on the job, allow their jobs to be subcontracted to non-union employers, abandon the eight-hour day, and work seven days a week—all to make their employer "internationally competitive." When they refused to work under these conditions and struck, they were met by the importation of strikebreakers, restrictive injunctions, squadrons of state police, hundreds of arrests, and astronomical fines. But among the leaders of the strike were notorious labor history buffs who were well aware of ways workers had coped with such attacks in the past. They mobilized massive support: 46,000 miners in ten states joined sympathy strikes and 30,000 people from all over the country—as well as international delegations—came to the strikers' "Camp Solidarity" to demonstrate their support. Strike organizers had studied the factory occupations of the 1930s. When miners occupied Pittston's key coal treatment plant, they dubbed their occupation "Operation Flintstone" after the great sit-down strike in Flint, Michigan, half a century before. Faced with such mobilized power, Pittston finally backed down and agreed to conditions acceptable to its workers.

Ultimately this book is about power. Many people feel powerless to affect what goes on in our society. The official channels through which they are supposed to be able to do so—elections, pressure groups, and the like—often appear useless. And yet ordinary people—together—have potentially the greatest power of all. It is their activity that makes up society. If they refuse to work, if they withdraw their cooperation, every social institution can be brought to a halt. By taking control of their own activity, they have the power to reshape society. That power is far different from the power we are familiar with in corporations and other institutions of authority. It is not the power of some people to tell others what to do. It is the power of people directing their own action cooperatively toward common purposes. It is that power we see rising in this book.

•

This twenty-fifth anniversary edition of *Strike!* preserves the original edition's core historical chapters on the main periods of mass strike with only modest revisions. A recast chapter introduces the little-known labor dimension of the Vietnam-era revolt. "The Significance of Mass Strikes" chapter has been trimmed and revised. Two dated chapters called "From Mass Strike to New Society" and "A Challenge to Historians" have been cut. A new chapter interprets the rank-and-file labor struggles of the past twenty-five years, in a "first draft" of the labor history of our era. I have also added a brief note on where to go "For Further Reading and Viewing."

The world has continued to change since this book was written, and, naturally, so have I. This edition is in a sense a collaboration between myself of twenty-five years ago and myself of today. As in any collaboration, each of us brings something to the party, but we don't always see everything in exactly the same way. This is not the book either of us would have written alone, but I hope I have preserved most of what was of value in the original while incorporating some of what I have learned since.

•

This updated edition of *Strike!* is intended to help people connect the realities they currently face with the history of workers in the United States. I hope it will provide those working to revive the labor movement today a new sense of their heritage. This book is dedicated to them.

Prologue

Visiting the United States in 1831, the French traveler Alexis de Tocqueville accepted as unsurprising the subordination of women, blacks, and Indians. But he was astonished not to find the extremes of rich and poor, aristocrat and peasant that were also taken for granted in Europe.

In the United States, the great majority of men were not landless peasants, but farmers working their own land, primarily for their own needs. Most of the rest were self-employed artisans, merchants, traders, and professionals. Other classes—wage earners and industrialists in the North, slaves and planters in the South—were relatively small. The great majority, de Tocqueville found, were independent and free from anybody's command.

Yet the forces that were to undermine this relative equality—and to produce the mass strikes that are the subject of this book—were already visible. De Tocqueville noted with concern "small aristocratic societies that are formed by some manufacturers in the midst of the immense democracy of our age."[1] Like the aristocratic societies of former ages, this one tended to divide Americans into classes made up of "some men who are very opulent and a multitude who are wretchedly poor,"[2] with few means of escaping their condition.

Further, de Tocqueville saw that production tended to become more and more centralized, for "when a workman is engaged every day upon the same details, the whole commodity is produced with greater ease, speed, and economy."[3] Thus, "the cost of production of manufactured goods is diminished by the extent of the establishment in which they are made and by the amount of capital employed."[4] The large, centralized companies naturally won out.

This process shaped both the worker and the employer. "When a workman is unceasingly and exclusively engaged in the fabrication of one thing, he ultimately does his work with singular dexterity; but at the same time he loses the general faculty of applying his mind to the direction of the work."[5] Thus, "in proportion as the workman improves, the man is degraded ... [H]e no longer belongs to himself, but to the calling that he has chosen."[6] But, de Tocqueville argued, while "the science of manufacture lowers the class of workmen, it raises the class of masters,"[7] until the employer more and more resembles the administrator of a vast empire.

De Tocqueville believed that "the manufacturing aristocracy which is growing up under our eyes is one of the harshest that ever existed in the world."[8] And he concluded that "if ever a permanent inequality of conditions and aristocracy again penetrates into the world, it may be predicted that this is the gate by which they will enter."[9]

Alexis de Tocqueville's dire predictions soon proved all too true. American industry grew at an incredible rate. In the fifty years following the start of the Civil War, investment in manufacturing grew twelve-fold. The distance covered by railroads grew from 30,000 miles to more than 200,000. By the turn of the century, more than three-fourths of manufactured products came from factories owned by corporations and other associations of stockholders. In 1860, only one-sixth of the American people lived in cities of 8,000 or more; by 1900 it was one-third. The number of wage-earners, meanwhile, grew from 1.5 million to 5.5 million. The United States became a full-fledged capitalist society with an economy driven by the pursuit of private profit in a virtually unregulated market.

Looking back on how these changes had affected workers during his lifetime, a labor leader wrote in 1889:

> With the introduction of machinery, large manufacturing establishments were erected in the cities and towns. Articles that were formerly made by hand, were turned out in large quantities by machinery; prices were lowered, and those who worked by hand found themselves competing with something that could withstand hunger and cold and not suffer in the least. The village blacksmith shop was abandoned, the road-side shoe shop was deserted, the tailor left his bench, and all together these mechanics [workers] turned away from their country homes and wended their way to the cities wherein the large factories had been erected. The gates were unlocked in the morning to allow them to enter, and after their daily task was done the gates were closed after them in the evening.

Silently and thoughtfully, these men went to their homes. They no longer carried the keys of the workshop, for workshop, tools and keys belonged not to them, but to their master. Thrown together in this way, in these large hives of industry, men became acquainted with each other, and frequently discussed the question of labor's rights and wrongs.[10]

Out of these experiences and discussions, many workers concluded that they were no longer free and equal citizens; more and more they felt like wage slaves, able to live only by working for someone else, left to walk the streets destitute when no employer would hire them. No longer possessing the keys to the workshop, they were left virtually helpless. Yet they possessed a weapon that gave them power—the strike. For without their labor, all the factories and offices, railroads and mines could produce nothing.

Strikes seem to have occurred ever since some people were forced to work for others. There are records of strikes by workers on the Great Pyramids of Egypt thousands of years ago. Strikes occurred in North America as early as 1636, but for the next two centuries they were rare, small, and local. Strikers and their organizations were often prosecuted as illegal conspirators.

Starting around 1800, workers gradually became an organized presence in American life. Workers in such trades as printing, shoemaking, and cabinetmaking began to organize craft unions in American cities. By the 1830s, many craft unions had held national conventions, local unions in many cities had formed central trades councils, and these city councils had held their first national convention. Workers also experimented with labor parties, producer and consumer co-ops, and even cooperative communities.

Yet until after the Civil War, the great majority of workers were self-employed. They might protest by voting, by demonstrating, by rioting, even from time to time by armed rebellion, but they could not strike.

Thus this book starts a dozen years after the Civil War, with the Great Upheaval of 1877—the first event in U.S. history to bring to the country's attention the vast new class of workers who possessed neither workshops nor farms, and thus had to work for those who did, the new class of industrial capitalists.

Railroads, factories, and farms grew at breakneck speed in the years following the Civil War. What had been largely a local and regional economy became a truly national one. The frontier moved steadily westward as one after another territory formerly possessed by Indians was opened to homesteaders and land speculators. The railroads bribed politicians and received land grants the size of whole countries. The attention of the nation turned away from politics and toward the astonishing advance of industry. It seemed a "Gilded Age," and the magnates who amassed great fortunes and vast enterprises were widely viewed as the conquering heroes of a new industrial civilization.

The government established the conditions for economic growth—from land grants for railroad corporations to high tariffs on imported products—but did little to cope with the consequences. Chaos resulted when industrialists used their control of the nation's resources to increase their own fortunes by any means necessary. The result was an unorganized, disorderly society. The social institutions that later would function to moderate social conflict, ease distress, and defuse discontent were virtually non-existent. Only those on whose backs the industrialists rode to power considered them not knights in shining armor but "robber barons."

Then the bubble burst. In September 1873, the leading American banking house, Jay Cooke and Company, suddenly declared bankruptcy. The stock market tumbled, and by the end of the month the stock exchange had closed its doors. In 1873 alone, 5,183 businesses worth over $200 million failed.

Depressions had been a regular feature of capitalist society since its start. But by 1877, the depression had lasted longer than any other in American history. For workers, conditions were quite desperate. Wages throughout industry had been cut more than 25 percent, below subsistence in many cases, while an estimated one million industrial workers were unemployed. Large numbers of the unemployed hit the road looking for work, often traveling in bands of what were referred to as "tramps."

The wealthier classes observed these conditions and trembled. Only six years before, the workers of Paris had arisen, taken over the city by armed force, and established the famous Paris Commune. Now it was not only Europe that was haunted by the "specter of communism." A Workingman's Party, dedicated to the overthrow of capitalism, had arisen in America as well. Meanwhile, sallow, sullen-faced men, women, and children walked the streets with little in their stomachs and hardly a place to lay their heads. An English visitor found wealthy Americans "pervaded by an uneasy feeling that they were living over a mine of social and industrial discontent with which the power of the government, under American institutions, was wholly inadequate to deal: and that some day this mine would explode and blow society into the air."[11]

That explosion came with the Great Upheaval of 1877.

Pittsburgh, July 22, 1877. The interior of the Pennsylvania Railroad upper roundhouse the day after a battle between strikers and the Philadelphia militia. The image is part of a series of stereographs taken by S.V. Albee, "The Railroad War." (Photo courtesy of the American Social History Project.)

Chapter 1

The Great Upheaval

In the centers of many American cities are positioned huge armories, grim nineteenth-century edifices of brick or stone. They are fortresses, complete with massive walls and loopholes for guns. You may have wondered why they are there, but it has probably never occurred to you that they were built to protect America not against invasion from abroad but against popular revolt at home. Their erection was a monument to the Great Upheaval of 1877.

July 1877 does not appear in many history books as a memorable date, yet it marks the first great American mass strike, a movement that was viewed at the time as a violent rebellion. Strikers seized and closed the nation's most important industry, the railroads, and crowds defeated or won over first the police, then the state militias, and in some cases even the federal troops. General strikes brought work to a standstill in a dozen major cities and strikers took over authority in communities across the nation.

It all began on Monday, July 16, 1877, in the little railroad town of Martinsburg, West Virginia. On that day, the Baltimore and Ohio Railroad cut wages 10 percent, the second cut in eight months.[1] Men gathered around the Martinsburg railroad yards, talking, waiting through the day. Toward evening the crew of a cattle train, fed up, abandoned the train, and other workers refused to replace them.

As a crowd gathered, the strikers uncoupled the engines, ran them into the roundhouse, and announced to B&O officials that no trains would leave Martinsburg until the pay cut was rescinded. The mayor arrived and conferred with railroad officials. He tried to soothe the crowd and was booed. When he ordered the arrest of the strike leaders they just laughed at him, backed up in their resistance by the angry crowd. The mayor's police were helpless against the population of the town. No railroad workers could be found willing to take out a train, so the police withdrew and by midnight the yard was occupied only by a guard of strikers left to enforce the blockade.[2]

That night, B&O officials in Wheeling went to see Governor Henry Matthews, took him to their company telegraph office, and waited while he wired Col. Charles Faulkner, Jr., at Martinsburg. Matthews instructed Faulkner to have his Berkeley Light Guards "prevent any interference by rioters with the men at work, and also prevent the ob-struction of the trains."[3]

The next morning, when the Martinsburg master of transportation ordered the cattle train out again, the strikers' guard swooped down on it and ordered the engineer to stop or be killed. He stopped. By now, hundreds of strikers and townspeople had gathered, and the next train out hardly moved before it was boarded, uncoupled, and run into the roundhouse.

About 9 a.m., the Berkeley Light Guards arrived to the sound of a fife and drum; the crowd cheered them. Most of the militiamen were themselves railroaders.[4] Now the cattle train came out once more, this time covered with militiamen, their rifles loaded with ball cartridges. As the train pulled through the yelling crowd, a striker named Wil-liam Vandergriff turned a switch to derail the train and guarded it with a pistol. A soldier jumped off the train to reset the switch. Van-dergriff shot him and in turn was fatally shot himself.[5]

At this, the attempt to break the blockade at Martinsburg was abandoned. The strikebreaking engineer and fireman climbed down from the engine and departed. Col. Faulkner called in vain for volun-teers to run the train, announced that the governor's orders had been fulfilled, dismissed his men, and telegraphed the governor that he was helpless to control the situation.

With this confrontation began the Great Upheaval of 1877, a spon-taneous, nationwide, virtually general strike. The pattern of Martinsburg—a railroad strike in response to a pay cut, an attempt by the companies to run trains with the support of military forces, and the defeat or dissolution of those forces by amassed crowds rep-resenting general popular support—became the pattern for the nation.

With news of success at Martinsburg, the strike spread to all divi-sions of the B&O, with engineers, brakemen, and conductors joining with the firemen who provided the initial impetus. Freight traffic was stopped all along the line, while the workers continued to run passenger and mail cars without interference. Seventy engines and six hundred freight cars were soon piled up in the Martinsburg yards.

Governor Matthews, resolved to break the strike, promised to send a company "in which there are no men unwilling to suppress the riots and execute the law."[6] He sent his only available military force, sixty Light Guards from Wheeling. But the Guards were hardly reliable, for the sentiment in Wheeling was strongly in favor of the strike.

The Guards marched out of town surrounded by an excited crowd, who, a reporter noted, "all expressed sympathy with the strikers."[7] Box-makers and can-makers in Wheeling were already on strike and soon people were discussing a general strike of all labor. When the Guards' train arrived in Martinsburg, it was met by a large, orderly crowd. The militia's commander conferred with railroad and town officials, but dared not use the troops, lest they "further exasperate the strikers."[8] Instead, he marched the Guards away to the courthouse.

At this point the strike was virtually won. But hardly had the strike broken out when the president of the B&O began pressing for the use of the U.S. Army against the strikers in West Virginia. "The loss of an hour would most seriously affect us and imperil vast interests," he wrote. With federal troops, "the rioters could be dispersed and there would be no difficulty in the movement of trains."[9] The railroad's vice-president wired his Washington agent, saying that the governor might soon call for federal troops, and instructing him "to see the Secretary of War and inform him of the serious situation of affairs, that he may be ready to send the necessary force to the scene of action at once."[10] Although a journalist on the scene at Martinsburg reported "perfect order,"[11] and other correspondents were unable to find violence to report, Col. Faulkner wired the governor:

> The feeling here is most intense, and the rioters are largely cooperated with by civilians.... The disaffection has become so general that no employee could now be found to run an engine even under certain protection. I am satisfied that Faulkner's experiment of yesterday was thorough and that any repetition of it today would pre-

cipitate a bloody conflict, with the odds largely against our small force.[12]

On the basis of this report, the governor in turn wired the president:

> To His Excellency, R.B. Hayes,
> President of the U.S.
> Washington, D.C.:
> Owing to unlawful combinations and domestic violence now existing at Martinsburg and at other points along the line of the Baltimore and Ohio Railroad, it is impossible with any force at my command to execute the laws of the State. I therefore call upon your Excellency for the assistance of the United States military to protect the law abiding people of the State against domestic violence, and to maintain supremacy of the law.[13]

The president of the B&O added his appeal, wiring the president that West Virginia had done all it could "to suppress this insurrection" and warning that "this great national highway [the B&O] can only be restored for public use by the interposition of U.S. forces."[14] In response, President Hayes sent 300 federal troops to suppress what his secretary of war was already referring to publicly as "an insurrection."[15]

This "insurrection" was spontaneous and unplanned, but it grew out of the social conditions of the time and the recent experience of railway workers. The tactics of the railroad strikers had been developed in a series of local strikes, mostly without trade union support, that occurred in 1873 and 1874. In December 1873, for example, engineers and firemen on the Pennsylvania Railroad system struck in Chicago, Pittsburgh, Cincinnati, Louisville, Columbus, Indianapolis, and various smaller towns, in what Ohio's *Portsmouth Tribune* called "the greatest railroad strike" in the nation's history.[16]

Huge crowds gathered in depot yards and supported the strikers against attempts to run the trains. State troops were sent into Dennison, Ohio, and Logansport, Indiana, to break strike strongholds.[17] At Susquehanna Depot, Pennsylvania, three months later, shop and repair workers struck. After electing a "Workingmen's Committee," they seized control of the repair shops; within twenty minutes the entire works was "under complete control of the men."[18] The strike was finally broken when 1,800 Philadelphia soldiers with thirty pieces of cannon established martial law in the town of 8,000.[19]

The railroad strikes of 1873 and 1874 were generally unsuccessful; but, as historian Herbert Gutman wrote, they "revealed the power of the railroad workers to disrupt traffic on many roads."[20] The employers learned that "they had a rather tenuous hold on the loyalties of their men. Something was radically wrong if workers could successfully stop trains for from two or three days to as much as a week, destroy property, and even 'manage' it as if it were their own."[21] And, Gutman continued, "the same essential patterns of behavior that were widespread in 1877 were found in the 1873-1874 strikes. Three and a half years of severe depression ignited a series of local brush fires into a national conflagration."[22]

The more immediate background of the 1877 railroad strike also helps explain why it took the form of virtual insurrection, for this struggle grew out of the failure of other, less violent forms of action. The wage cut on the B&O was part of a pattern initiated June 1 by the Pennsylvania Railroad. When the leaders of the Brotherhoods of Engineers, Conductors, and Firemen made no effort to combat the cut, railroad workers on the Pennsylvania system took action themselves. A week before the cut went into effect, the Newark, New Jersey, division of the Engineers held an angry protest meeting against the cut. The Jersey City lodge met the next day, voted for a strike, and contacted other workers; by the day the cut took effect, engineers' and firemen's locals throughout the Pennsylvania system had chosen delegates to a joint grievance committee, ignoring the leadership of their national unions.

The wage cut was not the workers' only concern; the committee proposed what amounted to a complete reorganization of work. They opposed the system of assigning trains in which the first crew into town was the first crew out, leaving them no time to rest or see their families; they wanted regular runs to stabilize pay and work schedules; they wanted passes home in case of long layovers; and they wanted the system of "classification" of workers by length of service and efficiency—used to keep wages down—abolished.[23]

But the grievance committee delegates were easily intimidated and cajoled by Tom Scott, the masterful ruler of the Pennsylvania Railroad, who talked them into accepting the cut without consulting those who elected them. A majority of brakemen, many conductors, and some engineers wanted to repudiate the committee's action; but, their unity broken, the locals decided not to strike.[24]

Since the railroad brotherhoods had clearly failed, the workers' next step was to create a new, secret organization, the Trainmen's Union. It was started by workers on the Pittsburgh, Fort Wayne and Chicago line. Within three weeks, lodges had sprung up from Baltimore to Chicago, with thousands of members on many different lines. The Trainmen's Union recognized that the privileged engineers "generally patched things up for themselves,"[25] so it included conductors, firemen, brakemen, switchmen, and others as well as engineers. The union also realized that the various railroad managements were cooperating against the workers, one railroad after another imitating the Pennsylvania with a 10 percent wage cut. The union's strategy was to organize at least three-quarters of the trainmen on each trunk line, then strike against the cuts and other grievances. When a strike came, firemen would not take engineers' jobs and workers on nonstriking roads would not handle struck equipment.[26]

But the union was full of spies. On one railroad the firing of members began only four days after the union was formed, and other railroads followed suit. "Determined to stamp it out," as one railroad official put it, the company issued orders to discharge all men belonging to "the Brotherhood or Union."[27] Nonetheless, on June 24 forty men fanned out over the railroads to call a general railroad strike for the following week. The railroads learned about the strike through their spies, fired the strike committee in a body, and thus panicked part of the leadership into spreading false word that the strike was off. Local lodges, unprepared to act on their own, flooded the union headquarters with telegrams asking what to do. Union officials were denied use of railroad telegraphs to reply, the companies ran their trains, and the strike failed utterly.[28]

Thus the Martinsburg strike broke out because the B&O workers had discovered that they had no alternative but to act on their own initiative. Not only were their wages being cut, but, as one newspaper reported, the men felt they were "treated just as the rolling stock or locomotives"—squeezed for every drop of profit. Reduced crews were forced to handle extra cars, with lowered pay classifications and no extra pay for overtime.[29]

A similar spontaneous strike developed that same day in Baltimore in response to the B&O wage cut, but the railroad had simply put strikebreakers on the trains and used local police to disperse the crowds of strikers.[30] What made Martinsburg different? The key to the strike, according to historian Robert Bruce, was that "a conventional strike would last only until strikebreakers could be summoned." To succeed, the strikers had to "beat off strikebreakers by force, seize trains, yards, roundhouses."[31] This was possible in Martinsburg because the people of the town so passionately supported the railroad workers that they collectively resisted the state militia. It was the support of workers elsewhere that would soon allow the strikers to resist the federal troops as well.

On July 19, four days into the strike, 300 federal troops arrived in Martinsburg to quell the "insurrection" and bivouacked in the roundhouse. With militiamen and U.S. soldiers guarding the yards, the company was able to move a few trains loaded with U.S. regulars through the town. When 100 armed strikers tried to stop a train, the sheriff and the militia marched to the scene and arrested the leader. No one in Martinsburg would take out another train, but with the military in control, strikebreakers from Baltimore were able to run freights unimpeded. The strike seemed broken.

But the population of the surrounding area also now rallied behind the railroad workers. Hundreds of unemployed and striking boatmen on the Chesapeake and Ohio Canal lay in ambush at Sir John's Run, where they stoned the freight train that had broken the Martinsburg blockade, forced it to stop, and then hid when the U.S. regulars attacked. The movement soon spread into Maryland, where a crowd of boatmen, railroaders, and others swarmed around the train at Cumberland and uncoupled the cars. When the train finally got away, a mob at Keyser, West Virginia, ran it onto a side track and took the crew off by force—while the U.S. troops stood by helplessly.[32] Just before midnight, the miners of the area met at Piedmont, four miles from Keyser, and resolved to go to Keyser in the morning and help stop trains. Coal miners and others—"a motley crowd, white and black"—halted a train guarded by fifty U.S. regulars after it pulled out of Martinsburg.[33] At Piedmont a handbill was printed warning the B&O that 15,000 miners, the united citizenry of local communities, and "the working classes of every state in the Union" would support the strikers. "Therefore let the clashing of arms be heard … in view of the rights and in the defense of our families we shall conquer, or we shall die."[34]

The result was that most of the trains sent west from Martinsburg never even reached Keyser. All but one, which was under heavy military escort, were stopped by a crowd of unemployed rolling-mill men, migrant workers, boatmen, and young boys at Cumberland, Maryland; on the one that went through, a trainman was wounded by a gunshot. When two leaders of the crowd were arrested, a great throng went to the mayor's house, demanded the release of the prisoners, and carried them off on their shoulders.

Faced with the spread of the strike through Maryland, the president of the B&O now persuaded Governor John Carroll of Maryland to call up the National Guard in Baltimore and send it to Cumberland. They did not expect, however, the reaction of Baltimore to the strike. "The working people everywhere are with us," said a leader of the railroad strikers in Baltimore. "They know what it is to bring up a family on ninety cents a day, to live on beans and corn meal week in and week out, to run in debt at the stores until you cannot get trusted any longer, to see the wife breaking down under privation and distress, and the children growing up sharp and fierce like wolves day after day because they don't get enough to eat."[35]

The bells rang in Baltimore for the militia to assemble just as the factories were letting out for the evening, and a vast crowd assembled as well. At first they cheered the troops, but then severely stoned them as they started to march. The crowd was described as "a rough element eager for disturbance; a proportion of mechanics [workers] either out of work or upon inadequate pay, whose sullen hearts rankled; and muttering and murmuring gangs of boys, almost outlaws, and ripe for any sort of disturbance."[36] As the 250 men of the first regiment marched out, 25 of them were injured by the stoning of the crowd, but this was only a love-tap. The second regiment was unable even to leave its own armory for a time. Then, when the order was given to march anyway, the crowd stoned them so severely that the troops panicked and opened fire. In the bloody march that followed, the militia killed ten and seriously wounded more than twenty of the crowd, but the crowd continued to resist, and one by one the troops dropped out, went home, and changed into civilian clothing. By the time they reached the Baltimore train station, only 59 of the original 120 men remained in line.[37] Even after they reached the depot, the remaining troops were unable to leave for Cumberland, for a crowd of about 200 drove away the engineer and firemen of the waiting train and beat back a squad of policemen who tried to restore control.

The militia charged the growing crowd, but were driven back by brickbats and pistol fire. It was at that stage that Governor Carroll, himself bottled up in the depot by the crowd of 15,000, desperately wired President Hayes to send the U.S. Army.

•

Like the railroad workers, others joined the "insurrection" out of frustration with other means of struggle. Over the previous years they had experimented with one means of resistance after another, each more radical than the last.

The first to prove their failure had been the trade unions. Craft unions had grown rapidly during and after the Civil War and had organized nationally. The number of national unions grew from six in 1864 to about thirty-three in 1870, enrolling perhaps 5 percent of nonfarm workers. Railroad workers formed the Brotherhoods of Locomotive Engineers, Railway Conductors, and Firemen. But the depression devastated the unions. By 1877 only about nine of these unions survived. Total membership plummeted from 300,000 in 1870 to 50,000 in 1876.[38]

Under depression conditions, the unions were simply unable to withstand the organized attack levied by lockouts and blacklisting. Unemployment demonstrations in New York had been ruthlessly broken up by police. Then the first major industrial union in the

United States, the Workingmen's Benevolent Association of the anthracite miners, led a strike that was finally broken by the companies, one of which claimed the conflict had cost it $4 million. Next the Molly Maguires—a secret organization Irish miners developed to fight the coal operators through terrorist methods—were infiltrated and destroyed by agents from the Pinkerton Detective Agency, which specialized in providing spies, agents provocateurs, and private armed forces for employers combating labor organizations.[39] Thus, by the summer of 1877 it had become clear that no single group of workers—whether through peaceful demonstration, tightly-knit trade unions, armed terrorism, or surprise strikes—could stand against the power of the companies, their armed guards, the Pinkertons, and the armed forces of the government.

Indeed, the Great Upheaval had been preceded by a seeming quiescence on the part of workers. The general manager of one railroad wrote on June 21: "The experiment of reducing the salaries has been successfully carried out by all the Roads that have tried it of late, and I have no fear of any trouble with our employees if it is done with a proper show of firmness on our part and they see that they must accept it cheerfully or leave."[40] The very day the strike was breaking out at Martinsburg, Governor John Hartranft of Pennsylvania was agreeing with his adjutant general that the state was enjoying a calm it had not known for several years.[41] In less than a week, it would be the center of the insurrection.

Three days after Governor Hartranft's assessment, the Pennsylvania Railroad ordered that all freights eastward from Pittsburgh be run as "double-headers"—with two engines and twice as many cars. This meant in effect a speed-up—more work and increased danger of accidents and layoffs. Pennsylvania trainmen were sitting in the Pittsburgh roundhouse listening to a fireman read them news of the strike elsewhere when the order came to take out a "double-header." At the last minute a flagman named Augustus Harris, acting on his own initiative, refused to obey the order. The conductor appealed to the rest of the crew, but they too said no. When the company sent for replacements, twenty-five brakemen and conductors refused to take out the train and were fired on the spot. When the dispatcher finally found three yard brakemen to take out the train, a crowd of twenty angry strikers would not let the train go through. One of them threw a link at a strikebreaker, whereupon the volunteer yardmen gave up and went away. Said flagman Andrew Hice, "It's a question of bread or blood, and we're going to resist."[42]

Freight crews joined the strike as their trains came in and were stopped, and a crowd of mill workers, tramps, and boys began to gather at the crossings, preventing freight trains from running while letting passenger trains go through. The company asked the mayor for police, but since the city was nearly bankrupt the force had been cut in half, and only eight men were available. Further, the mayor had been elected by the strong working-class vote of the city, and shared with the city's upper crust a hatred for the Pennsylvania Railroad and its rate discrimination against Pittsburgh. The railroad was given no more than seventeen police, whom it had to pay itself.[43]

As elsewhere, the Trainmen's Union had nothing to do with the start of the strike. Its top leader, Robert Ammon, had left Pittsburgh to take a job elsewhere, and the president of the Pittsburgh Division didn't even know that trouble was at hand; he slept late that morning, didn't hear about the strike until nearly noon—his first comment was "Impossible!"—and then busied himself persuading his colleagues to go home and keep out of trouble.[44]

The Trainmen's Union did, however, provide a nucleus for a meeting of the strikers and representatives of such groups as the rolling-mill workers. "We're with you," said one rolling-mill man, pledging the railroaders support from the rest of Pittsburgh labor. "We're in the same boat. I heard a reduction of ten percent hinted at in our mill this morning. I won't call employers despots, I won't call them tyrants, but the term capitalists is sort of synonymous and will do as well."[45] The meeting called on "all workingmen to make common cause with their brethren on the railroad."[46]

In Pittsburgh, railroad officials picked up the ailing sheriff, waited while he gave the crowd a *pro forma* order to disperse, and then persuaded him to appeal for state troops. That night state officials ordered the militia to be called up in Pittsburgh, but only some of the troops arrived. Some were held up by the strikers, while others simply failed to show up. Two-thirds of one regiment made it; in another regiment not one man appeared.[47] Nor were the troops reliable. As one officer reported to his superior, "You can place little dependence on the troops of your division; some have thrown down their arms, and others have left, and I fear the situation very much."[48]

Another officer explained why the troops were unreliable.

Meeting an enemy on the field of battle, you go there to kill. The more you kill, and the quicker you do it, the better. But here you had men with fathers and brothers and relatives mingled in the crowd of rioters. The sympathy of the people, the sympathy of the troops, my own sympathy, was with the strikers proper. We all felt that those men were not receiving enough wages.[49]

Indeed, by Saturday morning the militiamen had stacked their arms and were chatting with the crowd, eating hardtack with them, and walking up and down the streets with them, behaving, as a regular army lieutenant put it, "as though they were going to have a party."[50] "You may be called upon to clear the tracks down there," said a lawyer to a soldier. "They may call on me," the soldier replied, "and they may call pretty damn loud before they will clear the tracks."[51]

The Pittsburgh Leader came out with an editorial warning of "The Talk of the Desperate" and purporting to quote a "representative workingman":

This may be the beginning of a great civil war in this country, between labor and capital. It only needs that the strikers ... should boldly attack and rout the troops sent to quell them—and they could easily do it if they tried.... The workingmen everywhere would all join and help ... The laboring people, who mostly constitute the militia, will not take up arms to put down their brethren. Will capital, then, rely on the United States Army? Pshaw! These ten or fifteen thousand available men would be swept from our path like leaves in the whirlwind. The workingmen of this country can capture and hold it if they will only stick together.... Even if so-called law and order should beat them down in blood ... we would, at least, have our revenge on the men who have coined our sweat and muscles into millions for themselves, while they think dip is good enough butter for us.[52]

All day Friday, the crowds controlled the switches, and the officer commanding the Pittsburgh militia refused to clear the crossing with artillery because of the slaughter that would result. People swarmed aboard passenger trains and rode through the city free of charge.[53] The sheriff warned the women and children to leave lest they be hurt when the army came, but the women replied that they were there to urge the men on. "Why are you acting this way, and why is this crowd here?" the sheriff asked one young man who had come to Pittsburgh from Eastern Pennsylvania for the strike. "The Pennsylvania [Road] has two ends," he replied, "one in Philadelphia and one in Pittsburgh. In Philadelphia they have a strong police force, and they're with the railroad. But in Pittsburgh they have a weak force, and it's a mining and manufacturing district, and we can get all the help we want from the laboring elements, and we've determined to make the strike here."

"Are you a railroader?" the sheriff asked.

"No, I'm a laboring man," he replied.[54]

Railroad and National Guard officials, realizing that the local Pittsburgh militia units were completely unreliable, sent for 600 fresh troops from its commercial rival, Philadelphia. A Pittsburgh steel manufacturer came to warn railroad officials not to send the troops out until workingmen were back in their factories. "I think I know the temper of our men pretty well, and you would be wise not to do anything until Monday.... If there's going to be firing, you ought to have at least ten thousand men, and I doubt if even that many could quell the mob that would be brought down on us."[55]

These words were prophetic. But, remembering the 2,000 freight cars and locomotives lying idle in the yards, and the still effective blockade, the railroad official replied, "We must have our property." He looked at his watch and said, "We have now lost an hour and a half's time." He had confidently predicted that "the Philadelphia regiment won't fire over the heads of the mob."[56] Now the massacre he counted on—and the city's retaliation—was at hand.

As the imported troops marched toward the 28th Street railroad crossing, a crowd of 6,000 gathered, mostly spectators. The troops began clearing the tracks with fixed bayonets and the crowd replied with a furious barrage of stones, bricks, coal, and possibly revolver fire. Without orders, the Philadelphia militia began firing as fast as it could, killing twenty people in five minutes as the crowd scattered.[57] Meanwhile, the local Pittsburgh militia members stood on the hillside and ran for cover when they saw the Philadelphia regiment's Gatling gun come forward. Soon most militia members went home or joined the mob.[58]

With the crossing cleared, the railroad fired up a dozen double-headers, but even trainmen who had previously declined to join the strike now refused to run the trains, and the strike remained unbroken. Their efforts in vain, the remaining members of the Philadelphia militia retired to the roundhouse.

Meanwhile, the entire city mobilized in a fury against the troops who had conducted the massacre and against the Pennsylvania Railroad. Workers rushed home from their factories for pistols, muskets, and butcher knives. A delegation of 600 workingmen from nearby Temperanceville marched in with a full band and colors. In some cases the crowd organized itself into crude armed military units, marching together with drums. Civil authority collapsed in the face of the crowd; the mayor refused to send police or even to try to quiet the crowd himself.

The crowd peppered the troops in the roundhouse with pistol and musket fire, but finally decided, as one member put it, "We'll have them out if we have to roast them out."[59] Oil, coke, and whiskey cars were set alight and pushed downhill toward the roundhouse. A few men began systematically to burn the yards, despite rifle fire from the soldiers, while the crowd held off fire trucks at gunpoint. The roundhouse caught fire and the Philadelphia militia was forced to evacuate. As it marched along the street it was peppered with fire by the crowd and, according to the troops' own testimony, by Pittsburgh policemen as well.[60] Most of the troops were marched out of town and found refuge a dozen miles away. The few left to guard ammunition found civilian clothes, sneaked away, and hid until the crisis was over. By Saturday night, the last remaining regiment of the Pittsburgh militia was disbanded. The crowd had completely routed the army.

On Sunday morning, hundreds of people broke into the freight cars in the yards and distributed goods they contained to the crowds below—on occasion with assistance from police. Burning of cars continued. (According to first U.S. Commissioner of Labor Carroll D. Wright, "A great many old freight cars which must soon have been replaced by new, were pushed into the fire by agents of the railroad company," to be added to the damages they hoped to collect from Allegheny County.[61]) The crowd prevented firemen from saving a grain elevator, though it was not owned by the railroad, saying, "It's a monopoly, and we're tired of it,"[62] but workers pitched in to prevent the spread of the fire to nearby tenements.[63] By Monday, 104 locomotives, more than 2,000 cars, and all of the railroad buildings had been destroyed.

Across the river from Pittsburgh, in the railroad town of Allegheny, a remarkable transfer of authority took place. Using the pretext that the governor was out of the state, the strikers maintained that the state militia was without legal authority, and therefore proposed to treat them as no more than a mob. According to the mayor, the strikers armed themselves by breaking into the local armory, dug rifle pits and trenches outside the Allegheny depot, set up patrols, and warned civilians away from the probable line of fire. The strikers took possession of the telegraph and sent messages up and down the railway. They took over management of the railroad, running passenger trains smoothly, moving the freight cars out of the yards, and posting regular armed guards to watch over them. Economic management and political power had in effect been taken over by the strikers. Of course, this kind of transfer of power was not universally understood or supported, even by those who approved of the strike. For example, a meeting of rolling-mill workers in Columbus, Ohio, endorsed the railroad strikers, urged labor to combine politically and legislate justice, but rejected "mobbism" as apt to destroy "the best form of republican government."[64]

The strike spread almost as fast as word of it, and with it came conflict with the military. In the Pennsylvania towns of Columbia, Meadville, and Chenago, strikers seized the railroads, occupied the roundhouses, and stopped troop trains. In Buffalo, New York, the militia was stoned on Sunday but scattered the crowd by threatening to shoot. The next morning a crowd armed with knives and cudgels stormed into the railroad shops, brushed aside militia guards, and forced shopmen to quit work. They seized the Erie roundhouse and barricaded it. When a militia company marched out to recapture the property, a thousand people blocked it and drove it back. By Monday evening, all the major railroads had given up trying to move anything but local passenger trains out of Buffalo.

Court testimony later gave a good picture of how the strike spread to Reading, Pennsylvania. At a meeting of workers on the Reading Railroad, the chairman suggested that it would not be a bad idea to do what had been done on the B&O. "While it is hot we can keep the ball rolling," someone chimed in. After some discussion, men volunteered to head off incoming trains.[65]

The next day a crowd of 2,000 assembled while twenty-five or fifty men, their faces blackened with coal dust, tore up track, fired trains, and burned a railroad bridge. That evening seven companies of the National Guard arrived. As they marched through a tenement district to clear the tracks, the people of the neighborhood severely stoned them, wounding twenty with brickbats and pistol shots. The soldiers opened fire without orders and killed eleven.[66]

As in Pittsburgh, the population grew furious over the killings. They plundered freight cars, tore up tracks, and broke into an arsenal, taking sixty rifles. The next day the National Guard companies that had conducted the massacre marched down the track together with newly arrived troops; the crowd stoned the former and fraternized with the latter. When the Guard that had conducted the massacre turned menacingly toward the crowd, the new troops announced that they would not fire on the people, turned some of their ammunition over to the crowd, and proclaimed, "If you fire at the mob, we'll fire at you."[67]

Such fraternization between troops and the crowd was common. When the governor sent 170 troops to Newark, Ohio, they were so unpopular that the county commissioners refused to provide their rations. The strikers themselves then volunteered to feed them. By the end of the day, strikers and soldiers were socializing in high good humor. Similarly, when the governor of New York sent 600 troops to the railroad center of Hornellsville in response to the strike on the Erie, the troops and strikers fraternized, making commanders doubtful of their power to act. When the entire Pennsylvania National Guard was called up in response to the Pittsburgh uprising, a company in Lebanon, Pennsylvania, mutinied and marched through town amid great excitement. In Altoona, a crowd captured a westbound train carrying 500 militiamen. The troops gave up their arms with the best of will and fraternized with the crowd. The crowd refused to let them proceed but was glad to let them go home—which one full company and parts of the others proceeded to do. A Philadelphia militia unit straggling home decided to march to Harrisburg and surrender. They entered jovially, shook hands all around, and gave up their guns to the crowd.

Persuasion worked similarly with would-be strikebreakers. When a volunteer started to take a freight train out of Newark, Ohio, a striking fireman held up his hand, three fingers of which had been cut off by a railroad accident. "This is the man whose place you are taking," shouted another striker. "This is the man who works with a hand and a half to earn a dollar and a half a day, three days in the week, for his wife and children. Are you going to take the bread out of his mouth and theirs?"[68] The strikebreaker jumped down amid cheers.

By now, the movement was no longer simply a railroad strike. With the battles between soldiers and crowds drawn from all sectors of the working population, it was increasingly perceived as a struggle between workers as a whole and employers as a whole. This was now reflected in the rapid development of general strikes. After the burning of the railroad yards in Pittsburgh, a general strike movement swept through the area. At nearby McKeesport, workers of the National Tube Works gathered and marched all over town to martial music, calling fellow workers from their houses. From the tube works the strike spread first to a rolling mill, then a car works, and then a planing mill. In mid-morning, 1,000 McKeesport strikers marched with a brass band to Andrew Carnegie's great steel works, calling out planing-mill and tin-mill workers as they went. By mid-afternoon, the Carnegie workers and the Braddocks car workers joined the strike. At

Castle Shannon, 500 miners struck. On the South Side, laborers struck at Jones and Laughlin and at the Evans, Dalzell and Co. pipe works.[69]

In Buffalo, New York, crowds roamed the city trying to bring about a general strike. They effectively stopped operations at planing mills, tanneries, car works, a bolt and nut factory, hog yards, coal yards, and canal works. In Harrisburg, Pennsylvania, factories and shops throughout the city were closed by strikes and crowd action. In Zanesville, Ohio, 300 unemployed men halted construction on a hotel, then moved through town shutting down nearly every factory and foundry and sending horse-cars to the barns. The next morning a meeting of workingmen drew up a schedule of acceptable wages. In Columbus, a crowd growing from 300 to 2,000 went through town inciting a general strike, successfully calling out workers at a rolling mill, pipe works, fire clay works, pot works, and a planing mill. "Shut up or burn up" was the crowd's slogan.[70] An offshoot of a rally to support the railroad workers in Toledo, Ohio, resolved to call a general strike for a minimum wage of $1.50 a day. The next morning a large crowd of laborers, grain trimmers, stevedores, and others assembled and created a committee of safety composed of one member from every trade represented in the movement. Three hundred men formed a procession four abreast while a committee called on the management of each factory; workers of those not meeting the committee's demands joined in the strike.

In San Francisco, 7,000 attended a rally called by the Workingmen's Party, a national organization that had been formed the year before by predominantly immigrant followers of Karl Marx and Ferdinand Lassalle. The speakers demanded the eight-hour day and government operation of the struck railroads. But the movement soon was swamped by burgeoning hostility to the 50,000 Chinese workers who had been brought to California to build the railroads, many of whom had then been abandoned by the railroad companies and were finding their way into other occupations. At the Workingmen's Party rally someone in the crowd proposed the appointment of a committee to demand the discharge of Chinese workers from the Central Pacific, but the chair refused to entertain the motion. The rally ended peacefully, but in its wake gangs began attacking Chinese laundries and residences. Several nights of anti-Chinese rioting were finally brought to an end by police and a Committee of Safety.

In Chicago, the Workingmen's Party called a series of mass rallies. At the same time, forty switchmen struck on the Michigan Central Railroad. The switchmen roamed through the railroad property with a crowd of 500 others, including strikers from the East who had ridden in to spread the strike, calling out other workers and closing down those railroads that were still running. Next the crowd called out the workers at the stockyards and several packinghouses. Smaller crowds spread out to broaden the strike; one group, for example, called out 500 planing-mill workers, and with them marched down Canal Street and Blue Island Avenue closing down factories. Crews on several lake vessels struck. With transportation dead, the North Chicago rolling mill and many other industries closed for lack of coke and other supplies.

The next day the strike spread still further: streetcars, wagons, and buggies were stopped; tanneries, stoneworks, clothing factories, lumberyards, brickyards, furniture factories, and a large distillery were closed in response to roving crowds. A day later the crowds forced officials at the stockyards and gasworks to sign promises to raise wages to $2 a day, while more dock and lumberyard workers struck.[71] In the midst of this burgeoning activity, the Workingmen's Party proclaimed: "Fellow Workers ... Under any circumstances keep quiet until we have given the present crisis a due consideration."[72]

•

The general strikes spread even into the South, often starting with black workers and spreading to whites. Texas and Pacific Railroad workers at Marshall, Texas, struck against the 10 percent pay cut. In response, black longshoremen in nearby Galveston struck for and won pay equal to that of their white fellow workers. Fifty black workers marched down the Strand in Galveston, persuading construction men, track layers, and others to strike for $2 a day. The next day committees circulated around town supporting the strike. White workers joined in. The movement was victorious, and $2 a day became the standard wage in Galveston. In Louisville, Kentucky, black workers made the round of sewers under construction, urging a strike for $1.50 a day. By noon, sewer workers had quit everywhere in town. On Tuesday night a group of 500 stoned the depot of the Louisville and Nashville Railroad, which was refusing a wage increase for laborers. By Wednesday, most of Louisville's factories were shut down by roving crowds, and Thursday brought further strikes by coopers, textile workers, plow factory workers, brick makers, and cabinet workers.

The day the railroad strike reached East St. Louis, the St. Louis Workingmen's Party marched 500 strong across the river to join a meeting of 1,000 railroad workers and residents. Said one of the speakers: "All you have to do, gentlemen, for you have the numbers, is to unite on one idea—that the workingmen shall rule the country. What man makes, belongs to him, and the workingmen made this country."[73] The St. Louis General Strike, the peak of the Great Upheaval, for a time nearly realized that goal.

The railroad workers at that meeting voted for a strike, set up a committee of one man from each railroad, and occupied the Relay Depot as their headquarters. The committee promptly posted General Order No. 1, forbidding freight trains from leaving any yard.

That night, across the river in St. Louis, the Workingmen's Party called a mass meeting, with crowds so large that three separate speakers' stands were set up simultaneously. "The workingmen," said one speaker, "intend now to assert their rights, even if the result is shedding of blood.... They are ready to take up arms at any moment."[74]

The next morning, workers from different shops and plants began to appear at the party headquarters, requesting that committees be sent around to "notify them to stop work and join the other workingmen, that they might have a reason for doing so."[75] The party began to send such committees around, with unexpected results. The coopers struck, marching from shop to shop with a fife and drum shouting, "Come out, come out! No barrels less than nine cents."[76] Newsboys, gasworkers, boatmen, and engineers struck as well. Railroadmen arrived from East St. Louis on engines and flatcars they had commandeered, moving through the yards enforcing General Order No. 1 and closing a wire works.

That day, an "executive committee" formed, based at the Workingmen's Party headquarters, to coordinate the strike. As one historian wrote, "Nobody ever knew who that executive committee really was; it seems to have been a rather loose body composed of whomsoever chanced to come in and take part in its deliberations."[77]

In the evening, 1,500 men, mostly molders and mechanics, armed themselves with lathes and clubs and marched to the evening's rally. To the crowd of 10,000 the first speaker, a cooper, began, "There was a time in the history of France when the poor found themselves oppressed to such an extent that forbearance ceased to be a virtue, and hundreds of heads tumbled into the basket. That time may have arrived with us."[78] Another speaker called on the workingmen to organize into companies of ten, twenty, and a hundred, to establish patrols to protect property, and to "organize force to meet force." Someone suggested that "the colored men should have a chance." A black steamboatman spoke for the roustabouts and levee workers. He asked the crowd if they would stand behind the levee strikers, regardless of color. "We will!" the crowd shouted back.[79]

The general strike got under way in earnest the next morning. The employees of a beef cannery struck and paraded. The coopers met and discussed their objectives. A force of strikers marched to the levee, where a crowd of steamboatmen and roustabouts "of all colors" forced the captains of boat after boat to sign written promises of 50 percent higher pay.[80] Finally everyone assembled for the day's great march. Six hundred factory workers marched behind a brass band; a company of railroad strikers came with coupling pins, brake rods, red signal flags, and other "irons and implements emblematic of their calling."[81] Strikers' committees went out ahead to call out those still working, and as the march came by, with a loaf of bread on a flag-staff as its emblem, workers in foundries, bagging companies, flour mills, bakeries, chemical, zinc, and white lead works poured out of their shops and into the crowd. In Carondolet, far on the south side of the city, a similar march developed autonomously, as a crowd of iron workers closed down two zinc works, the Bessemer Steel Works, and other plants. In East St. Louis there was a parade of women in support of the strike. By sundown, nearly all the manufacturing establishments in the city had been closed. "Business is fairly paralyzed here," said *The Daily Market Reporter*.[82]

But economic activities did not cease completely; some continued under the control or by permission of the strikers. The British Consul in St. Louis noted how the railroad strikers had "taken the road into their own hands, running the trains and collecting fares"; he added, "It is to be deplored that a large portion of the general public appear to regard such conduct as a legitimate mode of warfare."[83] It was now the railroad managers who wanted to stop all traffic. One official stated frankly that by stopping all passenger trains, the companies would cut the strikers off from mail facilities and prevent them from sending committees from one point to another along the lines.[84] Railroad officials, according to *The St. Louis Times*, saw advantage in stopping passenger trains and thus "incommoding the public so as to produce a revolution in the sentiment which now seems to be in favor of the strikers."[85] From the strikers' point of view, running nonfreights allowed them to coordinate the strike and show their social responsibility.

The strikers had apparently decided to allow the manufacture of bread, for they permitted a flour mill to remain open. When the owner of the Belcher Sugar Refinery applied to the executive committee for permission to operate his plant for forty-eight hours, lest a large quantity of sugar spoil, the committee persuaded the refinery workers to go back to work and sent a guard of 200 men to protect the plant. According to one historian of the strike, "The Belcher episode revealed ... the spectacle of the owner of one of the city's largest industrial enterprises recognizing the *de facto* authority of the Executive Committee."[86]

But the strikers in St. Louis and elsewhere failed to hold what they had conquered. Having shattered the authority of the status quo for a few short days, they faltered and fell back, unsure of what to do. Meanwhile, the forces of law and order—no longer cowering in the face of overwhelming mass force—began to organize. Chicago was typical: President Hayes authorized the use of federal regulars; citizens' patrols were organized ward by ward, using Civil War veterans; 5,000 special police were sworn in, freeing the regular police for action; big employers organized their reliable employees into armed companies, many of which were sworn in as special police. At first the crowd successfully outmaneuvered the police in the street fighting that ensued, but after killing at least eighteen people the police finally gained control of the crowd and thus broke the back of the movement.[87]

Behind them stood the federal government. "This insurrection," said General Winfield Hancock, the commander in charge of all federal troops used in the strike, must be stifled "by all possible means."[88] Not that the federal troops were strong and reliable. The Army was largely tied down by the rebellion of Nez Perce Indians, led by Chief Joseph. In the words of Lieutenant Philip Sheridan, "The troubles on the Rio Grande border, the Indian outbreak on the western frontier of New Mexico, and the Indian war in the Departments of the Platte and Dakota, have kept the small and inadequate forces in this division in a constant state of activity, almost without rest, night and day."[89] Most of the enlisted men had not been paid for months, because Congress had refused to pass the Army Appropriations Bill to force the withdrawal of Reconstruction troops from the South. Finally, the Army included many workers driven into military service by unemployment. As one union iron molder in the Army wrote, "It does not follow that a change of dress involves a change of principle."[90] No mutinies occurred, however, as the 3,000 available federal troops were rushed under direction of the War Department from city to city, wherever the movement seemed to grow out of control. "The strikers," President Hayes noted emphatically in his diary, "have been put down by *force*."[91] More than 100 of them were killed in the process.

•

The Great Upheaval was an expression of the new economic and social system in America, just as surely as the cities, railroads, and factories from which it had sprung. The enormous expansion of industry after the Civil War had transformed millions of people who had grown up as farmers, self-employed artisans, and entrepreneurs into employees, growing thousands of whom were concentrated within each of the new corporate empires. Their work was no longer individual, but collective; they no longer directed their own work, but worked under control of a boss; they no longer controlled the property on which they worked or its fruits, and therefore could not find gainful employment unless someone with property agreed to hire them. The Great Upheaval grew out of workers' intuitive sense that they needed each other, had each other's support, and together were powerful.

This sense of unity was not embodied in any centralized plan or leadership, but in the feelings and action of each participant. "There was no concert of action at the start," the editor of *The Labor Standard* pointed out. "It spread because the workmen of Pittsburgh felt the same oppression that was felt by the workmen of West Virginia and so with the workmen of Chicago and St. Louis."[92] In Pittsburgh, concludes historian Robert Bruce, "Men like Andrew Hice or Gus Harris or David Davis assumed the lead briefly at one point or another, but only because they happened to be foremost in nerve or vehemence."[93] In Newark, Ohio, "no single individual seemed to command the … strikers. They followed the sense of the meeting, as Quakers might say, on such proposals as one or another of them … put forward. Yet they proceeded with notable coherence, as though fused by their common adversity."[94]

The Great Upheaval was in the end thoroughly defeated, but the struggle was by no means a total loss. Insofar as it aimed at preventing the continued decline of workers' living standards, it won wage concessions in a number of cases and undoubtedly gave pause to would-be wage-cutters to come. Insofar as it aimed at a workers' seizure of power, its goal was illusory, for workers as yet formed only a minority in a predominantly agrarian and middle-class society. But the power of workers to virtually stop society, to counter the forces of repression, and to organize cooperative action on a vast scale was revealed in the most dramatic form.

It was not only workers who drew lessons from the Great Upheaval. Their opponents began building up their power as well, symbolized by the National Guard armories whose construction began the following year, to contain upheavals yet to come.

•

Certain periods, wrote historian Irving Bernstein, bear a special quality in American labor history. "There occurred at these times strikes and social upheavals of extraordinary importance, drama, and violence which ripped the cloak of civilized decorum from society, leaving exposed naked class conflict."[95] Such periods were analyzed before World War I by Rosa Luxemburg and others under the concept of mass strikes. The mass strike, Luxemburg wrote, signifies not just a single act but a whole period of class struggle:

> Its use, its effects, its reasons for coming about are in a constant state of flux … [P]olitical and economic strikes, united and partial strikes, defensive strikes and combat strikes, general strikes of individual sections of industry and general strikes of entire cities, peaceful wage strikes and street battles, uprisings with barricades—all run together and run alongside each other, get in each other's way, overlap each other; a perpetually moving and changing sea of phenomena.[96]

The Great Upheaval was the first—but by no means the last—mass strike in American history.

Polish strikers attack Pennsylvania Coal and Iron Police—called "the Cossacks"
by the miners—in the Schuylkill region in 1888.
(Permission of Historical Picture Service.)

Chapter 2

May Day

Labor discontent was not long in re-emerging after the suppression of the Great Upheaval. By the mid-1880s, "labor agitation" was coursing from the largest cities to the smallest towns. Perhaps typical were the groups that developed in the obscure railroad town of Sedalia, Missouri, in 1884. Led by a cobbler and a railroad machinist, they would meet night after night, discussing the condition of workers and how to change it, debating various labor philosophies and their implications for immediate action. From these groups came the leaders of future strikes in the area.

The discontent frightened Terence Powderly, the somewhat bumbling head of the Knights of Labor—soon to become the most important labor organization in the land—and in December 1884 he issued a secret circular charged with fear that workers might try a "repetition of 1877 on a larger scale."[1]

"A change is slowly but surely coming over the whole country," he wrote.

> The discussion of the labor question takes up more of the time and attention of men in all walks of life at the present time than it ever did before.... The number of unemployed at the present time is very great, and constantly increasing. Reduction in wages, suspension of men, stoppage of factories and furnaces are of daily occurrence.... Under such circumstances as I have pointed out it is but natural for men to grow desperate and restive. The demonstrations in some of our large cities testify to that fact.[2]

Of course, history never repeats the same external events, and the strike wave of 1886—like each subsequent one—developed on a pattern of its own. No other period of mass strike in American history developed quite the character of a national insurrection seen in the Great Upheaval of 1877. Nonetheless, historians have generally considered the mid-1880s a more revolutionary period, even though it was marked by less insurrectionary violence. As in the Great Upheaval, workers were responding to a general depression that led to unemployment and declining wages. But they responded with a far higher level of planning, organization, and thought-out goals.

According to John Commons' classic *History of Labour in the United States*:

> All the peculiar characteristics of the dramatic events of 1886 and 1887, the highly feverish pace at which organizations grew, the nationwide wave of strikes, ... the wide use of the boycott, the obliteration, apparently complete, of all lines that divide the laboring class, whether geographic or trade, the violence and turbulence which accompanied the movement—all of these were the signs of a great movement by the class of the unskilled, which had finally risen in rebellion. This movement, rising as an elemental protest against oppression and degradation, could be but feebly restrained by any considerations of expediency or prudence.... The movement bore in every way the aspect of a social war. A frenzied hatred of labor for capital was shown in every important strike.... Extreme bitterness toward capital manifested itself in all the actions of the Knights of Labor, and wherever the leaders undertook to hold it within bounds they were generally discarded by their followers, and others who would lead as directed were placed in charge. The feeling of "give no quarter" is illustrated in the refusal to submit grievances to arbitration when the employees felt that they had the upper hand over their employers.[3]

Two months after Powderly's circular, a 5 percent wage cut was added to a previous 10 percent reduction for shopmen on the Missouri Pacific Railroad; the Missouri, Kansas and Texas; and the Wabash—the lines composing Jay Gould's Southwest System. The Wabash shopmen struck spontaneously the day after they received their wage cuts, and the strike rapidly spread to the shopmen on the other Southwest System roads. By the first week of March, the strike had spread to all the important shops of the system in Missouri and Texas, involving 10,000 miles of railroad.

Railroad officials tried to move the hundreds of freight cars that piled up, but without success, for the trainmen supported the strike.

When an engine was fired up and attached to a train, the engineer was approached by the strikers with the plea: "For the sake of your family and ours, don't take out that engine."[4] On March 15, 1885, the Missouri Pacific retracted the cut and agreed to other demands.

In the course of the strike, the railroad workers on the Union Pacific Railroad, who were members of the Knights of Labor, sent $30,000 and an organizer to support the Wabash strike. As a result, the Southwest System strikers began organizing local assemblies of the Knights of Labor; soon there were thirty locals with thousands of members. The railroads decided to move against the Knights. They fired shopmen on the Wabash, then closed the railroad shops altogether and opened them up again with fifty strikebreakers armed with revolvers and brass knuckles.

In reply, all Knights of Labor on the Wabash struck. The workers on the rest of the Southwest System demanded support from the leaders of the Knights of Labor, who reluctantly instructed all members to refuse to handle Wabash rolling stock: "If this order is antagonized by the companies through any of its officials, your executive committee is hereby ordered to call out all K. of L. on the above system without any further action."[5]

The Southwest System was controlled by Jay Gould, known as "The Wizard of Wall Street," and perhaps the most hated of the robber barons of his day. Faced now with a strike that would equal the dimensions of the 1877 railroad strikes and close down his entire system, Gould decided instead to come to terms, at least for the time being. He met with the executive board of the Knights of Labor and, according to the board, advised the general manager of the Wabash to agree to its demands. The manager agreed to reinstate those fired and promised that "no official shall discriminate against the K. of L."[6]

•

John Commons' *History of Labour in the United States* put well the significance of the victory:

Here a labor organization for the first time dealt on an equal footing with the most powerful capitalist in the country. It forced Jay Gould to recognize it as a power equal to himself, a fact which he amply

conceded when he declared his readiness to arbitrate all labor difficulties that might arise. The oppressed laboring masses finally discovered a champion which could curb the power of a man stronger
even than the government itself. All the pent-up feeling of bitterness and resentment which had accumulated during the two years
of depression, in consequence of the repeated cuts in wages and the
intensified domination by employers, now found vent in a rush to
organize under the banner of the powerful Knights of Labor.[7]

The result of these victories—headlined across the country—was
the sudden explosive growth both of strikes and of the Knights of Labor. "Every week," wrote a contemporary labor journalist, "trade unions are turned into local [Knights of Labor] assemblies or assemblies
are organized out of trade unions, and every day new mixed assemblies [which included workers of different trades] spring into existence. The numerous strikes East and West during the past twelve
months have added greatly to its growth." The usual pattern was to
"strike first and then join the Knights of Labor."[8]

The growth of the Knights of Labor was phenomenal. On July 1,
1884, there were 71,326 members. A year later there were 111,395. By
July 1, 1886 there were 729,677.[9]

The Noble and Holy Order of the Knights of Labor had been
founded by nine obscure garment cutters in Philadelphia in 1869. It
combined the functions of a trade union with an opposition to the
wage system as a whole, and originally had a deep religious strain as
well. As one of its founders, Uriah Stephens, put it:

Knighthood must base its claims for labor upon higher ground than
participation in the profits and emoluments, and a lessening of the
hours and fatigues of labor. These are only physical effects and objects of a grosser nature, and, although imperative, are but the step-
ping-stone to a higher cause, of a nobler nature. The real and
ultimate reason must be based upon the more exalted and divine
nature of man, his high and noble capability for good. Excessive labor and small pay stints and blunts and degrades those God-like
faculties, until the image of God, in which he was created and intended by his great Author to exhibit, are scarcely discernible.[10]

The one great sentiment embodied in the Knights of Labor was the idea of solidarity among all workers, whether white or black, skilled or unskilled, men or women. As historian Norman Ware put it: "The solidarity of labor was fast becoming an economic reality if not a psychological fact … The Order tried to teach the American wage-earner that he was a wage-earner first and a bricklayer, carpenter, miner, shoemaker, … a Catholic, Protestant, Jew, white, black, Democrat, Republican after."[11] The Order's motto, "An injury to one is the concern of all," captured the popular imagination. This feeling was expressed over and over again by the head of the Knights of Labor, Grand Master Workman Terence Powderly:

> The belief was prevalent until a short time ago among workingmen, that only the man who was engaged in manual toil could be called a workingman. The man who labored at the bench or anvil, the man who held the throttles of the engine or delved in the everlasting gloom of the coal mine did not believe that the man who made the drawings from which he forged, turned, or dug could be classed as a worker. The draughtsman, the timekeeper, the clerk, the school teacher, the civil engineer, the editor, the reporter, or the worst paid, most abused and illy appreciated of all toilers—women—could not be called a worker…. Narrow prejudice, born of the injustice and oppressions of the past, must be overcome, and all who interest themselves in producing for the world's good must be made to understand that their interests are identical.[12]

This sense of class unity developed in opposition to the spirit of the trade unions, which at that time generally represented only the most highly skilled craftsmen, the "aristocracy of labor," and fought to maintain their privileged position. According to Powderly, "The sentiment expressed in the words, 'The condition of one part of our class can not be improved permanently unless *all* are improved *together*,' was not acceptable to trade unionists, who were selfishly bound up in the work of ameliorating the condition of those who belonged to their own particular callings alone."[13]

"The failure which really led to the organization of the Knights of Labor, was the failure of the trade union to grapple, and satisfactorily deal with, the labor question on its broad, far-reaching basic principle: the right of all to have a say in the affairs of one.... The rights of the common, every-day laborer were to be considered by the new order," whereas the trade unions' attitude was, "we will not associate with the common, every-day laborers in any organization of labor." [14]

Trade unions also differed from the Knights, Powderly pointed out, in that they accepted the wage system. "Many of the members of these organizations seemed to regard themselves as being hired for life; they were content with demanding and obtaining from their masters better conditions in the regulation of workshops and wages; beyond that they did not think they had a right to venture." [15] The Knights—and many other workers at the time—felt differently:

> We are the willing victims of an outrageous system.... We should not war with men for being what we make them, but strike a powerful, telling blow at the base of the system which makes the laborer the slave of his master.... So long as a pernicious system leaves one man at the mercy of another, so long will labor and capital be at war.... Far be it from me to say that I can point out the way ... I can only offer a suggestion that comes to me as a result of experience ... to abolish the wage system. [16]

Although they had no clear idea of how to put it into practice, the Knights sought a society based on cooperative production as the alternative to wage slavery. "The fundamental principle on which the organization was based was co-operation; not a co-operation of men for the mere purpose of enhancing the value of their combined contributions to any productive enterprise alone, but a co-operation of the various callings and crafts by which men earned the right to remain upon the earth's surface as contributors to the public good." [17] Indeed, the idea of a class of permanent wage workers—so distant from the ideal that every man could become an independent entrepreneur—still seemed positively un-American to many workers of the 1880s. As Norman Ware wrote, "The reluctance of the labor movement to accept collective bargaining as its major function was due largely to the fact that this involved an acceptance of the wage system." [18]

Yet, despite their opposition to the wage system, the leaders of the Knights of Labor opposed strikes and revolutionary activities even more.

"I will never advocate a strike," Powderly wrote, "unless it be a strike at the ballot-box, or such a one as was proclaimed to the world by the unmistakable sound of the strikers' guns on the field of Lexington. But the necessity for such a strike as the latter does not exist at the present. The men who made the name of Lexington famous in the world's history were forced to adopt the bullet because they did not possess the ballot."[19] Powderly still hoped that the former position of workers as independent producers could be restored by creating producers' cooperatives and using the government to control monopolies. He feared that strikes distracted from this task and threatened to generate revolutionary disorder. Much of Powderly's energy, as we shall see, went into forestalling and weakening strikes.

But this opposition to strikes did not stop workers who wanted to strike from joining the Knights. As John Swinton, perhaps the leading contemporary labor journalist, wrote, "While the order is opposed to strikes, the first news we are likely to hear after … [a strike's] close is of the union of the men with the K. of L."[20] Nor did the Knights stop its members from striking, for while in theory it was highly centralized, in practice each local assembly acted on its own initiative, striking despite disapproval from on high.

During the same years as the Knights' rapid growth, a revolutionary tendency began developing within the labor movement, generally referred to as anarchism. The anarchists called upon all "revolutionists and armed workingmen's organizations in the country" to prepare to "offer armed resistance to the invasions by the capitalistic class and capitalistic legislatures."[21]

The growth of anarchism in the United States was a response to the evident failure of political action and trade unionism in the face of the growing misery of the depression. Indeed, one of the leading anarchists at the time, Albert Parson, had only a few years before spent his time running for political office in Chicago and lobbying in Washington, D.C., for the eight-hour day for federal employees.

The anarchist program, as set forth by a national congress in 1883, read in part:

> By force our ancestors liberated themselves from political oppression, by force their children will have to liberate themselves from economic bondage. "It is, therefore, your right, it is your duty," says Jefferson, "to arm!"
>
> What we would achieve is, therefore, plainly and simply:
>
> First—Destruction of the existing class rule by all means—i.e., by energetic, relentless, revolutionary and international action.
>
> Second—Establishment of a free society based upon co-operative organization of production.
>
> Third—Free exchange of equivalent products by and between the productive organizations without commerce and profit-mongery.
>
> Fourth—Organization of education on a secular, scientific, and equal basis for both sexes.
>
> Fifth—Equal rights for all, without distinction to sex or race.
>
> Sixth—Regulation of all public affairs by free contracts between the autonomous (independent) Communes and associations, resting on a federalistic basis.[22]

In many places the anarchists were only a small sect, but in Chicago a significant section of the workers joined this revolutionary current. In 1884, under anarchist influence, a large number of Chicago cigar-makers called for "open rebellion of the robbed class," pulled out of the existing Amalgamated Trades and Labor Assembly, and organized the Central Labor Union along with German metalworkers, carpenters and joiners, cabinetworkers, and butchers. By the end of 1885 the new Central Labor Union was nearly as large and strong as the old Assembly, and by April 1886 it included the eleven largest unions in the city.

•

Eighteen-eighty-six was a year of tumult. One contemporary aptly called it "the year of the great uprising of labor."[23] Historians have called it a "revolutionary year,"[24] and the "great upheaval," "more deserving of this title than even the convulsive events of 1877."[25]

This movement took a form originally promoted by neither the anarchists nor the Knights of Labor—an enormous strike wave culminating in a virtual nationwide general strike. These statistics suggest what happened:

Year	Strikes	Establishments	Participants
1881	471	2,928	129,521
1882	454	2,105	154,671
1883	478	2,759	149,763
1884	443	2,367	147,054
1885	645	2,284	242,705
1886	1,411	9,891	499,489

To summarize, the number of workers engaged in strikes in 1886 tripled compared with the average for the previous five years, and the number of establishments struck nearly quadrupled. The strikes were in every trade and in every geographical area.[26]

Further, the character of strikes changed radically. Through the depression years that preceded 1886, strikes had mostly been defensive ones in resistance to wage cuts. Now, with the beginnings of business recovery, they became above all offensive strikes for power over such issues as the hours of labor, terms of hiring and firing, the organization of work, and the arbitrary power of foremen and superintendents.

The wave began late in 1885 with "spontaneous outbreaks of unorganized masses."[27] Typical was a strike for the ten-hour day in the Saginaw Valley in Michigan. The legislature had passed a ten-hour law that proved unenforceable. In response, with little previous organization, the predominantly Polish and American workers in the lumber and shingle mills struck for the immediate introduction of a ten-hour day with no reduction in pay. The strikers marched in a body from mill to mill, demanding that the men quit work, and shut down the entire lumber industry, turning off steam and banking fires, including seventeen shingle mills, sixty-one lumber mills, and fifty-eight salt blocks. Although the employers imported more than fifty

Pinkerton detectives and a large militia was poised to intervene, the strike was won after two months.

The workers on Jay Gould's Southwestern Railroad System exemplified the new strike wave. They had discovered their power in previous strikes and had developed their own organization and coordination. Yet they still were subject to the arbitrary power of their employers: their wages were constantly cut or chiseled; they were arbitrarily transferred from one job to another; they were harassed by local railroad officials; and they could get no answer to their grievances. When one of their members was fired for attending a union meeting, even though he had been given permission, the strike they had long felt was inevitable broke out March 6, 1886.

A letter from one of the strikers to a contemporary labor journal gives the spirit in which they struck:

> Tell the world that the men of the Gould Southwest System are on strike. We strike for justice to ourselves and our fellowmen everywhere. Fourteen thousand men are out.... I would say to all railroad employees everywhere ... make your demands to the corporation for the eight-hour day and no reduction of pay. Demand $1.50 per day for all laboring men. Demand that yourselves and your families be carried on all railways for one cent a mile. Bring in all your grievances in one bundle at once, and come out to a man and stay out until they are all settled to your entire satisfaction. Let us demand our rights and compel the exploiters to accede to our demands.[28]

The objective of the strikers, according to Ruth Allen, a historian of the strike, was to be recognized by management as "men equally powerful in and responsible for the conduct of the Gould Southwest System." Recognition, according to the worker whose firing triggered the strike, meant that corporation officials, instead of holding all authority themselves, would "recognize and treat with the committee appointed by the Order to settle by arbitration the difficulties or grievances that might arise."[29] (The term "arbitration" at that time included any settlement reached through negotiation or collective bargaining.) H.M. Hoxie, Gould's top official on the scene, agreed that the time had come "when the question had to be decided whether he should run his own railroad or have the Knights of Labor run it."[30]

When the strike began on the Texas and Pacific Railroad, Joseph Buchanan, one of the most radical leaders of the Knights of Labor, tried to dissuade others on the Southwest System from striking in sympathy:

> Let us say the strike is ordered and the shops closed, though the trains are running. You know as well as I do that you cannot defeat a railroad company if the trains continue to run; therefore you will attempt to stop the trains. The police, deputy United States marshals, deputy sheriffs, and constables will swarm in the yards and on the tracks; you must drive them off. You are husky fellows and full of fight, so I'll admit that you can whip the police and deputies. Then the militia of the various states through which the roads run will be called out to oppose you. Who are the militiamen? Only a lot of spindle-legged counter-jumpers, but they are well trained and armed for business. Still, guns are plentiful in your part of the country and most of you are pretty good shooters yourselves; besides, you will be battling for a principle and the welfare of "Betty and the babies." If you are brave men and have intelligent leadership, you can clean out the militia. Now what happens? The Federal judges, under whom the roads are being operated, appeal to the President of the United States for assistance, and the regulars are sent to put down what has by this time become an armed revolution—rebellion, in fact.[31]

Nonetheless, the shopmen, switchmen, trackmen, and telegraph operators, and even coal heavers and miners throughout Missouri, Kansas, Arkansas, Nebraska, and the Indian Territory joined the strike.

According to *The New York Times*, the "striking mania" in Missouri had even extended to

> a class of laborers who it was supposed would be the last to fall into line. The farm hands of these counties have demanded of their employers an increase from $15 and board to $20 and board per month. The demand was at first refused, when no less than 50 men quit work. The employers have conceded their demands ... and the projectors hope to have the demand become general throughout the State.[32]

The Great Southwest Strike began March 1, 1886, with an occupation of the shops similar in some ways to the sitdown strikes of later years. When the men walked out, trusted strikers were placed in control of the shops and rolling stock to prevent them from being used and to protect them from violence. But soon the railroads secured dozens of injunctions, bench warrants, and writs of assistance, thus putting the strikers in contempt of court. Special police paid by the railroads and large numbers of extraordinary deputies were sworn in to enforce the orders.

To break the strike, the companies advertised widely for strike-breakers. In one bizarre episode, nine young men were recruited in New Orleans and sent to Marshall, Texas, on the assurance there was no strike in progress. On arrival they were sworn in as deputy United States marshals to protect company property. The next morning they wrote in the local paper that, "After due investigation, and hearing both sides of the question, we found undeniable proof of a strike ... [M]an to man we could not justifiably go to work and take the bread out of our fellow-workmen's mouths, no matter how much we needed it ourselves."[33] The United States marshal for East Texas arrested the men for contempt and intimidation and defrauding the company for refusing to work after accepting transportation from New Orleans; they received sentences of three to four months in the Galveston County jail.

The characteristic response of the workers to the attempts to break the strike was the "killing" of engines. This was done by putting out the engine's fire, letting out the water, displacing engine connections, and destroying part of the machinery. The workers also tried to prevent operation by strikebreakers by tampering with the rails and setting fires at terminals, water tanks, and shops.

A dispatch from Atchison, Kansas, gave a vivid example: "At 12:45 this morning the ten men on guard at the Missouri Pacific round-house were surprised by the appearance of 35 or 40 masked men. The guards were corralled in the oil room by a detachment of the visitors, who stood guard with pistols ... drawn, while the rest of them thoroughly disabled 12 locomotives which stood in the stalls."[34]

Another from Dallas, Texas, illustrated the widespread court action against strikers' tactics: "Charles Wilson, charged with displacing a switch for the purpose of derailing an engine at Denton on March 27, was sentenced to five months' imprisonment in the county jail; C. Bishop, for taking possession of a switch at Forth Worth on April 2, was found guilty and remanded to await sentence; Richard Gordon, striking a switchman with a stone at night, three months' imprisonment in the county jail."[35]

In addition, the railroads relied upon armed force to break the strike. They started in Palestine, Texas, where 300 links, 500 couplings, and 500 "draw-heads" had been removed, and where, of thirty-seven engines, two had been thrown from the track, eight were held by the strikers, and twenty-seven had been "killed." When the strikers gave notice that no trains would be allowed to move, the sheriff summoned a posse of 200 armed men and cleared the tracks; the first train was sent out guarded by armed men.[36] In Fort Worth, an old-style western gunman (who had once fled arrest in New Mexico because his methods of "freeing the land of 'squatters'" resulted in two deaths) was acting city marshal. He engaged in a shoot-out to get a train through in which half a dozen officers and strikers were killed or wounded. Afterward, a vigilante group of 100 was formed in Fort Worth and nearly 300 state militia troops were rushed in. A news dispatch described one scene there:

> Lawlessness and disorder have won in Fort Worth. One thousand desperado men have set the law and its executors at defiance, and their sweet will rules.... As early as 8:30 o'clock citizens who had been summoned by the Sheriff began to repair to the Missouri Pacific yards. Strikers and Knights of Labor, with sympathizers to the number of at least 400, were already there. Many of them had been there all night.... By 9:00 o'clock not less than 3,000 people were gathered in the yards of the road.
>
> At 10:00 o'clock a train was made up on a side track. A Missouri Pacific locomotive left the Texas and Pacific roundhouse, and the strikers yelled "Here she comes." On this locomotive and tender were a dozen officers.... About the locomotive was a squad of officers. The strikers surged about the train, but were forced back by the officers. Pistols flashed in the sunlight in an ominous manner.

"Kill the engine, kill the engine!" yelled a striker, and the bulk of the crowd rushed forward to the locomotive.

"Back! I'll kill the first man who touches this engine," cried out the Chief Deputy. The officers stationed along the train left their posts and, throwing the strikers to right and left, gathered about the locomotive. That engine wasn't touched, but the strikers, seeing their opportunity, rushed between the cars, pulled the pins, and even took the nuts out of the drawheads. Sheriff Maddox ordered the engineer to pull up, but not a car followed the engine, and the strikers yelled themselves hoarse with derision.[37]

This process reached its peak in East St. Louis, where on April 9 a group of deputies fired into a crowd, killing nine and wounding many. The crowd in fury retaliated by burning the shops and yards, destroying $75,000 of railroad property. According to *The New York Times*, it started when one member of a crowd stepped on railroad property. He was arrested, and as part of the crowd surged forward to rescue him,

there was a pistol shot, which in a few seconds was followed by the ringing reports of Winchester rifles. The shrieks and yells that rose from the crowd could be heard on the bridge, a third of a mile away. "Crack, crack" went the deadly rifles. The crowd split into two unequal parts and ran like mad in opposite directions.... Terror was king and drove all before him. The deadly ball had been fired at short range against a solid wall of flesh and blood.... On the bridge and roadway lay Mrs. John Pfeffer, shot through the spine and mortally wounded; John Bonner, a coal miner, dead; Oscar Washington, a painter, dead; Patrick Driscoll, a Wabash section hand, dead, and Major Rychman, a rolling mill employee, shot in the head and shoulder, mortally wounded.

When the fleeing mob recovered from its terror, and turning saw its assailants in full flight toward the Louisville and Nashville freight house, shouts of "To arms, to arms," rose from it, and men who stood over the dead and wounded vowed they would have a terrible revenge. Some of the wildest spirits rushed through the town calling on the strikers and their friends to arm themselves and kill all deputy sheriffs on sight. Pale-faced men soon appeared on the streets armed with revolvers and shotguns. Here and there a man could be seen carrying a small coil of rope. The cry of "Hang them" kept pace with that of "Kill them all."[38]

Leaders of the Knights of Labor tried to head off the crowd. One of them addressed the crowd: "Brothers, I appeal to you, be calm and disperse to your homes.... I beg of you please do nothing rash.... Don't forget how hard we worked to build up our organization, do not tear it down in ruins by one rash act." Nonetheless, *The New York Times* reported, a few hours later "the sky was reddened by the burning of the Louisville and Nashville freight house. The mob had begun the work of what it considered retaliation. The fire was not long confined to cars, for at midnight the Cairo Short Line freight depot was in flames."[39] The governor responded by sending in 700 National Guardsmen and putting East St. Louis under military law.

The participants in the Great Southwest Strike held out for two months in the face of such opposition, but as the company increasingly eroded their blockade with strikebreakers and armed violence, the workers ultimately were forced to return to work defeated. The final call to end the strike came May 4, but most of the strikers were refused their jobs, which had been taken by strikebreakers.

•

Shorter hours had long been a major objective for labor in the United States and worldwide, both to decrease the burden of toil and to cut unemployment by spreading work. Ever since the 1830s, labor reform societies had pushed for legislation establishing first the ten-hour and then the eight-hour day. But even when such legislation passed, it remained a dead letter, unenforced. Some trades had tried to shorten hours by strikes and negotiation, but with limited success, since unless the eight-hour system was adopted everywhere it put those firms that accepted it at a competitive disadvantage.

In 1884, a dying organization called the Federation of Organized Trades and Labor Unions, which had tried unsuccessfully to bring together national trade unions outside the Knights of Labor, passed a resolution that "eight hours shall constitute a legal day's work from and after May 1, 1886."[40] According to historian Norman Ware, "By a stroke of fortune, a resolution passed in the dull times of 1884 reached fruition in the revolutionary year of 1886 and became a rallying point and a battle cry for the aggressive forces of that year.... It was little more than a gesture which, because of the changed conditions of 1886, became a revolutionary threat."[41]

As a resolution passed by the federation in December 1885 suggests, the idea of a general strike for the eight-hour day developed out of the failure of other methods. The resolution noted that "it would be in vain to expect the introduction of the eight-hour rule through legislative measures ... [A] united demand to reduce the hours of labor, supported by a firmly established and determined organization, would be far more effective than a thousand laws, whose execution depends upon the good will of aspiring politicians or sycophantic department officials." Its call for a general strike was based upon the view "that the workmen in their endeavor to reform the prevailing economic conditions must rely upon themselves and their own power exclusively."[42]

The May Day strike movement received little support from existing labor organizations. The federation that originally suggested the May 1 deadline was so weak that when it polled its members on the plan only about 2,500 even voted. Terrence Powderly, the head of the Knights of Labor, opposed the May Day strike from the start. In a secret circular dated December 15, 1884, he proposed that instead of striking, each Knights of Labor assembly should "have its members write short essays on the eight-hour question."[43]

Anarchist groups at first argued that the eight-hour movement was a compromise with the wage system. The Chicago anarchist newspaper *The Alarm* declared that "it is a lost battle, and ... though the eight-hour system should be established the wage workers would gain nothing."[44]

But the idea of a general strike for the eight-hour day had caught the imagination of tens of thousands of workers. Despite the opposition of national leaders, the movement burgeoned locally across the country. Local Knights of Labor organizers, over protest of the national organization, established new local assemblies around the eight-hour issue; one formed three new assemblies in one night, despite a rule that an organizer must attend five weekly meetings before chartering a local. In the one month of February 1886, 515 new locals were organized. The Knights of Labor secretary for the Boston District Assembly reported on April 19, 1886, that in the Boston area district there were four times as many members as thirteen weeks before.[45]

The leadership was alarmed at the militance of the new members. Powderly complained that "the majority of the newcomers were not of the quality the Order had sought for in the past."[46] They suspended organizing of new assemblies for forty days, but the organizers continued, simply holding back charter fees until the forty days expired. In an attempt to halt the growth of their own organization, the Knights of Labor leaders next refused to approve 300 new organizers' commissions and finally suspended all their organizers.

Powderly gives a vivid picture of what was happening locally: "In the early part of 1886 many of the new local assemblies began to pass resolutions favoring the 'action of the General Assembly in fixing the first of May, 1886, as the day on which to strike for eight hours.' They sent them to the General Master Workman, who saw at once that a grave danger threatened the Order through the ignorance of the members who had been so hurriedly gathered into the assemblies. They were induced to come in by a false statement. Many organizers assisted in keeping up the delusion for the purpose of making 'big returns.'"[47]

At this point, Powderly tried deliberately to sabotage the movement. He issued a secret circular to Knights of Labor locals saying, "The executive officers of the Knights of Labor have never fixed upon the first of May for a strike of any kind, and they will not do so.... No assembly of the Knights of Labor must strike for the eight-hour system on May 1st under the impression that they are obeying orders from headquarters, for such an order was not, and will not, be given."[48] The movement represented a kind of class conflict that Powderly abhorred. The Knights of Labor leadership was unable to stop the strike, or even to stop widespread participation of Knights of Labor locals, but it did severely disrupt the unity and effectiveness of the movement.

Preparatory agitation for the strike built up to major proportions in March and came to a head in April. A considerable number of eight-hour strikes broke out ahead of time; the eight-hour demand was injected into labor struggles over other issues; and massive eight-hour demonstrations were held throughout the country. The movement centered in the major industrial cities of Chicago, New York, Cincinnati, Baltimore, and Milwaukee, with Boston, Pittsburgh, St. Louis, and Washington, D.C., affected to a lesser degree.

Even before May 1, almost a quarter of a million workers throughout the country were involved in the eight-hour movement. Some 30,000 had already been granted an eight-hour day or at least a reduction in working hours. At least 6,000 were on strike during the last week of April. It was estimated in April that not less than 100,000 were prepared to strike to secure their demand.[49]

The movement proved even bigger than anticipated. By the second week in May, some 340,000 workers had participated, 190,000 of them by striking. Eighty thousand struck in Chicago, 45,000 in New York, 32,000 in Cincinnati, 9,000 in Baltimore, 7,000 in Milwaukee, 4,700 in Boston, 4,250 in Pittsburgh, 3,000 in Detroit, 2,000 in St. Louis, 1,500 in Washington, D.C., and 13,000 in other cities. Nearly 200,000 workers, according to *Bradstreet's*, won shorter hours.[50]

Socialist satirist Oscar Ameringer, writing half a century later, described the May Day strike in Cincinnati. Ameringer had just arrived from Germany and secured a job in a furniture factory, which he found totally different from his father's carpentry shop:

> Here everything was done by machine. Our only task was assembling, gluing together, and finishing, at so much a chair or table, the two specialties of the factory. Speed came first, quality of workmanship last ....
>
> The work was monotonous, the hours of drudgery ten a day, my wages a dollar a day. Also, spring was coming on. Birds and blue hills beckoned. And so, when agitators from the Knights of Labor invaded our sweatshop preaching the divine message of less work for more pay, I became theirs.[51]

Ameringer joined a woodworkers union affiliated with the Knights of Labor. "The membership was almost exclusively German and seasoned with a good sprinkling of anarchists," he wrote. Before the May Day strike, "there had been groups of older or more militant members manufacturing bombs out of gas pipes. All of us expected violence, I suppose." At the kickoff march, "only red flags were carried … [T]he only song we sang was the 'Arbeiters Marseillaise' … [A] workers' battalion of 400 Springfield rifles headed the procession. It was the Lehr and Wehr Verein, the educational and protective society of embattled toil."[52]

Such brigades of armed workers had grown up in a number of cities, largely in response to the use of police and military forces in 1877. By 1886 they existed not only in Cincinnati, but in Detroit, Chicago, St. Louis, Omaha, Newark, New York, San Francisco, Denver, and other cities, adding to the feeling that a bitter conflict was at hand.

In Milwaukee, an enormous labor agitation was launched well in advance of May Day. In February 1886, the local assemblies of the Knights of Labor, despite the national leadership's objections, organized an Eight Hour League and in the following month were joined by the local trade unions. A mass meeting of 3,000 built pressure for the change.[53]

The Wisconsin commissioner of labor and industrial statistics reported that "the agitation permeated our entire social atmosphere. Skilled and unskilled laborers formed unions or assemblies. Men, and even women, contributed money and time to its promulgation. It was *the* topic of conversation in the shop, on the street, at the family table, at the bar, in the counting rooms, and the subject of numerous able sermons from the pulpit."[54]

As May 1 approached, workers in 200 workshops and factories made their demands. On April 29, the workers at the large John Plankinton and Co. packing house and several hundred workers from the sash and door shops struck for eight hours.

By May 1, 3,000 brewers, 1,500 carpenters and other construction workers, and large numbers of bakers, cigar-makers, brickyard workers, slaughterhouse workers, laborers, and others had struck—a total of about 8,000. On Sunday, May 2, 2,500 workers held a parade through downtown Milwaukee complete with several bands and ending with a picnic. The strike continued to spread on Monday, as workers from smaller shops left their jobs. By the end of the day, 14,000 were on strike and victories began appearing. The master masons and bricklayers granted a 20 percent wage increase and allowed their men to work eight or ten hours, as they preferred; and the Filer-Stowell foundry granted eight hours. Best Brewing met the workers' wage and hour demands, but total victory seemed at hand and the workers refused to go back unless the company fired those workers who had not struck.

The strike now began to spread in the pattern of the general strikes of 1877. Monday morning, 1,000 striking brewers lined up in front of the Falk Brewery, the only large brewery not on strike, to prevent employees from going to work. The Falk workers quit when the local assembly of the Knights of Labor called them out. That afternoon a crowd of several hundred strikers tried to force 1,400 men at the West Milwaukee Railway shops to quit. Turned away by the police, they marched on the still-running Allis works, where they were dispersed after being doused with streams of water from the mill. Fearing further violence, Allis decided to close the works, charging that "this afternoon a band of Polish laborers marched from the West Milwaukee shops ... to my works, and with brandished clubs endeavored to force an entrance. Although the mob of men with clubs marched directly before the eyes of the police at the south side station, who had been notified of their coming and of their purpose, not a policeman moved to keep them from attack."[55] The Chicago, Milwaukee, and St. Paul Railroad shops likewise closed to avoid violence.

The next morning one crowd gathered in the Menomonee River valley and moved along the river trying to close plants. Seventy-five policemen were powerless to control the crowd. Another group of 1,500 workers moved on the Brandt and Co. stove works and forced the men to quit work. Still another crowd gathered at St. Stanislaus Church in the Polish district and decided to march to the North Chicago Rolling Mills plant at Bay View, the largest plant in the city still in operation. When a strike committee presented the mill officials' explanation that the workers were paid by the ton, not by the hour, and asked if they were satisfied with it, the crowd yelled back "Eight hours!" They felt that it was no longer a matter between individual workers and employers, but rather a test of power between workers and employers as a whole. As one of the employers they attacked put it, the issue had become more than hours and wages. It was a question, he said, of "my right to run my works and your right to sell me your time and labor. Our whole civilization and independence hangs on these."[56]

Alarmed, Governor Jeremiah Rusk of Wisconsin called up the militia and sent them to Bay View. Three companies arrived by train and were stoned by the crowd as they marched onto the mill grounds. About 350 militiamen stayed in the mill overnight.

At 6 a.m. the next morning, a crowd of 1,500 gathered again at St. Stanislaus Church to return to the Bay View mills. A *Milwaukee Journal* reporter who spent the night with the rioters reported, "They have no organization or leaders, and act merely under pressure of momentary excitement."[57] The men assured reporters "that they had no intention of making an attack on the militia or the company's property, and simply wished to show that they had not been intimidated by the presence of the militia."[58] They marched to the mill in an orderly fashion, led by a red, white, and blue banner with a clock set at eight o'clock in the middle. They carried clubs, iron bars, broken scythes, stones, and a few guns.

According to General Charles King of the Wisconsin National Guard, Governor Rusk was telephoned and gave the order, "Fire on them!"[59] As the crowd approached the mill, the commander of the militia gave them an inaudible warning to stop, then ordered the militia to fire. "As if by a common impulse the entire crowd fell headlong to the ground, and for a minute it appeared as though nearly all had been killed or wounded by the first discharge. When the troops ceased firing, all who were uninjured turned and ran pell-mell back to the city, leaving six dead or dying in the dusty road."[60] The shooting broke the back of the eight-hour movement in Milwaukee, and gradually the strikers returned to work, mostly at the old terms.

The eight-hour movement was launched in New York with a rally of 20,000 in Union Square under a heavy police guard: "About 600 police officers were visible to the naked eye and over 100 more were hidden from view in the buildings surrounding the square. Not many blocks away 200 or 300 more officers might have been quickly called."[61] Nearly 4,000 furniture workers established shorter hours simply by reporting for work at 8 and leaving at 5. One thousand pi-ano workers, 750 furriers, 500 carriage and wagon makers, and 250 marble workers, to select a few examples, struck for shorter hours. Those winning their demands included:

Eight Hours

Brownstown Cutters	1,600
Cigar-makers and Packers	11,000
Cabinet and Furniture Makers	4,000
Piano Makers	3,000
Fresco Painters	700
Furriers	750
Typographers	360
Wagon and Carriage Makers	600
Total	22,010

Nine Hours

Coopers	1,500
Machinists and Pattern Makers	20,000
Bricklayers and Building Trades	40,000
Metal Workers (including Brass)	2,000
Clothing Cutters	1,500
Total	65,000

"Besides the above trades there are numerous others, such as the bakers and brewers, and salesmen of all kinds that have reduced their hours of labor from fifteen to twelve and ten."[62] The street railway men reduced their working day by as much as five hours—to twelve a day.

From Baltimore, *John Swinton's Paper* reported:

The third of May will be remembered in Baltimore as witnessing the largest and most imposing street parades of organized workingmen ever seen in this section.... Twenty thousand is the estimated number ... a monster mass meeting ... in the eight-hour interest was held at Concordia Opera House. About 10,000 organized working-men were in line of procession.... The streets along the road were a blaze of light, lit up by thousands of torches and lanterns carried by the men in line.[63]

In Pittsburgh, cabinetmakers struck for a 20 percent advance in wages and a reduction from ten to eight hours; the carpenters struck for nine hours and a 10 percent increase; and stonecutters quickly won nine hours. Bakers closed 120 of 160 bakeries demanding shorter hours in Pittsburgh and Allegheny; coal miners in Imperial, Pennsylvania, struck for an advance of half a cent per bushel; 1,500 colliers won wage increases. "The horseshoers are happy," a labor paper reported. "Hereafter they quit work at 4:00 p.m. Saturdays."[64]

In Troy, New York, 5,000 went out on strike for eight hours, including 2,000 stove molders and all the building trades. Three hundred Italian railroad laborers struck for a wage increase, and "after stopping work they tied red handkerchiefs to their pickaxes and shovels and marched down the track in a body to another place where a second gang was at work and induced them to join the strikers."[65]

In Grand Rapids, Michigan, several thousand furniture workers held a mass meeting demanding the eight-hour day; manufacturers accepted eight hours only with comparable wage reductions and were struck. There were a number of strikes in Detroit. On May 10, sixty policemen were drawn up in a line in front of the Michigan Car Works in an attempt to break a strike there.

The street in front of the works was thronged with strikers waiting to see how many of their number would, as had been announced, return to work when the whistle sounded. Several "spotters" were stationed near the gates leading into the works. These closely scrutinized each workman who entered, apparently taking notes for future reference. Every time a man in working garb turned from the sidewalk to pass through the gate, loud cries of "Come out of that,"

"Coward," "shame," &c., went up from the waiting and watching strikers.... The net result of all this effort was that nine-tenths of the men were eventually kept out.[66]

In St. Louis, plumbers and water works employees struck for eight hours without wage cuts; carpenters imposed the eight-hour rule; and furniture manufacturers agreed to eight hours, but with no wage adjustment. In Indianapolis, furniture workers struck for eight hours, and wheel works employees were locked out. In Louisville, Kentucky, furniture workers were shut out for demanding eight hours with adjusted pay. In Washington, D.C., the building trades decided to impose the eight-hour day and were soon seen at quitting time brushing shoulders with the government clerks who already had attained it. The tinners of Fort Worth, Texas, adopted the eight-hour system. Ten thousand miners at Wilkes Barre, Pennsylvania, demonstrated for the eight-hour day. From New Haven, Connecticut, *The New York Times* reported: "This town has picked up the reputation lately of having more strikes than any other city of its size in the country. Very likely it deserves it; at any rate the labor problem is in everybody's mouth. There are two societies devoted to its discussion," drawing hundreds of participants.[67] In Portland, Maine, cigarmakers struck for wage increases.

Of course, in a number of cities the eight-hour movement failed to catch on. From Boston, for example, *John Swinton's Paper* reported, "Although there [has] been a great deal of agitation, discussion and argument in this city for the last seven months over the adoption of the eight-hour day"—indeed 100 meetings on the question had been held by May 1—"when the third of May arrived only four trades struck for the proposed change ... the carpenters, plumbers, painters and masons."[68] And from Pennsylvania it reported, "The short hour movement has caused several strikes, most notably among the furniture workers and cabinet makers.... But the whole movement is dull as ditch water in Philadelphia."[69]

The heart of the eight-hour movement was in Chicago. Local Knights of Labor, trade unionists, and anarchists—reversing their previous opposition—all supported the Eight-Hour Association, which agitated for the strike. Through April, a series of huge mass demonstrations drew more than 25,000 people each. "Nearly every-one was certain that with this display of spirit and the excellent or-ganization of the Chicago workers, the movement would succeed."[70]

The other side prepared as well. More than a year before, newspa-pers had reported the formation of military bodies by businessmen, who armed their employees in wholesale houses, and the enlarge-ment of the National Guard. "In one large business house alone there is an organization of 150 young men who have been armed with Remington breech-loading rifles and pursue a regular course of drill-ing.... This is by no means an isolated case." The police were readied for emergency action; the militia was equipped for instant participa-tion in street disorders; and leading businessmen created a committee of the Citizens' Association of Chicago to hold almost continuous ses-sions "for the purpose of agreeing upon a plan of action in case the necessities of the situation should demand [its] intervention in any way."[71]

On the eve of the strike, *The New York Times* reported from Chicago that "within the past forty-eight hours nearly $2,000 has been sub-scribed by various members of the Commercial Club, with which it is proposed to purchase some sort of a machine gun for the First Infan-try, Illinois National Guard. The idea was suggested at the inspection and drill of the regiment Tuesday night and was readily adopted, when it was hinted that in case of a riot such a piece would prove a valuable weapon in the hands of the Guardsmen."[72]

By May Day, the movement in Chicago had already won impres-sive concessions: 1,000 brewers reduced their hours from sixteen to ten and 1,000 bakers who formerly worked fourteen to eighteen hours gained a ten-hour day. A good proportion of furniture workers won the eight-hour day with a 25 percent increase in hourly wages, while 1,600 clothing cutters won ten hours' pay for eight hours' work. Some tobacco, shoe, lard, packing, and other companies likewise re-duced hours. A great many more workers, however, were expecting a hard fight to win the eight-hour demand.

On May 1, *The Illinois State Register* reported: "The supreme officers of the police department have ceased in the attempt to smooth over the fears of the last few weeks regarding the labor movement. Their sole idea now is that ... there will be a great deal of trouble."[73] That day 30,000 struck in Chicago, including 10,000 lumbermen, 2,500 freight handlers, and 5,000 carpenters and woodworkers.[74] Perhaps twice that number watched or took part in demonstrations.[75] Freight handlers met and made a tour of the railroad freight depots, bringing out their fellows on all but two railroads. About 10,000 Bohemians, Poles, and Germans employed in and about the lumberyards marched through the streets with music and flags.[76] Perhaps because of their overwhelming numbers, there were no violent conflicts with the police.

By May 3, more and more workers were joining the strike. A correspondent for *John Swinton's Paper* reported jubilantly: "It is an eight-hour boom, and we are scoring victory after victory. Today the packing houses of the Union Stock Yards all yielded ... Men ... are wild with joy at the grand victory they have gained."[77]

But that day the police fired on a crowd that was attacking strikebreakers at the McCormack factory, killing four and seriously wounding many. With this the atmosphere turned bitter, and the next day repeated street fighting took place between the crowd and police. The anarchists issued an appeal for workers to take up arms, and many labor gatherings were called for that night, including a rally at Haymarket Square to protest police brutality.

Only about 1,200 people attended the Haymarket rally and all but about 300 of them had left as rain began to fall. The last speaker was just saying, "In conclusion ..." when to everyone's amazement a body of 180 policemen marched in and ordered the meeting to disperse. As the speakers climbed down from their platform, a dynamite bomb suddenly flew through the air and exploded among the police, killing one and wounding almost seventy. The police reformed ranks and fired into the crowd, killing one demonstrator and wounding many others.

Popular hysteria followed. The next day, wrote a Chicago lawyer, "I passed many groups of people ... whose excited conversations about the events of the preceding night, I could not fail to overhear. Everybody assumed that the speakers at the meeting and other labor agitators were the perpetrators of the horrible crime. 'Hang them first and try them afterwards,' was an expression which I heard repeatedly.... The air was charged with anger, fear and hatred."[78]

The press throughout the country did everything possible to stir up such emotions. *The New York Times*, for example, wrote: "No disturbance of the peace that has occurred in the United States since the war of the rebellion has excited public sentiment through the Union as it is excited by the Anarchists' murder of policemen in Chicago on Tuesday night. We say murder with the fullest consciousness of what that word means. It is silly to speak of the crime as a riot. All the evidence goes to show that it was concerted, deliberately planned, and coolly executed murder."[79]

The hysteria aroused by the bombing was turned against labor in general. As an anonymous Chicagoan wrote at the time, "The newspapers have taken advantage of the trouble to lump the socialists, anarchists, and strikers all together, making no distinction between them, and the consequence is that the labor cause will have to suffer. There will be a lull, and then a terrible reaction."[80]

"The bomb," John Swinton wrote, "was a godsend to the enemies of the labor movement. They have used it as an explosive against all the objects that the working people are bent upon accomplishing, and in defense of all the evils that capital is bent upon maintaining."[81]

The predicted reaction was not long in coming. Mayor Carter Harrison of Chicago issued a proclamation declaring that, since crowds, processions, and the like were "dangerous" under existing conditions, he had ordered the police to break up all such gatherings. An enormous police dragnet was organized. No less than fifty supposed radical "hangouts" were raided within two days, and those under even the slightest suspicion of radical affiliation were arrested. It was reported that "the principal police stations are filled with anarchists and men who were arrested out of the mobs Tuesday night. At Desplaines Street alone there are over fifty, at the Armory nearly seventy-five, and about twenty-five at the Twelfth Street Station."[82] Most of those arrested were taken without warrants, and for some time no specific charges were lodged against them. As a Chicago socialist wrote to the British socialist and author William Morris at the time:

> One week ago freedom of speech and of the press was a right un-
> questioned by the bitterest anti-Socialist.... Today all this is
> changed.... Socialists are hunted like wolves.... The Chicago papers
> are loud and unceasing in their demand for the lives of all promi-
> nent Socialists. To proclaim one's-self a Socialist in Chicago now is
> to invite immediate arrest.... All the *attachés* of all the Socialist pa-
> pers have been seized and the papers broken up.[83]

The Haymarket hysteria gave the signal for the law-and-order forces
throughout the country to act. Oscar Ameringer describes its effects
on the eight-hour strike in Cincinnati. At first, it had been a "jolly
strike." Victory had seemed certain, for "the forces of the opposition
kept in the background, and did not almost everyone belong to the
Knights of Labor?" As the strike benefits ran out, however, morale
began to decline. Then suddenly newsboys were crying, "Anarchist
bomb-throwers kill one hundred policemen in Haymarket in Chicago."

"The bad news from Chicago," Ameringer wrote, "fell like an exceedingly cold blanket on us strikers. To our erstwhile friends and
sympathizers the news was the clarion for speedy evaporation. Some
of our weaker Knights broke rank.... The police grew more numerous and ill-mannered."[84]

The First Regiment militia was stationed in the Cincinnati Armory
and three regiments from Columbus and Springfield were camped at
Carthage, ten miles out, with special trains on hand to bring them
into the city in twenty minutes if necessary. Most of the trades had
compromised by May 10 on nine hours' pay for eight hours' work.
Only the furniture makers remained out; but their strike was gradually broken and the men returned to work.

The pattern of demoralization and compromise was the same
throughout the country.

Seven of the anarchists seized in Chicago after the Haymarket
bombing were tried in an atmosphere of hysteria and sentenced to
death. Four were eventually hanged, although there was virtually no
evidence connecting them with the bombing. In 1893, the remaining
prisoners were pardoned by Governor John Peter Altgeld. His par-
don message acknowledged the charge that:

the record of this case shows that the judge conducted the trial with malicious ferocity … ; also, that every ruling throughout the long trial on any contested point, was in favor of the State; and further, that page after page of the record contains insinuating remarks of the judge … with the evident intention of bringing the jury to his way of thinking … ; that the judge's magazine article recently published, although written nearly six years after the trial is yet full of venom.… It is urged that such ferocity of subvervience is without a parallel in all history.

"These charges," Governor Altgeld concluded, "seem to be sustained by the record of the trial and the papers before me."[85]

•

The mass strike of 1886 was an attempt by the new class of industrial workers to use their power to gain some control over the conditions of their life and work. The Southwest strike was a direct bid for dual power over the operation of the railroads. The eight-hour strike was both an assertion that the worker was a human being whose life should not be consumed in toil and an attack on the deliberate policy of keeping hours long and unemployment high to get the most work for the least wages.

The movement was met with a fierce wave of reaction, taking the Haymarket hysteria as its starting point and utilizing the techniques that had been developed against the Southwest strikes.

There developed a "tidal wave of formation of employers' associations to check the abuses of unionism, even to crush it."[86] By September, a leading labor journalist wrote that "Since May last, many corporations and Employers' Associations have been resorting to all sorts of unusual expedients to break up the labor organizations whose strength has become so great within the past two or three years."[87]

To take two cases out of scores, the association of shirt manufacturers of Jamesburg, New Jersey, locked out 2,000 employees who it discovered had joined the Knights of Labor, and the manufacturers of silver goods in New York, Brooklyn, and Providence formed an association and locked out 1,200 workers for the same reason.[88] Thousands were not only fired but blacklisted, and thus kept from finding work elsewhere. The "Iron-Clad Oath" (later known as the "Yellow-Dog Contract"), which forced workers to swear they would not join a labor organization, became widely required for employment. The movement for labor solidarity and power was broken for the time, but it would arise again in less than a decade.

•

The 1886 May Day movement produced echoes worldwide. Within a few years, May 1 became an international workers holiday.

Chapter 3

The Ragged Edge of Anarchy

Late in 1892, Henry Clay Frick, the chairman of the Carnegie Steel Company, wrote a letter to Andrew Carnegie. In it he complained, "The mills have never been able to turn out the product they should owing to being held back by the Amalgamated men."[1] The Amalgamated men were a small number of highly skilled steelworkers who belonged to the Amalgamated Association of Iron and Steel Workers, the strongest trade union the country had ever seen.

The Amalgamated was affiliated with the American Federation of Labor (AFL), which had been formed by craft unions hostile to the inclusive membership and broad social goals of the Knights of Labor. Samuel Gompers, the first president of the AFL and its dominant force for forty years, held that the survival of the labor movement required a "pure and simple unionism" that would shun social reform and labor political parties. The AFL was a loose confederation that defined the jurisdiction of national craft unions and then allowed them almost complete autonomy. AFL unions generally included only highly skilled craft workers, excluding—in practice and often by deliberate intent—African Americans, women, many immigrants, and non-craft workers.

The power of AFL unions was rooted in the culture of craft workers, who controlled the skills necessary for production, trained the apprentices who entered the craft, and set rules for proper worker behavior. A hostile historian described the power the skilled steelworkers held over the actual process of production at Carnegie's Homestead Works near Pittsburgh:

> The method of apportioning the work, of regulating the turns, of altering the machinery, in short, every detail of working the great plant, was subject to the interference of some busybody repre-

senting the Amalgamated Association.... The heats of a turn were
designated, as were the weights of the various charges constituting
a heat. The product per worker was limited; the proportion of scrap
that might be used in running a furnace was fixed; the quality of
pig-iron was stated; the puddlers' use of brick and fire clay was prohibited; nor might one lend his tools to another.[2]

This power was exercised by committees in each department. When
investigator John Fitch inquired years later, he was told by both older
workers and a prominent Carnegie official that the union had actually run the Homestead Works.[3]

In 1889, Carnegie had moved to break the union's power, propos-
ing a 25 percent wage reduction and individual contracts for each
worker, putting an end to collective bargaining. In response, the
workers struck. The company hired detectives and tried to bring in
strikebreakers, but was defeated by mass picketing. As Frick described it later: "The posse taken up by the sheriff—something over
100 men—were not permitted to land on our property; were driven
off with threats of bodily harm, and it looked as if there was going to
be great destruction of life and property."[4]

In the face of sympathetic strike movements against other Carnegie
plants, its subsidiary, the H.C. Frick Coke Company, and the railroads handling Carnegie products, the company backed down and
signed a three-year contract with the Amalgamated, to expire in 1892.

The contract, however, was clearly only a truce, and the Carnegie
Company grew more determined than ever to eliminate the union.
David Brody, in his *Steelworkers in America: The Non-Union Era*, points
out that the great objective of the steel masters was to drive down
costs. "The maximization of labor savings required complete freedom
from union interference."[5] As a Carnegie partner put it, "The Amalgamated placed a tax on improvements, therefore the Amalgamated
had to go."[6]

In January 1892, the company proposed a new wage scale that
would reduce Amalgamated men's wages 18 percent, tipping off the
workers that another conflict was approaching. Early in May,
Carnegie drafted a statement that read:

These Works having been consolidated with the Edgar Thomson and Duquesne, and other mills, there has been forced upon this Firm the question whether its Works are to be run "Union" or "Non-Union." As the vast majority of our employees are Non-Union, the Firm has decided that the minority must give place to the majority. These works, therefore, will be necessarily Non-Union after the expiration of the present agreement.... This action is not taken in any spirit of hostility to labor organizations, but every man will see that the firm cannot run Union and Non-Union.[7]

Frick, however, understood that he could break the union without making this the ostensible issue of the conflict, simply by making impossible demands. A congressional committee later concluded that Frick was "opposed to the Amalgamated Association and its methods, and hence had no anxiety to contract with his laborers through that organization ... [T]his is the true reason why he appeared to them as autocratic and uncompromising in his demands."[8]

Following Carnegie's advice, Frick began his preparations for the anticipated strike by stepping up production to record levels. He ordered the construction of a great fence, twelve feet high and three miles long, around the works. Three-inch holes were bored at shoulder height every twenty-five feet, and the fence was topped with three strands of barbed wire. It was quickly dubbed "Fort Frick" and immortalized in verse:

There stands today with great pretense
Enclosed within a whitewashed fence
A wondrous change of great import,
The mills transformed into a fort.[9]

Finally, Frick wrote to Robert Pinkerton of the Pinkerton Detective Agency:

We will want 300 guards for service at our Homestead mills as a measure of precaution against interference with our plan to start operation of the works July 6th, 1892.

The only trouble we anticipate is that an attempt will be made to prevent such of our men with whom we will by that time have made satisfactory arrangements from going to work, and possibly some demonstration of violence upon the part of those whose places have been filled, or most likely by an element which usually is attracted to such scenes for the purpose of stirring up trouble....

These guards should be assembled at Ashtabula, Ohio, not later than the morning of July 5th, when they may be taken by train to McKee's Rocks, or some other point upon the Ohio River below Pittsburgh, where they can be transferred to boats and landed within the enclosure of our premises at Homestead. We think absolutely secrecy essential in the movement of these men.[10]

The Pinkerton Agency was well able to supply the men. In the previous decades it had provided its services for management in seventy major labor disputes; its 2,000 active agents and 30,000 reserves totaled more than the standing army of the nation.[11]

Frick issued an ultimatum that unless the union accepted his terms by June 24, the company would deal with the men only as individuals. Four days later, the company closed down departments in which 800 men worked; by July 2, it had laid off the entire workforce. The battle was on in earnest.

In preparation for the strike, the Amalgamated had formed an Advisory Committee of five delegates from each of its eight lodges. Since the Amalgamated Association included only 750 of the 3,800 workers at Homestead, the Advisory Committee called on the rest to support the strike. Three thousand workers packed into the Homestead Opera House and voted overwhelmingly that everyone would strike—for the semi-skilled and unskilled workers feared that their wages would be reduced as well. The Advisory Committee then circulated the following statement:

The Committee has, after mature deliberation, decided to organize their forces on a truly military basis. The force of four thousand men has been divided into three divisions or watches, each of these divisions is to devote eight hours of the twenty-four to the task of watching the plant. The Commanders of these divisions are to have as assistants eight captains composed of one trusted man from each of the eight local lodges. These Captains will report to the Division Commanders, who in turn will receive the orders of the Advisory Committee. During their hours of duty these Captains will have personal charge of the most important posts, i.e., the river front, the water gates and pumps, the railway stations, and the main gates of the plant. The girdle of pickets will file reports to the main head-quarters every half hour, and so complete and detailed is the plan of campaign that in ten minutes' time the Committee can communi-cate with the men at any given point within a radius of five miles. In addition to all this, there will be held in reserve a force of 800 Slavs and Hungarians. The brigade of foreigners will be under the command of two Hungarians and two interpreters.[12]

Military preparations began at once. Frick's plan for a naval land-ing of the Pinkertons had apparently been discovered by the Amalga-mated men, for they chartered a paddle steamer, the *Edna*, fitted with steam whistles to give the alarm. Day and night the boat cruised the Monongahela, supported by an armada of fifty two-man skiffs.

Every road leading to Homestead was blockaded. Armed guards surrounded the railroad depots. Sentries patrolled the waterfront and watched from the peaks of surrounding hills. A communications sys-tem was created, using flags, skyrockets, and a steam whistle, with telegraph facilities at the strike headquarters. The picket line grew steadily, until 1,000 men were patrolling ten miles of the river on both sides.

Meanwhile, the Advisory Committee took over authority in the town. It directed the running of the gas, water, and electric stations. It shut the saloons, kept the peace, and issued ad hoc laws. When eleven deputy sheriffs arrived to occupy the works, they were sur-rounded by 1,000 pickets and told, "No deputy will ever go in there alive."[13] The *Edna* then politely ferried the deputies back to Pitts-burgh.

When Sheriff McCleary of Allegheny County himself visited, the Advisory Committee gave him a guided tour of the plant and sug-gested that he deputize 500 strikers to guard it and keep out trespass-ers. He refused. The Advisory Committee offered to let fifty deputies take over the works—fearing the illegality of its own acts. But the sheriff was unable to raise a posse, for nobody in Allegheny County wanted to fight the Homestead workers. The few men he was able to recruit refused to bear arms, interfere with picketing, or escort strike-breakers. McCleary was powerless.

By late June, the Homestead workers had been informed by supporters in Chicago and New York that Pinkerton guards were on the
way. The guards arrived five miles downriver from Pittsburgh on the
night of July 5 and boarded the two Pinkerton barges that had been
prepared for them. The union was immediately informed by telegraph that several hundred strangers had arrived.

As the barges passed Pittsburgh a little after 3 a.m., a union lookout
wired headquarters: "Watch the river. Steamer with barges left
here."[14] The river patrol was intensified, and a union skiff almost run
down by the Pinkerton's tug fired revolvers at the barges. A little before 4 a.m., the Advisory Committee pulled the steam whistle with
the signal indicating a river landing was threatened and a mounted
sentry burst into Homestead shouting, "The Pinkertons are coming!"[15] Workers and their families piled from their beds. By the time
the barges approached the landing, the crowd that met them numbered 10,000. Several hundred carried carbines, rifles, shotguns, pistols, and revolvers, while most of the rest carried sticks, stones, and
nailed clubs.

The Pinkertons, armed with Winchester repeaters, threw out a
gangplank and began to land. "Don't step off that boat," someone
yelled from the jeering crowd. One striker lay down on the gangplank. When the first Pinkerton detective tried to shove him aside, he
pulled a revolver and shot the detective through the thigh, knocking
him over backward. Gunfire instantly raked the Pinkertons, killing
one and wounding five. A force of additional Pinkertons rushed on
deck and began firing steadily into the crowd, hitting over thirty and
killing at least three. The fire from the crowd quickly drove the Pinkertons back below decks. When they tried again to land a few hours
later, four more were shot down instantly and the attempt was abandoned.

The strikers, joined by large numbers of armed supporters from
other towns, now tried to find a way to drive the Pinkertons out of
the barges. First they built barricades of steel and pig iron from which
they could fire with safety on the barges. Skiffs swarmed around the
barges, firing at point-blank range. Half-pound sticks of dynamite
were hurled onto the barges, blowing holes in the sides but failing to

sink them. A twenty-pound brass cannon used for holiday celebrations and a smaller one residing in a veterans' hall were wheeled out and trained on the barges. Workers flooded the river around them with oil, but were unable to set them afire. A flaming raft was floated toward them, but the current carried it past. A natural gas main was directed toward the barges and the gas ignited with Fourth of July firecrackers, but only a small explosion was triggered.

By the end of the day, the Pinkertons were faced with a mutiny of their own men. Most of those on the barges were not regular company detectives but guards hired under false pretenses, then shipped to Homestead at gunpoint against their will. Many were wounded and all were terrified; the July heat in the barges was unbearable; the chance of escape was nil. Under these conditions, the men voted almost unanimously to surrender.

After surrendering, the Pinkertons were marched out, disarmed, and made to run a bloody gauntlet in which all were injured, many seriously. The crowd, enraged by the deaths it had suffered, initially demanded that "Not one must escape alive!"[16] The Advisory Committee, fearing the public reaction to a massacre, finally persuaded the workers to let the Pinkertons go.

The battle electrified the nation. On the strikers' side, forty were shot and nine killed. On the Pinkertons', twenty were shot, seven died, and nearly three hundred were injured running the gauntlet.[17] Reporters from all over the country—and even other countries— poured into Homestead. A song, "Father Was Killed by the Pinkerton Men," became an overnight hit.

For several days, the strikers held the works unchallenged. The sheriff, with no effective force of his own, appealed again and again to Governor Robert Pattison to call out the militia. Pattison stalled, stating: "I am of the opinion that there would not have been a drop of blood shed if the proposition had been accepted to let the locked-out men guard the premises."[18] But pressure on him mounted, and finally he ordered the militia to Homestead. It arrived July 12.

In the wake of the Great Upheaval of 1877, the Pennsylvania militia had been reorganized and brought to a high state of efficiency. By

1892, it included well over 8,000 officers and men, well armed with Springfield .45s and Gatling guns.

The strikers at first wanted to oppose the militia, but the Advisory Committee persuaded them to welcome it instead. As the troops marched off the train, they were met by a welcoming committee, complete with band. A spokesman for the Advisory Committee stepped up and said, "On the part of the Amalgamated Association, I wish to say that after suffering an attack of illegal authority, we are glad to have the legal authority of the State here."

General George Snowden, in command of the troops, replied: "I do not recognize your association, sir. I recognize no one but the citizens of this city. We have come here to restore law and order and they are already restored."[19]

The general's conception of law and order soon became apparent. That same day he was asked, "General, is it intended to use your troops for the protection of non-union men?" Snowden answered, "The gates are open and you may enter if the company permits it."[20]

Strikers maintained massive armed picket lines around the works, but the company began ferrying in small groups of strikebreakers by barge. The guards prevented retaliation. At first the militiamen fraternized with the strikers, but Snowden quickly put an end to this by forbidding those in his charge to consort with workers or enter town without an officer. "Pennsylvanians can hardly appreciate the actual communism of these people. They believe the works are theirs quite as much as Carnegie's," Snowden stated.[21]

In response to the killings and the dispatch of the militia, the strike soon spread to the rest of the Carnegie works in the Pittsburgh area. At the Union Iron mills, the men declared July 14 that they would not return to work until the Homestead dispute was settled. The company gradually resumed production there with strikebreakers. The next day, workers at the Beaver Fall mills refused to work until the company opened negotiations with the Homestead strikers. Frick declared a lockout and the strike continued for four months. Workers at Duquesne joined the Amalgamated and struck a week later, following appeals from the Homestead strikers. The state militia in August escorted repairmen, mechanics, and other strikebreakers into the plant, suppressed a riot, and allowed production to resume.

On July 16, the company posted a notice giving Homestead workers until July 21 to apply for rehiring: "It is our desire to retain in our service all of our employees whose past record is satisfactory, and who did not take part in the attempts which have been made to interfere with our right to manage our business."[22] But not a single one of the locked-out men applied.

The company was forced to adopt other tactics. Its law firm brought warrants for murder against leading Advisory Committee members. At least 160 other strikers were charged with lesser crimes. They were no sooner acquitted than the entire Advisory Committee was re-arrested for treason against the state of Pennsylvania. The chief justice of the state personally charged the grand jury:

> When a large number of men arm and organize themselves by divisions and companies, appoint officers, and engage in a common purpose to defy the law, to resist its officers and to deprive any portion of their fellow citizens of the rights to which they are entitled ... it is a levying of war against the State, and the offense is treason ... The men had no further demand upon its property than has a domestic servant upon the household goods of his employer when he is discharged.[23]

In the end, no Pittsburgh jury ever found a striker guilty on any charge. But the prosecutions nonetheless served their purpose. They tied up enormous funds in bail and legal costs. After bail money ran out, they kept large parts of the strike leadership in jail awaiting trial. By all accounts they also confused and demoralized the strikers at Homestead. The Amalgamated men had considered themselves conservative, patriotic citizens—most were solid Republicans—defending their rights against Frick's private army, the Pinkertons. The trials made them doubt the legitimacy of what they had done. Were they in fact just a murderous, treasonous mob?

The Carnegie Company continued bringing strikebreakers into Homestead, but had great difficulty recruiting the scarce, highly skilled steelworkers most needed to resume operations. In many cases, strikebreakers had to be virtually kidnapped. Fifty-six men hired in Cincinnati, for example, were offered easy work and good pay at another Carnegie steelworks. They boarded a train and only after the doors and windows were locked did the armed guards tell them their real destination. They battled with the guards and forced the doors; only twenty-one remained by the time they reached Homestead.

Once in Homestead, a strikebreaker reported, "We were made prisoners in the works and guarded like convicts. The more ignorant were told by the foreman that if they ventured outside the union men would shoot them like dogs…. At least half of them are sick from heat, bad water and poor food."[24]

A local paper reported that desertions were occurring "at such a lively rate … as to threaten to depopulate the mill in a week."[25] Strikers threw pamphlets from a train into the works, promising good treatment and free train fare home for deserting strikebreakers. There followed a grand rush for the exit, and company officials were powerless to stop a large number from leaving. Nonetheless, by September nearly every department of the plant was running, albeit poorly.

The strike held solid for four months. Frick wrote Carnegie, "The firmness with which these strikers hold on is surprising to everyone."[26] But with the company restoring production and winter coming on, morale finally began to decline. On November 18, the unskilled workers asked to be released from their strike pledge. The Amalgamated, knowing the end was at hand, agreed, and two days later called off the strike. The men returned to work as individuals—with the leaders blacklisted forever. Frick cabled Carnegie: "Strike officially declared off yesterday. Our victory is now complete and most gratifying. Do not think we will ever have any serious labor trouble again."[27]

In the wake of the Homestead defeat, the once powerful Amalgamated Association was practically driven out of the steel industry. By 1895, it retained but half its pre-Homestead membership, little of it in steel. The steel masters had created a seemingly impenetrable arsenal of weapons against unionism—an arsenal we shall meet again in 1919.

In the final analysis, the strikers were defeated by the new technology of the steel industry. In earlier days, it had been impossible to run the mills without the skilled labor of the Amalgamated, and so all that was necessary to defeat an employer was "to withhold our skills from them until such time as they agree."[28] But with the increasing mechanization of the mills, employers could start up with new men and only a nucleus of experienced workers. The new giant national corporations with many plants could easily shift work from a struck plant to an unstruck one and thus limit the effect of a strike. Only a movement embracing all steelworkers, skilled and unskilled, and supported by workers in allied industries could have stood a chance against a corporation as powerful as the Carnegie Company. As we shall see, many workers, especially on the railroads, drew this conclusion. But the Amalgamated, like the rest of the AFL, refused to adapt to the new realities of industrial America.

The employers made substantial gains from their victory in the Homestead strike. They were enabled without resistance to reduce labor costs and introduce new machinery to increase productivity. In 1897, a Carnegie executive reported "a marked reduction in the number of men employed." The Homestead Works "can now be run full with about 2,900 men," a 25 percent decrease from 1892.[29] In the two decades after 1890, David Brody points out, "the furnace worker's productivity tripled in exchange for an income rise of one-half; the steelworker's output doubled in exchange for an income rise of one-fifth." (Much of these wage increases merely compensated for inflation.) At bottom, "the remarkable cost reduction of American steel manufacture rested on those figures.... The accomplishment was possible only with a labor force powerless to oppose the decisions of the steel men."[30]

In the depression year of 1893, wages in iron and steel fell an average of 25 percent. With the union smashed, the cuts went practically unopposed. A Carnegie official, announcing wage cuts, stated, "With this new scale in force the firm will be in a position to compete more successfully than ever before and will probably have a material advantage over many of its competitors in cost sheets."[31] In the period from 1892 to 1907, the daily earnings of highly skilled plate-mill workers at Homestead shrank by one-fifth, while their hours increased from eight to twelve a day.[32]

But the most important result of the Homestead strike was its effect on American workers. Secretary of the Treasury Charles Foster, campaigning in Ohio, reported "trouble among laboring men." "They were talking about Homestead, and about Carnegie being too rich, while they were poor."[33]

The bloody battle of July 6 stirred a deep sense of identification in workers throughout the country. For example, 90,000 workers in Chicago had celebrated a "Homestead Day" and raised $40,000 for the strikers. Other contributions had poured into Homestead.

The defeat of the nation's most powerful trade union at the hands of a private army, the state militia, and the Carnegie Company started workers everywhere on a search for new solutions and a broader solidarity.

•

Almost simultaneously with Homestead, armed conflict broke out in the Coeur d'Alenes mining district of Idaho. In January 1892, the companies of the district began closing down their mines; the ostensible reason was to force cheaper railroad rates, but as one mine owner confided, "such is not the main issue, and you will find when the mines resume operation, wages will be $3.00 per day for shovelers and car men," a 15 percent reduction.[34] The workers, including the skilled miners whose wages had not been cut, refused to accept the new scale. Soon the owners began bringing in strikebreakers protected by armed detectives, but workers often persuaded incoming strikebreakers to leave. In one case, sympathetic railroad men assigned eighty strikebreakers from California to ride in boxcars, then shipped them 250 miles in the opposite direction.

In May, the governor was still complimenting union officials on holding their members in check, but this restraint was not to last. Tension built between miners and guards, breaking out in fistfights and peaking June 10, when the miners gathered with their guns in response to a rumor that the militia was on its way. Early the next morning a miner was fired on by guards at the Frisco mill; as the miners gathered, "a general cry went up to capture the Mill."[35] The miners circled the hill, dodging the fire of the guards until they climbed above them. Then, as the battle raged, they loaded a car with powder and sent it down the hill with a short fuse, demolishing the old mill. No one was injured, but the strikebreakers hoisted a white flag and surrendered. They were marched as prisoners down to the union hall. The strikers then peacefully took possession of other mines and plants in the district, taking as prisoners the strikebreakers occupying them.

The governor immediately declared martial law and sent in the militia. When it proved totally inadequate, President Grover Cleveland sent in federal troops at the governor's request. But the strikers occupied the Bunker Hill and Sullivan concentrator and threatened to destroy it unless the strikebreakers departed.

Martial law meant military repression of the strike. The sheriff and marshal, who had been elected by miners' votes, were removed and a hated company doctor was installed as sheriff. Four hundred and eighty people were indicted (although none was ever convicted of any crime) and numbers of strikers and sympathizers were arrested and imprisoned in "bull pens"—stockade enclosures. Two mines running with union workers were closed by order of an army colonel, ostensibly because union men used them as a meeting place.

The conflict at Coeur d'Alenes erupted again seven years later. When the governor on that occasion declared the strike an insurrection beyond the power of the state to control, it was quelled by the U.S. Army.

•

The conflicts of 1892 reached far into the South. Early in that year, streetcar drivers in New Orleans had won a reduction in hours from sixteen to twelve. The street railways, however, in an attempt to break the union, quickly discharged sixteen of the workers who had sponsored the twelve-hour movement. The workers struck, demanding a "closed shop" in which all workers would be union members. The issue polarized the city.

On the side of labor, "Sentiment in favor of a sympathetic strike swept the rank and file of other unions, and was checked only by the conservative leaders who took charge of the car-drivers' fight."[36]

On the side of business, a committee of fifty merchants from the Board of Trade and the commodity and security exchanges—"representing the commercial capital of New Orleans"[37]—came to the aid of the railways, denounced the closed shop, and, despite the absence of significant violence, appealed to the governor to send the militia. The leaders of the strike were arrested on conspiracy charges. The issue stalemated, both sides agreed to arbitration, and the workers were finally granted a preferential closed shop.

In the wake of this victory, workers flooded into the AFL unions of the city. Thirty new unions were chartered. A Workingmen's Amalgamated Council with two delegates elected from each of forty-nine unions, representing more than 20,000 workers, was established. Most important was the creation of the Triple Alliance of recently organized Teamsters, Scalesmen, and Packers. These three unions included both white and black members. They were potentially very powerful because they performed the manual labor essential to the commerce of the city.

On October 24, 1892, at the peak of the business day, the members of the Triple Alliance struck, demanding a ten-hour day, overtime pay, and a preferential closed shop. The Workingmen's Amalgamated Council appointed a Labor Committee of five from the most conservative unions, including one black worker, to direct the strike. Not one member of the committee came from the striking unions.

The strikers faced the unified opposition of all New Orleans employers. The Board of Trade centralized its decision making in a committee of five merchants, backed by the four railway systems entering New Orleans; the cotton, sugar, and rice exchanges; the clearing house; and the mechanics' and dealers' exchanges. It raised a defense fund of several thousand dollars and pushed for intervention by the militia and the courts. For a week it refused to recognize the existence of the Triple Alliance or to enter negotiations.

The stalemate paralyzed the city. The Labor Committee, "moved to action by the indignation of the rank and file,"[38] called a general strike. Under this threat, the unity of employers cracked and those not yet struck pressured the Board of Trade to negotiate. An agreement to resume work pending a final agreement was reached. But the agreement collapsed when many workers did not return to work and others were refused their jobs. There was bitterness on both sides. The employers' position hardened, and they refused to consider arbitration until every striker had returned to work.

The Amalgamated Council again ordered a general strike: "The unions polled their members in heated meetings which generally ratified the strike order. Despite such eagerness for a demonstration of strength, the Labor Committee did all in its power to avoid it."[39]

The strike was twice postponed, but on November 8 more than 20,000 workers walked out. This was only in part a sympathetic strike; each union on strike demanded recognition, a closed shop, and in many cases wage and hour gains for its own members. The strike was joined by associations of such non-industrial workers as musicians and hat, clothing, and shoe clerks. Gas and water workers, electric light trimmers, and other public utility workers had recently been organized with a full understanding of their critical importance. When they joined the strike, the Labor Committee at the behest of the governor ordered them back, but was twice defied by the workers. Streetcar drivers and printers broke their union contracts to join the strike, but the strike did not become a full general strike because other trades with such agreements continued to work. Nevertheless, the strike was highly effective; business came almost to a standstill and bank clearings were cut in half.

Employers moved to break the strike. With the assistance of the railroads, they telegraphed Birmingham, Memphis, Mobile, and Galveston and began bringing in strikebreakers. They pressured the mayor to call for special deputies, but only fifty-nine citizens responded. They began training their own clerks for riot duty, and offered to pay all the costs of the state militia if the governor would call it up. Under their pressure, the governor issued a proclamation ordering citizens not to congregate in crowds. The proclamation implied that the militia would be called if the strike continued, virtually declared martial law, and warned labor of possible bloodshed.

The unions, unwilling to stake their existence on a collision with the militia, decided after three days to bring the strike to an end. An agreement was worked out granting the wage and hour demands of the Triple Alliance, but refusing recognition to the unions. New Orleans continued as an open-shop city. Forty-five strike leaders were indicted in federal court for violating the Sherman Anti-Trust Act.

The New Orleans general strike revealed an extraordinary solidarity. The close cooperation and loyal mutual support of skilled and unskilled and black and white workers suggest that racism was not always insurmountable, even in the deep South. The strike indicates how widespread labor insurgency was in 1892. And it stands as a monument to lost opportunities in the South.

Meanwhile, in Tennessee, another little-known struggle was culminating. Throughout much of the South, convicts from the state penitentiaries were leased out to politically powerful employers at extremely low rates. An investigation by the Tennessee legislature reported that the branch prisons were "hell holes of rage, cruelty, despair and vice."[40] A conservative newspaper added that "employers of convicts pay so little for their labor that it makes it next to impossible for those who give work to free labor to compete with them in any line of business. As a result, the price paid for labor is based on the price paid convicts."[41]

Colonel Arthur Colyar, the Tennessee Democratic leader and general counsel for the Tennessee Coal, Iron and Railroad Company, an employer of convict labor, noted: "For some years after we began the convict labor system, we found that we were right in calculating that free laborers would be loath to enter upon strikes when they saw that the company was amply provided with convict labor."[42]

In spring 1891, miners in Briceville, Anderson County, turned down a contract that would forbid strikes against grievances, give up the right to a check weightman, and provide pay in "scrip" redeemable only at the company store (even though the last two were illegal under Tennessee law). On July 5, the operators imported a carload of forty convicts. The convicts tore down the miners' houses and erected stockades for themselves.

Ten days later, the miners decided at a mass meeting to act before the main body of convicts arrived the next day. Just after midnight 300 armed miners advanced on the stockade in a massed line, demanding the release of the convicts. The officers and guards realized that resistance was futile. The miners marched convicts, guards, and officers to the depot at Coal Creek and packed them on the train to Knoxville.

The next day, the governor came to Anderson County at the head of three companies of the militia and reinstalled the convicts. After the governor departed, the miners entertained the soldiers in their homes and slipped food into their barracks. The militia requested leaves of absence and one whole detachment nearly deserted. It was generally doubted that the militiamen would have taken any action against the miners. Similarly, according to the state superintendent of prisons, "nearly all the citizens of Anderson County around [the] mines are in sympathy with the mob."[43]

At 6 a.m. on July 20, miners from the surrounding counties, including some from Kentucky, armed with shotguns, Winchester rifles, and Colt pistols, began pouring into Briceville and Coal Creek on trains and mules and even on foot. They formed a line and marched on the offending mine, spreading out into the mountain ranges and taking cover behind rocks and trees as they drew close. They sent a committee forward to demand the expulsion of prisoners. When a militia colonel moved as if to capture the committee, one of its members waved a handkerchief as a signal to the miners, who sprang from cover. The 2,000 armed miners had little difficulty persuading the militia and guards to accompany them to the railroad station with the convicts and return with them to Knoxville. Meanwhile, the Briceville miners marched on another mine and sent guards and convicts packing.

The governor immediately ordered fourteen companies of militia, including 600 men, to Anderson County. The miners were talked into accepting a truce if the governor would call a special session of the legislature to repeal the convict lease law. The session convened, but the leasing companies were too powerful and nothing resulted. The miners then appealed to the courts for relief, but when they received none they turned again to direct action.

At a mass meeting on October 28, 1891, the committee that represented the miners at the legislature resigned and was replaced by a more radical leadership. The miners then held a series of secret meetings to prepare their action. On the evening of October 31, the miners filed up to the stockade and demanded the release of the prisoners. Officials turned the 163 convicts over to the miners, who set them free. The miners then marched to another mine and released 120 more convicts in the same manner. Two nights later, the miners rode on horseback to the stockade at Oliver Springs, battered down the door with a sledge hammer, and quickly released the convicts. In each case, the stockades were burned to the ground.

For a time it looked as if the miners had won. All available miners were hired full-time with their own check weightman; other objectionable features were removed from their contracts as well. "Peace and prosperity," a historian later observed, "had descended upon the entire valley from Coal Creek to Briceville."[44] But in the middle of December, the governor announced that the convicts would be sent back into the mine stockades at Briceville, Oliver Springs, and Coal Creek. Fort Anderson, a permanent military camp, was established, with 175 civil and military guards, surrounding trenches, and a Gatling gun overlooking the valley. The miners deeply resented this virtual military occupation.

The climax of the miners' struggle against the convict lease system came in summer 1892. In July, an operator in Tracy City, Grundy County, put regular miners on half-time and brought in 360 convicts to work full-time. The miners began holding secret meetings to discuss how to respond. On the morning of August 10, the miners converged on the convict stockade, overpowered the guards, captured the mines, and put the prisoners on the train to Nashville. The miners then marched to the Inman mine and repeated the same maneuvers.

This triggered renewed conflict in Anderson County. On August 15, 100 miners marched on the convicts' quarters at Oliver Springs and demanded their release. For the first time the guards, instead of submitting, opened fire on the miners, wounding several. In response, miners from the surrounding area poured into Coal Creek, commandeered two freight trains, and ordered the engineers to Oliver Springs at gunpoint. Bands of fifty to one hundred miners continued to arrive and mass into formation. They marched to the stockade, disarmed the guards, burned the blockhouse, and returned guards and convicts to Knoxville. They then laid siege to the militia at Fort Anderson, firing on it from the surrounding hills. Only when an army of 500 soldiers was organized and marched to Anderson County was the siege ended.

Large numbers of local citizens were arrested and locked up in railroad cars, the schoolhouse, and the Methodist church. In the end, nearly all were released by local juries. Although the militia succeeded in crushing the revolt, the convict lease system was thoroughly discredited and was abolished soon after.

•

The struggles at Homestead, Coeur d'Alenes, and Briceville all involved organized, armed resistance by groups of workers to military attack. The New Orleans General Strike revealed an extraordinary solidarity among all races and strata of labor. But these struggles provide only a prelude to the bitterness and unity of the conflicts of 1894. The strikes of 1892 revealed to workers everywhere their own capacity for cooperation and resistance. But 1892 also revealed that struggles by isolated, local groups of workers could be defeated by the superior force of the corporations. In 1894, 750,000 workers struck— more than in any previous year in U.S. history—and half of them did so simultaneously in overlapping national strikes of miners and railroad workers.

In 1893, the United States entered a serious depression. By 1894, *Bradstreet's* estimated that three million people were unemployed in the country; the mayor of Chicago reported 200,000 unemployed in that city alone. Wages were slashed in coal districts thoughout the country. In the Pittsburgh district, for example, the pay scale fell from seventy-nine to fifty cents or less per ton.[45] Miners were cut to parttime. Their desperation was voiced by a miner at Minerton, Ohio: "I have never seen as discouraged a set of men as the miners in this neighborhood have been since the last reduction was made. They know it matters not how steady they work they cannot make enough money to keep a small-sized family in the necessary food, and they have concluded that if they are to starve they prefer doing so at once and not by degrees."[46]

Thus it is not surprising that when the United Mine Workers convention declared a nationwide "suspension," *The New York Times* reported from one mining field, "The miners are elated by the action taken by their delegates at Columbus in declaring for a general suspension to go into effect on April 21st."[47] The aim of the strike was to end the coal glut, thereby forcing prices up and allowing the operators to raise wages to the old rate.[48]

The United Mine Workers had no more than 20,000 members in 1894, but on April 21 more than 125,000 miners struck.[49] The strike eventually reached from Tacoma, Washington, and Birmingham, Alabama, to Springhill, Nova Scotia, including many areas where the UMW had no organization whatever. Andrew Roy, a miners union official, reports that even "the general officers were surprised at the magnitude of the strike."[50] According to the UMW, no more than 24,000 bituminous miners remained at work in the entire country.

The extent of the strike made the workers optimistic. After ten days, President John McBride of the UMW announced: "Already operators are offering to pay the price asked, and in some instances more than has been demanded to get men to resume work, but the men are true to the orders issued by the National Convention, and refuse to work at any price until a general settlement has been made.... Your power having once been demonstrated, you are masters of the situation, and can command anything within reason."[51]

The miners of Thompson Run, Pennsylvania, illustrate what McBride meant. They were granted an increase of wages and were guarded by deputy sheriffs but nonetheless went out on strike in sympathy with the other miners.[52]

The miners organized themselves into bands of a few dozen to many thousands and engaged in widespread direct action that became, at times, virtual guerrilla warfare. They began with marches to spread the strike to unaffected areas. Two thousand miners from Spring Valley, Illinois, headed by two brass bands, marched into La Salle, Illinois, and organized a mass meeting "addressed in a dozen languages" to persuade miners there to strike.[53] A delegation of Clearfield, Pennsylvania, miners went to West Virginia to induce their fellows to join the action. At Pomeroy, Ohio, 500 miners chartered a steamboat and started down the river with a brass band, appealing to the miners along the valley in Ohio and West Virginia to strike.[54]

These activities were usually peaceful, until many operators began trying to reopen with strikebreakers, generally under the protection of special deputies. Under these circumstances, the bands of miners developed into what the press called "armies of intimidation."[55] The miners "have been on short time for two years, and are in poor condition to stand a long lockout," *The New York Times* reported on the first day of the strike. It added a week later: "The most alarming feature of the strike at present is the extreme destitution among the strikers. It is estimated that fully one-third or more of the families at the various plants are in destitute circumstances, and do not know where their next meal is to come from. Many of them proclaim their circumstances, and boldly announce that they will either have to go to work or steal."[56]

One center of disturbance was the Connellsville, Pennsylvania, coke region. Strikebreakers were imported early there, the *Times* reported: "Rainey and Cochran, who own the plants in the Vanderbilt region, say they will work tomorrow, and have asked Sheriff Wilhelm for protection. A large force of deputies was sent to Vanderbilt tonight. Rainey put fifty Italians in his Elm Grove mines yesterday, and will, it is reported, employ Italians at the coke plant if his employees join the strike."[57]

At Scottsdale, Pennsylvania, a crowd of women marched to the coke ovens determined to drive out strikebreakers. A mine official fired a rifle at them. The striking men then rushed the mine. Several were shot, but they captured and severely beat the official. Several strikers who had been shot were subsequently arrested.[58] Another plant was fired up with a large force of men under a strong guard of deputies. An hour later, strikers armed with clubs, stones, and coke forks advanced under cover of darkness and attacked the men at work. The attack was so sudden that the deputies were caught by surprise and the strikebreakers fled in terror.[59] A few weeks later, when an agent imported black workers from Virginia to Mount

Pleasant, Pennsylvania, to work in Frick's Standard Works, the wives of the strikers caught him and tore out most of his beard.[60]

Conflict in the coke region culminated in a massacre at a mine that was being operated by strikebreakers under guard of more than fifty deputies. Two thousand strikers from mining camps along the Monongahela and Youghiogheny Rivers assembled near the mine. *The New York Times* reported that the miners were armed with rifles, shotguns, revolvers, and clubs, though this was subsequently denied by strikers.[61] Squads of strikers marched up and down the road to the music of brass bands and fifes and drums.

Delegations visited the strikebreakers and deputies with messages such as this: "We are fully prepared to resist every attempt to start these mines. We know the workmen here would join the strike if they were not intimidated by armed mercenaries. We are heavily armed and will return bullet for bullet if the deputies fire on us. We are American citizens and demand the protection that is afforded the company."[62]

The next morning when the strikebreakers, guarded by deputies, marched to the mines, the strikers yelled to them to go home. The strikebreakers turned around and started back, to the cheers of the strikers. Instantly, the deputies rushed out of the mines and began "escorting" the strikebreakers to the mines. When the strikers moved forward a deputy fired, perhaps in the air. Soon bullets were flying in all directions. "The strikers fled down the road. The deputies followed closely upon them, and continued firing at them. The narrow defile of the road prevented the strikers from scattering or getting away.... The deputies neared the surging mass of men, and continued to shoot directly at them."[63]

Four of the strikers were killed outright, an unknown number wounded. Sixty-six strikers were captured and one hundred fifty were in jail by the next day.[64] *The New York Times* reported from the coke region:

> The prospect of a speedy settlement of the strike by peaceable means has been swept away by the riot at the Washington Run mines. The news of the killing of strikers has caused the men to become very angry.... The leaders realize the danger of an outbreak in

any part of the region and are doing all in their power to hold the men in check. Numerous appeals were issued from headquarters today to the men to abstain from violence and to keep within the bounds of the law.... The leaders themselves now admit their inability to control the angry strikers. [65]

In Spring Valley, Illinois, about 200 striking miners marched on a mine and drove out the strikebreakers. "A battle with clubs and stones ensued."[66] The strikers banked the fires and nailed up the entrances to the mines. Fifty deputies charged the strikers and captured one of the "ringleaders." "The mob followed the deputies to the jail, and, after breaking down the door, liberated their fellow-striker."[67]

At La Salle, Illinois, strikers held a mass meeting, then proceeded to the La Salle mine and engaged in a gun battle with the sheriff and his deputies. Running out of ammunition, the deputies fled. Three of them were shot, the rest beaten. Having driven them off, the crowd occupied the town. When they learned that two of their number had been taken prisoner, they marched on the jail, forcing the mayor to release the strikers.[68] The sheriff wired Governor John Altgeld for the militia, concluding, "Mob surrounding hotel where I am wounded."[69] A day later troops arrived. They intercepted 250 miners who had captured a railroad train at Ladd and were passing through La Salle on the way to Ottawa to release miners imprisoned there.[70]

At Duquoin, Illinois, 700 miners captured a freight train and forced the engineer to take them to Centralia, where they sabotaged a mine that had begun work there. "The shaft was filled with loose material, the belting on the machinery was cut, and the oil cups knocked from all the shafting."[71] The militia was sent in and at least eighty-eight men were arrested.

The bands of strikers ranged over a considerable area. At Coal Bluff, Indiana, 5,000 miners at a mass meeting decided to march *en masse* to Pana, Illinois, to force miners there to quit. That same day in Grant, Indiana, 1,000 men captured a freight train and took it to Terre Haute, on their way to Pana for the same purpose.[72]

Of course, violence was by no means always necessary to persuade strikebreakers to quit. When the Baltimore and Ohio Railroad ordered its shopmen and its Italian trackmen to replace striking miners, they refused and were fired.[73] At the Elm Grove mines near Wheeling, West Virginia, the operators imported four lots of strikebreakers, only to have them quit one after another.

Whenever it proved impossible to prevent the mining of coal, the miners turned to blockading coal trains as a way to enforce the suspension. At Oglesby, Illinois, strikers piled rails across the tracks of the Illinois Central Railroad in front of a coal train, causing a wreck.[74] At Minonk, Illinois, miners put ties, bolts, and the like across the tracks and forbade the passage of coal cars. In response, Governor Altgeld sent in the militia; he was also appealed to for arms, but reported he had none left.[75] Strikers at Shelburne, Indiana, stopped and examined all trains passing through. "If no coal was found, the trains were allowed to proceed; but when coal was found the cars were sidetracked."[76] At Fontanet, women took over the coal chutes on the Big Four Railroad and refused to let the company fuel its engines.[77] At Lyford, miners climbed on coal cars and set the brakes.[78] Governor Claude Matthews called out the Indiana National Guard to enforce the passage of trains through Cannellsburg.[79] At Jackson, Ohio, 5,000 miners held a mass meeting to decide how to prevent passage of coal. They paraded the town with half a dozen bands. "Communications from the various railroads were read, many of which were to the effect that the railroads will not haul any more non-union coal."[80] At Martin's Ferry, Ohio, strikers burned two railroad bridges. "They had prepared a stone as large as an engine tender at Barton tunnel to drop on a coal train should it succeed in passing the miners' fort."[81] Striking miners from Will and Grundy Counties in Illinois burned a bridge near Carbon "as a warning to the company to stop transferring coal."[82]

Miners at Terre Haute, Indiana, were stopped from blockading coal trains by the arrival of the state militia. When the militia moved to another town, miners resumed searching trains. "Their policy now is to stop the trains whenever the militia is not present, and, if the militia is sent to where they are, they will congregate at another point on the road."[83]

At Salineville, Ohio, 500 miners captured a coal train that had been released by troops earlier in the day. They soaped the tracks so that the train wheels would spin on the rails, backed the train onto a siding, and spiked the switch. "Within an hour the coal was scattered all over the ground and the cars were empty."[84] In the Kanawha Valley of West Virginia, miners burned a drum house and trestle at a working mine, stopped all traffic on one local railroad, and dynamited a railroad bridge. Another railroad simply gave up hauling coal.[85]

In all, the militia was called out in at least five states. At Erisley, Alabama, fifteen companies were encamped, but the strikers found new allies as well: "Several hundred idle mechanics and other laborers in Birmingham contemplate going to the Pratt Mines and encamping there, so as to be on hand to aid the miners in case of a conflict with the troops."[86]

But elsewhere the militia was effective in breaking the strikers' spirit. From Indiana a journalist reported, "The formidable force of militia has awed the strikers."[87] Another journalist wrote from Maryland: "The coming of the militia had a most satisfactory effect on the strikers at all the mines. The men seem to realize that unless they at once resume work new help will be employed to fill their places. At the Eckhart Mine, guarded by three companies of the Fifth Regiment, seventy-five men went to work this morning.... The outlook for the return of all the strikers under guard of the militia is exceedingly good."[88]

When the strikers interfered with trains, the United States government entered the fray. On May 28, a railroad lawyer arrived in Terre Haute with a restraining order from a U.S. judge forbidding the blocking of trains. This allowed the U.S. marshal to organize a force against the strikers. "The power of the federal government being behind the writ, all the force necessary to move the train will be used."[89] A week later, the U.S. marshal at Chicago went with a large body of deputies to Coal City and Streator to enforce an injunction against blockading trains on railroads under federal receivership.[90]

Coal shortages quickly appeared. By April 28, for example, the Colebrook furnaces in Lebanon, Pennsylvania, were banked for want of coal.[91] "It will not be long," McBride remarked April 30, "until there will not be coal enough left in the general market to boil a tea kettle with."[92] From Bellaire, Ohio, it was reported on May 5 that nine blast furnaces and four steel plants and nail mills in the area were closed for want of coal.[93] The Baltimore and Ohio Railroad Company "seized for the road's use all soft coal in transit to customers."[94] On the Chicago, Burlington and Quincy railroad, many of the engines were reduced to burning wood instead of coal.[95] In Des Moines, Iowa, the waterworks of the city were shut down for lack of coal to run them.[96] All departments but one of the great Edgar Thomson Steel Works in Braddock, Pennsylvania, closed down for lack of iron and coal.[97] In St. Louis, by May 24 the coal dealers were simply unable to fill orders in many cases[98]; all but five of the city's flour mills were shut down for want of coal, and the five still in operation were burning wood.[99] The Philadelphia and Erie Railroad was forced to switch to anthracite coal. The Missouri River steamers switched to wood. By May 27, the railroads were reported to be confiscating "all the coal in sight."[100] In Lincoln, Illinois, the electric streetcars were obliged to stop running.[101] Local coal dealers at Carthage reported that it was almost impossible to get coal.[102]

As the strike kept on week after week, the condition of the miners grew severe. From Minonk, Illinois, *The New York Times* reported on May 30, "The miners say their wives and children are at the point of starvation. They are subsisting mainly on dandelions, but have no flour, meat or other provisions."[103]

Despite starvation conditions, the workers held out. When union officials accepted a new pay scale below the old one, large numbers of miners continued the strike anyway. A mass meeting of miners near Camden, Pennsylvania, on June 13 voted unanimously that the new rate was unacceptable. From Punxsutawney, Pennsylvania, the miners were reported to be "indignant at the settlement." At Glenroy, Ohio, 2,000 miners met and decided to continue the strike. At Bellaire, Ohio, the miners said "they will starve before accepting the sixty-cent rate" that UMW officials had agreed to. At Spring Valley, Illinois, a mass meeting adopted resolutions "denouncing the action of the convention and calling upon the executive officers to resign." A mass meeting at La Salle resolved to accept nothing less than a return to the previous pay scale.[104]

But the strikers were defeated in the end by their inability to make the strike universal. As Andrew Roy wrote, "vast train-loads of coal from the anthracite fields of Pennsylvania, the New River and Pocahontas fields of West and Old Virginia (whose miners had not suspended work) were being poured into the markets which the suspension had been inaugurated to deplete."[105]

In Fairmont, West Virginia, for example, "The leading mine operators in this section state that over 200 percent more coal is being mined in the valley between this place and Clarksburg than was ever mined before. Large numbers of miners are flooding in and every pit is being worked to its full capacity. Over 3,500 men are now at work, where a month ago there were only about 1,200."[106] Under such conditions, the strike was finally defeated. After more than two months, the starving miners returned to work under the lower pay scale.

Simultaneously with the coal suspension, strikes had spread among the metal miners. The iron mines of the Eastern Mesaba Range in Minnesota were closed by strikes on May 2. "An armed gang of 300 foreign miners ... marched through the streets of Iron Mountain ... forced the miners in the Iron Mountain and Rathbone Mines to stop work and join their ranks, and also stopped work in White & McDevitt's saw mill. The rioters declare that work in all industries must cease. Fifty deputy sheriffs have been sworn in."[107] Two days later, thirty armed miners marched to Iron Mountain and prevented the opening of mines there.[108]

Especially dramatic was the conflict at Cripple Creek, Colorado. Some mine owners there had tried to lengthen the working day from eight to ten hours; the workers at various mines replied by organizing a union and declaring that all mines would have to adopt eight hours by February 7, 1894. In response, the largest mines shifted to ten hours and the men walked out. After a month of quiet, tension began to rise as some of the mines reopened with strikebreakers guarded by armed deputies. The district court judge issued an injunction against interfering with the operation of the mines, and the president of the union was arrested for violating the injunction.

The mine owners now pledged money and arms to the county if it would enroll a large body of deputies to protect the opening of the mines. The county commissioners accepted the offer, and Sheriff M.F. Bowers soon recruited and imported an army of 1,200 men.[109]

The strikers in turn organized on a military basis, establishing a headquarters and camp on Bull Hill under direction of a miner with three years' training at West Point. Taking the initiative, the miners marched under the noses of the deputies and cut them off from a number of the mines. Next they attacked and captured without bloodshed the Strong mine, which was guarded by a squad of deputies, confiscating their arms and ammunition. Early the next morning, the strikers tried to raid the deputies' camp to obtain more guns and ammunition; one deputy and one striker were killed in the battle that followed.[110]

Meanwhile, groups of armed men were forming in mining towns throughout Colorado, planning to march to Cripple Creek to support the strikers. At Rico, for instance, a hundred fully armed men seized a train and rode 100 miles toward Cripple Creek before they were stopped. In Colorado Springs, the mine owners' citadel, rumors were widely believed that the city was about to be attacked.

The Populist governor of the state finally negotiated a settlement establishing the eight-hour day, but the army of deputies remained in Cripple Creek.[111] Only by sending the militia and interposing them between the strikers and the deputies was a new engagement prevented. Under militia guard, work began again, but it was only a truce. In less than ten years, Cripple Creek and Colorado would again be the center of a bloody mine war.

•

The wage cuts and layoffs of the depression of the mid-1890s extended far beyond the miners. An extreme example of the prevalent wage cuts occurred at the works of the Pullman Palace Car Company in Pullman, Illinois. The entire town—land, houses, stores, churches, and all—was owned by George Pullman. Rents were deducted from wages by the company, and were not reduced as wages fell. The result, according to the minister of the Pullman Methodist-Episcopal Church, was that "after deducting rent the men invariably had only from one to six dollars or so on which to live for two weeks. One man has a pay check in his possession of *two cents* after paying rent.... He has it framed."[112]

During March and April 1894, a majority of the workers at Pullman joined a new organization called the American Railway Union, which had started at the beginning of the depression. The Pullman employees, although not railroad workers, were able to join because Pullman owned a few miles of railroad and anyone who worked for a railroad company—even a coal miner or longshoreman—was eligible. Indeed, the whole purpose of the ARU was to overcome the disunity among railroad workers by uniting them—and eventually all labor—into a single organization. As its president, Eugene Victor Debs, who would later be the five-time U.S. presidential candidate of the Socialist Party, put it: "The forces of labor must unite. The dividing lines must grow dimmer day by day until they become unperceptible, and then labor's hosts, marshaled under one conquering banner, shall march together, vote together and fight together, until working men shall receive and enjoy all the fruits of their toil."[113]

Despite this objective, the ARU maintained the railroad brotherhoods' traditional principle of including only white workers, with the consequence that some blacks gladly took railroad jobs during the great strike. That, however, did not prevent Chicago blacks from taking part in the movement to the extent of tipping over railroad cars in their own neighborhoods.[114]

The first major event in which the ARU was involved was a strike on the Great Northern Railroad, controlled by James J. Hill. Three times within a year the Great Northern had cut wages; three times the officers of the railroad brotherhoods had recommended that the men accept the cuts.[115] Disgusted, a number of the men had joined the ARU. Under its rules, in contrast to those of the brotherhoods, a strike could be called by a majority of members on the railroad line involved. After the third wage cut, the ARU members on the Great Northern declared a strike, although the ARU was so new that not a single lodge had as yet been organized.[116] The strike was supported not only by ARU members, but by a great many other workers, including even the rank and file of the railroad brotherhoods. Even though brotherhood officials helped the company recruit strikebreakers to run the trains, the strike stopped all freight traffic on the line without recourse to blockades. Within little more than two weeks, the company was forced to accept an arbitration decision that was practically a complete victory for the workers.

The victory over Jim Hill in 1894 had much the same results for the ARU that the victory over Jay Gould had had for the Knights of Labor in 1885. Coming in the midst of rising discontent and a series of defeats, the victory dramatized for workers everywhere the possibility and power of solidarity. Workers flooded into the ARU. According to Debs' biographer Ray Ginger:

> The officers were unable to pass out charters fast enough to keep pace with the applications. Entire lodges of the Railway Carmen and the Switchmen transferred to the A.R.U. Firemen, conductors, even engineers, joined the industrial union. But the great majority of recruits came from previously unorganized men who had been unable to meet the high monthly dues of the Brotherhoods. [Indeed, a large proportion of them were not even eligible for membership in the restricted brotherhoods.] The unskilled workers had been unprotected, underpaid, exploited; now the dikes snapped and a reservoir of bitterness and hope drove men pell-mell into the American Railway Union ... The officials did not have to coax or persuade; their main job was to sign cards and issue charters.[117]

Within a year, the ARU had 150,000 members, more than all the old brotherhoods together and only 25,000 fewer than the entire AFL.[118] The new spirit of unity that imbued the railroad workers was revealed when the auditing clerks on one western railroad wanted to organize, but were told by the company that any clerk joining the ARU would be fired on the spot. The switchmen called on the manager and warned him not to threaten the clerks. "During a grave depression, when unemployed men stood on every street corner, such action seemed suicidal, but the switchmen made it stick, and for the first time a railroad office was filled with union men."[119] This spirit made possible the great Pullman boycott of 1894.

The workers at Pullman sent a grievance committee to visit the company's manager. When three members of the committee were fired, sentiment for a strike reached a fever pitch. At an all-night session of the grievance committee, two top ARU officials strongly advised against a strike and Debs wired caution, but "Howard's oratory, Keliher's ebullient charm, and Debs' influence all went for nothing."[120] The committee voted unanimously to strike. The strikers held open meetings daily at which reports of committees were given and matters of policy decided; a central strike committee with representatives of each local union directed the strike. Three hundred strikers guarded the Pullman works day and night.

The strike was a desperation move. As a strike spokesman put it: "We do not expect the company to concede our demands. We do not know what the outcome will be, and in fact we do not care much. We do know we are working for less wages than will maintain ourselves and our families in the necessaries of life, and on that proposition we absolutely refuse to work any longer."[121]

A month after the strike began, the American Railway Union held its first regular convention in nearby Chicago. The workers at Pullman appealed to the convention for aid. For the 400 delegates, many of whom had visited Pullman, the issue became symbolic of everything they hated—the poverty of the workers, the arrogance of George Pullman, and the overwhelming power of the corporation. According to Ginger,

> Debs now used every rein of control in the hands of a chairman. His shrewdness, his eloquence, his influence, were all thrown into battle against headstrong action, and, in the end, they all went for nothing. The entire hall was filled with muffled, bitter comments: George Pullman had gone too far. It was time to show the bloodsucker. The A.R.U. should boycott all Pullman cars, not move a single sleeper until Pullman settled with his workers.... Finally one man spoke for dozens of men: A boycott against Pullman cars should be declared immediately. Debs, in his calmest voice, refused to entertain the motion.... Above everything else, he wanted to avoid a boycott on Pullman cars.[122]

The leadership of the union did everything possible to avoid what it feared would become a sympathetic strike. But when Pullman refused arbitration, saying there was "nothing to arbitrate,"[123] a committee of the ARU convention urged that a boycott of Pullman cars be instituted. When the delegates wired home for instructions, they found sentiment overwhelmingly in favor of the plan and voted unanimously to apply it.

Of course, it was not solely sympathy for the workers at Pullman that led the railroad workers to such an extraordinary decision. Debs himself put clearly the reasons for this sudden development of solidarity. The railroad employees had lost confidence in the brotherhoods because they "had failed, in a single instance, to successfully resist" the wage cuts gradually sweeping the country. All of the delegates, therefore, came to the ARU convention expecting to "restore their wages and to protect them in their rights and wages as employees. This is the reason that they were so ripe to espouse the cause of the injured Pullman employees.... While the injuries and grievances of the Pullman employees appealed to their sense of justice and to their sense of duty for redress, these further grievances of their own made the matter more binding upon them ... to do everything in their power to protect the Pullman employees, as well as their constituents."[124]

The testimony of workers from around the country gives a picture of those grievances. At La Salle, 100 miles west of Chicago, the workers had voted to strike even before the Pullman boycott was called, to protest the firing of ARU members.[125] At Des Moines, Iowa, the main grievance was "the radical change in the rules of the company concerning promotion and priority," putting extra workers on the employment rolls and using the surplus to drive down wages and forestall strikes.[126] At Rock Island, "some six or seven ... men were discharged, which caused a very restless feeling among the men ... and when it was learned that switchmen on the Rock Island had been discharged as members of the A.R.U., for refusing to handle Pullman cars, they took a vote in the local union and decided to take the same stand the members of the union did in Chicago."[127]

On the Grand Trunk railroad, one official "would get so drunk he did not know anything and then go around and dictate to men that did know their business," while another would "pry into the affairs of the men" and "cut the force down to such an extent that a man was dogged around and chased around as though he was not human in order to get the work done." In addition, the Grand Trunk used inexperienced road officials to do switching while laying off regular switchmen.[128]

On the B&O, the complaints were "favoritism, pets, and maladministration of some of the petty officers."[129] On the Pittsburgh, Fort Wayne and Chicago, engineers and foremen were deprived of paid dinner hours they had won in a previous agreement.[130] One fireman observed: "There was a feeling among railroad men in general that I had occasion to meet that there was going to be a reduction of wages on nearly every road throughout the country.... In a large number of roads there was a feeling among the employees that they were almost in a helpless condition to stand against the oppression of the petty officials, and the petty officials took advantage of that feeling and deviled the men."[131]

The boycott began on June 26, 1894, when switchmen on a number of lines out of Chicago refused to switch Pullman cars. They were instantly fired, leading other workers on the lines to walk off in protest. Two days later, four or five Chicago railroads were stopped, with 18,000 men on strike. This was what Debs and the other ARU officials had expected; but they were greatly surprised as committees and groups of railroad workers from all over started appearing at the strike headquarters, announcing that their local unions had decided to strike in support of the Pullman workers.[132] Soon virtually all twenty-six roads out of Chicago were paralyzed, and all transcontinental lines except the Great Northern—which carried no Pullman cars—were stopped. The struggle extended to twenty-seven states and territories. An estimated 260,000 railroad workers, nearly half of them not members of the ARU, joined the strike. *Bradstreet's* estimated that 500,000 were out of work because of the strike.

Coming at the same time as the coal strike, the Pullman boycott represented a social crisis of the first order. *The New York Times* saw in it "the greatest battle between labor and capital that has ever been inaugurated in the United States."[133] By July 3, *The Chicago Tribune* declared that the strike had attained the "dignity of an insurrection."[134]

Direction of the action moved on two levels. The ARU convention had left the conduct of the strike in charge of its president, Eugene

Debs, and its executive board. They rapidly set up a strike headquarters and threw themselves wholeheartedly into the strike in Chicago. These officials articulated the strikers' position, formulated aims, counseled non-violence, held daily mass meetings in Chicago, and sent out hundreds of telegrams a day encouraging the strikers. Operational control, however, rested in the strike committees that sprang up within each body of strikers.

As Debs explained it, "The committees came from all yards and from all roads to confer with us. The switchmen, for instance, would send a committee to us, and we would authorize that committee to act for that yard or for that road, and that committee would then go to that yard and take charge of the affairs."[135]

The ARU officials consulted daily with these committees in shaping strike decisions. The committees also served in part to contain the strike within the limits set by the leadership, although this was by no means always the case; for example, when the Mobile and Ohio Railroad offered not to run Pullman cars, the ARU advised the workers there to call off their strike, but they refused because they felt it would weaken the unity of the strike.[136] This informal structure of strike committees allowed the coordination of the strike over a vast area of the country despite the lack of organized preparations.

The Pullman conflict rapidly came to be understood as a general struggle between all workers and the corporations as a whole. The General Managers' Association (GMA), which represented the twenty-six Chicago railroads, served as a general staff for management, planning strategy, recruiting strikebreakers, and using its enormous power to influence public opinion and the government. As Debs wrote in an appeal to the railroad workers of America to support the strike,

> The struggle with the Pullman Company has developed into a contest between the producing classes and the money power of the country.... The fight was between the American Railway Union and the Pullman Company. The American Railway Union resolved that its members would refuse to handle Pullman cars and equipment. Then the railway corporations, through the General Managers' Association, came to the rescue, and in a series of whereases declared

to the world that they would go into partnership with Pullman, so to speak, and stand by him in his devilish work of starving his employees to death. The American Railway Union accepted the gage of war, and thus the contest is now on between the railway corporations united solidly upon the one hand and the labor forces on the other.[137]

The strike was effective beyond anyone's expectation. For the week ending June 30, 1894, ten trunk-line railroads out of Chicago carried 42,892 tons of eastbound freight; for the week ending July 7, they carried only 11,600; the Baltimore and Ohio carried fifty-two tons and the Big Four Railroad carried not one ton.[138] As Debs wrote later, the strike was won as far as beating the railroad companies was concerned: "The combined corporations were paralyzed and helpless."[139] Even John Egan of the General Managers' Association admitted by July 2 that the railroads had been "fought to a standstill."[140]

But by June 30 the legal committee of the GMA had worked out detailed plans to bring a power against the workers that the ARU had not reckoned on—the United States government. According to Almont Lindsey's careful study, *The Pullman Strike*: "A vital part of the strategy of the association was to draw the United States government into the struggle and then to make it appear that the battle was no longer between the workers and the railroads but between the workers and the government ... [I]t was the policy of the roads not to alleviate the inconvenience in transportation but rather to aggravate this condition wherever possible, in order to arouse the anger of the traveling public and thus hasten action by the federal authorities."[141]

In line with this policy, John Egan of the GMA on July 2 called for the use of federal troops, arguing there was no "other recourse left." With these troops, "the strike would collapse like a punctured balloon. It is the government's duty to take this business in hand, restore law, suppress the riots, and restore to the public the service it is now deprived of by conspirators and lawless men."[142]

President Grover Cleveland and his attorney general, Richard Olney, were more than happy to use the force of the U.S. government to crush the strike. Olney, for thirty-five years a railroad lawyer and still a director of several railroads (including one involved in the boycott), considered the strike an attack on railroad property and corporate control. The administration decided to break the strike in Chicago, for, as Olney confided to a trusted agent there, "if the rights of the United States were vigorously asserted in Chicago, the origin and center of the demonstration, the result would be to make it a failure everywhere else and to prevent its spread over the entire country."[143]

President Cleveland concurred in this strategy; as he wrote years later, "It was from the first anticipated that [Chicago] would be the seat of the most serious complications, and the place where the strong arm of the law would be needed. In these circumstances, it would have been criminal neglect of duty if those charged with the protection of governmental agencies and the enforcement of orderly obedience and submission to federal authority, had been remiss in preparations for an emergency in that quarter."[144]

Olney's first move was to appoint Edwin Walker, a member of the GMA's legal committee and general counsel for one of the struck railways, a special federal attorney in Chicago. His next was to secure a blanket injunction forbidding all strike activities—even attempting by persuasion to induce an employee to abandon his job.[145] Soon such blanket injunctions covered the country from Michigan to California, putting all strike supporters in contempt of court. One of the judges issuing the first injunction proudly called it a "Gatling gun on paper."[146]

"The object of the injunction," as the editor of *The Chicago Times* observed, was "not so much to prevent interference with the trains as to lay a foundation for calling out the United States troops."[147] On July 2, the federal marshal in Chicago read the injunction to a jeering crowd outside Chicago; the crowd responded by dragging baggage cars across the tracks to prevent the passage of trains. The next day, the marshal wired Olney, warning that a general strike was expected and saying, "I am unable to disperse the mob, clear the tracks, or arrest the men who were engaged in the acts named, and believe that no force less than the regular troops of the United States can procure the passage of the mail trains or enforce the orders of the court."[148] Over the protest of Governor John Altgeld of Illinois, federal troops marched into Chicago. Attorney General Olney told reporters, "We have been brought to the ragged edge of anarchy and it is time to see whether the law is sufficiently strong to prevent this condition of affairs."[149]

Until federal troops arrived, the strike in Chicago had been extraordinarily peaceful. Debs and the other ARU officials had told the workers that violence would play into the hands of the companies and that the strike could be won simply by the refusal of the railroad workers to work. With the U.S. Army on the scene to break the strike, however, such a peaceful victory was no longer possible, and the popular mood shifted rapidly. As an ARU official testified later, "the people of America have been treated so unfairly—I do not speak of myself, but from the experience we had in going through the country—that the very sight of a blue coat arouses their anger; they feel it is another instrument of oppression that has come, and they are liable to do things they would not do if the blue coats were kept away."[150]

The prevailing atmosphere is suggested by Debs' statement when troops were sent in: "The first shot fired by the regular soldiers at the mobs here will be the signal for a civil war. I believe this as firmly as I believe in the ultimate success of our course. Bloodshed will follow, and 90 percent of the people of the U.S. will be arrayed against the other 10 percent. And I would not care to be arrayed against the laboring people in the contest, or find myself out of the ranks of labor when the struggle ended. I do not say this as an alarmist, but calmly and thoughtfully."[151] General Nelson Miles, commander of the U.S. troops in Chicago, likewise believed there was danger that the civil government and authority of the United States would be paralyzed, if not overthrown, as a result of the conflict.[152]

Violent confrontation did in fact follow the arrival on July 4, 1894, of U.S. troops in Chicago. That night, crowds began to gather on railroad property, overturning boxcars and resisting authority. They were not composed of railroad workers, but of the most depressed part of the working class—immigrants, the unemployed, and unskilled laborers. The next day the crowds grew, throwing switches, changing signal lights, and blocking tracks with toppled boxcars. The largest crowd, numbering 10,000, started at the stockyards and moved slowly eastward along the Rock Island Line. The general sentiment was caught by a crowd that marched through railroad yards calling out workers, yelling that it was a "fight between labor and capital, and they must come out."[153] That night a great fire broke out, destroying seven structures at the World's Colombian Exposition, while at many other points railroad cars were burned.

The next morning, a railroad agent on the Illinois Central shot two members of a crowd. The crowd retaliated by burning the yards. The action spread to other lines, peaking that night when the crowd destroyed 700 cars at the Panhandle yards in South Chicago. In one day, the crowds destroyed railroad property valued at $340,000.

The total armed forces occupying Chicago, including federal troops, state militia, and deputy marshals hired and paid by the railroads, reached 14,000. In the course of the intermittent warfare, thirteen people were killed and fifty-three seriously wounded. Nonetheless, the strike remained firm. The Associated Press reported on July 6: "Despite the presence of the United States troops and the mobilization of five regiments of state militia; despite threats of martial law and bullet and bayonet, the great strike inaugurated by the American Railway Union holds three-fourths of the roads running out of Chicago in its strong fetters, and last night traffic was more fully paralyzed than at any time since the inception of the tie up."[154]

Meanwhile, the conflict spread across the country.

In Trinidad, Colorado, on July 1, a large crowd captured and disarmed forty-two deputy marshals coming into town to break the strike on the Santa Fe. The next morning, without even consulting the Populist governor of the state, the president ordered up five companies of U.S. troops from Fort Logan. The troops cleared the tracks and protected the deputy marshals as they arrested forty-eight "ringleaders" who had made "incendiary speeches" at a meeting of the strikers.[155] The deputy U.S. marshals were instructed to arrest without warrants anyone trying to induce railroad employees to quit and to ignore opposition from local magistrates and officials, arresting them if they tried to intervene. This, charged Governor David Waite, "allowed the U.S. Marshal to enlist a private army to suppress alleged state troubles ... waging an active war in Colorado without any declaration thereof by the U.S. ... and utterly in violation of law."[156]

The center of resistance on the Santa Fe next shifted to Raton, New Mexico, where 500 members of the ARU lodge were supported by the county sheriff and 300 striking coal miners, many of them armed. The U.S. marshal and eighty-five deputies entered Raton with instructions to arrest the sheriff if he interfered. They were met with such hatred in the town that hotel workers quit rather than serve them, and the hotels were thereafter staffed with deputy marshals. Meanwhile, a crowd in the little mining town of Blassburg, three miles above of Raton, launched sixteen cars down the grade, crashing in Raton and blocking the tracks. Even after the Tenth Infantry arrived, the railroads were unable to move trains because of insufficient crews.

In California, public hostility toward the railroad monopolies was so great that the special federal attorney at Los Angeles warned Olney that he believed open rebellion was an imminent possibility.[157] Five companies of California militia assembled at their armory and declared their sympathy for the strike. Troops were ordered into Los Angeles following a coded report from the U.S. attorney that heavily armed strike sympathizers were pouring into town and that in enforcing the injunction the U.S. government might encounter resistance from 5,000 armed men.[158] The strike was finally broken in the Los Angeles vicinity by putting a detachment of troops on each train.

Meanwhile, a large number of railroad workers at Sacramento joined the strike, while hundreds more poured in from up and down the lines—including a large, heavily armed party aboard a train that workers had seized at Dunsmuir. When the U.S. marshal and his deputies tried to protect a mail train containing Pullman cars, the strikers manhandled him and disconnected the train. He then called in two regiments of the state militia, some of whom simply deserted from the ranks in open defiance of orders, while the rest were unwilling to charge or fire out of sympathy for the strikers. Finally, 542 federal soldiers landed by boat in Sacramento, where they cleared the railroad tracks with fixed bayonets.

Similarly, in Oakland, a large crowd occupied the railroad yards, "killing" engines and leaving them to block the tracks. When 370 sailors and marines arrived, the wives and mothers of the strikers organized a Ladies' Relief Organization and turned a local hall into a hospital in anticipation of a battle that never occurred.

The struggle spread with great popular support throughout the western states of Nebraska, Wyoming, Utah, Nevada, and Montana. In Rawling, Wyoming, the city authorities ordered all deputy marshals combating the strike out of town. At Ogden, Utah, the strikers completely controlled the western terminal of the Union Pacific, uncoupling Pullman cars by force when necessary. They defied the U.S. marshal, who was able to raise only a small force of deputies and was afraid to make arrests lest he provoke a riot. When word came that federal troops were soon to arrive, fires were set simultaneously in seven different parts of the city. Railroad bridges were burned at Carlin, Nevada. The Great Northern, which used no Pullman cars, was the only transcontinental railroad not on strike, but when the army planned to move troops to Helena, Montana, on it, the workers threatened to strike. The order was withdrawn.

At Dubuque and Sioux City, Iowa, switches were spiked and tracks obstructed until the governor sent six militia companies into the latter. At Hammond, Indiana, the strikers sidetracked all Pullman cars despite the resistance of the sheriff, the federal marshal, and their deputies. Large crowds ranged over the tracks attacking strikebreakers, derailing trains, and seizing a telegraph office to prevent an appeal for the militia. On July 8, state militia and federal soldiers arrived in Hammond and cleared the tracks by firing indiscriminately into the crowd. "I would like to know," demanded the mayor, "by what authority U.S. troops come in here and shoot our citizens without the slightest warning."[159]

In Duluth, dockworkers struck in sympathy with the Pullman workers.[160] At Spring Valley, Illinois, striking miners provided the resistance; when a crowd stoned a train guarded by federal soldiers, the troops fired on them, killing two and wounding several. By the end of the Pullman strike, an estimated thirty-four people had been killed, and federal or state troops had been called out in Nebraska, Iowa, Colorado, Oklahoma, California, and Illinois.[161] General Miles maintained that only federal troops had saved the country "from a serious rebellion."[162]

Meanwhile, the U.S. government proceeded systematically with its plan to break the strike in Chicago. On July 10, 1894, Debs was arrested for conspiracy. The ARU office was ransacked by federal marshals, who seized all books and papers in a manner even the Department of Justice later admitted was illegal. The blockade out of Chicago was finally broken by sending trains, each escorted by forty deputy marshals and a contingent of U.S. troops, along the various lines. The eastbound freight on the ten trunk lines out of Chicago, which had fallen to 4,142 tons for the week ending July 14, rose to 29,146 tons by the following week.[163] As the United States Strike Commission, which later investigated the conflict, wrote, "The action of the courts deprived the ARU of leadership, enabled the General Managers' Association to disintegrate its forces, and to make inroads into its ranks. The mobs had worn out their fury, or had succumbed to the combined forces of the police, the U.S. troops and marshals, and the State militia."[164]

Besides the government, the General Managers' Association had another powerful ally—the established railroad brotherhoods. When 400 engineers had struck on the Wabash, the head of their union denounced them and announced that unemployed engineers would be permitted to serve as strikebreakers. The union head even went so far as to recommend particular men to replace striking engineers. The chief of the conductors took the same stand. The Brotherhood of Trainmen instructed its members to "perform their regular duties."[165] Its head declared, "The triumph of this railroad strike would be the triumph of anarchy."[166] It is no surprise that Everett St. John, chairman of the General Managers' Association and himself general manager of the Rock Island Line, testified of the railroad brotherhoods, "We have always gotten along comfortably well—in fact, in a very satisfactory manner—with the old orders as they exist."[167]

At the last moment, the strike was almost given a reprieve by the workers of Chicago. They supported the strikers passionately. Newsboys, for example, dropped newspapers that opposed the boycott into the sewers.[168] On June 30, the Chicago Trades and Labor Assembly had pledged the strength of its 150,000 members in support of the strike. It sent a committee to tell the ARU that, if necessary, every union member in Chicago would strike in sympathy; but Debs at that point considered the idea too extreme. Nonetheless, as the conflict deepened, pressures for a general strike continued to build. On July 7, the Building and Trades Council, representing 25,000 members, voted unanimously for a sympathetic strike and called for a nationwide general strike. The next day delegates from 100 Chicago unions met to decide on a strike.

While Chicago workers overwhelmingly supported such a move, many union officials objected because it would violate existing contracts with employers. But when the delegates heard that President Cleveland had issued a proclamation that seemed to put Chicago under martial law and declared that resistors would be considered "public enemies," all opposition to a general strike dissolved. Pullman was given until July 10, however, to accept arbitration before the strike went into effect. This delay proved fatal, for by July 11, Debs and the other ARU officials had been arrested, the military was in complete control of the city, and the strike was clearly doomed to defeat. The result was that only about 25,000 non-railroad workers joined the sympathetic strike in Chicago.[169]

At the request of the Chicago unions, AFL head Samuel Gompers came to Chicago, calling in twenty-four other national trade union officials for a conference at the Briggs House. During the first session, a committee from the Cigar Makers' Union of Chicago argued that, because the struggle of the ARU concerned the well-being of all workers and therefore required the complete solidarity of all labor, the conference should call for a nationwide general strike to force Pullman to arbitrate. Debs likewise suggested that a general strike be called if the railroad strikers were not permitted to return to their jobs. But the AFL leaders were suspicious of sympathetic strikes, opposed to the inclusive industrial unionism of the ARU, and allied with the railroad brotherhoods that opposed the strike. They believed that a head-on struggle between labor and capital should be avoided at all costs. Instead of appealing for a general strike, they recommended that $1,000 be given for Debs' legal defense and returned home.[170]

When the Chicago Building Trades Council called off its sympathetic strike in the wake of the AFL's decision, *The Chicago Tribune* declared jubilantly:

> DEBS' STRIKE DEAD
> It is Dealt Two Mortal Blows by Labor
> Federation Hits First
> Trades Council Follows with a Crusher[171]

(Perhaps the United States Strike Commission of 1894 had such actions in mind when it declared that trade unions "have promoted conciliation, arbitration, conservatism, and responsibility in labor contentions and agreements."[172])

How close at hand was a general strike? A number of locals in Chicago had already struck, and the Trades and Labor Assembly had come out for the idea. The Briggs House Conference statement said, "While we may not have the power to order a strike of the working people of our country, we are fully aware that a recommendation from this conference to them to lay down their tools of labor would largely influence the members of our affiliated organizations."[173] This would seem to be borne out by Gompers' testimony that "from St. Louis and various places throughout Missouri, Ohio, and Colorado, I was in receipt of telegrams that they had resolved to await the word that the A.F.L. conference would give as to determining their action."[174]

Instead of calling for such support, however, the Briggs House statement urged "that all connected with the A.F.L. now out on sympathetic strike should return to work, and those who contemplate going out on sympathetic strike are advised to remain at their usual vocations."[175] Gompers agreed that had the executive board of the AFL called a strike, even in its advisory capacity, its members would have struck[176] and that the strike thereupon "would have spread to a greater or lesser extent over the whole country."[177] Many coal miners were still on strike, and more workers joined strikes in 1894 than any previous year. Given the stormy atmosphere of the time, Gompers' judgment seems sound.

The workers at Pullman held out to the end. On July 6, the militia was sent in, replacing the strikers' guards at the works, but the strike remained firm. Once the railroad strike was broken, however, all hope was lost, and Pullman began to rehire his workers on his own terms, with the militia standing by.

The real issue of the strike, of course, had not been simply the wages of the workers at Pullman. George Pullman defined the issue as "the principle that a man should have the right to manage his own property."[178] The secret minutes of the General Managers' Association suggested that the question was whether the railroads would "determine for themselves" what cars they would or would not handle on their lines.[179] Or, as Vice-President George Howard of the ARU put it, "I always contended that the men had a right to handle or not handle anything they pleased," whereas the company announced publicly that it "would haul such cars as they chose regardless of what the delegates to the A.R.U. convention might say, or what their own employees might say."[180] The real issue was one of power; it was understood that this in turn would determine the other questions of wages, working conditions, and the like.

The Pullman strike showed that merely by making a non-violent strike against an industry—if the strike seriously challenged corporate power—workers might bring down upon themselves vast social forces, including military force. As Debs put it:

> We have only got a number, and a limited number, of poorly paid men in our organization, and when their income ceases they are starving. We have no power of the Government behind us. We have no recognized influence in society on our side.... On the other side the corporations are in perfect alliance; they have all of the things that money can command, and that means a subsidized press, that they are able to control the newspapers, and means a false or vitiated public opinion. The clergy almost steadily united in thundering their denunciations; then the courts, then the State militia, then the Federal troops; everything and all things on the side of the corporations.[181]

The lesson of the strike, as one railroad worker put it, was to "demonstrate to the laboring men that they must get together; that no single organization can win … [T]hey have seen the united press against them; they have seen the united clergy against them; they have seen the entire judiciary against them; they have seen the entire office holders of this country against them—the United States Government against them, and all the old-time [labor] organizations."[182]

The full mobilization of state power against the strikers created problems with which even the militant leadership of the American Railway Union was unprepared to deal. Although the ARU's structure allowed an unusual amount of initiative from below, local groups still looked to the national officers for leadership and direction. Consequently, when the leaders were jailed and their office broken up, the locals were unable to continue on their own. Debs gave a vivid picture of just how vulnerable the strike was to the loss of central leadership:

> Our men were in a position that never would have been shaken under any circumstances if we had been permitted to remain among them.… [B]ut once we were taken from the scene of action and restrained from sending telegrams or issuing the orders necessary, or answering questions; when the minions of the corporations would be put to work at such a place, for instance, as Nickerson, Kansas, where they would go and say to the men that the men at Newton had gone back to work, and Nickerson would wire me to ask if that were true; no answer would come to the message because I was under arrest, and we were all under arrest. The headquarters were demoralized and abandoned, and we could not answer any messages. The men went back to work, and the ranks were broken up by the federal courts of the United States.[183]

Even had the ARU officers remained at liberty, however, they would not have been able to win the strike against a state power resolved to crush it without a complete change of approach. The union was committed to "legal" and "orderly" tactics, even while it was being destroyed by the forces of "law and order." Initially, it made perfect sense for the workers to follow Debs' policy and "do everything in their power to maintain order, because … if there was perfect order there would be no pretext upon which [opponents of the strike] could call out the soldiers or appeal for the intervention of the court, and we would win without a question of a doubt."[184] But when the courts and army intervened despite the legal and non-violent policy of the strikers, the ARU did not change its approach. It was thus doomed to failure. Under such conditions, as Debs later pointed out, even "if all the railroad men in the country were organized within one brotherhood and acted together it would be impossible for them to succeed."[185]

When the troops came in, making legal success impossible, workers throughout the country responded with mass direct action. But for the ARU to adopt such a policy would have meant a challenge to the entire social order—a step from which it recoiled. Thus we are presented with the spectacle of Eugene Victor Debs, perhaps the greatest example of a courageous, radical, and uncorruptable trade union official in American history, trying to end the strike to prevent it from becoming an insurrection. For, as Debs testified, "We became satisfied that things were assuming too serious a phase, and that a point had been reached when, in the interest of peace and to prevent riot and trouble we must declare the strike off … It was in the crisis when everything was at stake, where possibly it might have eventuated in a revolution."[186]

•

However much of a defeat the Pullman strike may have been in terms of its immediate objectives, its real significance, as Debs saw, was the unprecedented sense of solidarity it reflected. This solidarity was not embodied in any particular organization, but in what he called "the spirit of organization." As Debs testified after the strike: "They might as well try to stop Niagara with a feather as to crush the spirit of organization in this country.… It may not come up in the form of the American Railway Union, but this spirit of resistance to wrong is there, it is growing stronger constantly, and it finds its outlet in labor disturbances, in strikes of various kinds. Even if the men know in advance that they are going to meet with defeat they are so impressed with a sense of wrong under which they are suffering that they strike and take the penalty."[187]

Chapter 4

Nineteen Nineteen

"The most extraordinary phenomenon of the present time," wrote *The Nation* in October 1919, "the most incalculable in its after effects, the most menacing in its threat of immediate consequences, and the most alluring in its possibilities of ultimate good, is the unprecedented revolt of the rank and file."

> It is a world-wide movement much accelerated by the war. In Russia it has dethroned the Czar and for two years maintained Lenin in his stead. In Korea and India and Egypt and Ireland it keeps up an unyielding resistance to political tyranny. In England it brought about the railway strike, against the judgment of the men's own executives. In Seattle and San Francisco it has resulted in the stevedores' recent refusal to handle arms or supplies destined for the overthrow of the Soviet Government. In one district of Illinois it manifested itself in a resolution of striking miners, unanimously requesting their State executive "to go to Hell." In Pittsburgh, according to [Samuel] Gompers, it compelled the reluctant American Federation [of Labor] officers to call the steel strike, lest the control pass into the hands of the [Industrial Workers of the World] and other "radicals." In New York it brought about the longshoremen's strike and kept the men out in defiance of union officials, and caused the upheaval in the printing trade, which the international officers, even though the employers worked hand in glove with them, were completely unable to control.
>
> The common man, forgetting the old sanctions, and losing faith in the old leadership, has experienced a new access of self-confidence, or at least a new recklessness, a readiness to take chances on his own account. In consequence, as is by this time clear to discerning men, authority cannot any longer be imposed from above; it comes automatically from below.[1]

It was this revolt that formed the underpinning for the mass strike of 1919.

In the quarter-century following the Pullman strike, American capitalism had changed profoundly. Such basic industries as steel and coal grew phenomenally, rivaling the railroads in size and economic importance. These basic industries developed an organized and controlled national market, usually dominated by one or a few firms. The United States became a great industrial exporter. It also became a world power engaged in war with Spain in 1898 and with the European Triple Entente in 1917. Its 1919 mass strike was part of the global crisis that followed World War I.

The trade unions had succeeded in expanding around the margins of this growth, while failing to organize more than a small minority of American workers. The American Federation of Labor remained a collection of highly exclusive unions of skilled craftsmen, scornful of the unskilled and semi-skilled majority. Its avowed objective was to gain concessions for its members while preserving the harmony of employers and employees. It was safe, sane, and conservative, and as hostile to industrial unionism and the mass-strike process as it had been in the days of the Pullman strike. As we shall see repeatedly, most AFL unions were usually more interested in preserving their own organizations than in responding to the broader needs of workers.

The radical Industrial Workers of the World (IWW) grew up in the vacuum left by the AFL. The "Wobblies" advocated "industrial unionism"—organizing all workers in an industry into one union—in contrast to the "craft unionism" of the AFL. The IWW organized the most depressed and unskilled, such as the migrant laborers of the West and the textile mill workers of the East. It proclaimed workers' ownership of industry its objective and saw every strike as a preparation for revolution. It was in many ways more of a social movement than a conventional union; though it was involved in many dramatic strikes, it generally scorned negotiating a continuing relationship with the employers. The Wobblies were brutally repressed by legal and illegal means during World War I; by 1919 they were rarely a significant force.

During World War I, the American economy was changed overnight to a system of state-coordinated planning and management. Government boards set prices and production levels; the railroads were placed under direct government management. With immigration cut off and an overwhelming need for production, labor was suddenly in a position of power. No longer could employers tolerate strikes for a few weeks or months, then easily hire strikebreakers from a steady supply of unemployed. Now strikes would halt critical war production and no unemployed workers were available as strikebreakers. As Alexander Bing, a wartime labor mediator and author of *War-time Strikes and Their Adjustment*, wrote: "The workers could, had they seen fit to do so, have taken advantage of the scarcity of labor and the enormous need for commodities, which the war produced, and have demanded radical changes in industry, and it is very difficult to see how such demands could have been successfully resisted."[2]

In this situation, business and government developed a new approach to trade unionism. Before World War I, employers, with some exceptions, had fought the establishment of trade unions, keeping workers under control by dealing with each one individually. Labor's new power made this strategy no longer serviceable. Consequently, employers and government turned to the unions to exercise such control. In effect, this policy took the form of a deal, in which the AFL agreed to oppose strikes in return for the right to organize, wherever the government had jurisdiction, without having its members fired. As a result, union membership increased by about two million during the war.[3] Both the AFL and the wartime employers agreed that wages were to be set, for the duration of the war, by boards composed of business, labor, and government.

Despite this deal, two factors pushed workers into action. First, the war was financed in large part by enormous inflation; the cost of living practically doubled from August 1915 to the end of 1919.[4] Second, as Bing noted, "the urgent need for production ... gave the workers a realization of a strength which before they had neither realized nor possessed."[5]

Despite the appeals of patriotism and the opposition of government, business, and the AFL, strikes mushroomed during the war. The war years from 1916 to 1918 averaged 2.4 times as many workers on strike as 1915.[6] Big strikes practically stopped spruce lumber production and closed down the most important copper areas early in the war. In Bridgeport, Connecticut, the most important munitions center in the United States, workers stopped production in defiance of the orders of both the National War Labor Board and their own national union leaders.

As so often before, workers developed a growing spirit of solidarity along with their increasing militance. For example, shipyard workers on the Pacific Coast tied up the yards for several months in sympathy with the lumber strikers in the Northwest, refusing to handle "ten-hour lumber." Four general strikes developed in different regions of the country. In Springfield, Illinois, a parade in support of striking streetcar workers was stopped by police; 10,000 union workers, especially miners, joined a general strike in protest. In Kansas City, Missouri, when laundry workers and drivers struck, a general strike developed in sympathy and lasted a week until the National Guard was called up to break it. In Waco, Texas, a general strike was called in support of streetcar men who had been locked out. And in Billings, Montana, icemen, city employees, gasmen, creamery workers, truck drivers, and others struck in sympathy with locked-out building trade mechanics.[7]

As World War I drew to a close, several additional factors shaped the climate of industrial conflict. The enormous patriotic sentiment generated by the war was deliberately and skillfully manipulated into a hysterical fear and hatred of the growing power of labor. Employers mobilized this sentiment in their efforts to roll back the powers gained by trade unionism during the war. The workers, on the other hand, felt that wartime propaganda had promised them a "new era"; now they were eager to receive what they felt they deserved for their sacrifices.

In the background of everyone's mind was the Russian Revolution and the wave of revolt sweeping the whole world in the wake of the incredible suffering, destruction, and disorganization resulting from the war. An astute characterization of the attitudes of American workers toward Soviet Russia was given in a study by the Interchurch World Movement, published in 1920: "The Russian Revolution was likely a bloody business and Bolsheviks are doubtless dangerous and wild, but the Russian Government is a laboring man's government and it has not fallen down yet. Two years of newspaper reports that the Russian republic was about to fall seem to have given workingmen, even here, a sort of class pride that it hasn't fallen."[8]

Business and government leaders, on the other hand, often felt their familiar world was under attack from all quarters and often saw Bolshevism as a unified conspiracy of all that threatened them—whether Soviet Russia or the AFL.

Real wages had risen considerably during the war as a result of the enormous demand for labor. With the end of the great wartime industrial expansion and the return to "normalcy," employers widely felt it necessary to reduce wages if profits were to be maintained. As the economist John Maynard Keynes later pointed out, this can be done with less resistance through inflation than by direct wage cuts. In 1919, the government simultaneously ended wartime price controls and allowed corporations to resume their traditional union-breaking policies. Between June 1919 and June 1920, the cost of living index (taking 1913 as 100) rose from 177 to 216.[9]

Anger, hope, and militance intensified. Nowhere did this radicalization go further than in Seattle. The radical IWW and the AFL Metal Trades Council cooperated in sponsoring a Soldiers', Sailors', and Workingmen's Council, taking the soviets of the recent Russian Revolution as their model. When a socialist and former president of the Seattle AFL, Hulet Wells, was convicted for opposing the draft during the war and then tortured in prison, the Seattle labor movement erupted with giant street rallies. Even the more conservative members of the Seattle labor movement supported the Bolshevik revolution and opposed the U.S. intervention against it.[10] In fall 1919, the Seattle longshoremen refused to load arms and munitions destined for Admiral Aleksandr Kolchak, leader of the counter-revolution in Siberia, and beat up the strikebreakers who tried to load them.[11] Seattle union membership increased from 15,000 in 1915 to 60,000 by the end of 1918—more than the total number of industrial workers.[12]

The Seattle trade unions were formally affiliated with the AFL, but their ideas and action differed greatly from AFL policy. As Harry Ault, editor of the union-owned *Seattle Union Record*, and a moderate in the local labor movement, put it: "I believe that 95 percent of us agree that the workers should control the industries. Nearly all of us agree on that but very strenuously disagree on the method. Some of us think we can get control through the Cooperative movement, some of us think through political action, and others think through industrial action."[13]

Pamphlets on the Russian Revolution circulated by the scores of thousands. A Seattle labor journalist later recalled:

> For some time these little pamphlets were seen by hundreds on Seattle's streetcars and ferries, read by men of the shipyards on their way to work. Seattle's business men commented on the phenomenon sourly; it was plain to everyone that these workers were conscientiously and energetically studying how to organize their coming power.
>
> Already, workers in Seattle talked about "workers' power" as a practical policy for the not far distant future. Boilermakers, machinists and other metal trades unions alluded to shipyards as enterprises which they might soon take over, and run better than their present owners ran them. These allusions gave life to union meetings.[14]

The militant spirit and trade union growth centered among the 35,000 workers in the shipyards. Seattle's shipbuilding industry had been built with federal funds and virtually created by the war. The Emergency Fleet Corporation of the United States government was the ultimate employer.

Less than two weeks after the armistice, the shipyard unions voted to authorize a strike. The unions proposed a pay scale that would raise wages for lower-paid workers and not for the skilled; the yard owners in turn tried to split off the skilled workers by offering them alone a wage increase. The skilled workers refused the bribe and on January 21, 1919, 35,000 shipyard workers struck.[15]

Charles Piez, representing the U.S. government as head of the Emergency Fleet Corporation, telegrammed the yard owners to resist any wage increase, threatening otherwise to withdraw their contracts. But "through the 'mistake' of a messenger boy," a reporter later recalled, "one of these telegrams was delivered not to the Metal Trades

Association [the employers], but to the Metal Trades Council [the workers]. The anger of the shipyard workers was thus directed against Washington."[16]

Faced by a government and employer determination to starve them out, the shipyard workers appealed to the Seattle Central Labor Council to call a general strike. The best-known local progressive and radical leaders were in Chicago at the time for a special conference to organize a national general strike to free Tom Mooney. (Mooney was an AFL official in San Francisco who had been convicted of throwing a bomb into a 1916 preparedness parade, despite the evidence of a photograph of him standing by a clock a mile away from the scene at exactly the time the bomb was thrown.) According to one of the leaders, Anna Louise Strong, the general strike in Seattle would probably not have occurred had they been in town. "They were terrified when they heard that a general strike had been voted.... It might easily smash something—us, perhaps, our well-organized labor movement."[17]

At a tumultuous session of the Central Labor Council, the shipyard unions' resolution that local unions poll their members on a general strike passed with virtually no opposition. The threat of a general strike was not taken seriously except by the workers themselves; as *The Seattle Times* wrote,

> A general strike directed at WHAT?
> The Government of the United States? Bosh!
> Not 15% of Seattle laborites would consider such a proposition.[18]

Yet within a day, eight local unions endorsed the strike at their regular meetings—most of the votes nearly unanimous. Within two weeks, 110 locals had endorsed the strike, with even some of the more conservative voting to do so by margins of five and ten to one.

In joining the strike, Seattle workers knew that they were risking more than a few days' pay. They risked punishment from their own national unions and the loss of established contracts with their employers. For example, the longshoremen's union imperiled and eventually lost a closed-shop agreement for the Seattle waterfront, and the president of the International Longshoremen's Association wired the local that he would rescind its charter if it took part in the general strike.

The Central Labor Council agreed that the strike would be run by a General Strike Committee of three members from each striking local, elected by the rank and file. The 300 members of the committee—mostly not officials but rank-and-filers with little previous leadership experience—started meeting four days before the strike; they and their fifteen-member executive committee were in daily session throughout the strike, forming virtually a counter-government for the city.

A study of the strike issued later by the General Strike Committee pointed out that "a general strike was seen, almost at once, to differ profoundly from any of the particular strikes with which the workers of Seattle were familiar.... If life was not to be made unbearable for the strikers themselves, problems of management, of selection and exemption, had to take the place of the much simpler problem of keeping everyone out of work."[19]

Workers in various trades organized themselves to provide essential services with the approval of subcommittees of the executive committee, which granted them exemptions from the strike. Garbage wagon drivers agreed to collect wet garbage that would create a health hazard, but not paper and ashes. Firemen agreed to stay on the job to handle emergencies. The laundry drivers and laundry workers developed a plan to keep one shop open to handle hospital laundry; before the strike they instructed the employers to accept no more laundry, then worked a few hours after the strike deadline to finish clothes in process so they would not mildew. Vehicles authorized to operate bore signs reading, "Exempted by the General Strike Committee."[20]

Employers and government officials, as well as strikers, came before the strike committee to request exemptions. According to one correspondent, "The extent to which the city recognized the actual rather than the titular government of the community is apparent enough to anyone who reads the carefully kept records of the strike committee, and observes what was actually done. Before the committee, which would seem to have been in well-nigh continuous session day and night, appeared a long succession of businessmen, city officials, and the Mayor himself, not to threaten or bully, but to discuss the situation and ask the approval of the committee for this or that step."[21]

Here are a few examples from the minutes:

King county commissioners ask for exemption of janitors to care for City-County building. Not granted.

F.A. Rust asks for janitors for Labor Temple. Not granted.

Teamsters' Union asks permission to carry oil for Swedish Hospital during strike. Referred to transportation committee. Approved.

Port of Seattle asks to be allowed men to load a government vessel, pointing out that no private profit is involved and that an emergency exists. Granted.

The retail drug clerks sent in a statement of the health needs of the city. Referred to public welfare committee, which recommends that prescription counters only be left open, and that in front of every drug store which is thus allowed to open a sign be placed with the words, "No goods sold during general strike. Orders for prescriptions only will be filled. Signed by general strike committee."

Communication from House of Good Shepherd. Permission granted by transportation committee to haul food and provisions only.

This is by no means all the business that came before the Committee of Fifteen in a single afternoon. Other topics included "An appointment of a committee of relief to look after destitute homes, the creation of a publicity bureau, an order that watchmen stay on the job until further notice."[22]

In some cases, workers improvised large-scale operations from scratch. For instance, the milk wagon drivers initially proposed to their employers that certain dairies remain open, but when the employers refused to open any dairies except in downtown Seattle, and attempted to take direction of the plan, the drivers decided to organize their own distribution system instead. They set up thirty-five neighborhood milk stations, purchased milk from small dairies near the city, and distributed it throughout Seattle. Even more impressive was the commissary department, which served 30,000 meals a day to the strikers and community. The cooks, waiters, and other provision trade workers purchased the food, located restaurant kitchens, and arranged to transport the cooked food to twenty-one eating places in halls throughout the city. This huge operation was running smoothly by the second day of the strike.

Two days before the strike, *The Seattle Union Record* asked union members who had served in the armed forces to come to a meeting to discuss "important strike work."[23] From this group was organized a "Labor War Veteran's Guard" designed to keep peace on the streets. Its principle was scrawled on the blackboard at one of its headquarters: "The purpose of this organization is to preserve law and order without the use of force. No volunteer will have any police power or be allowed to carry weapons of any sort, but to use persuasion only."[24]

On the eve of the general strike, an editorial in *The Seattle Union Record* tried to define the strike's significance:

On Thursday at 10 A.M.—There will be many cheering, and there will be some who fear.

Both these emotions are useful, but not too much of either.

We are undertaking the most tremendous move ever made by *LABOR* in this country, a move which will lead—*NO ONE KNOWS WHERE!*

We do not need hysteria.

We need the iron march of labor.

LABOR WILL FEED THE PEOPLE.

Twelve great kitchens have been offered, and from them food will be distributed by the provision trades at low cost to all.

LABOR WILL CARE FOR THE BABIES AND THE SICK.

The milk-wagon drivers and the laundry drivers are arranging plans for supplying milk to babies, invalids and hospitals and taking care of the cleaning of linen for hospitals.

LABOR WILL PRESERVE ORDER.

The strike committee is arranging for guards and it is expected that the stopping of the cars will keep people at home....

A few hot-headed enthusiasts have complained that strikers only should be fed, and the general public left to endure severe discomfort. Aside from the inhumanitarian character of such suggestions, let them get this straight—

NOT THE WITHDRAWAL OF LABOR POWER, BUT THE POWER OF THE STRIKERS TO MANAGE WILL WIN THIS STRIKE.

What does Mr. Piez of the Shipping Board care about the closing down of Seattle's shipyards, or even of all the industries of the northwest? Will it not merely strengthen the yards at Hog Island, in which he is more interested?

When the shipyard owners of Seattle were on the point of agreeing with the workers, it was Mr. Piez who wired them that, if they so agreed—

HE WOULD NOT LET THEM HAVE STEEL.

Whether this is camouflage we have no means of knowing. But we do know that the great eastern combinations of capitalists *COULD AFFORD* to offer privately to Mr. Skinner, Mr. Ames and Mr. Duthie a few millions apiece in eastern shipyard stock,

RATHER THAN LET THE WORKERS WIN.

The closing down of Seattle's industries, as a *MERE SHUT-DOWN*, will not affect these eastern gentlemen much. They could let the whole northwest go to pieces, as far as money alone is concerned.

BUT, the closing down of the capitalistically controlled industries of Seattle, while the *WORKERS ORGANIZE* to feed the people, to care for the babies and the sick, to preserve order—*THIS* will move them, for this looks too much like the taking over of *POWER* by the workers.

Labor will not only *SHUT DOWN* the industries, but Labor will *REOPEN*, under the management of the appropriate trades, such activities as are needed to preserve public health and public peace. If the strike continues, Labor may feel led to avoid public suffering by reopening more and more activities,

UNDER ITS OWN MANAGEMENT

And that is why we say that we are starting on a road that leads—*NO ONE KNOWS WHERE!*[25]

Mayor Ole Hanson of Seattle described the start of the strike on February 6, 1919: "Streetcar gongs ceased their clamor; newsboys cast their unsold papers into the street; from the doors of mill and factory, store and workshop, streamed 65,000 workingmen. School children with fear in their hearts hurried homeward. The life stream of a great city stopped."[26] The AFL strikers were joined by the IWW, the separately organized Japanese workers, and perhaps 40,000 non-union workers who did not go to work because of sympathy, fear, closed enterprises, or lack of transportation.[27] During the strike there was not a single arrest connected with it and general police court arrests sunk to less than half of normal. Major General John F. Morrison, in charge of U.S. troops in the city, said that in forty years of military experience he had not seen a city so quiet and orderly.[28]

The peacefulness of the strike did not prevent some in Seattle from seeing it as an attempted revolution. As Mayor Hanson put it,

> The so-called sympathetic Seattle strike was an attempted revolution. That there was no violence does not alter the fact.... The intent, openly and covertly announced, was for the overthrow of the industrial system; here first, then everywhere.... True, there were no flashing guns, no bombs, no killings. Revolution, I repeat, doesn't need violence. The general strike, as practiced in Seattle, is of itself the weapon of revolution, all the more dangerous because quiet. To succeed, it must suspend everything; stop the entire life stream of a community.... That is to say, it puts the government out of operation. And that is all there is to revolt—no matter how achieved.[29]

Local radicals thought revolution would take more; a widely circulated leaflet, often seized on as proof of the strike's revolutionary intent, read:

> The Russians have shown you the way out. What are you going to do about it? You are doomed to wage slavery till you die unless you wake up, realize that you and the boss have not one thing in common, that the employing class must be overthrown, and that you, the workers, must take over the control of your jobs, and through them, the control of your lives instead of offering yourself up to the masters as a sacrifice six days a week, so that they may coin profits out of your sweat and toil.[30]

Feeling the available National Guard inadequate for the situation, the Washington attorney general, acting for the governor, telephoned Secretary of War Newton Baker to send federal troops; by Friday,

February 7, 950 sailors and marines were brought into the city and carefully placed at strategic points. The mayor, dramatically portraying himself as the city's savior from Bolshevism, added 600 extra men to the police force and swore in 2,400 special deputies, many of them University of Washington students. By February 7, Mayor Hanson felt he had the necessary forces to issue an ultimatum to the strike committee: "I hereby notify you that unless the sympathy strike is called off by 8 o'clock tomorrow morning, Saturday, February 8, 1919, I will take advantage of the protection offered this city by the national government and operate all the essential enterprises."[31]

Whether to end the strike became the key issue. According to Anna Louise Strong, "As soon as any worker was made a leader he wanted to end that strike. A score of times in those five days I saw it happen. Workers in the ranks felt the thrill of massed power which they trusted their leaders to carry to victory. But as soon as one of these workers was put on a responsible committee, he also wished to stop 'before there is riot and blood.'"[32]

This dynamic was dramatized when the executive committee recommended thirteen to one on Saturday, February 8, to end the strike that night. The 300 members of the General Strike Committee were almost persuaded until they took a supper break and talked with members of their own rank and file. They returned to the meeting and voted overwhelmingly to continue the strike.

The heaviest pressures to end the strike now came from the international officials of the AFL unions. Telegrams ordering local unions to desert the strike poured into the Labor Temple. So did international officers, arriving from long distances to try to force their members back to work. These efforts began to take their toll. The streetcar men were ordered back to work by their executive committee under pressure from an international official, but said they would rejoin the strike if called by the General Strike Committee. The Teamsters likewise were ordered back by an international officer, but the rank and file called another meeting at which it was expected members would vote to rejoin the strike. The stereotypers returned "under severe pressure from their international officers"[33] and a false rumor that the strike had been called off.

With these breaks appearing and the power of the opposition growing ever stronger, the General Strike Committee finally voted to end the strike Tuesday, February 11, at noon. The strike was ended, as the General Strike Committee's history stated, by "pressure from international officers of unions, from executive committees of unions, from the 'leaders' in the labor movement, even from those very leaders who are still called 'Bolsheviki' by the undiscriminating press. And ... the pressure upon the workers themselves, not of the loss of their own jobs, but of living in a city so tightly closed."[34]

The immediate effect of the strike was inconclusive. The shipyard strike went on; the attack on unionism swelled in Seattle as elsewhere; the Socialist Party headquarters, a labor printing plant, and the IWW hall were raided and thirty-nine Wobblies arrested as "ringleaders of anarchy," although they played little role in the general strike.[35]

Perhaps the greatest effect of the strike was to suddenly bring American labor struggles into the context of the revolutionary conflicts sweeping the world in the wake of World War I. *The Seattle Union Record*, for example, noted afterward the similarity of the Seattle general strike to the workers' government just arising in Belfast:

> They are singularly alike in nature. Quiet mass action, the tying up of industry, the granting of exemptions, until gradually the main activities of the city are being handled by the strike committee.
>
> Apparently in all cases there is the same singular lack of violence which we noticed here. The violence comes, not with the shifting of power, but when the "counter revolutionaries" try to regain the power which inevitably and almost without their knowing it passed from their grasp. Violence would have come in Seattle, if it had come, not from the workers, but from attempts by armed opponents of the strike to break down the authority of the strike committee over its own members....
>
> Our experience, meantime, will help us understand the way in which events are occurring in other communities all over the world, where a general strike, not being called off, slips gradually into the direction of more and more affairs by the strike committee, until the business group feeling their old prestige slipping, turns suddenly to violence, and there comes the test of force.[36]

•

Soon after the armistice, an eight-hour movement swept the New England textile districts. The United Textile Workers, whose members were mostly skilled, decided to ask for an eight-hour day and the employers generally agreed to it, but with a corresponding reduction in pay. This was hardly satisfactory, however, to the unskilled majority of workers, mostly immigrants, who were not represented by the union and whose wages would have been reduced to intolerable levels by the agreement. In Lawrence, Massachusetts, which had seen a major textile strike in 1912, workers decided to strike for the shorter work week with no reduction in pay. The union refused to sanction the strike and ordered its members back to work. Nonetheless, the strike spread through New Bedford and Fall River, Massachusetts; Pawtucket, Rhode Island; Paterson, New Jersey; and other textile centers of New England and New Jersey. In all, 120,000 workers were out.[37]

In Lawrence, the strike was directed by a general strike committee of 100 composed of striking mill workers and a few others who met every morning to receive reports and make policies. Labor investigator John Fitch wrote: "They are delegates from the different nationalities and as they report each morning you seem to be listening to a roll call of the nations. Russians are there and Italians, Poles, Lithuanians, Greeks, Ukrainians, Syrians, Franco-Belgians, Finns and even Germans. Each nationality meets by itself in its own hall and every morning its delegates report to the strike committee."[38]

A local carpenter, "an extreme Socialist," was made chairman of the committee, and a radical minister, A.J. Muste, played an important part in leading the strike. He told the strikers "that they ought to learn everything they can about the business of making cloth so that they may have the knowledge and skill necessary when the time comes for them to operate the mills for themselves."[39]

Fitch described it as "a strike for wages carried on in a revolutionary atmosphere. That is, there are serious questionings of the justice of the existing economic order. In addition to that there is a feeling on the part of the strikers that the government is against them ... [T]o many of them American government is personified by the Lawrence police."

The strikers organized their own relief operation. Fitch describes a meeting in which a committee was considering the problems of milk distribution: "Arrangements had been made with a dairyman to supply milk in quantities at central points for the children of strikers' families. Depots were being established where the people of each nationality or group of nationalities could go for their supply. It was a business arrangement requiring cooperative effort ... [with] some of the delegates struggling with their English.[40]

The strike was met with opposition from the United Textile Workers and the Lawrence Central Labor Council, repeated brutality from the police, and fear of Bolshevism from much of the community, but after ten weeks it gained its demands.

The strike spread to Patterson with a somewhat different pattern. There, 30,000 silk workers tried to cut the work week for themselves—by arriving at work at eight o'clock instead of seven. When they arrived at the factories, however, they found themselves locked out. The silk workers organized on a factory-by-factory basis, with daily meetings of the delegates from more than 100 factories. The strike spread from Patterson to 10,000 unorganized wool workers in Passaic, New Jersey. For most of the strikers, the movement was victorious.[41]

The strike wave reached categories of workers often considered the model of labor docility. On April 15, for example, the telephone operators throughout New England walked off their jobs in a strike against the federal government, which still retained wartime control over the telephone companies. Unionization was primarily centered in Boston, but the strike spread to dozens of unorganized cities and towns. "I do not believe," wrote one observer, "that an industrial issue has ever before penetrated every village, hamlet or town of New England as has this strike of telephone girls."[42] The second day of the strike, 12,000 "inside men" of the telephone company struck in support of the operators. The next day the postmaster general, who was in charge of the companies, capitulated and came to a settlement with the operators.[43]

In Boston the local policemen's organization, known as the Boston Social Club, decided to affiliate with the AFL. When nineteen of their leaders were fired by the city police commissioner, the club members voted 1,134 to 2 to strike. The Central Labor Union ordered affiliated unions to vote on a general strike in support of the policemen. The president of Harvard University offered 1,000 students to replace the police, and many volunteers offered their services, but city officials preferred to let various minor disorders—looting of stores, stoning of trolley cars, and dice-playing on Boston Common—develop unopposed. The result was a huge public uproar over riot and revolution in Boston. "Lenin and Trotsky are on their way," stated *The Wall Street Journal.*[44]

On the second day of the strike the state guard occupied the city, then patrolled the streets for the next three months. The entire police force was fired and a new one gradually recruited. Against such pressures the strike was clearly doomed, and the Central Labor Union decided that "the time is not now opportune for the ordering of a general strike."[45] The main effect of the strike was to greatly increase fear of threats to "law and order" by showing that even the minions of law and order themselves were workers not immune to the spreading spirit of revolt.[46]

The strike wave was visible not only on a national but also on a city-by-city basis. On February 1, 1919, for instance, a magazine reported:

> In a small way New York City has lately been through a general labor crisis. To unemployment, daily growing more acute, have been added strikes following one another in rapid succession. The Amalgamated Clothing Workers, after several months of struggle, have won a substantial victory, the chief element of which was the achievement of a 44-hour week. The hotel workers are still on strike and 8,000 furriers have voted to go out if their demands are not granted. The harbor workers are awaiting the findings of the War Labor Board ... comfortable ... that at a day's notice they can tie up the whole vast traffic of New York harbor. The New York firemen ... are backing with all their force a Socialist resolution in the Board of Aldermen requesting the establishment of a three-platoon system in the New York Fire Department.... Whether the firemen will

strike, as they did in Cleveland, to win an eight-hour day, will probably depend upon the action of the city and the State. The most immediate and crucial symptom of the general labor unrest is the strike of some 35,000 ladies' garment workers for a 44-hour week, a 15 percent increase in wages, and "permission to a representative of the union to visit the shops once a month in order to ascertain whether the standards established by the protocol [contract] are observed." The deeper issue appears to be the future maintenance of the protocol. This treaty of industrial peace has in many respects proved galling to both sides. By cutting off the power of general and shop strikes it has tied the workers' hands; by depriving the employers of the right of arbitrary discharge it has interfered in a peculiarly irritating way with the direction of business.[47]

Another magazine reported in August that "in New York City a great variety of strikes is in progress. Cigarmakers, shirtmakers, carpenters, bakers, teamsters and barbers are out in large numbers. The most depressed trades are catching the strike infection, witness the walkout last week of women workers on feathers and artificial flowers, who want a forty-four-hour week and the abolition of home work. Even the scrubwomen employed in a downtown building struck and put strikebreakers to rout with their mop handles."[48]

An "Epidemic of Strikes in Chicago" was also reported. "More strikes and lockouts accompany the mid-summer heat than were ever known before at any one time … In rapid succession the 1,700 street sweepers, the 800 garbage collectors, drivers and workers at the reduction plant, the 900 bridge laborers, the 800 City Hall clerks and over 300 fire department engineers, with groups of workers in other departments, in all nearly 5,000 public employees, actually quit their jobs."[49]

Another strike occurred at the Corn Products Refining Company in Argo, a suburb of Chicago. "The attempt to operate the works led to an uprising of the cosmopolitan population, which resulted in bloodshed and a great popular demonstration at the funeral of the men who were killed, in which many returned soldiers in uniform participated."[50] At the McCormick works of the International Harvester Company, "without any notice whatever, without presenting any grievance or making any demands, 5,000 employees ceased work, and succeeded in persuading 800 in the adjoining twine mill and 1,800 in the tractor works not to continue working."[51]

Similarly, "The Crane Company, where good working conditions, including profit-sharing and an annual bonus, have been widely considered to be satisfactory for many years, also met with a spectacular surprise. At the noon hour one day a procession of employees started near one of the large buildings and soon numbered thousands of workers, including those of many crafts, who marched to an adjoining grove and did not return to work."[52] Sixteen thousand carpenters struck, closing down all construction, in violation of a contract running to May 1921. And "the threat of the surface and elevated streetcar men to strike ... has kept the public mind in keener suspense than all the other labor troubles—and with reason, because it would cause still more acute unrest and possibly much more serious and prevalent disturbance."[53]

•

The conflict that most held the nation's attention in 1919, however, was the great strike in the steel industry.

Trade unionism in the iron and steel industry, broken in the Homestead struggle of 1892 and faced with organized and violent opposition by the steel trust, remained quiescent until World War I. This did not prevent workers from striking, however, especially as labor became scarce toward the beginning of the war. An investigator reported that "[w]orkmen of the most docile tendencies have been making demands" and that "insignificant little rebellions verging on strikes" had been breaking out here and there.[54] In early 1916, an explosion came in Youngstown, Ohio. Laborers struck for a 25 percent increase at a Republic tube plant; the strike spread spontaneously to other steel plants in the town. On January 7, East Youngstown laborers gathered near a plant. As they pressed forward, a guard fired on them, the strikers replied with bricks, and the guards opened general fire. Enraged, the crowds marched through the streets and burned property worth $1 million. The National Guard was rushed in to suppress the movement. Twenty strikers were wounded, three fatally.[55]

A similar strike broke out four months later in the Pittsburgh district, the heart of the steel industry. Workers at Westinghouse in East

Pittsburgh struck in late April. They started marching from plant to plant spreading the strike, and steelworkers at points throughout the district began joining in. At the second march to the Edgar Thompson Works in Braddock, the company guards opened fire, killing two. The crowd's response, as at Youngstown, was fury. According to a local paper, they "charged plant after plant, and many of the places were wrecked." Some mills shut down to avoid trouble, and "the whole Pittsburgh district was threatened with industrial paralysis" until troops were sent in, the Westinghouse strike leaders arrested, and the strike suppressed.[56]

Frank Morrison, secretary of the AFL, visited Pittsburgh during this strike, but left in despair, considering the situation "too turbulent to be exploited by the AFL."[57] Nonetheless, the federation was interested in taking advantage of wartime conditions to expand its membership in the steel industry, and in August 1918 it established the National Committee for Organizing the Iron and Steel Workers. It was composed of twenty-four trade unions that claimed jurisdiction in the steel industry and was headed by John Fitzpatrick of the Chicago Federation of Labor, a liberal trade unionist. The unions, in the words of the Interchurch World Movement's (IWM) detailed and revealing *Report on the Steel Strike of 1919*, "had no doubt about what they wanted—more numbers for each of their separate craft organizations."[58]

The secretary-treasurer in charge of detailed work was William Z. Foster, who later became the leading trade union figure (and eventually chairman) of the American Communist Party. In 1919, Foster was a syndicalist who believed that trade unions should ultimately control the economy. For Foster, as historian Theodore Draper wrote, "if only the trade unions—even A.F. of L. unions—could become big and strong enough, the revolution would take care of itself."[59]

Meanwhile, the mills seethed. The IWM *Report* found that "three-quarters of steel employees [the unskilled] developed a frame of mind of more or less chronic rebellion, largely the physical reaction from exhaustion and deprivation. Rebellious reactions from having no 'say' in the conduct of the job was also chronic, though less so. These were fundamental facts in steelworkers' minds, of which they

were constantly reminded by endless 'grievances.'"[60] This discontent
was reflected at an individual level by high absenteeism and a phenomenal labor turnover—at Homestead, for example, 6,800 out of
11,500 workers in a year left the mills.[61] Further, a new psychology
had been created during the war. Steelworkers were the object of intensive propaganda stressing their essential role in the "battle for democracy." They expected after the war that their importance would
be recognized with some of the fruits of democracy; instead they
were met by renewed discrimination and repression.

In addition, the predominantly Eastern European steel laborers
were stirred by the overthrow of autocracy in their homelands. As the
IWM *Report* concluded on the basis of extensive interviews, the immigrant workers in general possessed little radical ideology, but had "a
vague idea that big rich people who run things 'arbitrarily,' even in
mills, are coming down in the world. Russia, moreover, means to
them the rise of workingmen to power. They have a vague idea that
poor people who have been run for a long time, on farms and in
mills, are coming up in the world and are beginning to run themselves."[62]

Under these conditions, an explosion was bound to come. But the
steel companies through long experience had developed powerful
techniques to prevent the steelworkers from organizing themselves.
The first key was the division of the labor force: thirty nationalities
worked in the mills, each speaking only its own language, segregated
in its own community, and isolated within its own traditions and customs. This was not a matter of chance: the divide-and-rule strategy
was understood as early as 1875 by a Carnegie plant manager who
wrote, "My experience has been that Germans and Irish, Swedes and
what I denominate 'buckwheats' [young American country boys], ju-
diciously mixed, make the most effective and tractable force you can
find."[63] The traditional leaders within the ethnic communities were
powerful, conservative, and often directly dependent on the steel
companies. Finally, the companies did everything possible to instill
fear in the workers—fear of firing, blacklists, labor spies, informers,
arrest, and deportation made steelworkers reluctant even to talk to

each other, let alone organize. They knew that as soon as workers started talking union they would be fired.

When the AFL began holding mass meetings in September, 1918 around the steel district, however, far from having to persuade workers to join, all it had to do was pass out membership cards; 1,200 steelworkers were signed up in one day in Joliet, 1,500 in South Chicago.[64] By the spring of 1919, nearly 100,000 steelworkers had signed up.[65]

Conflict soon arose over what form of organization the union should take. According to the IWM *Report*, "[I]n many plants the instinct of the immigrant recruit was to associate with his shopmates of different 'crafts' rather than with his 'craft' mates from other shops. He fell more easily into a shop or plant union."[66] The local leaders, "finding that organization by shops, departments and plants was often the most natural to their inexperienced fellow-workers ... followed that plan even though the result was industrial unionism in miniature."[67] This was heresy to the AFL. "The twenty-four crafts smothered this drift,"[68] and William Z. Foster "combated the natural tendency of sections of the rank and file toward industrial unionism."[69] The workers of each shop and plant were instead split up among the twenty-four unions.

The heart of the steel industry was the Pittsburgh district, including dozens of steel towns throughout western Pennsylvania. It was here that the decisive battles of the steel strike would be fought. But the mayors and burgesses of the Monongahela Valley met early in the campaign and decided to forbid all union meetings in their towns; as Mayor James S. Crawford of Duquesne put it, "Jesus Christ himself could not speak in Duquesne for the A.F. of L.!"[70]

The free speech fight in the district began in Monessen, where the burgess had forbidden union meetings for months. To break the ban, the local organizer called a meeting for April 1. On the date set, 10,000 miners from the surrounding coal country marched into Monessen, uniformed veterans at their head. The right to hold meetings was thereby established in fact if not by permission, and was gradually spread by similar tactics through the rest of the district.

The conflict between the steelworkers' rank and file and union officials became more evident the stronger the movement grew. The

IWM *Report* characterized their positions thus: "The raw recruits, particularly the immigrant workers, wanted to strike soon after they joined up, since they could conceive of both protection and 'results' only in a universal walkout.... The 24 old unions willingly put money into a campaign for new members but hesitated greatly over backing a strike in behalf of the new steel locals, which might possibly jeopardize their old membership outside the steel industry."[71]

The rank and file was particularly impatient to strike because the new union members were being fired by the hundreds up and down the steel district. In order "to give the men who have waited so long something tangible to look forward to" and to "pacify the restless spirits," the organizing campaign's National Committee called a conference May 25 with 583 representatives from local unions in eighty steel centers.[72] The representatives came with specific instructions from their own members. They assumed they were empowered to call a strike and tried to do so, but the national union representatives quickly asserted that only they had the authority to call a strike. The result was that workers began dropping out of the unions in large numbers.

The demand for a strike continued to mount. At the National Committee's meeting July 11 it was reported that "in Johnstown, Youngstown, Chicago, Vandergrift, Wheeling and elsewhere great strikes are threatening. The men are letting it be known that if we do not do something for them they will take the matter into their own hands. Where they are not threatening to strike they are taking the position that they will pay no more dues until they can see some results from their efforts."[73]

On July 20, the National Committee finally decided to authorize a strike vote, after they were faced with such ultimatums as this telegram from the Johnstown Steel Workers Council: "Unless the National Committee authorizes a national strike vote to be taken this week we will be compelled to go on strike here alone."[74]

Believing a strike was imminent, workers flooded back into the unions: membership increased 50 percent while the strike ballot was being taken.[75] The vote was virtually unanimous for the strike.[76]

Union organizers made a series of last-ditch efforts to head off a strike. John Fitzpatrick, who headed the nationwide organizing drive, believed that "if only both sides could get together around a table, it could all be straightened out,"[77] but labor's appeals to Judge Elbert Gary, head of U.S. Steel and spokesman for the industry, were repeatedly rebuffed. Finally an appeal was sent to President Woodrow Wilson, stating that a conference with management was the only demand. A week later, union leaders wired Wilson that "it is exceedingly difficult to withhold or restrain the men.... We cannot now affirm how much longer we will be able to exert that influence."[78] Finally, a strike date was set for September 22. President Wilson requested that the strike be postponed, but a flood of telegrams like this one forced the National Committee to go ahead with the strike:

> W.Z. Foster
> 303 Magee Bldg.
> Pittsburgh, Pa.
> We cannot be expected to meet the enraged workers, who will consider us traitors if strike is postponed.
> Organizers Youngstown District[79]

The extent of the strike surprised union leaders, as well as management. More than 350,000 walked out, crippling most of the steel industry. Many of those who struck were not union members. As Foster had predicted, "In iron and steel, where men work together in big bunches, we can get everybody to strike even though we have only 10 percent" organized.[80] The unskilled immigrants from southern and eastern Europe, who made up the great majority of the steelworkers, formed the backbone of the strike. Some of the skilled, predominantly native-born workers, long favored by the employers, joined the strike; others continued to go to work. In some places, even office workers joined the strike.

The strikers in western Pennsylvania, the heart of the industry, were met with a complete suppression of civil liberties and a reign of terror. Sheriff William S. Haddock of Allegheny County issued a proclamation forbidding outdoor meetings anywhere in the county, and swore in 5,000 strikebreaking employees of U.S. Steel as deputies.

Foster charged that the county had 50,000 deputies under arms. Indoor meetings in most steel centers were forbidden by local authorities. The isolation of the strikers, unable to meet with each other, undermined morale. Investigator George Soule, comparing towns, concluded that "the absence of the right to assemble naturally had its result in the non-effectiveness of the strike ... [T]he effectiveness of the strike was ... proportional to the amount of civil liberty permitted."[81]

The reign of terror was equally powerful. The IWM study, based on hundreds of affidavits and on-the-spot investigations, shows the strategy of the local officials:

> In Monessen, where the strikers held out solidly for a long time, with the exception of the arrest of many Russians on vague charges of "radicalism," the policy of the State Police was simply to club men off the streets and drive them into their homes. Very few were arrested. In Braddock, however, where some of the mills were partly operating, the State Police did not stop at mere beating. Ordinarily, when a striker was clubbed on the street he would be taken to jail, kept there over night, and then the Squire or the Burgess would fine him from $10.00 to $60.00. In Newcastle, the Sheriff's deputies carried the Braddock policy much further. Many of those arrested in Newcastle, who had lived in the town almost all their adult lives, were charged with being "suspicious" persons and were ordered not to be released until the strike was over. Others were released in Newcastle after they furnished bail ranging from $500 to $2,500 each. The other towns in western Pennsylvania generally followed one of the methods described above.[82]

In Newcastle, Pennsylvania, the sheriff (who was also chief of police) admitted to arresting 100 people the first week of the strike and planning to hold at least forty of them as "suspicious persons" until "the strike is over, even if we have to build a new jail to house them."[83] The state police, Foster admitted, felt free to brutalize the strikers because "they realize fully that they can depend upon trade-union leaders to hold the strikers in check from adopting measures of retaliation."[84]

The U.S. government, too, played its role in breaking the strike. It no longer needed labor's support for the war effort, and felt itself threatened by the revolutionary movements sweeping the world. The Department of Justice conducted "red raids" among the steelworkers, locking up and deporting immigrants. Attorney General A. Mitchell Palmer, architect of the nationwide roundup of radicals that became known as the "Palmer Raids," warned publicly that the strike harbored the threat of Bolshevism.

In Gary, Indiana, the National Guard occupied the city and forbade parades. Federal troops were sent in when the guard proved incapable of suppressing an "outlaw parade" of uniformed ex-soldiers and other strikers organized independently of the strike leadership. The commanding general, declaring that "the army would be neutral," had strikers arrested and picket lines broken up; soldiers were sent to arrest union officers in other trades for such offenses as threatening to call a strike on a local building operation. The army continued to occupy Gary until the strike was called off.[85] The strikers, who at the beginning had expected Wilson's publicly expressed support for trade unionism to be shown in action in the steel industry, became bitter and disillusioned, convinced that the federal government was on the side of the companies.

The repression in Pennsylvania threatened all workers in the state, and pressures for a general strike grew as the strike continued. Already the coal miners were out on their own strike. On November 1 and 2, the Pennsylvania Federation of Labor held a special convention, which resolved that "the Executive Council of the Pennsylvania Federation of Labor shall issue a call for a Statewide strike, when in its judgment it is necessary to compel respect for law and the restoration of liberty."[86] Such a general strike, of course, went against every AFL principle, and according to the IWM, William Z. Foster "was constantly complaining of fighting the 'radicals,' meaning those who wanted to have a general strike called."[87]

One critical element in the strike was the railroad workers on lines serving the steel plants; if they struck, production would be stopped throughout the Pittsburgh district. The railroaders' sentiment strongly supported the strike, but their national leaders did not. As one local strike leader explained, "If the railwaymen in the steel plant yards had struck, this strike would have been won. In October the railwaymen's locals near Pittsburgh voted to strike but got no assurance of support from their Brotherhoods."[88] In Youngstown and other places where railroad workers did join the strike, their unions gave them no strike benefits and allowed other members to take their jobs around the steel mills.

The leadership of the most important union in the industry, the Amalgamated Association of Iron and Steel Workers, constantly undermined the organizing campaign. In May, it tried to arrange separate negotiations with U.S. Steel, offering to help allay the "serious disturbing element in the industrial world at the present time, a great spirit of unrest that has spread over our common country."[89] Had Judge Gary not turned down this offer, it would have broken the entire strike. When the strike started, workers at mills where the Amalgamated Association had contracts generally joined the strike, but six weeks later the union ordered them back to work, saying the contracts would be honored "at whatever cost." Lodges that refused to break the strike had their charters revoked. According to *Iron Age*, the order "broke the strike in every plant in the [Youngstown] district with which the Amalgamated had a contract."[90] As a local strike leader described it, "When [Amalgamated Association president] Mike Tighe ordered back his men at that mill near Cleveland, he started an avalanche. One Amalgamated organizer got 400 men into one big union with an Amalgamated charter at a mill near Steubenville and they all struck. Mike ordered them all back and tore up that organizer's card."[91]

The employers played powerfully on the divisions among the workers. Native workers were bombarded with propaganda that it was just a strike of immigrant "hunkies"; immigrants were told that the Americans had already sold them out. The following written instructions to an operative of a labor detective firm hired to fight the strike give an indication of the company tactics:

> We want you to stir up as much bad feeling as you possibly can between the Serbians and the Italians. Spread data among the Serbians that the Italians are going back to work. Call up every question you can in reference to racial hatred between these two nationalities; make them realize to the fullest extent that far better results would

be accomplished if they will go back to work. Urge them to go back to work or the Italians will get their jobs.[92]

Such operatives were employed by the hundreds.

Between 30,000 and 40,000 black workers were brought into the steel districts as strikebreakers. They had few compunctions about this, since traditionally most AFL unions had been white-only. The only way blacks could enter unionized jobs was as strikebreakers. At Youngstown, one lone black machinist striker, though he stayed on strike to the end, was still not admitted to the machinists' local.

To pay strike benefits to 350,000 strikers was out of the question. To prevent workers with no resources from being starved back to work, though, an enormous commissary system handled food distribution for the entire strike zone. Goods were bought from grocery co-op suppliers, packaged into half-week allotments for large or small families, and shipped to forty-five local commissaries for distribution to those in need. The total commissary cost for the entire strike averaged less than $1.40 per striker.[93]

Few workers returned to the mills under the pressure of deprivation; as long as they were convinced that the strike was succeeding, they stayed out week after week, living on next to nothing. But the overwhelming power of the steel companies over communications gradually began to grind down the strikers' morale. The newspapers constantly reported that the mills had been reopened and the strike broken, for this was true in some places and therefore could be made to seem true generally. With little labor press, no public meetings, and visits to strikers' homes impossible without arrest for "intimidation," workers gradually came to believe that the strike no longer stood a chance and slowly began to filter back to work. By the end of ten weeks, the number of strikers was down from 365,000 to 110,000, and on January 8, 1920, the National Committee declared the strike over.

The objective of the strike from the point of view of the AFL unions involved was to establish trade union collective bargaining. As the IWM *Report* concluded, "It is possible that the workers throughout the whole steel industry might much more easily have been organized on a radical appeal. But the Strike Committee were opposed in principle to any such appeal … [T]he methods of organization used in the steel strike were old fashioned and became ostentatiously so as the organizers recognized the radical possibilities of the strike.… By the end of the year, it was evident that the strikers were getting an old-fashioned licking."[94]

The meaning of the strike to the strikers was different, both more vague and more radical. As David Saposs described it, based on an intensive study of immigrant communities in the steel district:

> The determination of the immigrant worker to assert himself in spite of all the opposition of dominant opinion in his own community, was the chief reason why the foreign and English press … considered the strike as having deeper motives than mere demands of ordinary trade unionism. Not only the mill managers, but all the governing classes in steel towns were accustomed to seeing the immigrant docile and submissive; to them any strike was indeed a revolution.… Thus the strike was also an outburst of the inhibited instincts for self-expression …. The immigrant wanted not only better wages and shorter hours. He resented being treated as a chattel or a "hunkie."[95]

The strike not only was for trade unionism, according to the IWM *Report*, but was "the workers' revolt against the entire system of arbitrary control."[96] The local strike leaders, in contrast to AFL officials, talked freely of the workers "sharing in industrial control." As Mary Heaton Vorse said after many interviews and discussions with the strikers, "What they believed was not formulated into a dogma. It was not narrowed down to trade union bargaining."[97]

Perhaps the most general sentiment of the strikers was expressed by an American steelworker in Youngstown: "If my boy could give his life fighting for free democracy in Europe, I guess I can stand it to fight this battle to the end. I am going to help my fellow workmen show Judge Gary that he can't act as if he was a king or a kaiser and tell them how long they have got to work!"[98]

The steel industry agreed. "If it came to a question of wage demands alone," *Iron Age* reported, the steel companies "might meet the union officials in a conciliatory spirit." But the real issue was whether unions "shall be allowed to dictate to the employer how he shall operate his plant."[99] Or, as *The Nation* concluded, the steel strike was "no mere squabble over wages and hours and collective bargaining and the open shop.... The real question is, Who shall control our steel industry?"[100]

•

Many of the strikes of 1919 were "outlaw" or wildcat strikes, opposed as heartily by the unions as by the employers. These spread even to such citadels of trade union authority as the printing trades. But the most important of all was on the railroads.

For practical purposes, the right of railroad workers to strike did not exist after the federal suppression of the Pullman strike. The unions generally supported this state of affairs. Thus those railroad strikes that occurred met the opposition not only of the railroads but of the unions and the government. This was all the more true during the war and post-war period because the railroads were under federal control until March 1920. Discontent rose with the cost of living; by April 1920, prices had risen 100 percent since 1914, railroad wages only 50 percent.[101] After April 1919, the government refused all requests for wage increases. According to Commons' *History of Labour in the United States*, "In the minds of the men the pent-up resentment against this injustice became directed not only against the dilatory government officials and railway managers but also against their own union officials who apparently bore this situation with a patience unbecoming."[102]

In this charged situation, a railroad worker named John Grunau, a leader of an insurgent Chicago Yardmen's Association, was demoted in the Chicago yards on April 2. The 700 switchmen on his line immediately walked out in protest. The strike crystallized the general discontent of the railroad workers, and within two days every railroad in the Chicago area was involved in the strike, with 9,000 switchmen out. By April 9, the strike had spread spontaneously across the country, reaching New York, San Francisco, Los Angeles, Pittsburgh, Memphis, St. Louis, Kansas City, Omaha, and Detroit. Engineers, conductors, and firemen joined the striking switchmen.

In the midst of the strike, the workers created several temporary organizations. For instance, 1,700 workers on nine railroads entering

Cleveland voted to form a Cleveland Yardmen's Association. Similar organizations developed in Chicago, New York, Pittsburgh, St. Louis, and Kansas City. Representatives from these various groups met in Washington, D.C., and formed a national alliance of striking switchmen and yardmen. Labor journalist Sylvia Kopald described the best known of the outlaw organizations, the United Railway Workers of America:

> Originating among the Jersey strikers, this organization, according to the statements of its accredited spokesmen, was not intended to continue after the strike. The organization had no central direction. At its head stood an Executive Committee of 15 men, including a chairman and a secretary who were chosen from the members of a General Strike committee. This latter committee in turn was composed of representatives elected from the various roads, each of which contributed 18, or three for each craft (yardmasters, engineers, firemen, conductors, road workmen and yard service men). The Executive Committee was vested with power to "conduct the strike and make such moves as seem advisable to carry it to a successful conclusion." Its actual power, however, was drastically limited by the fact that it could take no important action without the express authorization of a general meeting.[103]

The railway unions launched a bitter drive against the strike. Dozens of union officials concentrated in Chicago and other strike centers ordered the men back to work, on the grounds that the strike violated union rules and contracts—although no contracts with the employers existed, the roads having just been returned from federal control. They red-baited the strikers as Bolsheviks and charged them with destroying the union. They threatened the strikers with expulsion if they did not return to work, and actually applied this penalty to tens of thousands of workers.

Finally, the union leaders themselves recruited hundreds of strikebreakers. For example, a Chicago officer of the Brotherhood of Railway Trainmen wired all member unions outside Chicago to send switchmen to "break the strike of Grunau's rival organization."[104] An official of the Order of Railway Conductors wired members: "Strike is illegal, against our Brotherhoods and against railroads. Our existence is at stake. Our members [are] justified under the circumstances in working in yard and road service to help us save our organization."[105]

Even those who did not join the strike resented this practice, however; as a union official reported of his meetings with his rank and file: "Many members present showed a strong sympathy for the striking switchmen and said they would not work with 'scabs' or 'finks.' It was impossible to convince our members at this stage of the illegal strike that men who took the switchmen's places were not scabs or finks and that they were friends of bona fide organizations helping them to maintain their contracts which were made by their duly authorized representatives."[106] At another meeting, he reported, the principal topic was "the stated fear and undesire of our men to work with what they called 'finks.'"[107]

Finally, the power of the state was turned against the strikers. Attorney General A. Mitchell Palmer attacked the strike leaders as Wobblies and "reds." On April 15, he had twenty-three strike leaders in Chicago arrested on charges of violating the Sherman Anti-Trust Act and the Lever Act, which regulated the wartime economy. There were arrests and raids on meetings in Cleveland, New Orleans, and other cities as well.

The strike succeeded in forcing President Wilson to appoint a Railroad Labor Board. The board strengthened the hands of the official unions by agreeing to meet exclusively with them and refusing even to hear the outlaws. It granted a general wage increase in July. With the combined pressure of repression and concession, the strike gradually faded as positions were filled by strikebreakers or men returning to work.

•

The most protracted of all the struggles that followed the World War I was the mass strike in the coalfields, with sporadic strikes, national strikes, and armed battles running from 1919 into 1922.

During the week of July 4, 1919, strikes were held throughout the country to protest the imprisonment on dubious charges of San Francisco AFL official Tom Mooney. Strikes were widespread among the coal miners of the Belleville subdistrict of Illinois. In accordance with the union contract, thousands of miners found their pay docked for taking part in the wildcat protest.

When the miners in the invidiously named Nigger Hollow Mine No. 2 found they had been fined for the strike, they immediately requested that the operators return the fines. At the news of the operators' refusal, the miners gathered outside the mine for a spontaneous mass meeting. A petition was drawn up asking the local union chairman to call a meeting of the local; when he ignored the request, the miners marched up a nearby hill, selected one of their own number to preside, and held their own meeting. They resolved that the collection of the Mooney strike fines was unjustified and illegal, and voted to stop work in protest. Next the workers decided to send a committee and ask the miners of the equally invidiously named Nigger Hollow Mine No. 1, who had also been fined, to join the strike. The workers there quickly voted to do so, and proposed that a joint meeting be held that night.

At the meeting, a United Mine Workers official who urged the men to return to work was shouted down, and instead the miners decided to continue the strike. They called a meeting for workers from other mines that Sunday. Meanwhile, word of the strike began to spread around the district, and the men from nearby mines independently struck and held meetings to decide what action they would advocate at the Sunday meeting.

The men from the Nigger Hollow mines decided to propose two resolutions at the Sunday meeting. One was that the miners return to work and fight through regular channels rather than continue the strike. The second was a resolution on general policy reflecting the strong socialist tradition of the Illinois miners. It read:

> In view of the fact that the present-day system of Society, known as the capitalist system, has completely broken down, and is no longer able to supply the material and spiritual needs of the workers of the land, and in further view of the fact that the apologists for and the beneficiaries of that system now try to placate the suffering masses by promises of reforms such as a shorter workday and increases in wages, and in further view of the futility of such reforms in the face of the world crisis that is facing the capitalist system; therefore be it

… [r]esolved, that the next National Convention of the U.M.W.A. issue a call to the workers of all industries to elect delegates to an industrial congress, there to demand of the capitalist class that all instruments of industries be turned over to the working class to guarantee that necessities, comforts and luxuries be produced for the use of humanity instead of a parasitical class of stockholders, bondholders, and that the Congress be called upon to pass an amendment to the Constitution of the United States legalizing all such action in the aforementioned Congress.[108]

About 2,000 miners arrived for the Sunday meeting. They adopted the general policy resolution by a substantial majority. The fight came over continuing the strike. A local UMW official had earlier wired Illinois District President Frank Farrington:

Six mines in the Belleville District have struck this week. I have done my best to get them back to work. Three of them are still out. A mass meeting is called for Sunday at Priester's Park. The chances are a great many more miners will come out. Situation serious. If some one can come here Sunday it might have some effect.[109]

Farrington replied, "I have instructed Reynolds, Dobbins, Myers, Schaefer, Thomas, Walker and Mason to attend meeting to be held at Priester's Park Sunday afternoon and to use their every influence to curb the rebellious movement in the Belleville District."[110] The issue was debated for four hours, at the end of which both the UMW and the Nigger Hollow miners' resolution to end the strike was rejected, and instead it was decided to spread the strike further.

Two days later, a still larger body of strikers met for what was called a "general committee meeting." They established a "policy committee" of fifty miners to handle executive work of the strike.

Meanwhile, the issues of the strike were greatly expanded. It became not just a strike against the Mooney fines, but against the contract under which all miners were then working. This contract had been established during the war by the "Washington Agreement," which levied automatic fines for workers who struck. (It was under this provision that the Mooney strikers were punished.) The contract also provided maximum rates of pay, which the miners now considered inadequate in the face of post-war inflation.

Practically from the signing of the Washington Agreement, miners had demanded an increase in the wages it provided, and in the wake of the armistice, mass meetings were held in mining centers throughout Illinois demanding that the union abrogate the agreement. The union not only supported the agreement; it even prevented mine operators from paying bonuses above it.

The penalty clause levying fines for striking was likewise attacked from the start by the workers. The issue became critical after the armistice, when operators, especially in the Belleville area, began breaking down work practices the miners had long struggled to establish. When the miners retaliated by closing down the mines, they were fined under the penalty clause of the Washington Agreement.

The Washington Agreement was to run "during the continuation of the war not to exceed two years from April 1, 1918."[111] The U.S. government, the coal operators, and the national and state mine union leaders all agreed that despite the armistice, the contract would run until April 1, 1920, since no peace treaty had been signed. The rank-and-file miners throughout the country opposed continuing the old contract, and the Illinois miners' strike now became a strike to renounce the Washington Agreement and establish a new contract with a new wage scale and without the penalty clause.

Armed with this broadened program, the Belleville miners began systematically spreading their revolt across the state. They sent bulletins and posters giving word of the strike to other mining centers. Most important, they organized teams of "crusaders" who traveled across the state calling mass meetings of the miners in each area urging them to join the strike. As the strike spread, workers in each local elected representatives to a policy committee for their own subdistrict, and a state policy committee was formed from representatives of each of these. The insurgent state policy committee no longer merely petitioned the union for a state convention, but decided to go ahead and call one on its own account.

Meanwhile, the union officials counter-attacked. Illinois District President Frank Farrington issued a circular to the membership that began: "Our union is facing a crisis. The elements of destruction are at work. The issue is: Shall the forces of defiance and rebellion prevail and stab our union to death, or shall reason and orderly procedure dominate the affairs of the United Mine Workers of America?"[112]

Soon the union began supplying the operators with strikebreakers to reopen the mines that had been shut down. The union hired "loyal" workers to try to intimidate or stampede the strikers back to work. "Loyal" union men were sworn in as special deputy sheriffs, at least some of them apparently paid directly from the union treasury. Arrests of strikers by these deputies and other law officials were common. The crusaders were again and again held up on the public highways, beaten, and prevented from proceeding. The union eventually admitted having spent $27,000 to quell the rebellion, but refused to itemize the expenses.

The tactics of the union in suppressing the strike roused the ire of the miners even more. For example, a committee from Belleville was beaten up on the highway on the way to Springfield. When the committee subsequently appealed to the Springfield miners to join the strike for a new contract, the latter were wary—but when the committee referred to the beating they had received at the instigation of union officials, the miners voted to strike and remain on strike "until all the state officers resigned their jobs."[113] By the time of the insurgent state convention, perhaps half of the 90,000 miners in Illinois had joined the outlaw strike.

Although they had opposed the convention, the union officials understood how important it was to control it once it was called. They headed off the attempt to spread the movement to other states by excluding miners from Pennsylvania and other states. From then on, the union officials successfully asserted their authority, declaring the strike called off because contract negotiations had been scheduled to begin in a month. The contract demands of the insurgents were accepted, however, and became the basis of the rank-and-file program at the national UMW convention a month later. In addition, the convention recommended not that the mines be operated by the government—which had been the official UMW position—but that they be turned over to the miners.

When the national UMW convention met in Cleveland a month later, a completely new situation had been created by the Illinois insurgency, for Illinois was the heart of the union and reflected the mood of much of the rank and file. One observer described the convention as a "fight between the men and their officials."[114] The 2,000 delegates demanded a new contract, set a strike date for November 1 if it was not gained, and instructed their officers to demand a thirty-hour week and a 60 percent wage increase. The UMW officials were forced to negotiate for a new contract. When they failed to achieve one, the convention's strike order went into effect and 425,000 miners struck on November 1.

The U.S. government instantly leapt into the fray. President Wilson declared the strike "not only unjustifiable but unlawful."[115] At the request of the U.S. attorney general, a federal judge issued an injunction sequestering the union strike fund and prohibiting the union leaders from any action furthering the strike. Federal troops were moved into the coal fields of Utah, Washington, New Mexico, Oklahoma, and Pennsylvania. On November 8, the federal court further ordered the union officials to rescind the strike order and send the men back to work. Acting UMW President John L. Lewis ordered the strike call canceled, declaring, "We are Americans, we cannot fight our Government."[116]

But the coal miners disagreed, ignored the union order, and stayed out, refusing to return to work for nearly a month. They realized their power as they saw the U.S. government rationing coal, schools closing down for lack of heat, factories shutting down, and railroad operations drastically cut back. According to a report in *The Survey*,

> In not a few places where temperatures were below zero, a fuel famine existed. In the emergencies much volunteer coal mining was attempted. College and university students went into the surface mines in Kansas. In Montana on the other hand it was reported that Federal troops were used to drive miners to work. The Secretary of War announced that such an action was inconceivable, but there has been no public report on what actually occurred. In North Dakota Governor Frazier took over the mines under martial law and the union miners returned to work under the auspices of the state government.[117]

The miners reluctantly returned to work when President Wilson proposed an immediate 14 percent wage increase and an arbitration commission to grant further demands.

The miners remained discontented with the results of the settlement, however. By summer 1920, wildcats were common and all mining had stopped in Indiana and Illinois without declaration of a strike.

Insurgency developed even further in anthracite than in bituminous mining. In August 1919, a UMW convention formulated demands; negotiations dragged on fruitlessly until May 1920, when the union agreed to President Wilson's proposal for arbitration. The arbitration award was totally unsatisfactory to the miners, but the union recognized that having accepted the arbitration process, it was obliged to accept the results. While the union officials were drafting the contract, 85,000 miners struck under insurgent leadership, closing down half the anthracite collieries. Union officials earnestly endeavored to end the strike, but it continued for nearly a month.

Meanwhile, in response to the bituminous strike, the governor of Kansas called a special session of the legislature to establish compulsory arbitration in major industries by means of a labor court. As soon as the proposal was passed, 400 Kansas miners walked off their jobs in a wildcat strike to show their defiance of the law, but were ordered back to work by the union the next day. Soon a test case arose when miners in Crawford County refused to work with an engineer who had helped attempts to open the mines during the national coal strike. District union officials were ordered to appear before the new labor court and were arrested for contempt when they refused. In response, the miners struck, closing down 90 percent of the mines in Kansas. They then came into the town of Girard for a mass demonstration, where the UMW district president was allowed to address them from the prison balcony. The miners returned to work only when the officials were released on bond.

On December 11, 1921, hundreds of Kansas women held a meeting from which men were excluded and declared that, because their husbands were "striking against a law to enslave our children," they considered it their duty to stand "shoulder to shoulder" with the men. For the next three days, squadrons of up to 2,500 women, many with babies in their arms, blocked strikebreakers from entering Kansas mines. The Supreme Court of the United States eventually declared the Kansas Industrial Court unconstitutional, but in the same decisions sharply limited workers' right to strike.[118]

Meanwhile, events in West Virginia began developing toward civil war. During and after World War I, the West Virginia coalfields had expanded enormously. The northern fields were mostly unionized, but organization was completely blocked and union organizers were forbidden even to enter the southern counties of the state, whose local governments were under virtually complete control by anti-union mine operators. Miners who joined the union were fired and evicted from their homes; and deputy sheriffs on company payrolls ran union organizers out of town and arrested and beat up local union sympathizers.

At this time, a rumor spread around the state that women and children were being killed in Logan County. An investigator describes what happened:

> On Sept. 4 hundreds of miners assembled on Lens Creek ... 30 miles from Logan County. They trudged on over the hills and by the roads. Many of them carried guns; 5,000 miners had gathered by nightfall. There were no leaders. The miners were determined, apparently, to invade Logan County.[119]

The governor wired Frank Keeney, West Virginia UMW president, who rushed to Lens Creek to try to stop the miners. "On the outskirts of the crowd he was told that his presence was useless and he might as well go back home."[120] Next both Keeney and the governor addressed the strikers, but were only partially successful in persuading them to return home. The next day, 1,500 miners continued the march to Danville. Only when a committee they had sent to Logan County reported that all there was quiet did the miners disband and go home. But this was just a prelude.

In May 1920, a strike broke out in Mattewan, West Virginia, over the firing of members of a new union and rapidly spread through

Mingo County, West Virginia, and Pike County, Kentucky. Armed guards patrolled the Mingo County line "to prevent infiltration of union men."[121] In Mattewan, a shoot-out occurred between the local police chief, Sid Hatfield (an ex-miner and a Hatfield of the Hatfield-McCoy feud), and Baldwin-Felts detectives brought in by the operators to evict strikers. Two miners, the mayor of Mattewan, and seven Baldwin-Felts guards were killed in a matter of minutes. In response to this and other violence, the governor sent in state troops. On August 21, a three-hour gun battle between strikers and guards killed six. At the governor's request, 500 federal troops were rushed in. District President Keeney threatened a general strike throughout the state unless the federal troops stopped their strikebreaking activities.

The strike continued, with 1,700 people living in tent colonies. Battles flared intermittently; federal troops were withdrawn, rushed back, and withdrawn again. Finally at a meeting of miners in the small mining camp of Marmet on August 20, 1921, it was decided that since the union was kept out by the violence of guards, deputies, and troopers, the miners would have to open the area by force of arms. Thus a second miners' march was organized, led this time by war veterans.

"Patrols were flung out along the roads leading into Logan, a commissary was set up, and mess halls opened at various school houses near the front. Trains and automobiles were commandeered for the 'citizens' army' and the men, armed with all sorts of weapons, were accompanied by nurses in uniform.... The union men wore blue overalls with red handkerchiefs around their necks."[122] As the miners drew near to Logan County, their number reached 4,000. Frank Keeney, as before, tried to persuade them to disperse, but when word came that armed deputies had swooped down on a camp and killed five miners, the invasion was resumed. President Warren G. Harding issued a proclamation ordering the miners to disperse, but they ignored it. The miners took up position on a wide front and, advancing two miles, engaged in heavy battle at five points with deputies and volunteers defending the non-union counties. At that point, 2,100 troops of the 19th Infantry, together with machine guns and airplanes, were rushed into Logan County. The miners had no choice but to surrender to the federal troops, and with law and order of a sort restored the strike was easily defeated. Some 350 miners were indicted for treason but never convicted.

In April 1922, the UMW called strikes in both anthracite and bituminous fields. The strikes were joined by 75,000 non-union miners in the Connellsville coke region of Pennsylvania, as well. "With the zeal of new converts, the Connellsville miners became self-appointed organizers, looking to no one for orders, only anxious to spread the strike and the union gospel."[123]

After eight weeks of the strike, the Southern Illinois Coal Company began to reopen its mines in Williamson County with imported strikebreakers under heavily armed guards. When a group of miners tried to talk with the strikebreakers, they were fired on by machine guns and two of them were killed. Not only the miners themselves, but farmers and other workers of the area grew furious, and on June 21, when another striker was shot dead while standing in a farmyard half a mile from the mine, men began pouring into Williamson from as far as Kansas, Indiana, and Ohio.

The protesters were armed with weapons they had seized from hardware stores and American Legion halls. By dusk, 1,000 armed men advanced on the mine in skirmish waves directed by war veterans wearing trench helmets. An airplane, rented at a nearby field, flew overhead dropping dynamite bombs on the strongholds of the strikebreakers. According to a National Guard colonel, "It was a seemingly well-organized, remarkably sober, determined, resolute aggregation of men and boys."[124]

As the armed crowd approached they were met with continuous machine-gun fire from the mine guards. Just as they prepared to storm the mine, a white flag went up and the besieged offered to surrender. Armed miners marched them away, executing the mine superintendent along the way. They then were met by a mob from town who had not taken part in the battle. The mob took over the prisoners, told them to run for it, and then began shooting at them. In this and subsequent massacres, nineteen strikebreakers were killed. Juries of local farmers refused to convict anyone for the massacre.

In July, the federal government turned its strength against the nationwide coal strike. President Harding officially told the operators to go home and resume operations, and wired the governors of twenty-eight states to furnish them with protection, pledging the full support of the federal government. In response, the governors of Pennsylvania and Ohio ordered state troops to the mines, but the strike remained firm.

The union finally accepted a settlement at the expense of the 75,000 non-union miners who had joined the strike; they were abandoned to their fate. A committee appointed by the mayor of New York found their conditions "worse than the serfs of Russia or the slaves before the Civil War."[125] They continued their desperate strike for sixteen months until August 1923, when they were finally starved out. As the 1920s wore on, the war and post-war coal boom petered out and the industry developed a chronic coal glut. Under these conditions the United Mine Workers proved impotent. The rest of the 1920s was a period of steady decay as the union retreated or was broken in area after area.

•

In 1919, we see the energy of a mass strike working both through and against trade unionism. Where the rank and file was able to control existing unions—as in Seattle—the militance and class consciousness of the workers gave union action radical forms. Where unionization had been prevented, as in steel, establishing trade unionism was the logical objective of strike action. In the two basic industries that had been thoroughly unionized—coal and railroads—the unions tried desperately to head off or kill rank-and-file strike action, and the workers were forced to organize against their own unions. The unions as institutions strove to maintain their organizational security, while the workers pressed for changes that threatened that security; thus, such a conflict was inevitable.

Several important factors give mass strikes after 1900 a different character from those that had come before. The decline in the central role of railroads weakened the process by which railroad strikes in 1877 and 1894 rapidly became universal, nationwide struggles between labor and capital. The growth of a unionism based on collective bargaining contracts tended to counteract rank-and-file solidarity and made workers think of their struggle in terms of their own industry or workplace alone, rather than in terms of their class as a whole. Further, the contracts themselves operated as a powerful barrier to the tendency of strikes to spread to wider and wider groups. This contrasts markedly with such nineteenth-century labor organizations as the Knights of Labor and the American Railway Union, which considered sympathetic strikes and labor solidarity among their basic principles. The result is that twentieth-century mass strikes have been far less unified than those that came before. In 1919—as later—we see the spectacle of determined groups of workers, after great sacrifice, going down separately to defeat.

Another important change is that by the twentieth century, workers by and large accepted the wage system and their position of subordination within it as an accomplished fact. They were far less attracted by programs designed in one way or another to re-create a nation of small independent producers, such as the producers' cooperatives of the Knights of Labor or the cooperative colonies—somewhat like rural communes—to which the American Railway Union turned after its great defeat. This had two consequences. On the one hand, it meant that workers were far more willing to accept and indeed demand stable institutions of collective bargaining and union representation that would make life under capitalism more bearable. On the other hand, it meant that when the demand for workers' power arose, it no longer took the form of demanding a return to the system of small independent producers of the past. Instead, workers accepted and wanted to use the new industrial technology and the large-scale, coordinated production it made possible. The idea of workers' management of industry arose in many of the post-World War I labor struggles. It was spelled out by the workers in Seattle, in Lawrence, Massachusetts, and in Illinois, and it formed a background to the other conflicts. Of course, the strikes of 1919 were not in themselves attempts to establish such a system, but they were often seen by the participants—and their opponents—as part of a struggle for power that led in that direction.

Funeral of Henry Ness, a striker killed during the 1934 Minneapolis general strike. (Photo courtesy of the International Botherhood of Teamsters.)

A demonstrator injured by a flying missile during the Toledo Auto-Lite strike, May 23, 1934. (Photo permission of Archives of Labor and Urban Affairs, Wayne State University.)

Chapter 5

Depression Decade

Don't Starve-Fight

The 1920s were a period of great expansion for American capitalism. For the trade unions, it was a period of decline, which they met by trying to persuade employers to establish unionism to guarantee labor peace. By the late 1920s, one of America's leading economists was widely seconded when he declared that the country had entered an era of "permanent prosperity." Already, however, serious constriction had begun in such industries as coal and textiles, and with the collapse of the stock market in October 1929, depression—long believed a thing of the past—set in.

With the Depression came enormous misery—loss of jobs, homes, farms, savings, even the means to eat. Within three years, some fifteen million workers were unemployed. By early 1932, according to a New York journalist, groups of thirty or forty men would enter chain grocery stores and ask for credit: "When the clerk tells them business is for cash only, they bid him stand aside; they don't want to harm him, but they must have things to eat. They load up and depart."[1]

Out of this kind of desperation the unemployed began improvising a variety of forms of direct action to meet their needs. The most dramatic was direct action to stop evictions. A reporter described a typical anti-eviction "riot" in Chicago:

> A woman living in a certain block in Chicago has five children; her husband is a stockyards workman who has been out of a job a year and a half. But on ten dollars a month sent by her brother-in-law, and borrowing now and then from the neighbors' pantries, she has fed her family. There is no money left for rent. So after two warnings from the landlord—a crisis. She is to be evicted next Tuesday at five.

In the same block lives a member of the local branch of the Unemployed Council, who has been through it all before. He talks to
the men and women and together they call a meeting of all the
families on the block. Most of them have known Mrs. MacNamara
for years and know that the baby has tonsillitis. At 4:30 on Tuesday
you find them in an organized body outside the MacNamara flat.
The sheriff arrives and in the face of protest does his work. Mrs.
MacNamara's bed, bureau, stove, and children are translated to the
street. Then the Council acts. With great gusto the bed, bureau,
stove, and children are put back in the house. Then the neighbors
proceed to the local relief bureau, where a Council spokesman dis-
plays the children, presents the facts, and demands that the Relief
Commission pay the rent or find another flat for the MacNamaras.
The local relief worker expresses dismay but says the rent fund is
exhausted. The spokesman goes through the MacNamara story
again with a new emphasis, and repeats his demands. If the Commission is adamant, he leaves and reappears at general headquarters with a hundred Council members instead of fifty. Usually the
Commission digs up the $6 a month rent, or the landlord throws up
his hands, and Mrs. MacNamara's children have a roof over their
heads.[2]

Organizations of the unemployed sprang up city by city around
the country, often with initiative coming from Communist, Socialist,
or other leftist groups. Labor writer Charles R. Walker, who studied
them in various parts of the country, wrote:

The Unemployed Council is a democratic organ of the unemployed
to secure by very practical means a control over their means of subsistence. I find it is no secret that Communists organize Unemployed Councils in most cities and usually lead them, but the
councils are organized democratically and the majority rules. In one
I visited at Lincoln Park, Michigan, there were three hundred members of which eleven were Communists. The Council had a right
wing, a left wing, and a center. The chairman of the council, who
was of the right wing, was also the local commander of the American Legion. In Chicago there are forty-five branches of the Unemployed Council, with a total membership of 22,000.
     The Councils' weapon is democratic force of numbers and their
functions are: to prevent evictions of the destitute, or if evicted, to
bring pressure to bear on the Relief Commission to find a new

home for the evicted family; if an unemployed worker has his gas or his water turned off because he can't pay for it, to investigate the case and demand their return from the proper authorities; to see that the unemployed who are shoeless and clothesless get both; to eliminate through publicity and pressure discriminations between Negroes and white persons, or against the foreign born, in matters of relief; for individuals or families and children of the unemployed who have no relief as a penalty for political views or have been denied it through neglect, lack of funds, or any other reasons whatever, to march them down to relief headquarters and demand they be fed and clothed. Finally, to provide legal defense for all unemployed arrested for joining parades, hunger marches, or attending union meetings.[3]

By direct action the unemployed were able to stop many evictions. In Chicago and other cities, the public authorities were finally forced to suspend them entirely. Further, Walker reported, the amount of relief in cities he visited was directly proportional to the strength and struggle of the local unemployed council.

In many places the unemployed also made attempts to reorganize economic life on their own. In Seattle, the Unemployed Citizens' League organized self-help on a large scale. The unemployed were loaned fishing boats by the fishermen's union, allowed to pick unmarketable fruits and vegetables by nearby farmers, and permitted to cut wood on scrub timberland. Members throughout the city organized twenty-two locals, each with its own commissary at which the food and firewood thus acquired was exchanged with barbers who cut hair, seamstresses who mended clothes, carpenters who repaired houses, and doctors who treated the sick. With the end of the harvest season, however, self-help in Seattle lost its already marginal economic basis. The UCL then became the machinery for distributing relief. It also became a major political power in the city. Its candidate for mayor, named John Dore, won with the largest plurality in the city's history, whereupon he took relief administration away from the UCL and threatened to use machine guns against demonstrations of the unemployed; he quickly became known as "revolving Dore."[4]

By the end of 1932, there were 330 such self-help organizations in thirty-seven states with membership over 300,000. But by early 1933, most of them, including the Seattle UCL, were in disarray, as they began to discover the limitations of a self-help movement living off the scraps of an already collapsed economy.

The most dramatic—and illegal—form of self-help was the bootleg coal industry in Pennsylvania. Small teams of unemployed coal miners simply dug small mines on company property and mined out the coal, while others took it by truck to nearby cities and sold it below the commercial rate. A miner named William Keating composed a ballad in 1932 that typifies the attitudes of the "coal-leggers":

> While the woes of unemployment were increasing,
> While the price of foodstuff swelled the grocer's till,
> For to fix 'gainst next winter's chill breeze,
> Lest our poor families do freeze,
> We dug a wee coal hole on God's hill.
>
> But our terrible toil was wasted; we worked in vain,
> Two Cossack-mannered coal and iron cops came.
> On next winter's cold nights,
> We'll have no anthracite,
> 'Cause the cops caved in our wee coal hole.
>
> My mule-driving record proves at Oak Hill mine,
> I'm unfairly unemployed for four years' time.
> To no soup house I'll be led,
> Because I'll dig my family's bread,
> Or by cops be killed, in my wee coal hole.
>
> Right demands I keep my family fed and warm,
> God put coal 'neath these hills; here I was born.
> So call it bootleg or what,
> I'll have coal in my cot,
> While there's coal in Good God's coal vein.[5]

By 1934, coal bootlegging was an important industry, producing some five million tons of coal worth $45 million and employing 20,000 men and 4,000 vehicles. The coal companies fumed, but community opinion solidly backed the bootleggers—local officials would not prosecute the miners, juries would not convict, and jailers would not imprison. When company police tried to stop the bootlegging, the miners defended themselves by force. In Shamokin, when the company started stripping operations on the "Edgewood Bootleggers' Tract," where 17,000 illegal miners dug coal, the men promptly dynamited the steam shovel and told the company men to "beat it"; nobody was arrested. At Tremont, a thousand bootleggers prepared to battle fifty police until the latter withdrew. The private police of another company blew up more than 1,000 holes in 1934, but in that time at least 4,000 new ones were dug on the same property. An investigator reported several bootleggers telling him, "If they close our holes, we'll gang up on their collieries and close *them.*"[6]

In coal bootlegging the miners took over use of private property and began producing for themselves. But as long as the rest of the economic system remained unchanged, bootleg mining had severe limitations. Miners had little equipment save shovels, ropes and buckets; the primitive technology required much more labor for a given amount of coal. With bootleg coal priced below commercial coal, the bootleggers ended with a wage of about $14 a week. Had the bootleg competition cut seriously into regular producers' profits, the companies would have had to cut their workers' wages, thus worsening conditions of employed miners and turning them against the bootleggers. And with no money for safety devices, the bootleggers faced an accident rate far higher than that of ordinary miners.

•

Desperate revolt was by no means limited to the unemployed. As wages were cut again and again, strikes broke out and spread with little previous planning or organization. In High Point, North Carolina, for example, a few hundred stocking boarders walked out at six hosiery mills one July morning in 1932 when the second wage cut of the year was posted at their mills. Other hosiery workers joined and by the end of the day 1,600 had walked out. The next day bands of strikers and unemployed workers marched through High Point and nearby Kernersville, Jamestown, Lexington, and Thomasville, closing 100 factories of all kinds employing 15,000 workers. The next day twenty-five unemployed workers forced their way into a High Point movie house and demanded admission, saying that they were out of work and entitled to entertainment. When the police drove them out, they wrecked a motor and turned off the town's electricity, "to teach the big fellows that we ain't going to stand for no more bad treatment." The hosiery strike was finally settled through the intervention of the governor, with a revocation of the wage cut. Out of the conflict developed the Industrial Association of High Point, a union open to all industrial workers in the city, with 4,000 members and committees in each of the mills.[7]

Although trade union strikes were rare and ineffectual during the early years of the Depression, such spontaneous revolts developed in all parts of the country. As Charles R. Walker foresaw, there were

> increasing outbursts of employed and unemployed alike—a kind of spontaneous democracy expressing itself in organized demonstrations by large masses of people. I use the word organized and I use the word democracy advisedly. They will not be mobs—though the police will often break them up—but will march and meet in order, elect their own spokesmen and committees, and work out in detail their demands for work or relief. They will present their formulated needs to factory superintendents, relief commissions, and city councils, and to the government at Washington.... Another social tendency ... is to suppress by any means at hand this rough-and-ready democracy. Meetings, marches, unions, and councils will be greeted in many cases—as they were in Detroit—with bullets and not relief.... As long as the American crisis lasts these two political tendencies—"spontaneous but organized" protest, and suppression by violence—will fight it out.[8]

Leftist organizations received little support in the early years of the Depression, but it was widely felt that such spontaneous mass action would become a revolutionary movement if conditions continued to worsen. As one unemployed organizer wrote of the coal bootleggers,

> All that is really necessary for the workers to do in order to end their miseries is to perform such simple things as to take from where there is, without regard to established property principles or social-philosophies, and to start to produce for themselves. Done on a broad social scale it will lead to lasting results; on a local, isolated plane it will be either defeated, or remain an unsuccessful attempt unable to serve the needs of the working class. When the large

masses face a similar general situation as the Pennsylvania miners faced in their specific case, we have every reason to assume that they will react in the same way. The bootleg miners have shown in a rather clear and impressive way, that the so much bewailed absence of a socialist ideology on the part of the workers, really does not prevent workers from acting quite anti-capitalistically, quite in accordance with their own needs. Breaking through the confines of private property in order to live up to their own necessities, the miners' action is, at the same time a manifestation of the most important part of class consciousness—namely, that the problems of the workers can be solved only by themselves.[9]

At this point President Franklin Delano Roosevelt, the New Deal, and the National Recovery Administration offered many workers the hope that they would not have to solve their problems by themselves. From the day of his first inaugural address, Roosevelt captured the imagination and confidence of the nation with the promise of government action to meet the social crisis created by the Depression. He acted quickly to end the financial panic that had closed the nation's banks by putting the credit of the U.S. government behind them. He created a national relief system, which effectively prevented mass starvation in the face of the virtual breakdown of local welfare resources, and established public works programs to provide employment, going far to pacify the unemployed. Many workers developed an almost religious faith in the new president. From the Carolinas, Martha Gellhorn wrote: "Every house I visited—mill worker or unemployed—had a picture of the President. These ranged from newspaper clippings (in destitute homes) to large colored prints, framed in gilt cardboard. The portrait holds the place of honour over the mantel; I can only compare this to the Italian peasant's Madonna."[10]

One central feature of the early New Deal was the National Recovery Administration. The NRA was largely modeled on the War Industries Board of World War I, of which its head, General Hugh S. Johnson, had been an official. The National Recovery Act was in essence a suspension of the anti-trust laws, allowing trade associations for each industry to fix prices and establish production quotas for each company. A "Code of Fair Competition" was established for each industry, with a Code Authority to enforce the agreements and set minimum wages and maximum hours. Following the precedent of World War I (and with the tacit support of the U.S. Chamber of Commerce), labor support for the program was won by including as Section 7A of the National Recovery Act the provision that "employees shall have the right to organize and bargain collectively through representatives of their own choosing, and shall be free from the interference, restraint or coercion of employers."[11]

Until the formation of the NRA, the American trade union movement had become practically defunct. The AFL had failed to combat the layoffs and wage cuts that accompanied the Great Depression, and membership, far from increasing with popular discontent, went down with the slump. Workers had largely lost interest in trade unions and had turned on a considerable scale to various forms of direct action. But with Section 7A guaranteeing the right to organize and appearing to make trade unionism part of the president's plan for economic recovery, workers throughout the country rushed to join unions, with high hopes that Roosevelt and the AFL would cure their ills. In the Appalachian hills they sang:

> When you all work for the NRA
> You work shorter hours and get the same pay
> Sweet thing, baby mine.[12]

The great mass of unorganized industrial workers flooded into such industrial unions as the United Mine Workers, and where none existed, they joined the newly formed "federal locals" directly under the AFL. In 1933, the United Mine Workers used the NRA to sign up tens of thousands of members simply on the slogan, "The President wants you to join the union"—admitting only if challenged that they meant the president of the union, not of the United States.

Nineteen Thirty-Four

With the passage of Section 7A, longshoremen in San Francisco, like workers elsewhere, began pouring into the available unions. During July and August 1933, nearly 95 percent of the San Francisco longshoremen joined the International Longshoremen's Association.[13]

Their greatest grievance was the shape-up, a system of hiring that the longshoremen referred to as "the slave market." Every morning at 6 a.m., everyone seeking a day's work longshoring would crowd along the Embarcadero, where the foremen would pick out those they wanted for the day. The effect was that longshoremen could never count on steady work, had to suck up to or even bribe the foremen, and had to work to exhaustion or not be hired again.

When the ILA made no attempt to challenge the shape-up, the more militant workers began forming a rank-and-file movement within the union. (Its most prominent figure was an Australian, Harry Bridges, and it included many members of the Communist Party.) The rank-and-file movement forced the calling of a West Coast convention in February 1934, from which paid officers of the union were excluded as delegates, and pressured union officials to accept a program for which they had no desire to fight: abolition of the shape-up and its replacement by a union hiring hall, with a strike if this demand was not accepted within two weeks.

Faced with a strike, the Waterfront Employers Association made a somewhat vague offer to recognize the ILA and set up a dispatching hall whose control was not specified. The ILA leaders accepted the proposal, but the membership repudiated it and suspended the local president for being "too conservative." On May 9, longshoremen in Bellingham, Seattle, Tacoma, Aberdeen, Portland, Astoria, San Francisco, Oakland, Stockton, San Pedro, and San Diego struck, cutting off nearly 2,000 miles of coastland.

The lines of the conflict rapidly began to spread. The employers imported large numbers of strikebreakers—eventually 1,700, many of them recruited from the University of California—to unload the ships. The strikebreakers were housed in floating boarding houses (where union employees refused to work) and thus protected from pickets; those who sneaked ashore, however, were systematically brutalized by the strikers. Strikebreaking would have seriously threatened the strike, but within four days, mass meetings of Teamsters in San Francisco, Los Angeles, Oakland, and Seattle decided overwhelmingly not to haul goods to and from the docks, thus making the strikebreakers' efforts fruitless; many of the Teamsters joined the picket lines as well. In San Francisco, as much as 70 percent of the Teamsters' work was on the waterfront. The feelings stirred by seeing the struggle of the longshoremen, combined with their own fear that if the longshoremen were broken the Teamsters would be attacked next, gave them strong motivation for sympathetic action. Soon the strike began to idle unrelated industries; lumber mills shut down in Oregon, for example, because they were unable to ship their products.

At the same time, the strike spread to other maritime workers. As ships came to port, entire crews walked off and joined the longshoremen. By May 21, 4,500 sailors, marine firemen, water tenders, cooks, stewards, and licensed officers had struck. They established a Joint Marine Strike Committee with five representatives from each of the ten unions involved. Breaking a tradition of scabbing on each other, each agreed not to return to work until the others had settled.

Meanwhile, the longshoremen resisted numerous efforts by government and union officials to get them to work without the union hiring hall. At the outset, the strike had been postponed at the request of President Roosevelt, who appointed a Federal Mediation Board; the proposal this board worked out with the employers and West Coast leaders of the ILA was repudiated by the rank and file, who went ahead and struck anyway. Next, Assistant Secretary of Labor Ed McGrady, Roosevelt's top mediator, flew to San Francisco and asked the longshoremen to empower their negotiating committee to enter a final settlement; but the San Francisco local voted unanimously to refuse and to require any agreement to be ratified by the strikers themselves. Then Joseph Ryan, president of the ILA, flew to San Francisco and announced absurdly that "the only vital point at issue" was "recognition of the ILA." When Ryan negotiated a settlement similar to past proposals, he was met with catcalls and voted down almost unanimously by the ILA locals in Portland and San Francisco.[14]

Two weeks later, Ryan signed a new agreement to send the longshoremen back to work; Michael Casey and Dave Beck, San Francisco and Seattle Teamster bosses, guaranteed the agreement by promising to resume working on the docks; but Ryan was again booed by his own membership, which rejected the agreement by acclamation at a mass meeting in San Francisco. Finally, President Roosevelt appointed a National Longshoremen's Board to mediate the conflict.

Despite the efforts at pacification, the conflict grew steadily more violent. On the first day of the strike, police broke up a 500-strong picket line. On May 28, pickets armed with brickbats fought police, who ended the battle by firing directly into the pickets with sawed-off shotguns after failing to quell them with billy clubs and tear gas. As *The Clarion*, the organ of the conservative Central Labor Council, put it, "To parade strike-breakers through the streets on the way to the docks under police guard and to use public property and city employees in conveying these outcasts to their nefarious work was an invitation to violence."[15]

After forty-five days, San Francisco's economy was reeling and the business community decided the time had come to break the strike. At a meeting on June 23, representatives of the Employers' Industrial Association, the Chamber of Commerce, police commissioners, the chief of police, and harbor commissioners agreed to open the port, with the assurance of the chief of police that "every available police officer in San Francisco will be detailed to the waterfront to give the necessary protection."[16]

On July 3, a cordon of freight cars was set up, guarded by 700 policemen armed with tear gas and riot guns. A police captain brandishing a revolver declared, "The port is open," and five trucks manned by strikebreakers rolled from the pier toward the warehouses. Thousands of strikers and sympathizers on the picket line attacked the police lines. As *The New York Times* described it, "Mounted and foot police swung their clubs and hurled tear-gas bombs, strikers hurled bricks and rocks, battered heads with clubs and railroad spikes and smashed windows.... Mounted and foot police relentlessly drove the pickets behind these freightcar barriers. The safety line remained intact but on its fringes pandemonium raged."[17] Twenty-five people were hospitalized as a result of the battle, about half pickets and half police.

After the Independence Day holiday, the battle resumed July 5. In the morning, police charged 2,000 pickets who had gathered to stop trucks coming off the pier, and dispersed them after an hour and a half of street and barricade fighting. By the afternoon, a crowd of 5,000 gathered. When the police could no longer control them with gas, they switched to guns on a large scale. The crowd grew increasingly furious in the face of police shootings, and when the word spread that the National Guard would take over the waterfront that evening, pickets made a last concerted effort to seize the belt-line railway on the waterfront before the troops arrived. Unarmed demonstrators were no match for the police, however, and were driven back in a bloody battle. One reporter wrote, "It was as close to actual war as anything but war itself could be."[18] Two strikers and a bystander were killed and 115 people were hospitalized.

That night the governor of California ordered in 1,700 National Guard soldiers, who enclosed the Embarcadero with barbed wire and machine gun nests, patrolled the area with armored cars, and were given orders to shoot to kill. Under this protection, freight moved steadily from the docks to the warehouses. The balance of forces had shifted decisively against the strikers. As Harry Bridges said, "We cannot stand up against police, machine guns, and National Guard bayonets."[19]

But the conflict had generated a whole new body of allies for the strikers. In the early weeks of June, the feeling had begun to spread among San Francisco workers that a general strike might be necessary to back up the longshoremen. The strikebreaking activities of the police daily roused their ire. A general strike was felt to be a way of expressing their power against all employers. Even relatively conservative workers felt the need to protect themselves against the employer offensive. *The Clarion* reported: "Workers in other groups have been impelled to stand behind the marine and waterfront workers under the general belief that they represented the 'shock troops' in a general defense of the Trade Union position against the assault upon the union shop and for the installation of the 'open shop,' even in industries which had recognized union contracts for generations."[20]

In mid-June, the painters' local circulated a letter among AFL unions requesting support for a general strike if necessary. On June 20, the machinists' local voted to join such a strike if it were called. The longshoremen began sending small committees and then mass delegations of fifty to four hundred workers to other unions asking for support by a vote for a general strike.

The movement for a general strike received its strongest encouragement, however, from the violent opening of the port. The street fighting itself had roused a spirit of combat, and the killing of unarmed strikers by police roused the resentment of virtually all the city's workers; the sending in of the National Guard to break the strike aggravated them still further. With every other tactic defeated, many workers saw a general strike as the only way to save the longshoremen from defeat.

The day after the entry of the National Guard, the Joint Marine Strike Committee appealed for a general strike. The next day, fourteen unions in San Francisco voted to strike in sympathy with the longshoremen, while similar sentiment developed in Portland and Seattle. At the crucial meeting of the Teamsters, Local President Casey warned the drivers that their contract restricted and their union constitution forbade sympathetic strikes; but Teamsters voted 1,220 to 271 to strike Thursday, July 12, if the maritime strike had not been settled. "Nothing on earth," Casey said, "could have prevented that vote. In all my thirty years of leading these men I have never seen them so worked up."[21]

On July 9, a mass funeral procession for the strikers killed in the opening of the port rallied tens of thousands. As Paul Eliel, director of industrial relations for the Employers' Industrial Association, later wrote, "the funeral was one of the strangest and most dramatic that had ever moved along Market Street." It created a "tremendous wave of sympathy for the workers," and with it "a general strike ... became for the first time a practical and realizable objective."[22] By July 12, twenty-one unions had voted to strike, most of them unanimously. At a second mass meeting, Teamsters sang, "We'll hang Michael Casey from a sour apple tree," and shouted him down when he argued passionately against a strike.[23]

A partial general strike was under way by July 12. Four thousand Bay Area Teamsters walked out and picketed the roads entering the city, stopping all trucks except those carrying exempted goods, such as milk, bread, and laundry. In the city, Teamsters established a system of strike exemptions, as in Seattle in 1919:

> San Francisco's food and gasoline problems ... were taken to the Teamster's Union.... Emissaries of corporations and hospitals made their way through the crowd of striking truck drivers up the dingy stairs and waited their turn at the door behind which union officials sat.... Anyone not a representative in some way of a charitable institution or hospital was turned away with curt words before he reached that door, usually to the accompaniment of jeering laughter.... Union truck placards were granted without ado to the hospitals.[24]

Restaurants began to shut down. The next day, 2,500 taxi drivers were scheduled to walk out. Cleaners and dryers struck for their own demands. Boilermakers in sixty shops left their jobs.

The Central Labor Council was now faced with a general strike of which it wanted no part. Three weeks before, it had passed a resolution condemning the "Communist" leadership of the maritime strikers, and resolutions calling for a general strike had been ruled out of order at its meetings week after week. After the forcible opening of the port, when the Joint Maritime Strike Committee had appealed for a general strike, the Central Labor Council did not even take up the question. Instead, it appointed a "Strike Strategy Committee" of seven conservative union officials, none of them from the striking unions.

"The action of the conservative element in the labor council in naming the strike strategy committee ... successfully sidetracked the plan of more radical groups to incite and promote a general walkout immediately," *The New York Times* reported.[25] The committee was appointed to kill the strike, not to organize it.

The momentum of general strike sentiment was too great, however, for the city's AFL leadership to head off. When a convention called by the Strike Strategy Committee met Friday, July 13, the general strike, though not yet complete, was already a fact. The convention, with five members from each union, voted 315 to 15 for a general strike. By Monday, the strike deadline, virtually all San Francisco unions except the bakery wagon and milk wagon drivers—who were instructed to stay at work—had voted to join the strike. The Oakland Central Labor Council similarly voted for a general strike. The movement spread up the Pacific Coast. In Portland, the Central Labor Council voted for a general strike but left the date to a strategy committee.

Unable to stop the strike, the leadership of the San Francisco Central Labor Council decided to assume direction to bring it to an end as quickly as possible. They established a General Strike Committee of Twenty-five, all conservatives. The head was Edward Vandeleur, who as chairman of the Central Labor Council had consistently opposed the strike, and the vice-chairman was C.W. Deal. Deal was head of the ferryboatmen's union, one of the few in the city not to join the strike. Vandeleur was head of the municipal streetcar workers' union. When his members walked out on Monday, he ordered them back to work on the grounds that they were breaking civil service contracts; thus on the very first day of the strike he initiated the first return to work. The General Strike Committee made no provision for meeting the needs of the strikers and the city's population; instead it issued an ever-increasing number of strike exemptions, which created the impression that the strike was dissolving. The General Strike Committee also organized its own strike police to keep pickets from interfering with workers it had sent back to work.

According to the press, Harry Bridges planned to recommend "the immediate establishment of food distribution depots in every section of the city, with sub-committees of strikers to prevent profiteering, to regulate distribution of vegetables and fruit, and to prevent hardship."[26] But this system never developed. "The general strike was broken by the return of the carmen and the lifting of restrictions upon food and gasoline," Bridges concluded. And as an article in *Editor and Publisher* pointed out, the bitterly anti-strike newspapers fully understood and abetted the objective of the labor leaders: "Newspaper editorials built up the strength and influence of the conservative leaders and aided in splitting the conservative membership away from the radicals."[27]

Nevertheless, the strike effectively crippled the life of San Francisco. Some 130,000 workers were out. With taxis, trolleys, and street railway workers out and gasoline for private cars embargoed by the strikers, transportation in the Bay Area virtually stopped. Many small shops closed down in sympathy with the strike or because delivery of goods had been halted. Food trucks were given permits to enter the city and markets remained open; a limited number of restaurants were permitted to run; gasoline was supplied for doctors; electric power workers and newspaper printers continued to work. The violence that had raged for weeks came to a halt with the general strike.

The strike was met with a powerful counter-attack. Five hundred special police were sworn in and the National Guard contingent was raised to 4,500, complete with infantry, machine gun, tank, and artillery units. State officials were poised on the edge of declaring martial law The leading California publishers set up a headquarters at the Palace Hotel and undertook a coordinated attack on the strike, combining a desire to weaken trade unions with an effort to embarrass President Roosevelt.

In addition, they had a real fear that the general strike was the beginning of a revolt that might sweep the country. Typical was an editorial in *The Los Angeles Times*: "The situation in San Francisco is not correctly described by the phrase 'general strike.' What is actually in progress there is an insurrection, a Communist-inspired and led revolt against organized government. There is but one thing to be done—put down the revolt with any force necessary."[28]

The National Recovery Administration chief, General Hugh S. Johnson, arrived in San Francisco and after meeting with the publishers declared the general strike a "menace to the government" and a "civil war." The governor declared that the general strike "challenges the authority of government to maintain itself," and Senator Hiram Johnson, California's elder statesman, declared, "Here is revolution not only in the making but with the initial actualities."[29] President Roosevelt followed the strike closely, but felt it had been provoked by the employers and saw no need to intervene. Secretary of Labor Frances Perkins assured him that the General Strike Committee of Twenty-five was "in charge of the whole strike ... and represents conservative leadership."[30]

On July 17, Charles Wheeler, vice-president of the McCormick Steamship Lines, said that raids on radical centers would start soon, with government consent. That day, a series of vigilante raids began up and down the coast on the Marine Workers Industrial Union, the Ex-Service Men's League, *The Western Worker*, and many other radical organizations and gathering places. According to *The New York Times*, the vigilantes "were connected with the Committee of 500 organized by prominent citizens at the behest of Mayor [Angelo] Rossi."[31] The raids followed a regular pattern: men in leather jackets drove up, broke in, smashed windows, furniture, and typewriters, and beat up those within; the police invariably arrived just after the attackers departed and arrested those they had beaten. U.S. Army and immigration officials interrogated many of those arrested and held some of them for possible deportation. Radicals faced a virtual reign of terror.

The general strike succeeded in preventing the crushing of the longshoremen for the moment, but the Central Labor Council leadership began maneuvering to bring it to an end almost before it began. On July 18, President Green of the AFL disowned the strike. On the second day of the strike, the General Strike Committee called for arbitration of all issues, thus giving up the strike's basic demand, the union hiring hall. The third day, it reopened all union restaurants and butcher shops and ended embargoes on gasoline and fuel oil. This put enormous pressure on those still striking. As the strike strategy committee in the East Bay declared, "it would be unfair to the unions to continue the strike in view of the return of some San Francisco organizations to work." By the fourth day, the General Strike Committee voted 191 to 174 to end the general strike.[32]

With the end of the general strike, the longshoremen were forced to accept arbitration of all issues by the Longshoremen's Board. The board established jointly operated hiring halls with union dispatchers but employer choice among available workers. Each employer won the right "to introduce labor-saving devices and to institute such methods of discharging and loading cargo as he considers best suited to the conduct of his business."[33]

This far from ended the struggle on the waterfront, however, for the longshoremen now moved to direct action on the job to fight the speed-up authorized in the 1934 settlement. A journalist described the conflicts that followed:

> [E]very dock gang elected from among themselves a so-called gang or dock steward.... There were endless disputes, some resulting in "job action" on the part of workers or quick strikes ("quickies") localized to one dock. Suddenly, in the midst of unloading a ship, the longshore gang would walk off, causing the stubborn employer sailing delay, considerable additional expense, and general irritation....
>
> [T]he employer called the union hiring-hall for another gang, which came promptly enough, but as likely as not pulled another "quicky" an hour later; and so on, till the employer yielded to, say, a demand that the slingload be made two or three thousand instead of four thousand pounds.[34]

Between January 1, 1937, and August 1, 1938, more than 350 such work stoppages occurred in the maritime industry on the Pacific Coast.[35]

•

Another bloody struggle broke out at the Auto-Lite parts plant in Toledo, Ohio. The local AFL union struck, went back, and on April 12, 1934, struck again. Fewer than half the workers joined the strike, and the employers hired strikebreakers and kept the plants running. Under such conditions, the strike seemed doomed to failure, until a large number of unemployed workers began joining the picket lines. As a journalist in Toledo at the time wrote privately, "The point about Toledo was this: that it is nothing new to see organized unemployed appear in the streets, fight police, and raise hell in general. But usually they do this for their own ends, to protest against unemployment or relief conditions. At Toledo they appeared on the picket lines to help striking employees win a strike, though you would expect their interest would lie the other way—that is, in going down and getting the jobs the other men had laid down."[36]

The Lucas County Unemployed League was affiliated with the American Workers Party, a small radical organization led by Rev. A.J. Muste, which emphasized mutual support of employed and unem-

ployed workers. American Workers Party leaders played an important part in the conflict.

When the strikers and unemployed blocked the plant gates with
mass picketing, Auto-Lite obtained an injunction limiting them to
twenty-five pickets at each gate. The Unemployed League, determined to "smash the injunction," continued picketing, and when
leaders were arrested for contempt of court, hundreds of unemployed packed the courtroom and cheered and sang as the trial pro-
gressed. At noon on May 21, 1,000 rallied at the gates of the Toledo
Auto-Lite plant. The next day 4,000 came to the noon rally, and the
third day 6,000 rallied.

At this point, Sheriff David Krieger decided, as he later testified in
court, that the time had come to take the offensive. Unwilling to rely
on the local police, who were disaffected and sympathetic to the strikers, he deputized special police, paid for by Auto-Lite. Krieger then
began arresting pickets, and a deputy began beating an old man in
front of the crowd of 10,000 that had gathered. This was too much for
the crowd, which proceeded to surround the Auto-Lite plant, holding
1,500 strikebreakers inside. The special deputies dropped tear gas on
the crowd from the plant and attacked them with fire hoses, iron bars,
and some gunfire. The crowd systematically collected bricks and
stones, deposited them in piles around the streets, and heaved them
through the factory windows. Three times the strikers broke into the
factory and were driven out in hand-to-hand fighting. The battle
raged for seven hours.

At dawn the next morning, 900 National Guard troops, complete
with machine gun units, were rushed into Toledo from elsewhere in
the state, since Sheriff Krieger was unwilling to call up the local
guard. The guardsmen evacuated the strikebreakers from the plant,
but failed to intimidate the crowds, who stoned them and drove them
against the factory walls. The guardsmen advanced with bayonets.
The crowd drove them back again, and were in turn pushed back
with bayonets. As the crowd advanced the third time, the troops
were ordered to fire; they let go, killing two and wounding fifteen.
Even this did not disperse the crowd, which attacked again that night
and was again fired on by the National Guard.

Only the sending of four more militia companies to the plant—more troops than ever before seen in Ohio in peacetime—and the agreement of Auto-Lite to close down finally pacified the protesters.

Meanwhile, eighty-five local unions pledged to support a general strike in sympathy with another dispute, growing from the demands of workers at the electric power company. The strike was headed off when the electric power company offered a 22 percent wage increase and union recognition.

Next, the militia arrested leaders of the unemployed who had supported the Auto-Lite strike; one was seized and held incommunicado. But with their plants still closed, the auto parts makers finally agreed to recognize the union, grant a wage increase, and rehire the strikers. Rehiring proceeded slowly as the plants reopened until a crowd began gathering at the Auto-Lite gates and the company, fearing a renewal of direct action, rehired all the strikers at once.

•

Meanwhile, in Minneapolis a conflict developed that clearly demonstrated the process of polarization of social classes occurring throughout the country. Early in 1934, Teamsters who worked in Minneapolis coal yards struck, catching the employers by surprise, and closed down sixty-five of the town's sixty-seven coal yards. The employers capitulated in three days and granted recognition to Teamsters Local 574.

The local had a catch-all charter, making it virtually industrial in character, and truck drivers and helpers in all trades began pouring in after the strike. Unofficial leadership for the unions was provided by the Dunne brothers (Grant, Miles, and Vincent Raymond) and Carl Skoglund, who were members of the Communist League, American followers of Leon Trotsky. When the trucking companies refused to sign any agreement with the union, the Teamsters voted to strike at a mass meeting May 12. Most businesses were affected by the strike. As the sheriff later put it, "They had the town tied up tight. Not a truck could move in Minneapolis." The only exceptions were the unionized milk, ice, and coal companies, which were given strike exemptions.[37]

The key tactic of the strike was the "flying squadron," a system of mobile pickets operating out of the strike headquarters, an old garage rented for the strike. There were never less than 500 strikers at the headquarters, day or night. In the dispatchers' room, four telephones took in messages from picket captains throughout the city with instructions to call in every ten minutes:

> Truck attempting to move load of produce from Berman Fruit, under police convoy. Have only ten pickets, send help.
>
> Successfully turned back five trucks entering city.... Am returning Cars 42 and 46 to headquarters.[38]

On the basis of such information, the dispatchers sent cars from the garage wherever they were needed. A motorcycle squad cruised the city reporting trouble. The strikers listened to police radio instructions on a special short-wave radio, and conducted phone calls in code when their phones were tapped. Pickets guarded fifty roads into the city, turning back non-union trucks. A crew of 120 prepared food day and night; at the peak of the strike, 10,000 people ate at the headquarters in a single day. A hospital was established with two doctors and three nurses in constant attendance. And a machine shop with fifteen auto mechanics kept the 100 trucks and cars of the flying squadrons in repair. Guards policed the headquarters and stood watch on the roof with tommy guns. Constant PA announcements and nightly mass meetings attended by thousands of strikers and supporters kept strikers in touch.[39] A rank-and-file committee of 100 truck drivers formed the official strike authority.

Support for the strike among other Minneapolis workers was passionate. Thirty-five thousand building trades workers walked out in sympathy, as did all the taxi drivers in the city. The Farm Holiday Association, a militant farmers' organization, made substantial contributions of food, and other unions contributed to the strike fund. Hundreds of non-Teamster workers showed up at strike headquarters daily, saying, "Use us, this is our strike."[40]

The city polarized as the business forces, too, began to organize. Leading them was the Citizens' Alliance, one of the most powerful employers' associations in the country, with its own corps of undercover informers. It was dedicated to keeping unionism out of Minneapolis and for a generation it had been almost completely successful. Business leaders developed their own strike headquarters with barracks, hospital, and commissary. As the conflict deepened, they called for a "mass movement of citizens" to break the strike and began organizing a "citizens' army,"[41] many of whose members were deputized as special police.[42]

With an unusual clarity, two organized social classes stood face to face, poised for battle. The battle was seriously joined on Monday, May 21. A group of men and women pickets had been severely beaten when they were sent into a police trap by an informer who had infiltrated the strike headquarters. One striker described the effect: "Nobody had carried any weapon or club in the first days of the strike. We went unarmed but we'd learned our lesson. All over headquarters you'd see guys making saps or sawing off lead pipe."[43]

As the citizens' army began to occupy the market and move trucks, the strikers hit with military precision. A strike leader explained:

We built up our reserves in this way. At short time intervals during an entire day, we sent fifteen or twenty pickets pulled in from all over the city into the Central Labor Union headquarters on Eighth Street. So that although nobody knew it, we had a detachment of six hundred men there, each armed with clubs, by Monday morning. Another nine hundred or so we held in reserve at strike headquarters. In the market itself, pickets without union buttons were placed in key positions. There remained scattered through the city, at their regular posts, only a skeleton picket line. The men in the market were in constant communication through motorcycles and telephone with headquarters. The special deputies [citizens' army] were gradually pushed by our pickets to one side and isolated from the cops. When that was accomplished, the signal was given and the six hundred men poured out of Central Labor Union headquarters. They marched in military formation, four abreast, each with their clubs, to the market. They kept on coming. When the socialites, the Alfred Lindleys and the rest who had expected a little picnic with a mad rabble, saw this bunch, they began to get some idea what the score was. Then we called on the pickets from strike headquarters who marched into the center of the market and encircled the police. They [the police] were put right in the center with no way out. At intervals we made sallies on them to separate a few. This kept up for a couple of hours, till finally they drew their guns.

We had anticipated this would happen, and that then the pickets would be unable to fight them. You can't lick a gun with a club. The correlation of forces becomes a little unbalanced. So we picked out a striker, a big man and utterly fearless, and sent him in a truck with twenty-five pickets. He was instructed to drive right into the formation of cops and stop for nothing. We knew he'd do it. Down the street he came like a bat out of hell, with his horn honking and into the market arena. The cops held up their hands for him to stop, but he kept on; they gave way and he was in the middle of them. The pickets jumped out on the cops. We figured by intermixing with the cops in hand-to-hand fighting, they would not use their guns because they would have to shoot cops as well as strikers. Cops don't like to do that.

Casualties for the day included for the strikers a broken collar bone, the cut-open skull of a picket who swung on a policeman and hit a striker by mistake as the policeman dodged, and a couple of broken ribs. On the other side, roughly thirty policemen were taken to the hospital.[44]

The Monday battle was not decisive, however, and the reserves on both sides mobilized in the market again the next day. An extra 500 special police were sworn in, and according to labor expert Charles R. Walker's study of the strike, *American City*, "Nearly every worker who could afford to be away from his job that day, and some who couldn't, planned to be on hand in the market."[45] Twenty to thirty thousand people showed up. No battle was planned. The melee began when a merchant started to move crates of tomatoes and a picket threw them through his store window. The pickets, armed with lead pipes and clubs, fought viciously with the police, driving them out of the market within an hour, then continuing to battle them all over the city. By nightfall there were no police to be seen in Minneapolis. Strikers were directing downtown traffic.

After the "Battle of Deputies Run," a settlement of sorts was patched together by the governor and federal mediators, leaving the real issues unsettled, and events moved toward a second strike. The chief of police requested a virtual doubling of his budget to add 400 men to the force, maintain a training school, and buy machine guns, rifles, bayonets, steel helmets, riot clubs, and motorcycles. The employers sponsored an enormous press and radio campaign against the union, stressing an attack by the head of the International Brotherhood of Teamsters calling the local leadership communist. The workers laid in food for a forty-day siege.

On July 5, the largest mass meeting in the history of Minneapolis, preceded by a march of farmer and labor groups with two airplanes flying overhead, mobilized support for the Teamsters and displayed the forces that would support them in the event of another showdown. When the Teamsters struck again on July 16, they re-established in still more perfected form the strike organization, published a hugely popular strike daily paper, *The Organizer* (whose circulation went from nothing to 10,000 in two days), and kept farmer support by allowing all members of farmers' organizations to drive their trucks into town and establish their own market.

The first few days of the strike were peaceful, but the police then tried to break it by terror. On July 20, a truck accompanied by fifty police armed with shotguns started moving in the market. A second truck with ten pickets arrived and cut across the convoy's path. The police opened fire, and within ten minutes sixty-seven persons, including thirteen bystanders, were wounded, two fatally. A commission appointed by the governor to investigate the "riot" later concluded:

> Police took direct aim at the pickets and fired to kill.
> Physical safety of police was at no time endangered....
> At no time did pickets attack the police....
> The truck movement in question was not a serious attempt to move merchandise, but a "plant" arranged by the police.
> The police department did not act as an impartial police force to enforce law and order, but rather became an agency to break the strike.
> Police actions have been to discredit the strike and the Truck Drivers' Union so that public sentiment would be against the strikers. [46]

These actions were hardly accidental. As the secretary of the Citizens Alliance, whose leaders met with the police chief just before the attack, stated later, "Nobody likes to see bloodshed, but I tell you after the police had used their guns on July 20 we felt that the strike was breaking.... There are very few men who will stand up in a strike when there is a question of they themselves getting killed."[47]

That night an enormous protest meeting ended in a march on City Hall to lynch the mayor and police chief. The march was headed off by National Guard troops. This, together with a huge mass funeral for one of the killed pickets—attended by an estimated 50,000 to 100,000 workers—revealed that the massacre had strengthened rather than undermined the workers' determination and solidarity.

In this situation Farmer-Labor Party governor Floyd B. Olson—who had personally contributed $500 to the strike fund and stated, "I am not a liberal ... I am a radical"—declared martial law. The governor's official policy was that neither pickets nor trucks (except those delivering food) would operate; but by the second day of martial law, military authorities announced that "more than half the trucks in Hennepin County were operating."[48] Faced with the imminent breaking of the strike, the workers decided at a mass meeting attended by 25,000 to resume picketing in defiance of the governor and the National Guard. The governor replied by surrounding the strike headquarters at 4 a.m., August 1, occupying it, arresting most of the top strike leaders, and instructing the rank and file to elect new leaders. The strikers replied with intensified picketing. As the press reported: "Marauding bands of pickets roamed the streets of Minneapolis today in automobiles and trucks, striking at commercial truck movement in widespread sections of the city.... National Guardsmen in squad cars made frantic efforts to clamp down. The continued picketing was regarded as a protest over the military arrest of William Brown and the Dunnes, strike leaders, together with 68 others during and after Guardsmen raided strike headquarters and the Central Labor Union."[49]

Charles R. Walker wrote: "The strike's conduct had been such that a thousand lesser leaders had come out of the ranks and the pickets themselves by this time had learned their own jobs. The arrest of the leaders, instead of beheading the movement, infused it, at least temporarily, with demoniac fury."[50] "We established 'curb headquarters' all over the city," one worker said. "We had twenty of them."[51]

In the face of this situation, the governor was forced to back down. He released the captured leaders, turned back the strike headquarters, and raided the Citizens Alliance to save face with his labor constituents. The strike continued and with the city reeling after a month of conflict, the employers succumbed to the enormous pressures for a settlement and capitulated. The strike supporters celebrated with a twelve-hour binge.

•

The most extensive conflict of the NRA period was the national textile strike of 1934. The Depression hit the textile industry long before the rest of America and by early 1929 the mill towns, especially in the South, were seething with discontent. The great grievance was the "stretch-out." At one mill at Monroe, North Carolina, for example, spinners were required to work twelve rather than eight spindles, four doffers did the work of five, and crews of four carders were cut to three. The result, as labor researcher Herbert Lahne wrote in *The Cotton Mill Worker*, was that "a powder train of strikes flashed through an astonished South," many of them "without unionism at all and … under purely local leadership whose main concern was … the stretch-out."[52] We have described above one such explosion at High Point, North Carolina.

With the coming of the NRA, textile workers flooded into the United Textile Workers union. Its paper membership went from 27,500 in 1932 to 270,000 in 1934.

The NRA Cotton Textile Industry Committee was headed by George Sloan, who happened to be the chief industry spokesman as well. The code set a minimum wage of $12 per week in the South and $13 in the North. It utterly failed to prevent more stretch-out, or to stop employers from firing workers who joined the union.[53] Further, to restrict over-production, the NRA ordered a cut-back to thirty hours a week per shift, reducing wages 25 percent. The UTW threatened to strike the industry, but withdrew the threat in exchange for a seat on the Cotton Textile Industrial Relations Board and a government "study" of the industry.

Textile workers were furious at the union's backdown. For the Southern cotton mill workers, as labor historian Irving Bernstein put it, "NRA had become a gigantic fraud."[54] In Alabama, forty of forty-two UTW locals voted to strike, and 20,000 workers walked out on July 16, 1934. The president of the UTW advised workers in other states not to join the strike, adding to resentment at the cancellation of the previous strike. "He killed the other strike," a worker in Birmingham remarked. "We're not going to let him kill this one."[55]

The strike held firmly, revealing an unexpected commitment and solidarity, and a month later a UTW national convention, with the militant Southern rank and file in control, voted without opposition for a general strike in the industry, and required the officers to call it within two weeks. The workers condemned NRA bitterly and were kept from boycotting it only by a special appeal from union officers and prominent outsiders. The strike began in North Carolina on Labor Day, September 3, 1934, when 65,000 workers walked out. National Guardsmen were ordered to guard three mills that day in South Carolina where the strike was expected the next day. The workers not only quit work, but immediately formed "flying squadrons," which moved through the area, closing non-striking mills. A reporter described a typical example: "Workers in the Shelby, N.C., mills, thoroughly organized, refused to permit the opening of their plants early today, formed a motorcade which swept into King's Mountain, a dozen miles away, and succeeded in closing eleven plants. They met with no resistance and persuaded 2,800 non-union workers to quit their posts."[56]

The strikers showed creativity in other ways. For example, at Macon, Georgia (and later at various other points), a group of pickets, many of them women, sat down on a plant railroad track and prevented the movement of trains carrying finished goods. Before and at the start of the strike, mass demonstrations were held throughout the South, including a meeting of 1,000 at Charlotte, North Carolina, and a parade of 5,000 in Gastonia, North Carolina, designed to show the workers' strength.

The strike spread rapidly throughout the East Coast. Newspaper surveys reported 200,000 out on September 4 and 325,000 out the next day.[57] The flying squadrons were largely responsible: "Moving with the speed and force of a mechanized army, thousands of pickets in trucks and automobiles scurried about the countryside in the Carolinas, visiting mill towns and villages and compelling the closing of the plants ... Strikers in groups ranging from 200 to 1,000 assembled about mills and demanded that they be closed.... The speed of the pickets in their motor cavalcades and their surprise descent on point after point makes it difficult to follow their movements and makes impossible any adequate preparation by mill owners or local authorities to meet them."[58]

What happened when the flying squadrons arrived depended on conditions of the moment, the mood of the crowd, the degree of resistance, and similar factors. Sometimes they simply picketed peacefully, at other times they battled guards, and at times they entered mills, unbelted machinery, broke threads, and fought non-strikers.

Although the flying squadrons created a sensation throughout the country, they were a natural form of action in isolated mill towns. They were at first tolerated and perhaps encouraged by union officials, but as the squadrons led to confrontations, union officials tried to bring them to a halt. Francis Gorman, chairman of the UTW strike committee, repudiated their use and denied that they were ever sanctioned by the national leadership. [59]

Practically from the beginning of the strike, confrontations and small-scale violence developed in numerous places. In Fall River, Massachusetts, a crowd of 10,000 imprisoned 300 strikebreakers in a mill, and in North Carolina pickets stormed a mill in which strikebreakers were working. The flying squadrons and other mass actions developed a momentum of their own, and as early as September 5, *The New York Times* warned on page one: "The grave danger of the situation is that it will get completely out of the hands of the leaders. Indications of that were in evidence today." Women were reported to be "taking an increasingly active part in the picketing, egging on the men," with "the pickets apparently prepared to stop at nothing to obtain their objectives."[60] The *Times* added ominously, "The growing mass character of the picketing operations is rapidly assuming the appearance of military efficiency and precision and is something entirely new in the history of American labor struggles. Observers ... declared that if the mass drive continued to gain momentum at the speed at which it was moving today, it will be well nigh impossible to stop it without a similarly organized opposition with all the implications such an attempt would entail."[61]

The opposition was not long in starting. On September 5, the governor of North Carolina called out the National Guard to aid local authorities, declaring, "The power of the State has been definitely challenged" and "local authorities have proven unequal to the test." More National Guardsmen were ordered out in South Carolina, and on September 9, partial martial law was established in that state.[62] The governor declared that a "state of insurrection" existed.[63] Mills in the Carolinas were reported to be "feverishly preparing to resist ... by mobilizing special guards equipped with shotguns and tear gas bombs and by arming workers who remained at the looms."[64] But as a reporter wrote from the strike center in North Carolina, "Despite efforts of strike leaders to prevail upon the strike pickets 'to put on the brakes,' ... picketing activity showed no abatement."[65]

More than fifty strike squadrons were in action in the Carolinas, in detachments of 200 to 650. They moved south on a 110-mile front between Gastonia, North Carolina, and Greenville, South Carolina, garrisoning the towns along the line of battle to ensure that the mills would stay closed. As they approached Greenville, squadrons were met by National Guardsmen who informed them they had orders to "shoot to kill," but "the strikers, apparently undeterred by the presence of the troops, were determined to capture Greenville,"[66] where the strike had not yet spread.

The conflict quickly became more violent. Indeed, "the situation was rapidly assuming the character of industrial civil war."[67] On September 5, a striker and a special deputy were killed in a two-hour battle at a mill in Trion, Georgia (population 2,000); a policeman shot three pickets, one fatally, in Augusta; 2,500 textile workers rioted in Lowell, Massachusetts; and mill officials' cars were attacked in Danielson, Connecticut; Macon, Georgia; and other points.[68]

On September 6 at Honea Path, South Carolina, sheriff's deputies and armed strikebreakers fired on pickets: "Without warning came the first shots, followed by many others, and for a few minutes there was bedlam. Striker after striker fell to the ground, with the cries of wounded men sounding over the field and men and women running shrieking from the scene."[69]

Seven pickets were killed and a score wounded in the attack. The killings were seen as marking "the beginning of the second bloody phase of the strike," as "one town after another reported completion of preparations to resist the flying squads and the picketing activity of the strikers."[70]

Commissaries were set up in various textile centers, and hundreds of strikers canvassed for contributions of food and money. At Hazleton, Pennsylvania, 25,000 workers shut down the town in a one-day general strike in support of the textile workers on September 11. George Googe, chief AFL representative in the South, urged other workers to give support "without joining the strike," emphasizing that his appeal was not to be interpreted as "a move toward extending the strike to other industries."[71] Workers from other industries joined in many of the confrontations that occurred at mills throughout the country, turning them into community struggles.

Meanwhile, violent conflict spread through New England. The first strike shooting there occurred in Saylesville, Rhode Island, on September 10. A crowd of 600 pickets attempting to close a mill (particularly hated for having broken previous strikes) was driven back by state troopers with machine guns. A smaller group of pickets then tried to outflank the troopers and attack the rear of the plant; deputy sheriffs opened fire on them with buckshot. The next afternoon, a much larger crowd, estimated at 3,000 to 4,000, imprisoned strikebreaking employees in the mill. As the shift was due to end, the crowd surged forward, captured the mill gate, ripped up a fire hydrant, overturned a gate house, and appeared about to take possession of the plant. In reply, deputy sheriffs began firing buckshot into the crowd with automatic weapons, hitting five. Some 280 National Guard troops then rode into the scene on caissons. They were pelted with paving stones torn up by the pickets as they clubbed their way to the mill. The crowd tried unsuccessfully to capture the pumping station and set fire to the mill.

That night the pickets deployed themselves behind the tombstones of a nearby cemetery, and shouting "Let's get the militia!" 2,000 of them broke through police lines and battled the troops.[72] By the next afternoon, the crowd had grown to 5,000. Hurling pieces of gravestones from the cemetery, they charged the troops and drove them back behind the barbed-wire enclosure surrounding the plant. The National Guard troops fired into the crowd, critically wounding three. That night another crowd stoned the guard, which again fired on them. In the face of such serious disorder, the Sayles plant finally decided to shut down, giving the signal for many other plants in the area to do the same.

By September 12, National Guard members were on duty in every New England state except Vermont and New Hampshire. At Danielson, Connecticut, 1,500 pickets battled state troopers. A flying squadron of 200 from Fall River, Massachusetts, was turned back from a factory in Dighton, Massachusetts, when it found every approach barricaded with sandbags by police and seventy-five special deputies armed with shotguns. Other confrontations occurred at Lawrence and Lowell, Massachusetts, and Lewiston, Maine, but the New England violence reached its peak at Woonsocket, Rhode Island.

The mill that was the original scene of rioting in Woonsocket had been organized six months before, at which point the union members were fired, causing much bitterness. On the evening of September 12, Governor T.F. Green of Rhode Island read a proclamation over the radio urging rioters to return to their homes. Instead, ever-increasing masses began to pour down on the Woonsocket Rayon Mill in a "sullen and rebellious mood." At midnight, a crowd of about 500 let fly a barrage of bricks at the police guards at the plant, then attacked. The police replied with tear gas grenades, many of which were caught and thrown back "with telling effect" by the crowd. Word of the conflict spread, and the crowd grew quickly to 2,000. At this point, National Guardsmen took a hand, firing 30 shots into the front ranks of the crowd, hitting four, one fatally. At the shooting, a correspondent reported, "The crowd went completely wild with rage.... News of the shooting, carried back into the heart of the city, brought recruits to the strikers' forces.... Men and women and boys too, pounded up and down the business district, and where they ran the crash of broken plate glass and tearing splintering wood was heard."[73] The crowd

grew to 8,000 and was only quelled by the arrival of two more companies of National Guardsmen, who put the city under military rule.
The Woonsocket Rayon Mill, the source of the conflict, was closed.

Declaring that "there is a Communist uprising and not a textile
strike in Rhode Island," Democratic governor Green called the legislature into special session to declare a state of insurrection and request federal troops. Acting under secret orders from Washington,
detachments of regular Army troops began mobilizing at strategic
points, prepared to leave for Rhode Island "at a moment's notice."[74]

The union leadership agreed with the governor's assessment of the
riots: "Communists ... were solely responsible for the serious upris-
ings that took place in both Saylesville and Woonsocket.... [The
Rhode Island] strike committee has instructed each union to place
trustworthy men and women of their unions at strategic points in
strike areas for the sole purpose of cooperating with police and all
other law enforcement agencies in driving Communists not only
from strike areas but from the state."[75]

The textile strike—like the industry—was centered in New England and the South, but it spread through the rest of the East Coast as
well. In Pennsylvania, for example, 47,000 workers struck, eleven cars
filled with special guards were attacked and some of them overturned, and, in Lancaster, police charged that women strikers were
using "old-fashioned hat pins" to attack non-strikers.

Meanwhile, the struggle in the South reflected "a grim determination on both sides to hold on at any cost."[76] A road approaching the
Cherryville mill in Gaston County, North Carolina, was dynamited
September 10, as was a mill generator at Fayetteville, North Carolina,
a few days later. Five pickets in a crowd of 400 wearing "peaceful
picket" badges were bayoneted by soldiers as they yelled "scab" at
strikebreakers entering a mill in Burlington, North Carolina. Non-
striking workers in Aragon, Georgia, armed by their employer and
led by a deputy sheriff, dispersed a flying squadron by threat of force.

By September 17, the Southern textile employers were ready for
their big counter-offensive. They met in advance in Greenville, North
Carolina, and planned "a gigantic effort ... to break through the strike
lines and start the movement back to the mills."[77] An army of 10,000

National Guardsmen was mobilized in Georgia, South Carolina, North Carolina, Alabama, and Mississippi, supplemented by 15,000 armed deputies. Numerous Southern mills tried to reopen under heavy armed guard.

The New York Times described as typical the response of 1,000 pickets at the Hatch Hosiery Company in North Carolina: "Refusing to budge even when a wedge of troops with bayonets tried to cross the road to break their lines, the pickets shouted 'Boy Scouts!' and 'Tin Soldiers!' … A committee of four pickets was assured that the mill would not resume operations during the day and the picket line dispersed until tomorrow."[78] Such confrontations continued all week throughout the South. The employers' efforts to stampede the strikers back to work failed overwhelmingly. On September 18, the Associated Press reported 421,000 textile workers were on strike, 20,000 more than the week before.

In Georgia, Governor Eugene Talmadge declared martial law. National Guardsmen started mass arrests of flying squadrons and incarcerated them without charges in what was described as a concentration camp near the spot where Germans had been interned during World War I. Thirty-four key strike leaders in whose names strike funds were held were arrested and held incommunicado, thus crippling the strike relief system in the state. Organizers were beaten and arrested throughout the South. By September 19, the death toll in the South had reached thirteen. Union officials stated September 20 that "force and hunger" were sending strikers back to the mills, but only 20,000 of 170,000 on strike in the South had returned to work in the previous six days, many of them to mills still too understaffed to operate, and they were offset by many thousands of additional workers who had joined the strike.[79]

On September 20, the Board of Inquiry for the Cotton Textile Industry, which President Roosevelt had appointed toward the start of the strike, issued its report. A new Textile Labor Relations Board of "neutral" members should be established; it would set up a subcommittee to "study" workloads. The Federal Trade Commission should study the capacity of the industry to raise hours and employment and the Department of Labor should survey wages to see whether differentials had been maintained. As Irving Bernstein noted, "There was little of tangible benefit to either the textile workers or U.T.W. ... In fact, the only recommendation that was immediate and tangible in effect was imposed on the union: to terminate the strike."[80] Nonetheless, the UTW strike committee hailed the board's recommendation as "an overwhelming victory" and on September 22 ordered the strikers back to work.[81] Thus ended what labor economist Robert Brooks the next year described as "unquestionably the greatest single industrial conflict in the history of American organized labor."[82]

President Roosevelt urged textile firms to rehire strikers without discrimination, but by October 23, the UTW reported, 339 mills had refused to do so, leaving thousands of workers unemployed. Martha Gellhorn, a novelist then working as a government investigator, wrote from North Carolina that textile workers "live in terror of being penalized for joining unions; and the employers live in a state of mingled rage and fear."[83]

The textile workers felt an extreme disillusionment with both the government and the union. As Brooks concluded:

> The thousands of militiamen, sheriffs, and armed strikebreakers which were thrown into strike territories and the numerous deaths at the hands of drunken deputies and nervous guardsmen linked the forces of law and order so clearly with the interests of the textile employers that northern newspaper reporters repeatedly referred to the situation as "the employers' offensive." The significance of this was not lost upon the strikers. In the space of a few weeks thousands of workers received a practical education in the philosophy of class relations which was clearly reflected in conversation, tactics, and general attitude.[84]

Mill workers were likewise extremely bitter at the union and its officials for claiming a victory, calling off the strike, and putting their faith in government boards, when the employers had conceded nothing. Herbert Lahne, author of a study on the United Textile Workers Union, reported he found that "in many interviews ... with Southern cotton mill workers in 1938 this resentment was clearly expressed."[85]

Sitdown

The bloody conflicts of 1934 certified the failure of the National Recovery Act's Section 7A. By the end of the year, workers who had
previously looked to the NRA for a solution to their problems were
referring to it as the National Run-Around. Local radicals—Communists in San Francisco, Musteites in Toledo, Trotskyists in Minneapolis—played important parts in the strikes of 1934. Significantly, in
each case it was not their particular party line and party organization
that was responsible for this, but the fact that their own militance co-
incided with that of the workers.

Observing the strikes of 1934, United Mine Workers head John L.
Lewis, according to his biographer Saul Alinsky, "read the revolutionary handwriting on the walls of American industry"[86] and
moved to establish the Committee for Industrial Organization (CIO)
within the AFL to utilize the recently displayed working-class militance to establish unionism in the basic mass-production industries.
New Dealers in Congress began pushing for a National Labor Relations Act to enforce the system of orderly collective bargaining in
industry that the NRA had promised but had manifestly failed to
establish. Meanwhile, the workers themselves, largely fed up with
both the unions and the NRA, began to develop their own methods
of struggle. The key weapon they created was the sitdown. The cruci-
ble in which it was forged was Akron, Ohio.

By the time of the Depression, Akron was the rubber center of
America, home of the enormous Goodyear, Firestone, and Goodrich
plants and more than twenty factories of lesser companies. At peak
production, the Akron rubber industry employed nearly 40,000
workers, but by 1933 one-third to one-half of Akron's workers were
unemployed, Firestone and half a dozen smaller rubber companies
were closed down, and Goodyear was on a two-day week.[87]

With the passage of the NRA in 1933, Akron's rubber workers
poured into unions set up by local trade unionists. As journalist and
novelist Ruth McKenney wrote in her over-dramatized but percep-
tive account of the Akron labor movement, *Industrial Valley*, "the first

weeks of the new rubber union were something like a cross between a big picnic and a religious revival."[88] Forty to fifty thousand rubber workers, most of them in Akron, took out union cards in 1933. They expected the union, backed by the government, to save them:

> Always the cry was "join up." But nobody said what came after you joined. The rubber workers believed blindly, passionately, fiercely, that the union would cure all their troubles, end the speed-up, make them rich with wages. They had no clear idea, and nobody told them, just how the union would accomplish these aims. Vaguely, they thought President Roosevelt might just order the rubber bosses to raise wages and quit the speed-up.[89]

The next two years would see their disillusionment with that belief and their discovery of how to act on their own.

The AFL assigned an organizer, Coleman Claherty, to Akron. His first step was to try to separate the rubber workers, who had established locals representing all the workers in each plant, into various crafts. The workers joined the unions to which they were assigned but proceeded to ignore the divisions, coming to the meetings of their plant local anyway. Claherty's slogan was "Rome wasn't built in a day," and he did everything possible to "pack ice on the hot-heads" who were pushing in every union meeting for action. McKenney describes a Goodyear local meeting that Claherty addressed on the NRA:

> "We want action," a big tirebuilder bawled, bored with the NRA.
> "Sure you do," Claherty shot back, "and you're going to get it."
> Claherty never liked the curious atmosphere of Akron union meetings. He tried to prevent the back talk. He deplored the universal notion of rubberworkers that a man had a right to get up and have his say, whenever he felt like it, at his own union meeting.
> But the rubberworkers had carried over the technique of Baptist prayer sessions, where anybody was free to "testify" as the spirit moved him, to their union meetings. Tirebuilders rose in the Federal locals to "testify" about "why ain't this union gittin' anywheres," whenever the thought struck them.
> "We shall demand that the rubber industry recognize our unions," Claherty thundered this Sunday.
> "How you goin' to git' em to dew that?" somebody yelled....

"He asks a question like that," Claherty shot back, "when everybody in this room knows that President Roosevelt is for the unions."

It was a good answer. A lot of the men clapped and the millroom man in the back of the hall seemed satisfied....

"It won't be long now," some of the men said .... "Roosevelt will fix those bastards pushing up our rate schedules."

"Every labor gain," he [Claherty] told his assistant ... "is a gradual one. You can't expect to get everything the first five years. The fellows expect the moon on a platter all in a month."[90]

On June 19, 1934, tire builders at the General Tire and Rubber Company walked out when a foreman announced some wage rate changes—the first step in introducing the "Bedaux plan" to speed up production. The tire builders began cussing out the foreman. One of them yelled, "I ain't going to stand for it. Let's quit, boys," and the entire shift walked out. Outside the plant the men decided to have a meeting the next day and take a strike vote. At the meeting, the local union's executive committee recommended that the workers accept a wage increase the company had offered in response to the strike and go back to work. The committee was booed off the platform and physically attacked by the strikers. A local officer was hissed off the platform for saying the strike wasn't legal because the United Rubber Council executive board had to give permission to strike. "Who said they had to OK what we do? We ain't never heard anything about that before," a man yelled from the floor. The rubber workers voted to strike and established their own strike organization, selecting their own picket captains and organizing food committees. After a month, the company granted a number of the strikers' demands and they went back to work.[91]

By the end of 1934, the labor relations board of the NRA denounced the companies for refusing to bargain collectively and ordered representation elections in the Goodyear and Firestone plants. The government had ballots printed and polling places set up. The rubber workers fully expected the government to force the companies to recognize them. Then, two days before the election, the companies asked for and obtained an injunction against the election from a federal court, thus tying up the issue in the courts indefinitely. The rubber workers were shocked and bitterly disappointed; their belief that the government would solve their problems was killed at a blow. As McKenney put it, "Rubberworkers spent three passionate weeks hoping that the government would cure the speed-up and low wages in Akron—and then the NRA and its NLRB went blooey as far as the man on the tire machine was concerned."[92]

The final disillusionment with the union came in spring 1935. Workers were flooding out of the unions, and Claherty recognized that he had to give at least the appearance of doing something. On March 27, he announced a strike vote. By April 8, AFL president William Green was announcing to the press, "There is no hope of averting the strike."[93] The rubber workers were set to strike on April 15, and began feverish preparations. Then Claherty and the local presidents went to Washington and, at the last minute, signed a government-mediated agreement not to strike and to await court action on a representative election. As Goodyear announced, the agreement made "no change in employee relations since the provisions are in complete accord with the policies under which Goodyear has always operated."[94]

The rubber workers considered the agreement a complete sell-out. They stood on street corners tearing up their union cards, thinking it futile even to vote against the settlement. As one put it, "You can't do nothin' about that. They run the union, and they run it for the bosses, not for us. I'm through. I'd see myself in hell before I ever belong to another dirty stinking union."[95] Union membership in Summit County—mostly rubber workers—dropped from 40,000 to 5,000, with most of those remaining only paper members.

At the same time as this collapse of confidence in trade unionism and the government, work conditions remained intolerable. As a rubber worker in Akron wrote to the local paper:

> Only our machines are alive. We must treat them with respect or they turn against us. Last week one of the boys who had been back only a month grew a little careless, or maybe the long layoff had made him dull or maybe he had grown so accustomed to the change from sleeping at night to working at night—and his mill swallowed his hand and part of his arm....

The mills stopped only long enough for us to pull him out, and then they resumed their steady turn. Two of the boys carried him to the hospital and the foreman called for a Squad man to take his place.

Unbelievably it is 3 am, and we hastily gulp tasteless sandwiches, working and eating at once. The soapstone which is flying around everywhere clogs our throats and tongues and nostrils so that they seem dry. If we drink much water, we become fat and bloated, so we chew great handfuls of licorice-flavored tobacco.

Someone has grown drowsy. "Ha, ha," we laugh. "Old Bill has forgotten to weigh his batch. That's a good one, ha, ha." Bill doesn't laugh. He knows that to do this once more will cost him his job. The foreman has warned him....

We used to work eight hours and feel fine when the quitting whistle blew. Now we work six hours and are dead-tired.

We can't be cheerful, remembering the hard days of the past three years, and knowing that the work may not last much longer. We've nothing to look forward to. We're factory hands.[96]

Disillusioned with trade unionism and tormented by the speed-up, workers in Akron developed a new tactic—the sitdown—which they themselves could directly control without need for any outside leaders. When writer Louis Adamic visited Akron to find out how the sitdowns had begun, he was told that the first had occurred not in a rubber factory but at a baseball game. Players from two factories refused to play a scheduled game because the umpire, whom they disliked, was not a union man. They simply sat down on the diamond, while the crowd for a lark cheered the NRA and yelled for a union umpire, until the non-union umpire was replaced.[97]

Not long after, a dispute developed between a dozen workers and a supervisor in a rubber factory in Akron. The workers were on the verge of giving in when the supervisor insulted them and one of them said, "Aw, to hell with 'im, let's sit down." The dozen workers turned off their machines and sat down. Within a few minutes the carefully organized flow of production through the plant began to jam up as department after department ground to a halt. Thousands of workers sat down, some because they wanted to, more because everything was stopping anyway. What had happened, workers wanted to know? "There was a sitdown at such-and-such a department. A sitdown? Yeah, a sitdown; don't you know what a sitdown is, you dope? Like what happened at the ball game the other Sunday."[98]

Adamic describes the response:

Sitting by their machines, cauldrons, boilers, and work benches, they talked. Some realized *for the first time* how important they were in the process of rubber production. Twelve men had practically stopped the works! Almost any dozen or score of them could do it! In some departments six could do it! The active rank-and-filers, scattered through the various sections of the plant, took the initiative in saying, "We've got to stick with 'em!" And they stuck with them, union and non-union men alike. Most of them were non-union. Some probably were vaguely afraid not to stick. Some were bewildered. Others amused. There was much laughter through the works. Oh boy, oh boy! Just like at the ball game, no kiddin'. There the crowd had stuck with the players and they got an umpire who was a member of a labor union. Here everybody stuck with the twelve guys who first sat down, and the factory management was beside itself. Superintendents, foremen, and straw bosses were dashing about.... This sudden suspension of production was costing the company many hundreds of dollars every minute.... In less than an hour the dispute was settled—full victory for the men![99]

Between 1933 and 1936 this tactic gradually became a tradition in Akron, with scores of sitdowns—the majority probably not instigated even by rank-and-file union organizers, and almost invariably backed by the workers in other departments. It became an accepted principle that when one group of workers stopped work, everyone else along the line sat down, too.

To explain this, Adamic listed the advantages of the sitdown strike "from the point of view not so much of the rank-and-file organizer or radical agitator as of the average workingman in a mass-production industry like rubber." To begin with, the sitdown is the opposite of sabotage, to which many workers were opposed.

It destroys nothing. Before shutting down a department in a rubber plant, for instance, the men take the compounded rubber from the mills, or they finish building or curing the tires then being built or cured, so that nothing is needlessly ruined. Taking the same precautions during the sitdown as they do during production, the men do not smoke in departments where benzene is used. There is no drinking. This discipline ... is instinctive.[100]

Sitdowns were effective, short, and free of violence.

There are no strikebreakers in the majority of instances; the factory management does not dare to get tough and try to drive the sitting men out and replace them with other workers, for such violence would turn the public against the employers and the police, and might result in damage to costly machinery. In a sitdown there are no picket lines outside the factories, where police and company guards have great advantage when a fight starts. The sitdown action occurs wholly inside the plant, where the workers, who know every detail of the interior, have obvious advantages. The sitters-down organize their own "police squads," arming them—in rubber—with crowbars normally used to pry open molds in which tires are cured. These worker cops patrol the belt, watch for possible scabs and stand guard near the doors. In a few instances where city police and company cops entered a factory, they were bewildered, frightened, and driven out by the "sitting" workers with no difficulty whatever.[101]

The initiative, conduct, and control of the sitdown came directly from the workers involved.

Most workers distrust—if not consciously, then unconsciously—union officials and strike leaders and committees, even when they themselves have elected them. The beauty of the sitdown or the stay-ins is that there are no leaders or officials to distrust. There can be no sell-out. Such standard procedure as strike sanction is hopelessly obsolete when workers drop their tools, stop their machines, and sit down beside them.

Finally, the sitdown countered the boredom, degradation, and isolation of the factory.

Work in most of the departments of a rubber factory or any other kind of mass-production factory is drudgery of the worst sort—mechanical and uncreative, insistent and requiring no imagination; and any interruption is welcomed by workers, even if only subconsciously. The conscious part of their mind may worry about the loss of pay; their subconscious, however, does not care a whit about that. The situation is dramatic, thrilling.

The average worker in a mass-production plant is full of grievances and complaints, some of them hardly realized, and any vent of them is welcomed.

The sitdown is a social affair. Sitting workers talk. They get acquainted. And they like that. In a regular strike it is impossible to bring together under one roof more than one or two thousand people, and these only for a meeting, where they do not talk with one another but listen to speakers. A sitdown holds under the same roof up to ten or twelve thousand idle men, free to talk among themselves, man to man. "Why, my God, man," one Goodyear gum-miner told me in November, 1936, "during the sitdowns last spring I found out that the guy who works next to me is the same as I am, even if I was born in West Virginia and he is from Poland. His grievances are the same. Why shouldn't we stick?"[102]

Late in 1935, Goodyear announced that it was shifting from the six-hour to the eight-hour day, admitting that 1,200 workers would be laid off and that other companies would follow suit. The announcement created shock in Akron. Unemployment was still high and six hours under speed-up conditions were already so exhausting that rubber workers complained, "When I get home I'm so tired I can't even sleep with my wife."[103] As the companies began "adjusting" piece rates in preparation for introducing the eight-hour day, a wave of spontaneous work stoppages by non-union employees forced a slowing of production.

On January 29, 1936, the truck tire builders at Firestone sat down against a reduction in rates and the firing of a union committee member. The men had secretly planned the strike for 2 a.m. When the hour struck,

> the tirebuilder at the end of the line walked three steps to the master safety switch and, drawing a deep breath, he pulled up the heavy wooden handle. With this signal, in perfect synchronization, with

the rhythm they had learned in a great mass-production industry, the tirebuilders stepped back from their machines.

Instantly, the noise stopped. The whole room lay in perfect silence. The tirebuilders stood in long lines, touching each other, perfectly motionless, deafened by the silence. A moment ago there had been the weaving hands, the revolving wheels, the clanking belt, the moving hooks, the flashing tire tools. Now there was absolute stillness, no motion anywhere, no sound....

"We done it! We stopped the belt! By God, we done it!" And men began to cheer hysterically, to shout and howl in the fresh silence. Men wrapped long sinewy arms around their neighbors' shoulders, screaming, "We done it! We done it!"[104]

The workers in the truck tire department sent one committee around the plant to call out other departments, another to talk with the boss, and a third to police the shop. Within a day, the entire Plant No. 1 was struck; fifty-three hours later the workers at Plant No. 2 announced they had voted to sit down in sympathy. Management capitulated completely.

Two days later, pitmen at Goodyear sat down over a pay cut. They were persuaded to return to work by the company union; sat down again, were again cajoled back to work; sat down a third time, and then returned to work under threat of immediate replacement. A few days later, the tire department at Goodrich sat down over a rate reduction. The strike spread through the rest of the plant, stopping it completely within six hours, and management rapidly capitulated to the sitdowners. The sitdown had shaken each of the big three rubber companies within a ten-day period.

The crisis finally came February 14. A few days before, Goodyear had laid off 700 tire builders. The workers assumed that this was the signal for introducing the eight-hour day. At 3:10 a.m., 137 tire builders in Department 251-A of Goodyear's Plant No. 2—few if any of them members of the union—shut off the power and sat down. The great Goodyear strike was on.

Meanwhile, the rubber workers union had been regaining support. It had refused to accept Claherty as president, installed former rubber workers in office, and allied itself with the new CIO. With each sitdown, the union signed up the participants, and now workers flooded back into the union halls. The initiative for the sitdowns, however, did not come from the union; indeed, as Irving Bernstein has noted, "The URW … disliked the sitdown."[105] URW officials persuaded the Goodyear sitdowners to leave and marched them out of the plant. Goodyear offered to take the laid-off men back, but the rubber workers of the entire city were already up in arms, determined to make a stand against the eight-hour day. Fifteen hundred Goodyear workers met and voted unanimously to strike, but four days later the president of the local was still maintaining the strike was not a URW affair.

The workers made it their affair. They began mass picketing at each of the forty-five gates around Goodyear's eleven-mile perimeter, putting up 300 tar-paper shanties to keep warm. They elected picket captains who met regularly, coordinated strike action, and set the strike's demands. Inside Plant No. 1, hundreds of men and women staged a sitdown—until a union delegate marched them out. At the union hall, "committees sprang up almost by themselves" to take care of problems as they arose. A soup kitchen developed out of the sandwich-making and coffee-making crew, staffed by volunteers from the cooks' and waitresses' union. On the sixth day of the strike, the CIO sent in half a dozen of its top leaders, and the URW executive board finally sanctioned the strike.

Goodyear now tried to break the strike by force. The company secured an injunction against mass picketing, which the workers simply ignored. The sheriff put together a force of 150 deputies to open the plants, but 10,000 workers of all trades from all over the city gathered with lead pipes and baseball bats; a charge on the picket line was called off at the last possible second. Next, a Law and Order League, which claimed 5,200 vigilantes, was organized by a former Akron mayor with money from Goodyear. Word spread that an attack was planned for March 18. The union broadcast on the radio throughout that night, while workers gathered in homes across the city, ready to rush anywhere an attack was made. The Summit County Central Labor Council declared it would call a general strike in the event of a violent attack on the picket lines. In the face of such preparations, the vigilante movement was paralyzed.

President Roosevelt's ace labor mediator, Ed McGrady, proposed that the workers return to work and submit the issues to arbitration. To this and other proposed settlements, the workers at their mass meetings chanted, "No, no, a thousand times no. I'd rather die than say yes."[106]

After more than a month, Goodyear capitulated on most of the demands, including layoffs by seniority, six-hour shifts in the tire division, and meetings of company officials and foremen with union representatives, although the company did not agree to a signed contract. The rubber workers returned to work largely victorious and proceeded to strengthen their position with the sitdown. In the three months after the strike, nineteen recorded sitdowns at Goodyear alone took place, with many "quickies" unrecorded.

Louis Adamic described the situation he found in Akron late in 1936:

A week seldom passed without one or more sitdowns.... A typical one took place on November 17, when I was in Akron, in the huge Goodyear No. 1 plant. After an inconclusive argument with the management over an adjustment in wage rates, ninety-eight workers in one of the departments sat down, stopping the work of seven thousand men for a day and a half, at the end of which period the company promised speedy action on the adjustment.

Officials of rubber companies, with whom I talked, were frantic in their attempts to stop the sitdowns. They blamed them on "troublemakers" and the union movement in general. They tried to terrorize union sympathizers. The Goodyear management, for instance, assigned two non-union inspectors to a department with instructions to disqualify tires produced by known union men. After pelting them with milk bottles for a while, the men sat down and refused to work till the inspectors were removed. The company rushed in forty factory guards with clubs, but a 65-year-old union gum-miner met the army at the entrance and told them to "beat it." They went—and the non-union inspectors were replaced.

Akron sitdowns were provoked by various other causes. In the early autumn of 1936, S.H. Dalrymple, president of the U.R.W.A., was beaten by thugs employed by a rubber factory, whereupon the factory workers sat down in protest, forcing the company to close for a day. When work was resumed the next night, a K.K.K. fiery cross blazed up within view of the plant. This caused the workers to sit down again—and to dispatch a squad of "huskies" to extinguish the cross.[107]

Such use of the sitdown gave rubber workers virtually a dual power over the production process in Akron.

•

Machine Operator No. 8004 worked in the camshaft department of the Chevrolet factory in Flint, Michigan. The men he worked with produced 118 shafts per shift, naturally producing a few more in the first half, when they were fresh, than in the second. One day in 1935, the management suddenly announced that they would have to increase production in the second half to the level of the first, turning out 124 instead of 118 each shift. The workers accepted the increase, but then organized informally to prevent any further speed-up. As one of them put it, "Any man who runs over 124 every night is only cutting his own throat."[108] They also carefully planned not to produce more in the first half, lest management again use the differential against them. If workers ran past sixty-two shafts, they would hide the extras in the racks under the machines, covering them with rough stock. The pick-up man checked every hour to see how many shafts were completed and passed the information along, allowing the workers to keep a steady and equalized pace. If a worker turned out seventy shafts, he picked up only sixty-two of them.

Machine Operator No. 8004 fought the movement, telling his fellow workers to "knock the production out and forget about trying to set an amount for each man to run."[109] He was almost beaten up for his pains. This case of workers controlling the speed of production is documented—unlike thousands of other such actions that have remained unrecorded—because Machine Operator 8004 was a labor spy whose periodic reports were later published by the Senate Civil Liberties Investigating Committee, popularly known as the La Follette Committee.

As a study of the auto industry in 1934 by the NRA Division of Research and Planning revealed prophetically, the grievance "mentioned most frequently ... and uppermost in the minds of those who testified is the stretch-out. Everywhere workers indicated that they were being forced to work harder and harder, to put out more and more products in the same amount of time and with less workers doing the job.... If there is any one cause for conflagration in the Automobile Industry, it is this one."[110]

According to *Sitdown*, Sidney Fine's scholarly study of the great General Motors sitdown strike of 1936-1937, the speed-up was resented not only because of the absolute rate of production, but also because the mass-production worker "was not free, as perhaps he had been on some previous job, to set the pace of his work and to determine the manner in which it was to be performed."[111] A Buick worker complained: "You have to run to the toilet and run back .... If there wasn't anybody there to relieve you, you had to run away and tie the line up, and if you tied the line up you got hell for it."[112]

"You should see him come home at night, him and the rest of the men in the busses," the wife of a General Motors worker complained, "so tired like they was dead, and irritable. My John's not like that. He's a good, kind man. But the children don't dare go near him, he's so nervous and his temper's bad. And then at night in bed he shakes, his whole body, he shakes."

"Yes," replied another, "they're not men any more if you know what I mean. They're not men. My husband is only 30, but to look at him you'd think he was 50 and all played out."[113]

"Where you used to be a man ... now you are less than their cheapest tool," one worker complained, and another summed up, "I just don't like to be drove."[114]

The development of unionism in the auto industry followed closely that in rubber. Labor writer Herbert Harris estimated that 210,000 auto workers joined the AFL auto locals with the coming of the NRA. [115] Since the employers refused to give any significant concessions, important auto locals voted to strike; a strike throughout the industry seemed inevitable. Workers flooded into the unions to take part in the strike—20,000 in Flint alone.[116] The AFL leadership, however, wanted no part in a strike and managed to stall it.

Finally, William Collins, the leading AFL official in the auto industry, asked President Roosevelt to intervene. Roosevelt immediately demanded that the strike be postponed. Collins told union leaders,

"You have a wonderful man down there in Washington and he is trying hard to raise wages and working conditions."[117] According to Henry Kraus, editor of the union paper in Flint, "The attitudes of the auto workers toward the President those days bordered on the mystical."[118] Local representatives agreed to cancel the strike. Roosevelt then announced a settlement conceding nothing to the workers but an Automobile Labor Board to hear discrimination cases. The settlement legitimized company unions, and virtually exempted the auto industry from Section 7A.[119]

"We all feel tremendously happy over the outcome in Washington," a General Motors vice-president announced.[120] In the words of labor historian Sidney Fine, "The President made the victory of the automobile manufacturers complete on the issue of representation and collective bargaining."[121] Leonard Woodcock (later president of the United Auto Workers) recalls that when the workers in Flint heard of the settlement, they felt "a deep sense of betrayal" and began to tear up union cards. By October 1934, dues-paying membership in Flint had plummeted to 528. In several subsequent local auto strikes, the AFL played a strikebreaking role, even marching its members with a police escort into a motor products plant struck by another union.

Those few workers, mostly young and militant, who remained in the auto union bitterly fought AFL control. They eventually took control of the union and aligned it with the newly emerging Committee for Industrial Organization, an alliance of unions formed in 1935 to organize the unorganized basic industries. The AFL, dominated by craft unionists, suspended the unions affiliated with the CIO, including the UAW, in 1936. The CIO began to function as an independent labor center. Two years later it took the name Congress of Industrial Organizations.

Like the rubber workers, the auto workers turned to the sitdown and other forms of job action against the speed-up. Quickies occurred sporadically, especially in auto body plants in Cleveland and Detroit, from 1933 through 1935. By late 1936, the highly visible sitdowns in Akron were being imitated by auto workers throughout the industry, especially since it was the "grooving-in" period during which new models were introduced. Management as usual tried to increase speed and cut piece rates on new jobs, raising resentment to a peak. In Flint, the heart of the General Motors empire, seven work stoppages took place in the Fisher Body No. 1 plant in one week. One day the trim shop knocked off an hour early as a protest. Workers in another shop struck for an extra worker and got the line slowed from fifty to forty-five units. Another action won the restoration of a 20 percent wage cut. Henry Kraus described these workplace actions as "largely a spontaneous movement onto which the union had not yet securely attached itself."[122] Bud Simons, a union leader in the Fisher plant, pleaded with Bob Travis, the UAW organizer in Flint, "Honest to God, Bob, you've got to let me pull a strike before one pops somewhere that we won't be able to control!"[123]

The union tried to win the confidence of the workers by supporting the sitdowns and making itself the agency through which they could be spread. On November 12, 1936, for example, management reduced by one the number of "bow-men" who welded the angle irons across car roofs. The other bow-men were two brothers named Perkins and an Italian named Joe Urban; none of them was in the union, but they had been reading about a sitdown at Bendix. Adopting the idea, they simply stopped working. The foreman and superintendent rushed over and tried to talk them into returning to work, but the men just sat there arguing until twenty unfinished jobs had passed on the production line. The whole department followed the argument with intense excitement. The bow-men eventually agreed to go back to work until they could talk with the day shift about their griveance, but everyone left that night talking about the sitdown. The next day, when the Perkins brothers came to work, they were sent to the employment office and told that they were fired. They showed their firing slips to Bud Simons and he and the other union committee members ran through the "body-in-white" department where the main welding and soldering work was done, crying, "The Perkins boys were fired! Nobody starts working!" Henry Kraus detailed the microcosmic rebellion:

The whistle blew. Every man in the department stood at his station, a deep, significant tenseness in him. The foreman pushed the button and the skeleton bodies, already partly assembled when they got to this point, began to rumble forward. But no one lifted a hand. All eyes were turned to Simons who stood out in the aisle by himself.

The bosses ran about like mad.

"Whatsamatter? Whatsamatter? Get to work!" they shouted.

But the men acted as though they never heard them. One or two of them couldn't stand the tension. Habit was deep in them and it was like physical agony for them to see the bodies pass untouched. They grabbed their tools and chased after them. "Rat! Rat!" the men growled without moving and the others came to their senses.

The superintendent stopped by the "bow-men."

"You're to blame for this!" he snarled.

"So what if we are?" little Joe Urban, the Italian cried, overflowing with pride. "You ain't running your line, are you?"

That was altogether too much. The superintendent grabbed Joe and started for the office with him. The two went down along the entire line, while the men stood rigid as though awaiting the word of command. It was like that because they were organized but their organization only went that far and no further. What now?

Simons, a torch-solderer, was almost at the end of the line. He too was momentarily held in vise by the superintendent's overt act of authority. The latter had dragged Joe Urban past him when he finally found presence of mind to call out:

"Hey, Teefee, where you going?"

It was spoken in just an ordinary conversational tone and the other was taken so aback he answered the really impertinent question.

"I'm taking him to the office to have a little talk with him." Then suddenly he realized and got mad. "Say, I think I'll take you along too!"

That was his mistake.

"No you won't!" Simons said calmly.

"Oh yes I will!" and he took hold of his shirt.

Simons yanked himself loose.

And suddenly at this simple act of insurgence Teefee realized his danger. He seemed to become acutely conscious of the long line of silent men and felt the threat of their potential strength. They had been transformed into something he had never known before and over which he no longer had any command. He let loose of Simons and started off again with Joe Urban, hastening his pace. Simons yelled: "Come on, fellows, don't let them fire little Joe!"

About a dozen boys shot out of line and started after Teefee. The superintendent dropped Joe like a hot poker and deer-footed it for the door. The men returned to their places and all stood waiting. Now what? The next move was the company's. The moment tingled with expectancy.

Teefee returned shortly, accompanied by Bill Lynch, the assistant plant manager. Lynch was a friendly sort of person and was liked by the men. He went straight to Simons.

"I hear we've got trouble here," he said in a chatty way. "What are we going to do about it?"

"I think we'll get a committee together and go in and see Parker," Simons replied.

Lynch agreed. So Simons began picking the solid men out as had been prearranged. The foreman tried to smuggle in a couple of company-minded individuals, so Simons chose a group of no less than eighteen to make sure that the scrappers would outnumber the others. Walt Moore went with him, but Joe Devitt remained behind to see that the bosses didn't try any monkeyshines. The others headed for the office where Evan Parker, the plant manager, greeted them as smooth as silk.

"You can smoke if you want to, boys," he said as he bid them to take the available chairs. "Well, what seems to be the trouble here? We ought to be able to settle this thing."

"Mr. Parker, it's the speed-up the boys are complaining about," Simons said, taking the lead. "It's absolutely beyond human endurance. And now we've organized ourselves into a union. It's the union you're talking to right now, Mr. Parker."

"Why that's perfectly all right, boys," Parker said affably. "Whatever a man does outside the plant is his own business."

The men were almost bowled over by this manner. They had never known Parker as anything but a tough cold tomato with an army sergeant's style. He was clearly trying to play to the weaker boys on the committee and began asking them leading questions. Simons or Walt Moore would try to break in and answer for them.

"Now I didn't ask you," Parker would say, "you can talk when it's your turn!" In this way he sought to split the committee up into so many individuals. Simons realized he had to put an end to that quickly.

"We might as well quit talking right now, Mr. Parker," he said, putting on a tough act. "Those men have got to go back and that's all there is to it!"

"That's what you say," Parker snapped back.

"No, that's what the men say. You can go out and see for your-self. Nobody is going to work until that happens."

Parker knew that was true. Joe Devitt and several other good men who had been left behind were seeing to that. The plant manager seemed to soften again. All right, he said, he'd agree to take the two men back if he found their attitude was okay.

"Who's to judge that?" Simons asked.

"I will, of course!"

"Uh-uh!" Simons smiled and shook his head.

The thing bogged down again. Finally Parker said the Perkins brothers could return unconditionally on Monday. This was Friday night and they'd already gone home so there was no point holding up thousands of men until they could be found and brought back. To make this arrangement final he agreed that the workers in the department would get paid for the time lost in the stoppage. But Simons held fast to the original demand. Who knew what might happen till Monday? The Perkins fellows would have to be back on the line that night or the entire incident might turn out a flop.

"They go back tonight," he insisted.

Parker was fit to be tied. What was this? Never before in his life had he seen anything like it!

"Those boys have left!" he shouted. "It might take hours to get them back. Are you going to keep the lines tied up all that time?"

"We'll see what the men say," Simons replied, realizing that a little rank and file backing would not be out of the way. The committee rose and started back for the shop.

As they entered a zealous foreman preceded them, hollering: "Everybody back to work!" The men dashed for their places.

Simons jumped onto a bench.

"Wait a minute!" he shouted. The men crowded around him. He waited till they were all there and then told them in full detail of the discussion in the office. Courage visibly mounted into the men's faces as they heard of the unwavering manner in which their committee had acted in the dread presence itself. "What are we going to do, fellows," Simons asked, "take the company's word and go back to work or wait till the Perkins boys are right here at their jobs?"

"Bring them back first!" Walt Moore and Joe Devitt began yelling and the whole crowd took up the cry.

Simons seized the psychological moment to make it official.

"As many's in favor of bringing the Perkins boys back before we go to work, say Aye!" There was a roar in answer. "Opposed, Nay!" Only a few timid voices sounded—those of the company men and the foremen who had been circulating among the workers trying to influence them to go back to work. Simons turned to them.

"There you are," he said.

One of the foremen had taken out pencil and paper and after the vote he went around recording names. "You want to go to work?" he asked each of the men. Finally he came to one chap who stuck his chin out and said loudly, "Emphatically not!" which made the rest of the boys laugh and settled the issue.

Mr. Parker got the news and decided to terminate the matter as swiftly as possible. He contacted the police and asked them to bring the Perkins boys in. One was at home but the other had gone out with his girl. The police short-waved his license number to all scout cars. The local radio station cut into its program several times to announce that the brothers were wanted back at the plant. Such fame would probably never again come to these humble workers. By chance the second boy caught the announcement over the radio in his car and came to the plant all bewildered. When told what had happened the unappreciative chap refused to go to work until he had driven his girl home and changed his clothes! And a thousand men waited another half hour while the meticulous fellow was getting out of his Sunday duds.

When the two brothers came back into the shop at last, accompanied by the committee, the workers let out a deafening cheer that could be heard in the most distant reaches of the quarter-mile-long plant. There had never been anything quite like this happen in Flint before. The workers didn't have to be told to know the immense significance of their victory. Simons called the Perkins boys up on the impromptu platform. They were too shy to even stammer their thanks.

"You glad to get back?" Simons coached them.

"You bet!"

"Who did it for you?"

"You boys did."

Simons then gave a little talk though carefully refraining from mentioning the union.

> "Fellows," he said amid a sudden silence, "you've seen what you can get by sticking together. All I want you to do is remember that."[124]

Largely in response to this victory, United Auto Workers' membership in Flint increased from 150 to 1,500 within two weeks. The union's objective was to win recognition as the collective bargaining representative for the auto workers. Discontent was seething in the auto plants and breaking out in strikes throughout the country. Since the auto companies were not willing to recognize the union voluntarily, the obvious approach for the union was to "attach itself" to this strike movement, lead it on a company-wide basis, and use it to negotiate for recognition. As one UAW National Council member had argued earlier, "the only means we have now is to strike.... We must prove to the automobile workers we can help them."[125]

Although such "organizational strikes" became the basic tactic of the CIO unions in winning union recognition, the union leadership was ambivalent about an auto strike. According to J. Raymond Walsh, who was later the CIO research and education director, "The CIO high command, preoccupied with the drive in steel, tried in vain to prevent" a strike in the auto industry.[126] Leadership of the UAW believed a strike was necessary to gain union recognition, but wanted to postpone it until they were better organized—membership from April to December 1936 averaged only 27,000 for the entire industry—and resisted attempts to spread various strikes that broke out in November and December. This attitude was based on the fact that General Motors would be little hurt by strikes in peripheral plants, but if the Fisher Body plants in Cleveland and Flint could be closed, perhaps three-quarters of GM's production could be crippled.

Local leaders, in contrast, often reflected the turbulence of the workers in the shops. Adolph Germer, CIO representative for the auto industry, complained: "There is ... a strong undercurrent of revolt against the authority of the laws and rules of the organization.... It is not that the boys are defiant of the organization; I attribute it rather to their youth and dynamic natures. They want things done right now, and they are too impatient to wait for the orderly procedure involved in collective bargaining."[127]

The union finally requested a collective bargaining conference with General Motors, the key company in the industry. It also announced the goals with which it hoped to gain leadership of the workers: an annual wage adequate to provide "health, decency, and comfort," elimination of speed-up, spreading work through shorter hours, seniority, an eight-hour day, overtime pay, safety measures, and "true collective bargaining."[128] It expected events to move toward a head sometime in January. Events, however, did not wait. Workers throughout the industry began striking on their own. "It seems to be a custom for anybody or any group to call a strike at will,"[129] Germer complained.

In Atlanta, on November 18, the local called a sitdown over piece rate reductions, to the consternation of UAW national officials. A week later, the UAW local at the Bendix Corporation in South Bend, Indiana, won a contract after a nine-day sitdown, and a sitdown at Midland Steel Frame Company in Detroit won a wage increase, seniority, and time-and-a-half for overtime. In early December, a sitdown at Kelsey-Hayes Wheel Company in Detroit forced union recognition. In Kansas City on December 16, workers sat down over the firing of a union member for jumping over the conveyor to go to the toilet. Detroit experienced a virtual sitdown wave in December 1936, with workers at the Gordon Baking Company, Alcoa, National Automotive Fibers, and Bohn Aluminum and Brass Company all sitting down.

Those union leaders who wanted a strike against General Motors were most worried about whether the Fisher plant in Cleveland would come out. Many union workers there had lost their jobs in the wake of previous strikes, and no more than 10 percent of the workers were in the union. But resentment was running high over grooving-in speed-up, and when management postponed a long-awaited meeting to discuss grievances on December 28, workers in the quarter panel department said, "to hell with this stalling," and pulled the power switch. Workers in the steel stock, metal assembly, and trim departments quit work, and soon 7,000 workers were sitting down.[130] The local leadership was "taken completely by surprise."[131]

Meanwhile, events in Flint moved toward the decisive conflict. Two days after the Cleveland strike began, fifty workers sat down at the Fisher Body No. 2 plant in Flint to protest the transfer of three inspectors who had been ordered to quit the union and refused. Later that night, workers in Fisher plant No. 1 discovered that the company was loading dies—critical for the making of car bodies—onto railroad cars for shipment to plants elsewhere. (General Motors followed a policy described by its executive vice-president, William Knudson, as "diversification of plants where local union strength is dangerous"; half the machinery in the Toledo Chevrolet plant, for example, had been removed after a strike in 1935, leaving hundreds out of work.)

The workers were furious about the dies, and streamed over to the union hall across from the plant, where a meeting had been announced for lunchtime. Kraus, who was present, reports that "everybody's mind seemed made up before even a word was spoken."[132] When an organizer asked what they wanted to do, they shouted, "Shut her down! Shut the goddamn plant!"[133] They raced back into the plant, and a few minutes later one of them opened a third-story window and shouted to Flint UAW organizer Bob Travis, "Hurray, Bob! She's ours!"[134]

The occupiers rapidly faced the problem of organizing themselves for life inside the plant. Their basic decision-making body was a daily meeting of all the strikers in the plant. "The entire life of the sitdown came into review here and most of its ideas and decisions originated on the spot," Henry Kraus reported.[135] The chief administrative body was a committee of seventeen that reported to the strikers; available records indicate that virtually all its decisions were cleared with the general meeting of strikers. The strikers inside the plant, according to Sidney Fine, "displayed a fierce independence in their relationship with the UAW leadership on the outside." For example, Travis, though personally respected by the strikers, had to ask their permission to send one of his staff into the plant to gather material for the press, and he was only allowed in on the condition that his notes were cleared by the strike executive. A sitdowner told a reporter that he and his companions would not leave the plant even under orders from the union president or John L. Lewis, "unless we get what we want."[136]

Social groups of fifteen, usually men who worked together in the shop, set up house and lived together in their own corner of the plant, usually with close camaraderie. Each group had its own steward, and the stewards met together from time to time. The actual work of the strike was done by committees on food, recreation, information, education, postal services, sanitation, grievances, rumor control, coordination with the outside, and the like. Each worker served on at least one committee, and was responsible for six hours of strike duty a day. The sitdowners sent out their own representatives to recruit union members, coordinate relief, and create an "outside defense squad."

Special attention was paid to the question of defense. A "special patrol" made hourly inspections of the entire plant day and night, looking for signs of company attack. Security groups were assigned to doorways and stairwells. Strikers set up "a regular production line"[137] to make blackjacks out of rubber hoses, braided leather, and lead, and covered the windows with metal sheets with holes for fire hoses. The men conducted regular drills with the hoses, and collected piles of bolts, nuts, and door hinges for ammunition.

Sanitation likewise was stressed. At 3 p.m., a crane whistle would blow and all the men would line up at one end of the plant. The first wave would pick up refuse, behind it the second would put things in order, and the third would sweep the floor. The commissary floor was cleaned once an hour. The men showered daily. These measures were aimed at preserving both morale and health. Likewise, the workers protected the machinery, in some cases even oiling it, organized fire protection, and inspected for fire hazards. Food was prepared on the outside by hundreds of volunteers and brought to the sitdowners by striking trolley coach employees.

Workers established courts to punish infractions of rules. The most serious "crimes" were failures to perform assigned duties by not showing up, sleeping on the job, or deserting one's post. Others included failing to bus dirty dishes, littering, not participating in daily clean-up, smoking outside the plant cafeteria, failing to search everyone entering and leaving buildings, bringing in liquor, and making noise in sleeping areas or the "Quiet Zone," where absolute silence was available twenty-four hours a day. Punishments were designed to fit the crime; for example, men who failed to take a daily shower were "sentenced" to scrub the bathhouse. The ultimate punishment, applied only after repeated infractions, was expulsion from the plant. The courts were generally conducted with a good deal of humor and treated as a source of entertainment. For example, a striker who entered a plant without proper credentials was sentenced to make a speech to the court as his punishment. Reporter Edwin Levinson observed that "there is more substantial humor in a single session of the Fisher strikers' kangaroo courts than in a season of Broadway musical comedies."[138]

This kind of informal gaiety and creativity seemed to burgeon in the strike community. A favorite pastime was for the men to gather in a circle and call out the name of a member, who would then have to sing, whistle, dance, or tell a story. Each plant had its own band, composed of mandolins, guitars, banjos, and harmonicas. The strikers made up verse after verse about the strike to dozens of popular and country tunes. General meetings, by the strikers' decision, opened and closed with singing. The favorite was "Solidarity Forever."

"We are all one happy family now," a sitdowner wrote home. "We all feel fine and have plenty to eat. We have several good banjo players and singers. We sing and cheer the Fisher boys and they return it."[139] Another wrote, "I am having a great time, something new, something different, lots of grub and music."[140] "The atmosphere of cooperativeness," one psychologist declared, created "a veritable revolution of personality," indicated, for example, by workers more frequently saying "we" than "I."[141] As a reporter in Paul Gallico's novelette on the sitdown suggested, "They had made a palace out of what had been their prison."[142]

Outside the factories, a network of committees supported the strike, organizing defense, food, sound cars, picketing, transportation, strike relief, publicity, and entertainment. Women were particularly important in the outside organization. (The union leadership had decided that only men would occupy the plants, to the anger of some women workers.) Wives' support was essential to strike morale, a fact recognized by the company, which sent representatives calling on them to pressure their husbands back to work. But strikers' wives and women workers poured into the commissary and worked on the various committees. Following a street dance on New Year's Eve, about fifty women decided to form a Women's Auxiliary and set up their own speakers' bureau, day care center for mothers on strike duty, first-aid station, and welfare committee. After battles began with the police, women established a Women's Emergency Brigade of 350 members, organized on military lines, ready to battle police. "We will form a line around the men, and if the police want to fire then they'll just have to fire into us," announced Genora Johnson, one of the founders of the brigade.[143]

"A new type of woman was born in the strike," one of the women said. "Women who only yesterday were horrified at unionism, who felt inferior to the task of organizing, speaking, leading, have, as if overnight, become the spearhead in the battle of unionism."[144] Another recalled, "I found a common understanding and unselfishness I'd never known in my life. I'm living for the first time with a definite goal.... Just being a woman isn't enough anymore. I want to be a human being with the right to think for myself."[145]

The union coordinated the strike and put forward union recognition as its central demand. What recognition meant was never clarified, but workers assumed it meant a powerful say for them in industrial decisions and they supported it enthusiastically. The strike spread rapidly from Flint and other initial centers throughout the General Motors system. Auto workers sat down at Guide Lamp in Anderson, Indiana, at Chevrolet and Fisher Body in Janesville, Wisconsin, and Cadillac in Detroit. Regular strikes developed at Norwood and Toledo, Ohio, and Ternstedt, Michigan. General Motors was forced to halt production at Pontiac, Oldsmobile, Delco-Remy, and numerous other plants.[146] GM's projected production for January of 224,000 cars and trucks was cut to 60,000. In the first ten days of February, it produced only 151 cars in the entire country.

General Motors refused to bargain until the plants were evacuated and started a counter-attack on three levels: legal action, organization of an anti-strike movement, and direct violence against the strikers. The third day of the strike, GM lawyers requested and received an injunction from Judge Edward Black ordering strikers to evacuate the plants, cease picketing, and allow those wanting to work to enter. The sheriff read the injunction to the sitdowners, who jeered him menacingly until he fled. Then a quick-witted union lawyer checked and discovered that Judge Black owned 3,365 shares of General Motors stock valued at $219,900. This exposed the judge as an interested party and made the injunction worthless, as well as showing the corporation's power over government.

The company's next move was to organize the Flint Alliance "for the Security of Our Jobs, Our Homes, and Our Community." It was headed by George Boysen, a past and future General Motors official, and as a state police investigator reported, it was "a product of General Motors brains." The alliance worked in close cooperation with John Barringer, the Flint city manager.[147] It began anti-strike publicity and started recruiting anti-union workers, businessmen, farmers, housewives, schoolchildren, and anyone else who would sign a card. The Flint Alliance sought a large enrollment, according to Boysen, for "its moral effect toward smothering the strike movement."[148]

For almost two weeks, little violence occurred in Flint. But on January 11, supporters carrying dinner to the sitdowners in Fisher No. 2 were stopped at the gate by plant guards, whom the strikers had allowed to hold the ground floor of the factory. The pickets started taking food up a twenty-four-foot ladder, but the guards formed a flying wedge and seized the ladder. Suddenly police closed off all traffic approaches to the plant. An attempt was clearly under way either to starve out the sitdowners or evict them by force, and unless the workers took the gates it would succeed. Twenty sitdowners, armed with blackjacks, marched downstairs and demanded the key to the gate. "My orders are to give it to nobody," the company police officer in charge replied.[149] The sitdowners gave the guards to the count of ten, then charged the gate. The guards fled and locked themselves in the women's bathroom. The sitdowners put their shoulders to the wooden gates and splintered them, to the cheers of the pickets who had quickly gathered outside.

Then suddenly patrol cars drew up and city policemen began pouring out, throwing gas grenades at the pickets and into the plant. At this point, the earlier defensive preparations taken by the sitdowners came in handy; they opened firehoses on the officers and showered them with two-pound door hinges. Within five minutes, the police, drenched and battered, retreated from the vicinity. The police attacked again, but the outside pickets regrouped and drove them off. In retreat, the police began firing their guns, wounding thirteen.

The conflict was quickly dubbed the "Battle of the Running Bulls." It was considered a great victory for the strikers and a demonstration that they could hold out against police attack. In its wake, previously hostile workers flooded into the union. It also provoked Governor Frank Murphy to order the National Guard into Flint.

Murphy was a New Deal governor *par excellence*. In Detroit he had been one of the most liberal mayors in the country, providing exceptional public assistance to the unemployed and preventing the police from suppressing radicals. He was elected governor with overwhelming labor support, and had insisted on making welfare relief available to strikers. He was also on close terms with such auto magnates as Walter Chrysler and Lawrence Fisher of Fisher Body, whose plants were the chief target in Flint. Although it was not known at the time, Murphy was also the owner of 1,650 shares of General Motors stock worth $104,875.[150]

Murphy did not intend to use the National Guard to drive the sitdowners out by force. He was fully supported in this decision by General Motors, whose officials told Murphy privately that they did not want the strikers "evicted by force."[151] Knudson stated publicly that GM wanted the strike settled by negotiation rather than violence. Murphy, who believed the sitdown illegal but feared bloodshed in evicting the strikers, used the National Guard to prevent vigilante attacks while holding the threat of a starve-out over the workers' heads. Murphy even succeeded in arranging a truce in which the union would evacuate the plants in exchange for a company pledge not to remove machinery or open the plants for fifteen days. This would have given away the strikers' strongest point, their possession of the plants, but it was scotched when the union labeled GM's plans to negotiate with the Flint Alliance a double-cross and called off the truce.

Failing to evacuate the plants by other means, GM applied for a new injunction from a different judge. Meanwhile pressure built up as strikers were attacked by police in Detroit, vigilantes in Saginaw, and both in Anderson, Indiana.

At this point, the local leaders in Flint devised a bold initiative to shift the balance of forces by seizing the giant Chevrolet No. 4 plant. The problem was that union strength at Chevrolet No. 4 was limited and the plant was heavily protected by company guards. At a meeting of carefully selected Chevrolet workers, which deliberately included suspected company spies, Bob Travis announced a sitdown at Chevrolet No. 9 at 3:20 the next day, February 1. Key leaders at No. 9 were told that they need only hold the plant for half an hour, as the real target was No. 6. As expected, company guards had been tipped off by the company spies and shifted from the No. 4 to the No. 9 area. At 3:20, workers sat down at No. 9, company guards rushed in, and the diversionary battle began. Meanwhile, a handful of workers in Chevrolet No. 4 who knew the plan marched around the factory shouting, "Shut 'er down!"[152] but were too few even to be heard. Those in on the plan in No. 6, meanwhile, led a small group over to No. 4. They were still too few to close down the huge plant, however, and it seemed as if the plan had failed. But when they returned to No. 6, they found the whole plant on strike, and the workers marched en masse back to No. 4 to shut it down. About half the No. 4 workers joined the sitdown, the rest dropping their lunches in gondolas for the sitdowners as they left.

The capture of Chevrolet No. 4 changed the balance of forces. It demonstrated that the workers, far from being exhausted, were still able to expand their grip on the industry. As a result, General Motors agreed to negotiate without evacuation of the plants. The law-and-order forces tried one more offensive, however. Judge Gadola issued a new injunction ordering evacuation of the plants and an end to picketing within twenty-four hours. When the workers ignored it, he issued a writ of attachment and claimed authority to have the National Guard enforce it without approval of the governor. In the final crisis, thousands of workers poured into Flint from hundreds of miles around. Auto plants in Detroit and Toledo were shut down by the exodus of workers to Flint. To avoid the appearance of provocation, the mobilization was declared Women's Day and women's brigades came in from Lansing, Pontiac, Toledo, and Detroit. The crowd of perhaps 10,000 virtually occupied Flint, parading through the heart of the city, then surrounding the threatened Fisher No. 1 plant, armed with thirty-inch wooden braces provided from the factory.

Learning that the National Guard would not evict the sitdowners, City Manager Barringer ordered all city police on duty and decided to organize a 500-man "army of our own." "We are going down there shooting," he announced. "The strikers have taken over this town and we are going to take it back."[153]

The tenor of events is suggested by a plan worked out without union knowledge by the Union War Vets, who had taken responsibility for guarding strike leaders outside the plants. Had leaders been arrested under the Gadola writ, the veterans "would muster an armed force among their own number and in defense of the U.S. Constitution, of 'real Patriotism,' and the union, would take over the city hall, the courthouse and police headquarters, capture and imprison all officials and release the union men."[154]

The rug was pulled from under Barringer's "army" when a GM official asked him to demobilize, saying, "The last thing we want is rioting in the streets,"[155] a result the workers' mass mobilization would have made inevitable.

On February 11, General Motors agreed to recognize and bargain with the union in the struck plants and promised not to deal with any other organization in them for six months. As Sidney Fine wrote, "What the U.A.W., like other unions at the time, understood by the term 'recognition' has always been rather nebulous, but the union believed, and it had reason to, that it had been accorded a status of legitimacy in G.M. plants that it had never before enjoyed. It was confident that it would be able to consolidate its position in the 17 plants during the six-month period because it had no rivals to contend with."[156]

But if the agreement established the *union* firmly enough, it did little for the concrete grievances of the workers. When Bud Simons, head of the strike committee in Fisher No. 1, was awakened and told the terms of the settlement, he remarked, "That won't do for the men to hear. That ain't what we're striking for."[157] When the union presented the settlement to the sitdowners, they asked, "How about the speed of the line? How about the bosses—would they be as tough as ever?"[158]

The workers' forebodings were borne out by the negotiations that followed the evacuation of the plants. In the words of Irving Bernstein, "The corporation's policy was to contain the union, to yield no more than economic power compelled and, above all, to preserve managerial discretion in the productive process, particularly over the speed of the line."[159] The fundamental demand of the strike from the point of view of the workers had been "mutual determination" of the speed of production, but under the collective bargaining agreement signed March 12, local management was to have "full authority" in determining these matters. If a worker objected, "the job was to be restudied and an adjustment was to be made if the timing was found to be unfair."[160] Further, instead of having a shop steward for every twenty-five workers, directly representing those they worked with, the union agreed to deal with management through plant committees of no more than nine members per plant. Finally, the union agreed to become the agency for limiting workers' direct action against speedup and other grievances, pledging that "there shall be no suspensions or stoppages of work until every effort has been exhausted to adjust them through the regular grievance procedure, and in no case without the approval of the international officers of the union."[161]

Such agreements were not enough to control workers who had just discovered their own power. Workers assumed victory in the strike "would produce some radical change in the structure of status and power in G.M. plants," and they "were reluctant to accept the customary discipline exercised by management." They "ran wild in many plants for months."[162] As one worker later recalled, "every time a dispute came up the fellows would have a tendency to sit down and just stop working."[163] According to Knudson, there were 170 sit-downs in GM plants between March and June 1937.[164]

For example, on March 18, 200 women sat down in a sewing room in Flint Fisher Body No. 1 in a dispute over methods of payment. An hour later, 280 sat down in sympathy with them in another sewing room. Next, sixty men sat down in the shipping department. Soon the entire plant was forced to shut down. "Since the strike was clearly in violation of the agreement ... in which the union promised to pro-tect the company against sitdowns during the life of the agreement, union officials hurried to Flint to settle the matter."[165]

Two weeks later, 935 men struck in the final Chevrolet assembly plant. Then the parts and service plant struck in sympathy, closing Fisher Body No. 2. Finally, workers in all departments of the Chevrolet complex walked out in sympathy. Meanwhile, the Fisher Body Plant and the Yellow Truck and Coach Plant in Pontiac were closed by workers protesting discharge of fellow workers. In all, 30,000 workers were involved in the wildcats at this time.

These actions indicated that the workers had developed the ability to coordinate action between plants and even between cities without the union. Union officials told Governor Murphy that they were "mystified" by the sitdowns and that "their representatives in the plants told them they had been 'pushed into' the new sitdowns with-out union authorization."[166]

Equally important, the workers won control over the rate of pro-duction, despite the union contract that conceded this authority to management. "Production in the Chevrolet Motor plants has been slowed down to nearly 50 per cent of former output during the last several weeks by concerted action of the union workers, with key men on the mother line stopping work at intervals to slow down pro-duction," *The New York Times* reported April 2.[167]

Despite the failure of the union to win control over production rates, a Fisher No. 1 worker who had opposed the big strike wrote:

The inhuman high speed is *no more*. We now have a voice, and have slowed up the speed of the line. And [we] are now treated as hu-man beings, and not as part of the machinery. The high pressure is taken off.... It proves clearly that united we stand, divided or alone we fall.[168]

The top leadership of the union considered these wildcat work stoppages a serious threat to union authority. A *New York Times* article entitled "Unauthorized Sit-Downs Fought by C.I.O. Unions" described the steps they took against them:

(1) As soon as an unauthorized strike occurs or impends, international officers or representatives of the U.A.W. are rushed to the scene to end or prevent it, get the men back to work and bring about an orderly adjustment of the grievances.

(2) Strict orders have been issued to all organizers and representatives that they will be dismissed if they authorize any stoppages of work without the consent of the international officers, and that local unions will not receive any money or financial support from the international union for any unauthorized stoppage of, or interference with, production.

(3) The shop stewards are being "educated" in the procedure for settling grievances set up in the General Motors contract, and a system is being worked out which the union believes will convince the rank and file that strikes are unnecessary.

(4) In certain instances there has been a "purge" of officers, organizers and representatives who have appeared to be "hot-heads" or "trouble-makers" by dismissing, transferring or demoting them.[169]

John L. Lewis and UAW leaders blamed wildcats that idled tens of thousands in early April on Communist agitation, and *The New York Times* reported Lewis might soon "send some 'flying squadrons' of 'strong-arm men' from his own United Mine Workers to Flint ... to keep the trouble-makers in line."[170] But William Weinstone, Michigan secretary of the Communist Party, hotly denied the charges that Communists were responsible. He denounced "helter-skelter use of the sit-down."[171] He added, "I have personally visited Flint today ... and have not found a single Communist party member who countenanced or supported in the slightest the recent sit-down."[172]

The Communist Party's general attitude toward the sitdown closely followed that of the CIO. At a party strategy meeting an Akron Communist leader argued: "The sitdown is an extremely effective organizational weapon. But credit must go to Comrade Williamson for warning us against the danger of these surprise actions. The sitdowns came because the companies refused to bargain collectively with the union. Now we must work for regular relations between the union and the employers—and strict observance of union procedure on the part of the workers."[173]

The lengths to which union opposition to wildcat sitdowns went is illustrated by an incident in November 1937. Four workers were fired from a Fisher Body plant and several hundred of their fellow workers struck and occupied the plant in protest. United Auto Workers leaders denounced the strike but were unable to persuade the workers to leave, and therefore resorted to stratagem. They persuaded the workers to divide into two shifts and take turns occupying the plant, concentrated their supporters in one of these shifts, and marched the workers out of the plant, turning possession back to the company guards. When the other shift of strikers arrived to take their turn, they found themselves locked out.

It is not surprising that a *New York Times* reporter found the continuing sitdowns resulted in part from "dissatisfaction on the part of the workers with the union itself" and that workers were "as willing in some cases to defy their own leaders as their bosses."[174] Rank-and-file workers had not reckoned on the union becoming the agency for enforcing work discipline in the shops. Yet this had always been the essential policy of the CIO unions, however much they might utilize sitdowns as an organizing tactic.

CIO director John Brophy made this clear in a carefully worded statement issued before the General Motors strike: "In the formative and promotional stages of unionism in a certain type of industry, the sitdown strike has real value. After the workers are organized and labor relations are regularized through collective bargaining, then we do urge that the means provided within the wage contract for adjusting grievances be used by the workers."[175]

Len De Caux, editor of the CIO Union News Service, elaborated:

The first experience of the C.I.O. with sitdowns was in discouraging them. This was in the Akron rubber industry, after the Goodyear strike. C.I.O. representatives cautioned … the new unionists against sitdowns on the grounds that they should use such channels for negotiating grievances as the agreement provided.…

When collective bargaining is fully accepted, union recognition accorded and an agreement reached, C.I.O. unionists accept full responsibility for carrying out their side of it in a disciplined fashion, and oppose sitdowns or any other strike action while it is in force.[176]

John L. Lewis was even more blunt: "A C.I.O. contract is adequate protection against sit-downs, lie-downs, or any other kind of strike."[177] Held up as a model was the CIO's largest union, the United Mine Workers, whose "agreement with coal companies now includes guarantees that there shall be no cessation of work during the term of the contract, and [whose] constitution includes definite penalties, including fines, discharges and even a blacklist for anyone calling or participating in an unauthorized strike."[178]

"The new unions, it is held in C.I.O. quarters, must educate and discipline their members or invite a situation of chaos and anarchy which could very well be utilized by either Leftists or Rightists in seizing political power," the *Times* concluded ominously.[179]

Despite the efforts of the union and management, however, the wildcats in the auto industry continued—and continue to this day.

•

In the wake of the General Motors strike, people throughout the country began sitting down. Even excluding the innumerable quickies of less than a day, the Bureau of Labor Statistics recorded sitdowns involving nearly 400,000 workers in 1937.[180] It would be impossible to summarize them all here, but we can learn something of their range and pattern by examining a number of those that occurred in the peak of the wave during and just after the General Motors sitdown.

The most immediate spread was in the auto industry. The union began negotiations with Chrysler, and the company offered to accept the General Motors agreement. According to *The New York Times:*

[T]he union committee started the discussion on the issue of seniority, but said that the rank-and-file demanded that sole bargaining
be put first on the agenda.

Then the various union locals held meetings and passed resolutions ordering the union committee to present an ultimatum demanding a yes-or-no answer from the company on sole bargaining
by the following Monday.

When the company replied in the negative, according to the union, the men themselves sat down without being ordered out by
their leaders.[181]

The company secured an injunction ordering the 6,000 sitdowners to
leave, but as the evacuation hour came near, huge crowds of pickets
gathered—10,000 at the main Dodge plant in Hamtramck; 10,000 at
the Chrysler Jefferson plant; smaller numbers at other Chrysler,
Dodge, Plymouth, and DeSoto plants; 30,000 to 50,000 in all—demonstrating the consequences of an attempted eviction. "It is generally
feared," the *Times* reported, that an attempt to evict the strikers with
special deputies would lead to an "inevitable large amount of bloodshed and the state of armed insurrection."[182]

Governor Murphy warned that the state might have to use force to
restore respect for the courts and other public authority, to protect
personal and property rights, and to uphold the structure of organized society, emphasizing that the state must prevent "needless interruption to industry, commerce and transportation."[183] Murphy
established a law-and-order committee, but when top UAW officials
refused to serve on it, "strikers inside the plant could be seen waving
their home-made blackjacks in jubilation. Inside the gate about 150
women who had been serving meals in the company cafeteria engaged in a snake-dance, beating knives and forks against metal serving trays."[184]

Shop committees in the occupied plants voted not to leave the
plants until they had won sole bargaining rights. Nonetheless, on
March 24, John L. Lewis, representing the CIO, agreed to evacuate the
plants on the basis of the General Motors settlement, which Chrysler
had accepted even before the strike began. Many strikers considered
the settlement a surrender, but they reluctantly left the plants.

The Chrysler strike was merely the largest of dozens of simultaneous sitdowns in the Detroit area. About 20,000 additional auto workers were out as a result of a sitdown at the Hudson Motor
Company.[185] Wildcat sitdowns in General Motors plants occurred by
the score during this period, many of them involving tens of thousands of workers at a time. By April 1, there were more than 120,000
auto workers on strike in Michigan. Workers occupied the Newton
Packing Company in late February and, after eleven days, turned off
refrigeration of $170,000 worth of meat, stating they were "through
fooling."[186] In early March, clerks sat down in the Crowley-Milner
and Frank and Sedar department stores. Thirty-five women workers
seized the Durable Laundry, as the proprietor fired a gun over organizers' heads "to scare them away."[187] The same day, Detroit's four
leading hotels were all closed by sitdowns and lockouts, the auto
workers providing a mass picket line in one case. Women barricaded
themselves in three tobacco plants for several weeks; in one case, residents of the neighborhood battled their police guard with rock-filled
snowballs. Eight lumber yards were occupied by their workers. Other
sitdown strikes occurred at the Yale and Towne lock company and
the Square D electrical manufacturers.

Unable to challenge the giant Chrysler strike, police moved force-
fully against the lesser sitdowns. Early in the afternoon of March 20,
police evicted strikers from the Newton Packing Company. Three
hours later, 150 police attacked sitdowners at a tobacco plant: "Hysterical cries echoed through the building as, by ones and twos, the 86
women strikers, ranging from defiant girls to bewildered workers
with gray hair, were herded into patrol wagons and sped away,
while shattering glass and the yells of the street throng added to the
din."[188]

Such action could clearly be an entering wedge against the auto
workers, and the UAW responded by calling a mass protest rally in
Cadillac Square. The union also threatened to call a strike of 180,000
auto workers in the Detroit area (excluding those at GM for whom
they had just signed a contract) and hinted that it would ask for a
city-wide general strike unless forcible evictions of sitdowners in
small stores and plants were halted. In the judgment of Russell B.

Porter of *The New York Times*, "It is wholly possible that the automobile workers' union might get the support of the city's entire labor movement, now boiling over with fever for union organization ... for a city-wide general strike."[189] Telegrams went out to UAW locals in Detroit to stand by in preparation to strike, but the city quickly halted its drive against the more than twenty remaining sitdowns.

From March 7 to March 21, Chicago experienced nearly sixty sitdowns. Motormen on the sixty-mile freight subway under Chicago shut off controls and sat down when the employer decided to ship a greater proportion of goods above ground and laid off thirty-five tunnel workers. The motormen were joined by 400 freight handlers and other employees who barricaded their warehouses. On March 12, sitdowns hit the Loop, with more than 9,000 men and women striking—including waitresses, candy makers, cab drivers, clerks, peanut baggers, stenographers, tailors, truckers, and factory hands. Eighteen hundred workers, including three hundred office workers, sat down at the Chicago Mail Order Company and won a 10 percent pay increase; 450 employees at three de Met's tea rooms sat down as "the girls laughed and talked at the tables they had served" until they went home that night with a 25 percent pay increase[190]; and next day sitdowns hit nine more Chicago firms.

The range of industries and locations hit by sitdowns was virtually unlimited. Electrical workers and furniture workers sat down in St. Louis. Workers at a shirt company sat down in Pulaski, Tennessee. In Philadelphia, workers sat down at the Venus Silk Hosiery Company and the National Container Company. Leather workers in Garard, Ohio, sat down, as did broom manufacturing workers in Pueblo, Colorado. Workers sat down at a fishing tackle company in Akron, Ohio. Oil workers sat down in eight gasoline plants in Seminole, Oklahoma.

Sitdowns were particularly widespread among store employees, so easily replaced in ordinary strikes. Women sat down in two Woolworth stores in New York. Pickets outside one store broke through private guards, opened windows from a ledge fifteen feet above ground, and passed through cots, blankets, oranges, and food packets to the strikers, who ate with china and silver from the lunch counter.

Similar sitdowns occurred in five F. & W. Grant stores; in one, strikers
staged an impromptu St. Patrick's Day celebration and a mock mar-
riage to pass the time. Having no chairs to sit down on, 150 salesgirls
and 25 stock boys in Pittsburgh staged a "folded-arms strike" in four
C.G. Murphy five-and-ten stores for shorter hours and a raise; they
also complained that "we have to pay for our uniforms and washing
them and have to sweep the floor."[191] Twelve stores in Providence,
Rhode Island, locked out their employees to prevent an impending
sitdown, at which point the unions called a general strike of retail
trades.

Nor was the sitdown restricted to private employees. In Amster-
dam, New York, municipal ash and garbage men sat down on their
trucks in the city Department of Public Works garage when their demands for a wage increase were refused; when the mayor hired a private trucking firm, the strikers persuaded the men not to work as
strikebreakers. A similar strike occurred in Bridgeport, Connecticut,
when sixty trash collectors sat down, demanding immediate reinstatement of a fellow employee and the firing of the foreman who
had dismissed him. In New York, seventy maintenance workers, half
white, half black, barricaded themselves in the kitchen and laundry of
the Hospital for Joint Diseases; services were continued for patients,
but not for doctors, nurses, and visitors. A series of similar sitdowns
occurred in the Brooklyn Jewish Hospital.

Forty grave-diggers and helpers prevented burials in a North Ar-
lington, New Jersey, cemetery by sitting down in the toolhouse to secure a raise for the helpers. Seventeen blind workers sat down to
demand a minimum wage at a workshop run by the New York
Guild for the Jewish Blind, and were supported by a sympathy sitdown of eighty-three blind workers at a workshop of the New York
Association for the Blind. Draftsmen and engineers in Brooklyn sat
down against a wage cut in the office of the Park Department. Works
Progress Adminstration workers in California sat down in the employment office as flying squadrons spread a strike through the Bay
Area.

An important aspect of the sitdown was the extent to which it was
used to challenge management decisions. We have already seen vari-

ous examples of this, such as the Chicago freight subway workers' challenge to the decision to move more freight above ground. On March 11, workers at the Champion Shoe Company sat down when they found the company had secretly transferred fifty machines to a new plant. Two hundred and fifty workers, more than half of them women, occupied a Philadelphia hosiery mill that management intended to close and prepared to block efforts to move the machinery.

A hundred and fifteen workers at the Yahr Lange Drug Company in Milwaukee, who had resisted efforts to unionize them, sat down in protest against a company policy of firing workers as soon as their age and length of service justified a raise. Their sole demand was removal of Fred Yahr as general manager of the company. "The girls sat around and played bridge and smoked, and the men gathered in knots awaiting the results. The telephone was not answered, and customers were not served. Salesmen on the road were notified of the strike by wire and responded that they were sitting down in their cars until it was settled." After a long conference with the workers, management announced that Yahr had resigned. The strikers, in effect, had "fired the boss."[192]

Far from being limited to employer-worker relationships, sitdowns were used to challenge a wide range of social grievances. In Detroit, for example, thirty-five women barricaded themselves in a welfare office demanding that the supervisor be removed and that a committee meet with the new supervisor to determine qualifications of families for relief. Thirteen young men sat down in an employment agency where they had paid a fee for jobs that had then not materialized. In New York, representatives of fifteen families who lost their homes and belongings in a tenement fire sat down at the Emergency Relief Bureau, demanding complete medical care for those injured in the fire and sufficient money for rehabilitation, instead of token sums the bureau had offered. A few days later, forty-five people sat in at another relief office, demanding aid for two families and a general 40 percent increase for all families on home relief. In Columbus, Ohio, thirty unemployed men and women sat down in the governor's office, demanding $50 million for poor relief. And in St. Paul, Minnesota, 200 people staged a sitdown in the Senate chamber, demanding action on a $17 million relief plan. In the Bronx, two dozen women sat down in an effort to prevent the eviction of two neighbors by twenty-five policemen.

Prisoners in the state prison in Joliet, Illinois, sat down to protest working in the prison yard on Saturday afternoon, usually a time of rest, as did prisoners in Philadelphia against a cut in prison wages. Children sat down in a Pittsburgh movie theater when the manager told them to leave before the feature film, as did children in Mexia, Texas, when a theater's program was cut. At Mineville, New York, 150 high school students struck because the contracts of the principal and two teachers had not been renewed. Women students at the Asheville Normal and Teachers College in North Carolina sat down to protest parietal rules. In Bloomington, Illinois, wives went on a sitdown strike, refusing to prepare meals, wash dishes, or answer door bells until they received more compensation from their husbands. In Michigan, thirty members of a National Guard company that had served in Flint during the GM sitdown staged a sitdown of their own in March because they had not been paid.

The sitdown idea spread so rapidly because it dramatized a simple, powerful fact: that no social institution can run without the cooperation of those whose activity makes it up. Once the power of the sitdown was demonstrated, others could apply it to their own situation. On the shop floor, it could be used to gain power over the actual running of production. In large industries, it could be used for massive power struggles like the GM strike. In small shops, it could force quick concessions. Those affected by public institutions—schools, jails, welfare departments, and the like—could use similar tactics to disrupt their functioning and force concessions. The power and spread of the sitdowns electrified the country. In March 1937 alone, 170 industrial sitdowns with 167,210 participants were reported. No doubt a great many more went unrecorded.[193]

The sitdowns provided ordinary workers an enormous power that depended on nobody but their fellow workers. As Louis Adamic wrote of the non-union sitdowns in Akron:

> The fact that the sitdown gives the worker in mass-production industries a vital sense of importance cannot be overemphasized. Two

sitdowns which completely tied up plants employing close to ten thousand men were started by half a dozen men each. Imagine the feeling of power those men experienced! And the thousands of workers who sat down in their support shared that feeling in varying degrees, depending on their individual power of imagination. One husky gum-miner said to me, "Now we don't feel like taking the sass off any snot-nose college-boy foreman." Another man said, "Now we know our labor is more important than the money of the stockholders, than the gambling in Wall Street, than the doings of the managers and foremen." One man's grievance, if the majority of his fellow-workers in his department agreed that it was a just grievance, could tie up the whole plant. He became a strike leader; the other members of the working force in his department became members of the strike committee. *They* assumed full responsibility in the matter; formed their own patrols, they kept the machines from being pointlessly destroyed, and they met with management and dictated their terms. *They* turned their individual self-control and restraint into group self-discipline.... *They* settled the dispute, not some outsider.[194]

In the face of the sitdown wave, a great many employers decided to deal with unions voluntarily, and by World War II unions were recognized by practically all large industrial companies. Most significant was the largest corporation of them all, U.S. Steel, which reversed its bitter tradition of anti-unionism to recognize the CIO's Steel Workers Organizing Committee (SWOC). As Irving Bernstein wrote, it made sense for the corporation to engage in collective bargaining "on a consolidated basis with experienced and responsible union officials like Lewis and Murray rather than with disparate local groups led by men with no background in bargaining." U.S. Steel head Myron Taylor "had good reason to trust Lewis and Murray," whom he had bargained with already in the coal industry.[195]

The new contract cost U.S. Steel little—a wage increase it recouped twice over in a price increase, limitation on hours, which was already required to bid on government contracts, and some deference to seniority in laying off workers. In return, the contract provided that "differences ... should be taken up without cessation of work, with the final decision, if an agreement was not reached, to rest with an impartial umpire named by the company and union."[196]

The SWOC was in a strong position to enforce this strike ban: its officials were appointed by the CIO, not elected by the steelworkers; all initiation fees and dues went through the central office; and locals were forbidden to sign an agreement or call a strike without its approval. As Myron Taylor wrote a year after the contract went into effect, "The union has scrupulously followed the terms of its agreement."[197]

In early 1937, Louis Adamic had a revealing interview with the head of a small steel company that had voluntarily recognized the CIO soon after U.S. Steel, suggesting how union recognition looked to an employer faced with rising labor militancy. The employer described how he had been visited by a CIO organizer who "began to sell me on the idea of letting the CIO start a union in our plant." The organizer started to tell him "all about the petty troubles and pains-in-the-neck we'd had in the mill the past few weeks, which ... amounted to a lot of trouble and expense," which "were bound to increase as the years went by":

> Why? Because, he said, in shops where the union was fought and men belonged to it secretly all sorts of damned things happened all the time, which led to fear, nervousness, and jitters among the men, to secret sabotage and loafing on the job.... [H]e proceeded to tell me, too, that if we let the union come in, it would form a grievance committee consisting of workers in the mill; all the union men in the shop would be required, and others allowed, to take their grievances to the committee, which would assemble all the kicks and complaints and what-nots, then take them up with us—the management ... say once a week; and many, perhaps most, of the grievances would be smoothed out by the committee itself without bothering us with them.... We signed an agreement for a year, the union was formed, about half the men joined, a grievance committee was organized and sure enough, the thing began to work out.... It seemed to act as a sort of collective vent....
>
> The men bring their grievances to committee members, then argue about them, then the first thing they know, in many instances, the grievances disappear.
>
> The employer's only complaint was that grievance committee members "are new, green, inexperienced fellows, apt to get excited

about nothing at all. As yet they can't quite handle authority and responsibility. They 'get tough' with us over little matters."[198]

Workers had used the sitdown to establish a direct counter-power to management—freedom to set the pace of work, to tell the foreman where to get off, to share the work equitably, to determine their share of the product, and the like. They saw trade unionism as a way to guarantee this power. The new CIO unions—like any organization trying to win a following—presented themselves as the fulfillment of the workers' desires. The objective of the CIO organizing campaigns was that magical phrase "union recognition"—magical because it could mean different things to different people.

The CIO indicated to workers that union recognition meant shorter hours, higher wages, better working conditions, vacations with pay, seniority, job security, an end to speed-up, and—in the words of John L. Lewis—"industrial democracy." Furthermore—and here the CIO won over the great number made cynical about unionism by their experience with the AFL—it proclaimed that the union meant all the workers would be organized together to fight the employers. It was this image that allowed the CIO to appear as the champion of the great sitdown wave, even as it was systematically opposing and crushing sitdown movements.

Meanwhile, to management, the CIO was able to sell itself with equal honesty as a mechanism for disciplining the workforce, managing workers' discontent, and protecting "against sit-downs, liedowns, or any other kind of strike"—a claim whose validity it was able to demonstrate in practice. With the help of the government, which created a rigid institutional structure for collective bargaining through the Wagner Act and its National Labor Relations Board, the CIO was able to channel the sitdown movement back into forms of organization far less challenging to the power of the corporate managers.

Police break up a picket line at the General Electric plant in West Philadelphia, February 1946, after a court order had banned mass demonstrations in front of the plant gates. (Photo permission of Wide World Photos.)

Chapter 6

The War and Post-War Strike Wave

The institutional structures developed in the 1930s changed the relationships among workers, unions, employers, and government. Strikes during World War II and its aftermath share some but by no means all of the characteristics of earlier mass strikes.

With the coming of World War II, the divergence between unions and workers' own action deepened. When the United States entered the war, the leaders of both the American Federation of Labor and the Congress of Industrial Organizations pledged that there should be no strikes or walkouts for the duration of the war. Thus, at a time when profits were "high by any standard" and a great demand for labor meant "higher wages could be secured ... and a short stoppage could secure immediate results," the unions renounced the principal method by which workers could have gained from the situation. Instead, they took on the function of administering government decisions affecting the workplace, disciplining the workforce, and keeping up production.[1] "To cease production is to strike at the very heart of the nation," proclaimed the AFL. The CIO announced it would "redouble its energies to promote and plan for ever-increasing production."[2] Over the radio, Philip Murray of the CIO urged labor to "Work! Work! Work! Produce! Produce! Produce!"[3]

Interestingly, the unions with Communist leadership carried this policy furthest. As *Business Week* noted,

A more conciliatory attitude toward business is apparent in unions which once pursued intransigent policies. On the whole, the organizations involved are those which have been identified as Communist-dominated....

Since Russia's involvement in the war, the leadership in these
unions has moved from the extreme left-wing to the extreme right-
wing position in the American labor movement.

Today they have perhaps the best no-strike record of any section
of organized labor; they are the most vigorous proponents of labor-
management cooperation; they are the only serious labor advocates
of incentive wages.... In general, employers with whom they deal
now have the most peaceful labor relations in industry.

Complaints to the union's national officers usually will bring all
the organization's disciplinary apparatus to focus on the heads of
the unruly local leaders.[4]

As in World War I, the government established a tripartite National War Labor Board, empowered to impose final settlements on
all labor disputes. At the request of President Franklin Roosevelt,
Congress passed an Economic Stabilization Act, essentially freezing
wages at the level of September 15, 1942. The board retained power to
make exceptions in cases of maladjustment and substandard wages.

"We're going to have to call on the leaders of labor to put this
[wage stabilization] over," the chairman of the War Labor Board declared in an interview. "That is another reason for upholding the
hands of leaders of organized labor."[5] In exchange for enforcing the
no-strike pledge, unions had their hands upheld by being granted
rights that greatly aided their growth, while making them less vulnerable to pressure from their own rank and file. The unions' problem, as Joel Seidman put it in *American Labor from Defense to
Reconversion*, was this:

Since the right to strike was suspended, how could they produce
the rapid improvements in wages and working conditions and the
prompt and satisfactory settlement of grievances that would sell unionism to nonmembers and keep old members paying their dues?
How could they cooperate with management to boost production
as required by war needs, if their time and energy had to go, month
after month, into the routine but exhausting tasks of signing up new
members and keeping old ones satisfied, so that union strength
would be preserved and the treasury maintained? How could they
build the responsible type of unionism demanded by the nation at
war without the power afforded by a security clause to discipline

those who violated the contract or broke union rules? How could they afford to be discriminating on grievances, refusing to waste valuable time on those of little or no merit, if the workers thus offended were free to quit the union and persuade their friends to do likewise? If union leaders were to meet their responsibilities under wartime conditions, they argued, they had to be assured that their membership would remain high and their treasuries full.[6]

In most cases, the board met this need for "union security" by setting up maintenance-of-membership provisions, under which no union member could quit for the duration of the contract. Thus the union was "safe-guarded against a shrinkage of membership and relieved of the necessity of reselling itself to the membership every month."[7] Maintenance of membership "protected the union from those new employees who did not wish to join or those old employees who became dissatisfied."[8] By making the unions dependent on the government instead of on their members, it kept them "responsible." As the board decision on maintenance-of-membership put it:

> By and large, the maintenance of a stable union membership makes for the maintenance of responsible union leadership and responsible union discipline, makes for keeping faithfully the terms of the contract, and provides a stable basis for union-management cooperation for more efficient production. If union leadership is responsible and cooperative, then irresponsible and uncooperative members cannot escape discipline by getting out of the union and thus disrupt relations and hamper production.[9]

The board also declared:

> Too often members of unions do not maintain their membership because they resent the discipline of a responsible leadership. A rival but less responsible leadership feels the pull of temptation to obtain and maintain leadership by relaxing discipline, by refusing to cooperate with the company, and sometimes with unfair and demagogic attacks on the company. It is in the interests of management, these companies have found, to cooperate with the unions for the maintenance of a more stable, responsible leadership.[10]

Further, the board could hold the threat of refusing maintenance-of-membership as a club over any unions that did not cooperate. "Even a stoppage of a few hours, when engaged in deliberately by a union, was enough evidence of irresponsibility for the Board to deny it the protection of the membership maintenance clause."[11] For example, on September 19, 1942, the board denied a union security clause for an AFL union at the General Electric Company in Buffalo because it had gone on strike for a few hours in June.

The unions thrived under these conditions. By some measures the greatest growth of union membership in American history came in this period of collaboration with management and government. By 1946, 69 percent of production workers in manufacturing were covered by collective bargaining agreements, including almost all of the largest corporations.[12]

At first, the power of the government and the unions, combined with general support for the war, virtually put an end to strikes. The chairman of the War Labor Board called labor's no-strike policy an "outstanding success."[13] Five months after Pearl Harbor was bombed, he reported that there had not been a single authorized strike and that every time a wildcat walkout had occurred, union officials had done all they could to end it. With the exception of a series of successful strikes by the United Mine Workers in 1943, the unions continued to play this role until the end of the war.

Faced with this united front of government, employers, and their own unions, workers developed the technique of quick, unofficial strikes independent of and even against the union structure on a far larger scale than ever before. The number of such strikes began to rise in the summer of 1942, and by 1944, the last full year of the war, more strikes took place than in any previous year in American history,[14] averaging 5.6 days apiece.[15] Jerome Scott and George Homans, two Harvard sociologists studying wildcats, reported that "the responsible leaders of the unions were as weak as management in dealing with 'quickies,' and the government, for all its new machinery, almost as weak."[16]

Scott and Homans described a detailed study of 118 work stoppages in Detroit auto plants in December 1944 and January 1945: "[O]nly four strikes ... might be attributed to wages and more specifically attributable to union organization. Most of the strikes were protests against discipline, protests against certain company policies, or protests against the discharge of one or more employees."[17] Many involved all three. For example, one strike record read, "7 employees stopped work in protest of discharge of employee for refusing to perform his operation; 5 of this 7 were discharged when they refused to return to work; 320 employees then stopped work and left plant."[18] "If one added to this, that the international union was unsuccessful, and that the War Labor Board succeeded only after a time, in getting the men to go back to work, one would have the picture of a characteristic quickie," Scott and Homans concluded.[19]

The sense of solidarity was strong enough so that wildcats often expanded on a large scale. In February 1944, 6,500 Pennsylvania anthracite miners struck to protest the discharge of a fellow worker. Ten thousand workers at the Briggs Manufacturing Company in Detroit struck for one day over a cutback in work schedules. Ten thousand workers at the Timken Roller Bearing Company in Canton, Ohio, struck twice in June 1944 over the general refusal of the employer to settle grievances. In September 1944, 20,000 workers struck for two days at the Ford Willow Run bomber plant against the transfer of workers in violation of seniority rules.[20]

This form of resistance became an industrial tradition, into which new workers were initiated. For instance, one company set a high output standard in an operation in which many young and inexperienced workers were employed. The newcomers strove to meet the standard until an old-timer came and told them they ought to stick together and turn out a good deal less. The company fired the old-timer and several of the new workers; the other workers in the plant responded with a wildcat.[21]

Those who worked together functioned as an informal organization. As Scott and Homans found, "In almost all instances a wildcat strike presupposes communication and a degree of informal group organization. The strike had some kind of leadership, usually from within the group, and the leaders do some kind of planning, if only but a few hours or minutes ahead."[22] Many official labor leaders, in contrast, "were dealing more with War Labor Board decisions and policies relating to the union as a whole than with the feeling of the men in the lines.... [N]o company president could have been more bewildered and irritated than a representative of the central office of the union, called in to stop a wildcat strike."[23]

In many cases, the strikes were directed against decisions of the War Labor Board. For example, in October 1943, the union representing workers at the National Malleable and Steel Castings Company in Cleveland requested a wage increase from the board. After nine months, the board granted an increase of only two and one-half cents an hour; in late July, 1,100 workers struck against the decision. Similarly, maintenance workers in twenty Detroit-area auto plants struck in October 1944, idling 50,000, when their request for an eleven-cent increase in hourly wages sat before the board for nine months without action.[24]

The unions and the employers worked hand-in-hand to suppress the wildcats. For example, at the Bell Aircraft Corporation plant in Marietta, Georgia, employees in the electrical department, most of them women, left their jobs after the transfer of a supervisor. Union officials ordered them back to work, but the workers held out for six hours. Next they were called to a meeting in the plant labor relations office. Union officials told them they had forfeited union protection when they broke the no-strike pledge, then company officials handed out discharge slips to the seventy workers.[25] In the Akron rubber industry, "some plants had work stoppages almost daily over minor grievances, dissatisfaction with wage rates." In a typical response, United Rubber Workers president Sherman H. Dalrymple one week expelled seventy-two combat-tire-band builders who participated in a wildcat at General Tire and Rubber, and two mill-room workers blamed for leading a strike at Goodyear. This amounted to firing, *Business Week* reported: "[M]anagement was obliged to conform to the maintenance of membership clause in the rubber contracts and dismiss the expelled workers because they are no longer union members in good standing.... General and Goodyear are expected to notify the appropriate local draft boards of the dismissals, and the change in occupational status of the strikers may subject them to reclassification."[26] When Dalrymple's home local, Goodrich Local 5, retaliated by voting to expel him for violating the union constitution, the union's executive board backed down and reinstated all but seven of the wildcatters.

Detroit, the center of U.S. defense production, was likewise the center of the strike movement. Detroit papers had carried reports on a dozen strikes a week on the average for the first three months of 1944. At Ford, two or three a week were common. Occasionally they became violent. For example, a crowd of workers overpowered a plant protection man and demolished the office and records of a labor relations officer for whom they were searching. The president of the Ford local promised to take "whatever measures are necessary to wipe out rowdyism in Local 600." Twenty-six "ringleaders" were fired and ninety-five more were disciplined with the tacit approval of the UAW officials. "Implementation of this policy in the Ford case was hailed by management people, who feel that only a few examples of this kind are necessary to bring labor relations back to a level keel," *Business Week* reported.[27] When members of Local 600 moved for a strike vote against the penalties, the officers quickly adjourned the meeting.

During the forty-four months from Pearl Harbor to V-J Day, there were 14,471 strikes involving 6,774,000 strikers—more than during any period of comparable length in United States history.[28] In 1944 alone, 369,000 steel and iron workers, 389,000 auto workers, 363,000 other transportation equipment workers, and 278,000 miners were involved in strikes.[29] In many cases, the "quickie" tactics were extremely effective in improving working conditions and easing the burden of company discipline. Workers virtually made extra holidays for themselves around Christmas and New Year's, holding illicit plant parties and cutting production to a trickle. Workers often created free time for themselves on the job by other means. On one occasion, workers in an aircraft plant staged a necktie-cutting party in the middle of working hours, roaming through the plant snipping off ties of fellow workers, supervisors, and managers. The wildcat tradition and organization gave workers a direct counter-power over such management decisions as the speed of work, number of workers per task, assignment of foremen, and organization of work. While the effects are impossible to measure, industry representatives claimed a decrease of "labor efficiency" of 20 to 50 percent during the war period.[30]

•

No doubt most union leaders would have liked a continuation of wartime conditions—protection by government and cooperation with management—into the post-war period. Presidents Murray and Green of the CIO and AFL signed a "Charter of Industrial Peace" with Eric Johnston, president of the U.S. Chamber of Commerce, in March 1945. "It's Industrial Peace for the Post-War Period!" read the front-page headline of *C.I.O. News*.[31] But this was mostly wishful thinking. As early as July 1944, *The New York Times* acknowledged "labor-management antagonisms which forecast a post-war period of great turmoil in labor relations."[32] The real question was not whether there would be strikes, but whether they would be union-controlled or wildcats. *Business Week* found many who expected "large numbers of quickie strikes.... [T]hese analysts admit that the end results of such stoppages may prove as substantial as those of the premeditated, big-league strikes."[33]

Business was resolved to "restore efficiency" and raise productivity—in many cases below pre-war standards—by breaking the *de facto* control of production won by workers during the war. To this end, employers demanded from the unions "company security" against wildcats and a recognition of management's "right to manage." The unions' program after the war was, as industrial relations specialist Clark Kerr put it, "a continuation substantially of the *status quo*."[34] Union officials set as their main bargaining objective the maintenance of wartime incomes. Through loss of overtime and downgrading of workers, the weekly wages of non-war workers decreased 10 percent between spring 1945 and winter 1946; war workers lost 31 percent[35] and were making 11 percent less spendable income than they were in 1941.[36] A government study released in May 1946 found that "in most cases, wages during the first phase of reconversion were inadequate for the maintenance of living standards permitted by earnings in the year preceding the Pearl Harbor attack."[37] To compensate for these losses and to re-establish rank-and-file support, the unions bargained for substantial increases in hourly wages.

With the end of the war, the expected strike wave began. In September 1945, the first full month after the Japanese surrender, the number of work days lost to strikes doubled. It doubled again in October.[38] Forty-three thousand oil workers struck in twenty states on September 16.[39] Two hundred thousand coal miners struck on September 21 to support the supervisory employees' demand for collective bargaining. Forty-four thousand Northwest lumber workers, seventy thousand Midwest truck drivers, and forty thousand machinists in San Francisco and Oakland all struck. East Coast longshoremen struck for nineteen days, flat glass workers for 102 days, and New England textile workers for 133 days.[40] These were but a prelude to the great strikes of 1945 and 1946.

Three days after Japan surrendered, the United Auto Workers requested from General Motors a 30 percent increase in wage rates—without a price increase—to maintain incomes. The company offered a 10 percent cost-of-living increase and told the union its prices were none of the union's business. United Auto Workers president R.J. Thomas stated he hoped that a settlement could be reached "without a work stoppage," but by early September some ninety auto and auto parts plants around Detroit were already on strike, and the union decided to order a strike vote.[41] When GM failed to respond to a union offer to have all issues settled by arbitration if the company would open its books for public examination, 225,000 workers walked out November 21.

The auto strikers were soon joined by workers throughout industry. On January 15, 1946, 174,000 electrical workers struck. The next day, 93,000 meatpackers walked out. On January 21, 750,000 steelworkers struck, the largest strike in United States history. At the height of these and 250 lesser disputes, 1.6 million workers were on strike.[42] On April 1, 340,000 soft-coal miners struck, causing a nationwide brown-out. A nationwide railroad strike by engineers and trainmen over work-rule changes on May 23 brought "an almost complete shutdown of the nation's commerce."[43]

The first six months of 1946 marked what the U.S. Bureau of Labor Statistics called "the most concentrated period of labor-management strife in the country's history," with 2,970,000 workers involved in strikes starting in this period.[44] The strike wave was not limited to industrial workers. Strikes were unusually widespread among teachers, municipal workers, and utility workers, and there were more strikes in transportation, communication, and public utilities than in any previous year.[45] By the end of 1946, 4.6 million workers had been involved in strikes; their average length was four times that of the war period.[46]

The government moved in quickly to contain the strike movement. As President Harry Truman wrote, "it was clear to me that the time had come for action on the part of the government."[47] In the auto dispute, he appointed a "fact-finding board" and appealed to the strikers to return to work pending its decision; similar boards followed for numerous other industries. The findings of the General Motors strike board, generally followed by the other boards as well, recommended a 19.5 percent wage increase, six cents above the corporation's last offer and a little more than half of what the union demanded as necessary to retain wartime incomes. General Motors refused to accept the recommendation.

Where fact-finding boards were not sufficient to set limits to the strike wave, the government turned to direct seizures, still authorized under wartime powers. On October 4, 1945, President Truman directed the Navy to seize half the refining capacity of the United States, thus breaking the oil workers' strike.[48] On January 24, 1946, the packinghouses were seized on the grounds that the strike was impeding the war effort—months after the war's end—and the strike was thus broken. The nation's railroads were seized May 17 to head off a nationwide strike. Workers struck anyway on May 23, and only the president's threat to draft the strikers and call up the Army to run the railroads forced them back to work. On May 21, the government seized the bituminous coal mines; the miners continued to strike, however, forcing the government to grant demands unacceptable to the operators and continue its control of the mines for many months. On November 20, the miners struck again, this time directly against the government. The government secured an injunction against the United Mine Workers, and when the miners struck anyway the union was fined $3.5 million for contempt. As President Truman wrote, "We used the weapons that we had at hand in order to fight a rebellion against the government."[49]

The unions made little effort to combat the government's attack, despite their demonstrated power to stop virtually the entire economy. Except for the miners, workers returned to their jobs when the government seized their industries, and in most cases they accepted the recommendations of the fact-finding boards, even though these admittedly meant a decline in workers' incomes below wartime levels. Indeed, by May 1947—a year after the big strikes—the average worker had less purchasing power than in January 1941.[50] In March 1947, auto and basic steel workers were making almost 25 percent less than they were two years before.[51]

Nor did the unions generally attempt to combine their strength, even within the AFL or CIO. Each union made settlements without consideration of others still on strike. Thus the division of the working class that had been the source of so much criticism of craft unionism was reproduced on a larger scale by the new forms of industrial unionism. This contrasts with the high level of rank-and-file solidarity, indicated not only by the nationwide strikes of 1946 but also by general strikes in Lancaster, Pennsylvania; Stamford, Connecticut; Rochester, New York; and Oakland, California.

Indeed, most union leaders would have preferred to avoid the strikes of 1946 altogether. They led them only because the rank and file were determined to strike anyway, and only by leading the strikes could the unions retain control of them. In a widely cited *Collier's* article, business analyst Peter F. Drucker pointed out that in the major strikes of 1945 and 1946, "it was on the whole not the leadership which forced the workers into a strike but worker pressure that forced a strike upon the reluctant leadership; most of the leaders knew very well that they could have gained as much by negotiations as they finally gained by striking. And again and again the rank and file of the union membership refused to go back to work."[52]

The attitude of top union officials was embodied in the preamble to the 1947 U.S. Steel contract, in which company officials pronounced that they were not anti-union, and union officials stated they were not anti-company but were "sincerely concerned with the best interests and well-being of the business."[53]

Far from trying to break the unions, management in the large corporations had learned how to use them to control the workers. General Motors' foremost demand in 1946 auto negotiations was "union responsibility for uninterrupted production."[54] The unions were willing to continue their role in disciplining the labor force. Ninety-two percent of contracts in 1945 provided automatic arbitration of grievances,[55] and 90 percent of contracts pledged no strikes during the course of the agreement by 1947.[56] Wildcat action on the part of workers was the predictable result of this union-management cooperation. In U.S. Steel alone, there were sixty-three unauthorized strikes in 1946.[57]

The war integrated the American economy more than ever before. The conditions affecting workers in 1946 cut across industry lines, leading to the closest thing to a national general strike of industry in the twentieth century. The potential capacity of the workers to paralyze not just one company or industry but the entire country was demonstrated. At the same time, even simple wage settlements affected the entire economy. Therefore the government took over the function of regulating wages for the whole of industry. In this situation, the trade unions played an essential role in forestalling what might otherwise have been a general confrontation between the workers of a great many industries and the government, supporting the employers. The unions were unable to prevent the post-war strike wave, but by leading it they managed to keep it under control. Nonetheless, they were unable to prevent wildcat strikes and other direct challenges by workers to management control.

Chapter 7

The Unknown Labor Dimension of the Vietnam War Era Revolt

The late 1960s and early 1970s are remembered in American history as an era of revolt. University struggles that started with the Berkeley student strike of 1964 became a virtually national student uprising at the start of the U.S. invasion of Cambodia in 1970. Forty-five percent of high school teachers polled in 1970 reported "student unrest" in their schools. Black ghetto rebellions began with the Watts riot and became a nationwide movement in the 1967 upheaval following the assassination of Dr. Martin Luther King, Jr. Direct action developed over rent strikes, housing, and welfare issues in dozens of cities. The women's liberation movement launched a direct assault on the institutions of male dominance. Many American soldiers in Vietnam turned against the war and increasingly engaged in acts of resistance. In 1970 alone, the Pentagon reported 209 incidents of American servicemen using fragmentation grenades to kill other Americans, usually officers or non-commissioned officers.[1]

Often ignored in accounts of the Vietnam War era is the fact that it was also a period of labor revolt. The number of workers striking and the number of work days lost to strikes reached the highest level in the past half-century.[2] Despite the merger of the American Federation of Labor and the Congress of Industrial Organizations in 1955, the proportion of workers in unions gradually declined. Most employers accepted unions as part of the system, while unions made few attempts to challenge the status quo. As a result, workers' action in the late 1960s and early 1970s was increasingly independent of union leaderships, with wildcat strikes, contract rejections, informal direct action on the job, and rank-and-file caucuses all reaching their highest levels in the post-World War II era.

•

Early in 1970, United Auto Workers president Walter Reuther observed, "There is a new breed of workers in the plant who is less willing to accept corporate decisions that preempt his own decisions.... There is a different kind of worker than we had twenty-five or thirty years ago."[3]

The New York Times detailed the change:

The younger generation, which has already shaken the campuses, is showing signs of restlessness in the plants of industrial America.

Many young workers are calling for immediate changes in working conditions and are rejecting the disciplines of factory work that older workers have accepted as routine.

Not only are they talking back to their foremen, but they also are raising their voices in the union halls complaining that their union leaders are not moving fast enough.

Leaders and young workers ... said in recent interviews that they saw increasing dissatisfaction and militancy.

The new, younger workers, they say:

Are better educated and want treatment as equals from the bosses on a plant floor. They are not as afraid of losing their jobs as the older men and often challenge the foreman's orders.

Do not want work they think hurts their health or safety, even though old-timers have done the same work for years.

Want fast changes and sometimes bypass their own union leaders and start wildcat strikes.

And at the heart of the new mood, the union men said, there is a challenge to management's authority to run its plants, an issue that has resulted in some of the hardest-fought battles between industry and labor in the past.

"The worker wants the same rights he has on the street after he walks in the plant door," said Jim Babbs, a 24-year-old worker who is a U.A.W. officer at Wixom. "This is a general feeling of this generation whether it's a guy in a plant or a student on a campus, not wanting to be an I.B.M. number," he said....

[T]he president of U.A.W. Local 36 ... pointed to a paragraph in a 1967 contract and said:

"If there isn't a change in this section soon there's going to be a revolt against the union here."

The section says that the company retains the sole right to maintain order and efficiency in its plants and operations; to hire, lay off, assign, transfer and promote employees, and to determine the starting and quitting time and the hours worked.

"To the young guy this means the company has all the rights and he's just part of the machinery.... They want to equalize things a little."

The young fight back, he said, by challenging the orders of foremen in the sprawling assembly plant that turns out luxury Lincoln and Thunderbird cars....

When they challenge a foreman, he added, they may be disciplined, and that raises another cry of injustice.

The foreman can immediately discipline a worker by barring him from the plant but a worker who feels he has been punished unjustly must follow a grievance procedure that sometimes lasts up to a year.

"They're willing to strike to win that one.... They want to change the idea that you're guilty until proven innocent. And just like the students they want it changed now."

A steelworkers union official said:

"Most of the older workers in my area are immigrants. They're somewhat afraid of authority. When a foreman pushes them around they take it. The young generation coming in now won't take that. They want to be asked to do something, not to be told to do it."

He recalled that young workers had sparked several wildcat strikes over the way an employee had been treated by a foreman. Last month, he said, young workers led a three-day wildcat strike in a brick manufacturing plant after a foreman disciplined a worker for carelessness in operating a lift truck.

"The older generation would have filed a grievance," he said. "The young people have no faith in that. They want it settled right away. There's a big explosion coming in the industrial unions."

The argument that workers should be satisfied with the gains won by the unions in the past cut little ice with younger workers. I.W. Abel, president of the United Steel Workers union, said that one cause of the unrest was that "young workers don't appreciate what the union has built ... [T]hey didn't go through the rough times."

As UAW education director Brendan Sexton complained, "The style of the young is very different from that of the old-timers ... [T]hey understand a lot less about power, the potential and the limits." The young are impatient for change and more militant, Sexton said, while compromise is part of the union movement. "Even in the toughest unions there comes a time to settle."[4]

The result was the development of widespread action by workers—especially younger workers—independent of and even against the unions. It could be seen at many levels, including resistance to management and union authority on the job, work stoppages, wildcat strikes, strikes over "local issues," and opposition to union-negotiated contracts.

The Wall Street Journal reported in the summer of 1970 that workers were piling up so many grievances that "observers of the labor-management scene ... almost unanimously assert that the present situation is the worst within memory." An official of a large UAW local in Detroit complained, "I've had more grievances dumped on my desk in the past two months than I had all last year."

A large proportion of these grievances resulted from company efforts to cut labor costs in the face of the 1970 recession by laying off and downgrading workers and through speed-up. As a Chicago shop steward put it, "A foreman with a fast monkey wrench can speed up a line quite a bit. It's a constant battle you have to fight, and it's gotten much worse lately."[5]

Significantly, workers did not respond to the recession by driving themselves harder in their work. According to *The Wall Street Journal*, corporate officials were surprised to learn that "morale in many operations is sagging badly, intentional work slowdowns are cropping up more frequently and absenteeism is soaring."

Production workers in some facilities, long accustomed to fat paychecks due to overtime, began to stretch out their work to keep the overtime coming, and to forestall any layoff.... [M]en such as Mr. Burke at Otis [Elevator Co.] contend the problem [of declining worker productivity] is so widespread it's their major headache at the moment.

Another factor that contributed to lower productivity, according to Prof. Cummins at Case Western Reserve, is the pickup in "group therapy sessions," when employees gather around watercoolers and elsewhere to moan about layoffs, past or pending. An office worker at the Otis unit in Cleveland says he noticed that such sessions were well attended "almost every time I went to the men's room" ... [A] metallurgist at an Ohio steel plant that downgraded some workers says many felt the company was unfair to them and slowed down "to get even with the company."[6]

In 1968, a young man named Bill Watson went to work in an auto factory in the Detroit area. In the year he spent there he discovered what he considered a "new form of organization," informal, separate from the union, whose purpose was not negotiation with management but "taking control of various aspects of production," introducing a virtual "counter-planning" by the workers opposing the plans of management.

One dramatic example concerned a six-cylinder model hastily planned by the company without any interest in the life or precision of the motor. It ran roughly, workers in the motor-test area complained, and workers submitted dozens of suggestions for improving the motor and modifying its design. Workers throughout the plant became interested and were convinced that certain changes would solve the problems, but all suggestions were ignored.

[T]he contradictions of planning and producing poor quality, beginning as the stuff of jokes, eventually became a source of anger. In several localities of the plant organized acts of sabotage began. They began as acts of misassembling or even omitting parts on a larger-than-normal scale so that many motors would not pass inspection. Organization involved various deals between inspection and several assembly areas with mixed feelings and motives among those involved—some determined, some revengeful, some just participating for the fun of it. With an air of excitement, the thing pushed on.

Temporary deals unfolded between inspection and assembly and between assembly and trim, each with planned sabotage. Such things were done as neglecting to weld unmachined spots on motor heads; leaving out gaskets to create a loss of compression; putting in bad or wrong-sized spark plugs; leaving bolts loose in the motor assembly; or, for example, assembling the plug wires in the wrong firing order so that the motor appeared to be off balance during inspection. Rejected motors accumulated.

In inspection, the systematic cracking of oil-filter pins, rocker-arm covers, or distributor caps with a blow from a timing wrench allowed the rejection of motors in cases in which no defect had been built in earlier along the line. In some cases motors were simply rejected for their rough running.

There was a general atmosphere of hassling and arguing for several weeks as foremen and workers haggled over particular motors. The situation was tense, with no admission of sabotage by workers and a cautious fear of escalating it among management personnel.

In the end, the entire six-cylinder assembly and inspection operation was moved to an area at the end of the plant and staffed with new workers. "In the most dramatic way, the necessity of taking the product out of the hands of laborers who insisted on planning the product became overwhelming."[7]

Just before the time for model changeover, the company attempted to build the last V-8 engines with parts rejected during the year. The motor-test area protested, but management sent down representatives to insist that inspectors pass the motors.

It was after this that a series of contacts, initiated by the motor-test men, took place between areas during breaks and lunch periods. Planning at these innumerable meetings ultimately led to plant-wide sabotage of the V-8's. As with the 6-cylinder-motor sabotage, the V-8's were defectively assembled or damaged en route so that they would be rejected. In addition to that, the inspectors agreed to reject something like three out of every four or five motors.

The result was stacks upon stacks of motors awaiting repair, piled up and down the aisles of the plant. This continued at an accelerating pace up to a night when the plant was forced to shut down, losing more than 10 hours of production time. At that point there were so many defective motors piled around the plant that it was almost impossible to move from one area to another.

These actions aimed at partial control of what was produced. Others were designed to get control of working time.

> A plant-wide rotating sabotage program was planned in the summer to gain free time. At one meeting workers counted off numbers from 1 to 50 or more. Reportedly similar meetings took place in other areas. Each man took a period of about 20 minutes during the next two weeks, and when his period arrived he did something to sabotage the production process in his area, hopefully shutting down the entire line. No sooner would the management wheel in a crew to repair or correct the problem area than it would go off in another key area. Thus the entire plant usually sat out anywhere from 5 to 20 minutes of each hour for a number of weeks due to either a stopped line or a line passing by with no units on it.[8]

In other cases, large-scale contests and games, such as water fights with fire hoses on hot days, were organized "to turn the working day into an enjoyable event."[9]

Likewise, workers imposed counter-plans for getting the work done. For example, workers established

> a complete alternative break system … whereby they create large chunks of free time for each other on a regular basis. This plan involves a voluntary rotation of alternately working long stretches and taking off long stretches. Jobs are illegally traded off, and men relieve each other for long periods to accomplish this. The smuggling of men through different areas of the plant to work with friends is yet another regular activity requiring no small amount of organization.[10]

On one occasion, management scheduled an inventory that was to last six weeks.

> They held at work more than 50 men who otherwise would have been laid off with 90 per cent of their pay. The immediate reaction to this was the self-organization of workers, who attempted to take the upper hand and finish the inventory in three or four days so they could have the remaining time off. Several men were trained in the elementary use of the counting scales while the hi-lo truck drivers set up an informal school to teach other men to use their vehi-

cles. Others worked directly with experienced stock chasers and
were soon running down part numbers and taking inventory of the
counted stock. In several other ways the established plan of ranking
and job classification was circumvented in order to slice through the
required working time.[11]

Management forced this process to a halt, even though it would have
saved money, claiming that legitimate channels of authority, training,
and communication had been violated.

Watson noted that a majority of the workers participating in these
actions were either black or newly arrived Southern whites. "Despite
the prevalence of racist attitudes ... these two groups functioned together better than any other groups in the plant ... [W]omen were no
less active than men ... [W]orkers from eighteen to thirty-five were
the most militantly anti-union and the most willing to go beyond the
established channels in their work actions."[12]

> What stands out in all this is the level of cooperative organization of
> workers in and between areas. While this organization is a reaction
> to the need for common action in getting the work done, relation-
> ships like these also function to carry out sabotage, to make collec-
> tions, or even to organize games and contests which serve to turn
> the working day into an enjoyable event.... There is planning and
> counter-planning in the plant because there is clearly a situation of
> dual power.[13]

"Within these new independent forms of workers' organization,"
Watson suggested, "lies a foundation of social relations at the point of
production which can potentially come forward to seize power in a
crisis situation and give new direction to the society."[14]

•

Workers' desire for more control over workplace conditions led to
a steadily rising number of strikes over so-called "local issues." In
1970, General Motors, for example, received more than 39,000 "local
demands."[15] According to GM, demands included:

> shift schedules, vacations, work assignments, entertainment or rec-
> reation for employees, providing legal advice, additional wash-up
> facilities, nursery care for [children] of working parents in the plant,

employees' cars to be serviced and maintained at company expense, and health and safety.

Other demands dealt with assignment of overtime, speed of production lines, the amount of relief time, choices of work turns, the use of new technology and grievance procedures.[16]

These issues dealt with every aspect of life in the factory.[17]

The relation of local and national contracts in the auto industry had been established in 1955. A contract that had been hailed as a great union victory over GM had unexpectedly been followed by a coast-to-coast wildcat over "local issues" that crippled production. In response, union and management agreed to incorporate local issues into the national collective bargaining agreement in order to control such strikes. Nonetheless, as *The Wall Street Journal* observed, "To the auto companies and the UAW's top leaders, these [local] disputes have become a nightmare."[18] Indeed, while headlines during strikes focused on wage issues, "local issues" increasingly became the heart of labor disputes, in the auto industry above all. One measure of this was General Motors' estimate that between 1955 and 1967 it lost 14.9 million hours of work in strikes over national issues, but 101.4 million hours in "local disputes."[19]

The right to strike over local disputes even during the life of the contract also became a major issue in the steel industry. Typical was the complaint of the president of Local 2698 in Monessen, Pennsylvania, who said that management had refused to use a better grade of coal in its coke ovens to cut down pollution. When workers refused to work in the polluted area, the company used supervisors to replace them. To get more influence over company policy and regain control of such wildcat actions, the local union leadership demanded the right to strike. United Steel Workers president I.W. Abel persuaded a conference of 600 local presidents in March 1971 not to vote on a motion to allow such strikes, though Abel conceded that a majority would have voted for it.[20]

•

The Vietnam War era labor revolt responded to national as well as local conditions. Inflation, caused primarily by the escalating costs of the war, steadily reduced the living standards of most working people. Average take-home pay adjusted for inflation fell slowly but steadily from 1965 to 1970. Partially due to the pressures generated by the 1970 Teamsters wildcat (see below), real wages rose briefly in 1971 and 1972. But in 1973 and the first half of 1974 they fell nearly 7 percent. At the end of 1974, the economy went into a sharp recession. By January 1975, unemployment reached its highest level since the end of the Great Depression.[21]

The early 1970s saw a series of national strikes independent of the official labor movement. Perhaps the most dramatic of these—and the one most resembling the pattern of previous mass strikes—was the postal wildcat of March 1970, the first major strike in the history of the United States Post Office, indeed of the federal government.

A government study in 1968 reported "widespread disquiet" among postal workers as a result of "antiquated personnel practices … appalling working conditions … and limited career opportunities."[22] The explosion finally came in New York City, where high living costs forced many postal workers onto welfare to supplement incomes eroded by the inflation of the late 1960s. Several small wildcats had already occurred, including a "sick-out" the year before by more than seventy employees at the Kingsbridge Station in the Bronx.[23] Letter carriers voted to strike March 17, 1970, and set up picket lines around the city's post offices. Twenty-five thousand drivers and clerks honored the picket lines, bringing postal operations to a standstill. The strike began to spread almost instantly, with workers throughout New York, New Jersey, and Connecticut joining within a day or two. The strikers organized themselves through informal channels. By March 19, the New York local said it had received unsolicited telephone calls from letter carriers in fifty-eight communities in a number of states saying they would join the strike.[24]

Government and union officials moved quickly against the strike. The walkout was illegal from the start, since it is a felony for government employees to strike, and the courts quickly issued an injunction against the New York strikers. James Rademacher, head of the national letter carriers union, announced he would send a telegram to Gus Johnson, president of the New York local that launched the wildcat, warning that the union's executive council was considering expelling the local because of its strike action, which was contrary to union policy. Johnson in turn urged members to return to work.

Postmaster General Winton Blount stated that national leaders of the postal unions had assured him of their cooperation.[25] The government also promised concessions if the strikers returned to work. On March 20, "The Administration won an agreement from postal union leaders ... to urge their striking workers back to work in return for prompt consideration of their demands."[26] That night, however, 6,000 postal workers in Chicago—the postal system's central distribution point—ignored Rademacher's urgings and voted to join the strike. The next day New York postal workers voted almost unanimously to defy their leaders and the back-to-work agreement:

> Branding their national union leaders "rats" and "creeps" for urging a return to work, the rank and file ... roared their refusal to accept the proposed settlement.
>
> Signs behind the rostrum in a Manhattan armory where the employees met read "Hang Rat-emacher" and "We won't take rat poison." An effigy of the union president hung nearby.[27]

Despite this open defiance, Rademacher nonetheless predicted that "reason will prevail over emotion ... and ninety percent of the mail will be moving on Monday."[28] But the action of the New York letter carriers crystallized discontent throughout the country. By March 21, the strike had spread to more than 200 cities and towns, including Chicago, Detroit, Philadelphia, Cleveland, Pittsburgh, San Francisco, Minneapolis, Denver, and Boston. "We're very close to paralysis," said a postal official. "What is still functioning is hardly worthy of calling a postal system."[29] At the Post Office's emergency command center, "increasingly thick clusters" of flashing red lights indicating struck areas blinked in twelve states. "No blue lights—indicating struck areas where employees were returning to work—flashed on the big map."[30]

Even more alarming to government and union officials, the strike seemed on the verge of spreading to other public employees. John Griner, head of the American Federation of Government Employees, reported that he had to intervene personally to prevent several strikes by his locals. Nathan Wolkomer, head of the National Federation of Federal Employees, said that NFFE locals throughout the country had indicated that they wanted to strike in support of the postal workers.[31] "There's no doubt that our members are in complete sympathy with the postal workers. The strike definitely could spread throughout the Federal service."[32] Alan Whitney, vice-president of the National Association of Government Employees, reported that "tremendous pressure" was being put on the union to authorize strikes, especially in "one of our biggest locals whose primary duty is to supply our war effort in Southeast Asia." Whitney added: "We have been receiving phone calls from our various local presidents in various agencies throughout the government and throughout the country. They have watched events of the past days and have seen postal workers striking with a degree of impunity, and their question to us is, if they can do it, why can't we?"[33]

One government strike advocate, quoted in *The Washington Star*, said: "We've learned from the postal workers that if practically everybody strikes, then nobody is going to be hurt.… After all, they can't fire everybody."

The postal strike itself, meanwhile, continued to hold. In most cities, other postal workers refused to cross letter carriers' picket lines, ignoring another plea from the federal government and from the seven major postal unions that they return to work.[34] In all, more than 200,000 postal workers in fifteen states joined the wildcat, ignoring injunctions throughout the country.

President Lyndon Johnson, turning to his last resort, declared a national emergency and ordered the U.S. Army and National Guard into New York to break the strike at its most militant point. In a television address, he echoed Grover Cleveland's declaration in sending federal troops to break the 1894 Pullman strike that "the mails must go through," and stressed that the postal workers were striking "not only against the best interests and the best traditions of their service, but against the recommendations of their national union leaders."[35] Soon some 25,000 state and federal troops arrived and began to sort the most pressing commercial mail, whose stoppage had threatened to close business and even the stock exchange.

The troops, however, did not bring an end to the strike. As strikers observed, "You can't sort mail with bayonets." Many soldiers fraternized with strikers and deliberately created chaos inside to support them. Though the administration maintained its stance of refusing to negotiate until the postal workers returned to work, congressional leaders emphasized that they would act immediately on pay increases as soon as the strike was over.

In the midst of this squeeze play, Rademacher called 500 local union officials to Washington. These officials recognized that the strike was being forced to a close, but ordered Rademacher to call a new national strike unless their demands were quickly met. A week after they had struck, the postal workers returned to work and negotiations began, with the New York local constantly threatening to trigger another strike, even calling a rump meeting of local leaders throughout the country to discuss plans for a coordinated slowdown.[36]

In strictly financial terms, the strike was a modest success, forcing Congress to grant an immediate 6 percent pay increase to all government workers and an additional 8 percent for postal workers on passage of the postal reorganization plan in August 1970.

The strikers did not play by the rules of the game. The risks they took were considerable. Striking against the government was a felony, punishable by a year and a day in jail and a $1,000 fine.[37] For the unions, opposition to the strike was a matter of institutional survival. Rademacher warned that continuation of the strike would put the union "practically out of business," since government unions whose members strike lose their right to the dues check-off by which members' union dues are automatically collected by the employer. Fortunately, for the union officials, the government was fully aware of their efforts to break the strike and therefore tried to strengthen the unions' hand. Indeed, in the subsequent postal reorganization, the government went out of its way to reinforce the authority of the major unions that supported it against the postal strikers in 1970.

•

The development of rank-and-file independence from the trade union leadership and from orderly collective bargaining was likewise illustrated in the 1970 Teamsters wildcat. After what was described as the "most orderly series" of negotiations in Teamsters' history—which management officials credited to acting Teamsters president Frank Fitzsimmons[38]—union and management agreed to a new contract granting a $1.10-per-hour wage increase over thirty-nine months. But drivers in sixteen cities, including such central distribution centers as San Francisco, Los Angeles, St. Louis, Cleveland, Atlanta, Chicago, Detroit, Harrisburg, Akron, Columbus, Toledo, Buffalo, Kansas City, and Milwaukee quickly wildcatted against the agreement in what *The New York Times* described as "a revolt against the national union leadership and a $1.10-an-hour raise that has been accepted in a national contract."[39]

The strikers quickly established mobile pickets to enforce the strike. The head of Lee Way Motor Freight, Inc., complained, "We've been unable to operate into the East because of the Teamsters union in St. Louis, whose roving pickets have stopped all our drivers at various Mississippi River crossings." He said the company had tried to route its truckers across the Mississippi at Cairo, Illinois, but had been stopped there, too.[40]

The New York Times reported from Cleveland: "Strikers here have set up a roving patrol system that they say can muster 300 men within an hour to stop any truck moving goods in the area. The strikers are allowing trucks carrying food, drugs and beer to continue, but they have become outraged when they have found food trucks carrying other cargo. There has been rock throwing, windshields have been smashed, tires slashed and air hoses cut."[41]

Mayor Stokes of Cleveland stated that violence had been associated with the strike in two-thirds of the counties in Ohio.[42] The United Press International wire service estimated that 500,000 people were out of work as a result of the strike.[43]

Fitzsimmons had previously pledged, "We will never tie up the over-the-road freight operation of this country."[44] As the wildcat spread, he sent telegrams to 300 locals urging members to return to work.[45]

In response to the wildcat, a representative of the employers vowed, "We'll stay out till the snow falls," rather than accept the rank-and-file wage demands, and stated that the Teamsters union was "standing by" the agreement it had negotiated.[46] Local and national Teamsters officials unanimously endorsed the agreement, and the director of the Federal Mediation Service issued a statement urging all striking truck drivers to return to work pending a vote to ratify the contract—all to no avail.

Since none of the walkouts were legally sanctioned, trucking companies secured numerous injunctions against the strikers. In California, workers who were enjoined from striking simply called in sick.[47] Teamsters in St. Louis ignored an injunction against them for a month, then were cited for contempt until they returned to work.[48] In Los Angeles, where strikers ignored a court back-to-work order, the conflict developed a special bitterness. Teamsters initially struck over the "local issue" of lack of sick pay. The companies responded by sending 10,000 strikers telegrams telling them they were fired, presumably so they could rehire them without seniority. The workers responded by demanding not only ten days' sick leave with pay but full amnesty.[49]

Meanwhile, the governor of Ohio called 4,100 National Guard members to combat the strike, placing the remaining 13,000 on standby alert to counter what he called "open warfare" on the highways of Ohio.[50]

> Helmeted troops, armed with M-1 rifles, were stationed in pairs on some overpasses, while other guardsmen rumbled along on patrol in quarter-ton trucks.
>
> Guard officers said their men were also guarding truck terminals and, in response to requests from truck companies and the state police, had escorted about four convoys of from 5 to 20 trucks....
>
> 200 rock-throwing strikers drove back about 50 policemen and guardsmen and the three-truck convoy they were attempting to escort out of the Yellow Freight Line terminal.[51]

The 145th Infantry—which had intervened in several ghetto riots in the previous two years and was soon to be rushed to Kent State University—patrolled west of Akron, where a number of truck terminals were operating in defiance of the strike. "The Guard sought out and neutralized the strong points, identifying two bars where striking Teamsters hung about and from which they poured out to heave everything from invective to rocks whenever trucks moved out of nearby terminals. The National Guard simply set up squads to meet the Teamsters as they rushed out." One Guard member reported, "They'd pull up short, stare at us for a while, and then go back into the bar for another drink."[52]

Despite the combined opposition of union, employers, courts, and the military, the strike held firm. After twelve weeks, employers in Chicago capitulated, undermining the entire national contract and forcing a wage increase two-thirds higher than the original union and management agreement.

The Teamsters settlement broke national wage guidelines and had a broad impact on wage levels throughout the economy. In the year following the Teamsters wildcat, real after-tax wages for the average worker increased by 1.8 percent, despite high inflation and unemployment, "because of the large wage increases that have taken place." This reversed the decline in real wages of the previous four years. In August 1971, the Nixon administration moved from voluntary guidelines to compulsory wage and price controls. According to *The New York Times*, "the essential purpose of the whole complicated system of boards, commissions, and councils created to manage the drive against inflation" was to "tighten the knot on future wage settlements and increase pressure on unions to acquiesce in the arrangement."[53]

•

Wildcat actions became endemic in the coal industry, where, as a *Fortune* article pointed out, "the aims, interests, and policies of the union and the companies became inextricably intertwined ... and the threat of a strike in the coalfields disappeared from the land" during the 1950s and 1960s. According to the Catholic labor activist Monsignor Charles Owen Rice, "The union that once protected the men from the bosses has become the union that protects the bosses from the men." As union president Tony Boyle described union policy, "The U.M.W.A. will not abridge the rights of mine operators in running the mines. We follow the judgment of the coal operators, right or wrong."[54]

In response, the miners' traditional solidarity became divorced from the union and emerged in wildcat actions. As *Fortune* put it, "Pensions, health, and safety are issues so close to a miner's heart that he will strike for them at the sight of a single picket sign, whoever carries it."[55] Management was therefore faced with "the problem of dealing with a work force that is no longer under union discipline."[56]

Perhaps the most dramatic example of such "indiscipline" was the Black Lung wildcat in West Virginia. One cold morning in February 1969, a miner at Winding Gulf District Mine in Raleigh County, West Virginia, fed up with the lack of progress on health and safety conditions, spilled his water out on the ground. This act of rebellion was the traditional appeal to other miners to join a strike. His fellow workers quit working, and within five days the wildcat spread to 42,000 of West Virginia's 44,000 coal miners. They continued to strike for twenty-three days until the state legislature finally passed a bill to compensate victims of pneumoconiosis—black lung—the miners' most dreaded disease.[57]

Sporadic wildcats followed on other issues. Three thousand miners in southern Illinois struck and ignored union back-to-work orders in a dispute over filling a repairman's job.[58] On June 22, 1970, 19,000 miners in Pennsylvania, Ohio, and West Virginia struck to protest non-enforcement of the federal mine safety act. *The Wall Street Journal* reported that "the nation's coalfields are seething with anger and disappointment over the new law."[59] "Rebel miners and others charge that the Bureau [of Mines] is acting in concert with the Boyle leadership and coal operators" to undermine implementation of the law.[60] A court order drove many of the miners back to work.

Similarly, a series of three wildcats in Virginia, West Virginia, and Kentucky, eventually involving 15,000 workers at ninety mines, was met by union opposition and court restraining orders. The strikes' primary aim was union hospital benefits for disabled miners and widows.[61] A simultaneous wildcat in Pennsylvania was ended when a court ordered the miners to return to work "or go to jail."[62] All these cases followed the miners' traditional pattern of walking out of the mines when roving pickets appeared.

In other industries, discontent simmered without boiling over into large-scale wildcats. In March 1970, for example, railroad shopcraft workers were so fed up with repeated delays in settling work-rule issues that William P. Winpisinger, chief union negotiator, reported that they were "right on the rigid edge of being out of control" and warned of a "carbon copy of the current Post Office strike," in which, as *The Wall Street Journal* added, "the rank-and-file workers defy efforts of union leaders and the government to keep them on the job."[63] Nixon Administration labor secretary George Shultz agreed that "though wildcat strikes have been contained, thanks to the action of responsible union leaders, I fear another delay might fuel the fires of impatience."[64] Similar situations existed in a wide range of industries.

•

In the strikes of the early 1970s, union and management officials often appeared as partners trying to devise a formula and a strategy to get the workers back to work and keep them there. As *The New York Times* wrote of a July 1971 telephone strike, "Union and management ... were manifestly less concerned about any real differences between them than about how to fashion an agreement that would satisfy the inflated expectations of a restless union rank and file."[65]

The strike itself sometimes actually served as part of the strategy to control the workers—albeit a costly one. A fascinating series of articles in *The Wall Street Journal* described "union-management cooperation" to get the workers back to work and build up the authority of the union in the course of the 1970 General Motors strike.[66] According to *The Wall Street Journal*, after UAW president Walter Reuther died in a plane crash in May 1970, "G.M. had to consider the crisis at Solidarity House, the U.A.W.'s headquarters, and the problems of a new union president—problems that could influence U.A.W. control over the men in G.M. plants."[67] GM's "goal was union help to bolster productivity."[68]

From the union-management viewpoint, a strike was necessary for three reasons. First, a long strike would "help to wear down the expectations of members, expectations that in the current situation have been whetted by memories of recent good times and by the bite of inflation. This trimming of hopes eases the difficult task of getting members to ratify settlements leaders have negotiated. (More than one of every 10 agreements hammered out by union officials is rejected by union members.)"[69] As one UAW official put it privately, "The guys go out on strike expecting the moon. But after a few weeks of mounting bills and the wife raising hell about his hanging around the house all day watching TV while she works, the average worker tends to soften his demands."[70]

Second, a long strike would "create an escape valve for the frustrations of workers bitter about what they consider intolerable working conditions imposed by companies' single-minded drive for greater production and profits."[71]

Third, a long strike would "foster union loyalty and pull together various rank-and-file factions by uniting them against a common enemy" and "strengthen the position of union leaders, who must stand for re-election regularly by a membership that is constantly turning over and that is wary of leaders in general, union leaders included."[72]

The strike "permits union leaders to assert their manhood—at least in the eyes of their followers. It is the best way they have to demonstrate that they are 'tough' and thus to refute the assertion, common among workers, that the union's leaders are really in bed with management."[73]

But, *The Wall Street Journal* pointed out, it was not only union leaders who recognized these functions of official strikes: "Surprisingly, among those who do understand the need for strikes to ease intra-union pressures are many company bargainers.... They are aware that union leaders may need such strikes to get contracts ratified and to get re-elected. In fact, some company bargainers figure strikes actually help stabilize fragmented unions and, by allowing workers to vent their 'strike need,' actually buy peace in future years."[74]

Unfortunately, from the union-management point of view, this approach nearly backfired in the General Motors strike. To generate pressure for settlement of "local issues," "top negotiators for both sides ... indicated they won't return to serious bargaining on national issues until the bulk of the union's 155 local bargaining units reach agreement with G.M.,"[75] even though "company and union officials say they can reach a national agreement after settling local issues in about ten days."[76]

Labor-management cooperation was so close that General Motors lent the UAW $30 million to pay the medical insurance bills of the striking workers.[77] "Both sides want G.M. to be able to resume operations quickly after a national agreement is reached."[78] But workers simply refused to agree to local settlements, raising the specter of a long strike going out of union control and defeating the original purpose of the plan.

"Both sides agree that if the strike had dragged on past Thanksgiving, it would have paved the way for an epic dispute continuing into the new year. Such a possibility could have tipped the scales within the U.A.W. from a ... strengthening of [UAW president Leonard] Woodcock to a messy strike beyond the control of the top leaders."[79]

To forestall this threat, top GM and UAW negotiators entered secret talks to settle the national contract despite the unresolved local disputes. The contract did not fulfill GM's dream of cutting labor costs by strengthening work discipline, but, wrote *The Wall Street Journal*, the company received as "consolations" "the knowledge that peace is probably assured when it next bargains with the U.A.W., in 1973, and perhaps for many years thereafter (at least over national contract issues); [and] the prospect that the U.A.W. ... emerged stronger and thus may be able to speak more confidently for its members who are younger, less loyal and increasingly distrustful of employer and union alike."[80]

•

Throughout the last years of the Vietnam War, the government repeatedly pitted its power against workers through injunctions, wage policies, and the National Guard and Army. Police, National Guard, and Army civil disturbance programs were greatly expanded, coordinated, and given the latest of technical gadgetry—often modeled on that developed for counter-insurgency in Vietnam. A secret directive issued by the Army in February 1968, and later uncovered by a Senate committee, revealed that senior officers at that time feared the development of "a true insurgency." Another directive, from May 1968, ordered surveillance of "strikes and labor and civil disturbances of sufficient magnitude to indicate a probable employment of Federal troops to preserve or restore order." The order was based on what the Army called a long-standing tradition of rendering assistance to state or local authorities in peacetime.[81] A command center was established "to procure, evaluate, interpret, and disseminate ... intelligence relating to any actual, potential or planned demonstrations or other activities related to civil disturbances within the continental U.S. which threaten civil order or military security."[82] Testimony of Assistant Secretary of Defense Robert Froehike revealed that the program was initiated and supervised by the very highest civilian officials, including Attorney General Ramsey Clark, Secretaries of Defense Robert McNamara and Clark Clifford, and presidential special assistant Stephen Pollak.[83]

In the twenty-nine months from January 1968 through May 1970, the National Guard was used on 324 occasions to suppress civil disorders—including many "labor disturbances."[84] By 1970, 680,000 members of the Armed Forces and Reserves had been trained for civil disturbance duty.[85]

All of the wildcat movements of the early 1970s were eventually brought back under control. Workers did not develop ways to maintain resistance independent of union leadership even though union leaders did not effectively protect their members' economic interests. In 1973 and the first half of 1974, average take-home pay fell nearly 7 percent.

Falling real incomes produced what was undoubtedly the largest mass protest in American history—the consumer meat boycott of 1973. As a newspaper account described it: "The boycott is being organized principally at the grass-roots level rather than by any overall committee or national leadership. It is made up mainly of groups of tenants in apartment buildings, neighbors who shop at the same markets in small towns, block associations and—perhaps most typical—

groups of women who meet every morning over coffee. All have been spurred into action by the common desire to bring food prices back to what they consider a manageable level." A Gallup poll taken at the end of the boycott found that over 25 percent of all consumers—representing families with fifty million members—had participated in it. The boycott represented, in the words of one reporter, "an awareness that, for a whole new class of Americans like themselves, push has finally come to shove."[86]

At the end of 1974, the economy entered a sharp recession. By January 1975, unemployment reached its highest level since the end of the Great Depression.[87] Nearly one-quarter of all UAW members at the "Big Three" auto plants were on indefinite layoff; similar conditions prevailed throughout American industry.[88] In many cases, the militant young workers who had spearheaded wildcats and on-the-job resistance were among the first laid off, due either to low seniority or management (and at times union) desire to get rid of "troublemakers." As in the recession of 1921, sudden mass layoffs took the steam out of labor insurgency.

What a recent study found for UAW members was true for many other workers as well:

> The UAW rank and file was decimated by high levels of unemployment after 1973. This did not heighten worker militancy—it destroyed it. Instead of more dramatic, collective solutions to more desperate problems, workers turned inward. Increasingly, they conceived of their problems in individual terms—concerned with their own job security, workers put their heads down and thought a fight against concessions was hopeless.[89]

The result was a period of decline for the labor movement that rivaled that of the 1920s.

•

The Vietnam War era labor upheaval resembled, if on a smaller scale, the great mass strikes of earlier periods. At the cell level of production, work groups resisted management authority and established the ability to act on their own behalf. Through informal control of production and strikes over "local issues," they reached out for control over the production process itself. Where established union structures and leaders failed to pursue the rank and file's agenda, workers acted independent of and even against them. Strikes spread rapidly from one group of workers to another and often involved mass direct action; community-based actions like the 1973 national consumer meat boycott complemented workplace-based action. Police, military, and other government forces intervened to repress workers' actions. As in previous wartime mass strikes, the government also imposed direct wage controls, putting the power of the law behind employers' efforts to hold down workers' incomes.

The Vietnam War era labor revolt was part of a broader movement that challenged many of the fundamental structures of American society. The idea of participatory democracy—that ordinary people should participate in making the decisions that affect them, rather than leaving decision-making to their rulers—echoed from black ghettos to university campuses to the consciousness-raising groups of the women's liberation movement. As we have seen, it also echoed in the workplace and the union hall.

The labor revolt of the late 1960s and early 1970s, like the other movements of the era, embodied new social values. Many young workers scorned identification with work that was merely a way to make a living and rejected the idea that workers should serve the production process rather than the other way around. At the most fundamental level, this was a response to the fact that modern technology had made the subordination of life to the needs of production obsolete and irrational. Industrial expansion and the imperative to accumulate wealth were increasingly seen as the source of many of American society's greatest problems—its environmental pollution, its stressful and atomized way of life, and its constant international conflicts. The movements of the Vietnam War era were unable to solve these problems, and the questions they posed have yet to be answered.

Sitdown strike at the St. Louis Chevrolet plant in March 1937.
(Photo permission of Wide World Photos.)

Chapter 8

The Significance of Mass Strikes

The United States has often been described as a society without classes and therefore without class struggle. In 1888—two years after the May Day general strike and six years before the Pullman strike—the famous British jurist, historian, and analyst of American society James Bryce observed:

> There are no struggles between privileged and unprivileged orders, not even that perpetual strife of rich and poor.... Not one of the questions which now agitate the nation is a question between rich and poor. Instead of suspicion, jealousy, and arrogance embittering the relations of classes, good feeling and kindliness reign.... The poor have little to fight for, no grounds for disliking the well-to-do, few complaints to make against them.[1]

It is difficult to reconcile such a view with the history of repeated and often violent mass strikes recounted in this book. Periods of mass strike, it is true, are not typical of American history. But as Charles R. Walker wrote regarding the Minneapolis general strike of 1934, "Frequently more can be learned of the character of an individual, a class or a community in a few hours of crisis than a lifetime of routine living."[2] It is at such times that the veil of stasis is rent and the forces maintaining and undermining the existing structure of society are revealed.

The United States, while founded in revolution and proclaiming itself based on the consent of the governed, reveals under its democratic veneer an ambiguous reality. Its original inequalities of race and gender are now widely acknowledged. But the emergence in the nineteenth century of a class system whose main actors are workers and corporate capitalists and the persistence of that system through the twentieth century violate the cherished tenets of the American myth. Instead of a society based on freedom and consent, we find a small, circumscribed realm of protected liberties, surrounded by vast—and now increasingly global—hierarchical institutions based on command and backed by force.

American government, while ostensibly embodying the collective will of the citizenry, in reality reflects the disproportionate power of corporations and those who own them. The threat—and employment—of private armies, police, and military force has been a continuing factor molding the so-called "American consensus." According to a study prepared for the Commission on Violence in the United States, "The United States has had the bloodiest and most violent labor history of any industrial nation in the world."[3] Control by violence, as Marcus Raskin has pointed out, is often hardly visible but is "the central fact of human relations in American society. It dictates the contours of the political structure and announces that no social contract exists."[4] Only by ignoring the most serious challenges to that structure—notably mass strikes—is it possible to ignore the central role of repression in American society.

Class is only one of many dimensions of social life; individuals' identities are rooted in family, gender, race, ethnic, national, religious, and many other relations. While some American workers are imbued with a sense of themselves as workers and as part of the working class through traditions and experiences, for many others the fact that they are workers is not incorporated in their sense of personal identity. But the realities of class impose themselves on people whether they identify with their class situation or not. Even in times of relative stability, working people to a greater or lesser extent assimilate those realities from their daily life, from the ideas of those around them, and from historical events that occasionally expose the character of class. In periods of mass strike, the realization that they are workers, that they are part of a working class, and that their problems and the potential solutions are shaped by their class situation becomes suddenly salient.

Most of the time a kind of equilibrium exists among classes. This reflects a formal or informal class compromise, which most members of the respective classes conform to whether they like it or not. This equilibrium reflects the unequal power of classes, but rarely a total domination of one over the other; it provides each with certain guarantees that they consider their entitlement. This balance is often embodied in rules and institutions ranging from minimum-wage laws to collective bargaining agreements.

Periods of mass strike reflect the disruption of such equilibriums. This may occur because the underlying power relations have shifted or because the aspirations of the parties have changed. Mass strikes challenge the subordinate position of workers and foreshadow transformations of their position in society.

In periods of mass strike, workers act outside of institutionally prescribed roles. They reinvent themselves as historical actors and as part of a group making history together. When workers strike and otherwise withdraw their cooperation from existing institutions, they reveal that those institutions are not the fixed things they appear—that in reality they depend on the living human beings whose activity makes them up. Win or lose, mass strikes reveal the truth about social relations hidden in an alienated society.

The Mass Strike Process

If, as Rosa Luxemburg wrote, mass strikes form "a perpetually moving and changing sea of phenomena," how is it possible to make sense of them? What ties together the disparate local, national, and general strikes, occupations, street fights, armed confrontations, and other actions we have seen arise during peak periods of class conflict in the United States? While every mass strike is different, certain patterns run through them all.

Let us start by isolating three related processes: the challenge to existing authorities, the tendency of workers to begin taking over direction of their own activities, and their development of solidarity with each other.

These processes often begin in the cell-unit of production, the group of those who work together. As Elton Mayo discovered in a famous study of American factories, "In every department that continues to operate, the workers have—whether aware of it or not—formed themselves into a group with appropriate customs, duties, routines, even rituals; and management succeeds (or fails) in proportion as it is accepted without reservation by the group as authority and leader."[5]

The development of such work groups was studied in 1946 by the Committee on Human Relations in Industry at the University of Chicago. In a number of factories in the Chicago area, the committee's researchers found that most work groups established a "quota" beyond which the group expected no individual worker to produce. The new employee was systematically "indoctrinated" by the work group, which expected the employee "to conform to its system of social ethics."[6] This system was backed by the workers' knowledge that management would use higher production by one of them to speed up the others. As one worker expressed it, "They begin by asking you to cut the other guy's throat, but what happens is that everybody's throat is cut, including your own."[7] The workers worked intensively for a short time to meet the quota, then used the remaining free time as their own.

> Much of the time accumulated in this fashion was used "shooting the breeze" or reading newspapers in the toilet. The observers, however, believe ... that the greater part was spent in "government work." Such work included making the "illegal" devices and fixtures which served as shortcuts in production, repairing parts damaged by men in other departments so that repair tickets might be avoided, and making equipment for their automobiles and homes. Most workers did not like to be idle for too great a time, but all of them preferred "government work" to production work.[8]

The workers saw the cooperation and sociable relaxation created by such action as valuable in themselves. As one put it,

> Sure, I think most of us would admit that we could double our take-home if we wanted to shoot the works, but where's the percentage? A guy has to get something out of life.... The way it works out none of us are going to be Van-Asterbilts so why not get a little pleasure out of living together and working together.[9]

The work groups also created their own ways of getting the work done, contradicting those indicated by management. The scheduling of work was often reorganized so that machine operators could eliminate extra time setting up their jobs. Each work group had special cutting tools, jigs, and fixtures, usually made on "government time," through which operations could be performed in a fraction of the time allowed for them. As the study concluded, "Such restrictive (and, from management's point of view, illegal) devices make necessary a system of social controls imposing, upon the individual, responsibility to the group. Essentially what results is an informal secret organization ... [W]orkers employ a social ethic which requires that each individual realize his own goals (social and pecuniary) through cooperation with the work group."[10]

It is largely in these groups that the invisible, underlying process of the mass strike develops. They are communities within which workers come into opposition to the boss, begin acting on their own, realize their need to support each other, and discover the collective power they develop in doing so. The end product of this process is precisely the rejection of management as "authority and leader," and the transformation of the work group into what one industrial sociologist described as a guerrilla band at war with management.[11]

Although the unofficial actions of these groups generally go unnoticed and unrecorded, we have been able to catch glimpses of them—from the cooperative action of the railroad workers in each town in 1877, to the wildcat strikes and informal control of production by factory workers during World War II, to the "counter-planning on the shop floor" of the Vietnam War era auto plants.

The large-scale struggles of periods of mass strike develop out of the daily invisible and unrecorded skirmishes of working life in normal times. Clayton Fountain, later a United Auto Workers official, but at the time an auto worker so untouched by unionism that he didn't hesitate to cross picket lines, described such a conflict at a Briggs auto plant in 1929, one of the quietest years for industrial conflict in American history:

According to the theory of incentive pay, the harder and faster you worked, and the more cushions you turned out, the more pay you received. The employer, however, reserved the right to change the rules. We would start out with a new rate, arbitrarily set by the company time-study man, and work like hell for a couple of weeks, boosting our pay a little each day. Then, bingo, the timekeeper would come along one morning and tell us that we had another new rate, a penny or two per cushion less than it had been the day before.

One day when this happened we got sore and rebelled. After lunch the whistle blew and the line started up, but not a single worker on our conveyor lifted a hand. We all sat around on cushions waiting to see what would happen.

In a few minutes the place was crawling with big-shots. They stormed and raved and threatened, but our gang stood pat. We just sat on the cushions and let them rant and blow. When they got too abusive, we talked back and told them to go to hell. We told them that the Briggs plant was run by a bunch of rats who did nothing but scheme how to sweat more production out of workers and that we didn't care a damn how many of us they fired; we just weren't going to make any more cushions or backs at the new low rate.

We didn't belong to a union and we had no conception of organization. There were no leaders chosen by us to deal with the angry bosses; we all pitched into the verbal free-for-all with no epithets barred. Some of the workers threatened to take the bosses outside and beat the hell out of them—in fact, they had a damn good notion to do it right then and there inside the plant.

Finally, after about forty-five minutes of confusion, the bosses relented. They agreed to reinstate the previous piecework rate. With this assurance, we went back to work. Looking back, I can see that, in a small and disorganized fashion, we tasted the power of the sitdown strike on that far-away day in the Briggs plant in 1929.[12]

This miniature revolt and innumerable ones like it, unknown to all but those directly involved, form the submerged bulk of the iceberg of industrial conflict, of which the headline-making events of mass strikes are the visible tip. Because workers do not direct production, they find it is directed to their disadvantage—in a way that tries to hold down their income, extract more labor from them, and increase the power of their employers. Against this, as in the example above, workers are forced to fight back, thus discovering their own power.

In many workplaces at different points in history, workers have organized or joined unions as a vehicle for dealing collectively with their employers. Their unions over time developed bargaining relationships with employers, operated within a legal framework established by government, and acquired an institutionalized position in the workplace and in society. In periods of mass strike, workers often organize unions or use existing unions as vehicles for coordinating their activity and confronting management and government. But they also frequently find existing unions and their leadership unsupportive or even opposed to their actions. In such cases, they may create new unions; create or use other forms of organization; or link informal work groups outside of official union channels.

Whether or not unions are present, and whether unions support or oppose it, workers at times turn to the strike. Day-to-day conflict in the workplace, the exploitation revealed in inadequate wages, and a general resentment against subordination promote strike sentiment.

As the Interchurch World Movement's report on the 1919 steel strike put it, "It cannot be too strongly emphasized that a strike does not consist of a plan and a call for a walkout. There has been many a call with no resultant walkout; there has been many a strike with no preceding plan or call at all. Strike conditions are conditions of mind."[13]

Whether triggered by a relatively trivial incident or by a strike call, at some point in the accumulation of resentment workers quit work. Already this is a kind of revolt, or, in the words of sociologist Alvin Gouldner, "a refusal to obey those socially prescribed as authorities in that situation, that is, management."[14]

When workers strike, they immediately face the problem of making the strike effective by preventing production. This means in effect denying the owners free use of their own property. The result is a frequent tendency toward *de facto* seizure of the productive apparatus by sitdown strikes, crowd action, and mass picketing. We find this as early as 1877, when railroad workers and supporting crowds virtually took possession of the railroad system of the country; it was dramatically illustrated again by the sitdowns and mass picketing of the 1930s.

When strikes seriously disrupt production for a significant period of time, they generally call forth state intervention. As the official *History of Violence in America*, published in 1969 by the President's Commission on Violence, noted, "Today, as always, employers have the legal right to move goods and people freely across a picket line and the duty and practice of police has tended to safeguard this right."[15] Further, the government has generally been held to have the right and responsibility to end strikes which create an "emergency" by disrupting the ordinary functioning of society. Finally, the government has frequently defined strikes as insurrections to be suppressed by military action. According to the *History of Violence in America*, there have been no fewer than "160 occasions on which State and Federal troops have intervened in labor disputes."[16] (Many more have occurred since its publication.) Leon Wolff hardly exaggerated in his study of the Homestead strike when he concluded that "the decisive effect of militiamen cannot be overemphasized; one searches United States labor history in vain for a single case where the introduction of troops operated to the strikers' advantage. In virtually all conflicts before and after 1892 the state guard acted, in effect, as a strikebreaking agency."[17]

Use of guards, deputies, police, militia, and army in turn has generated frequent large-scale battles between crowds and occasionally armed bands of strike supporters and the forces of "law and order." Thus by a progression we have observed dozens of times, strikes in the United States have moved toward miniature civil wars between workers and the state.

Even in workplace conflicts over the speed and organization of production, workers take over part of the management function and coordinate their own action to a degree. In a strike, the normal power of the employer to shape daily life is broken, and workers are put in a position to think, act, and coordinate their actions for themselves. Once a strike begins, it involves a tremendous amount of activity, including picketing; countering employer and government violence;

providing food, health care, and other vital needs of the strikers; co-ordinating activity; and setting strike strategy. If the strike seriously affects the population, the strikers often find it necessary to continue part of their usual work to show their social responsibility and keep public sympathy; for example, railroad strikers have generally run passenger and mail trains. This tendency of strikers to conduct social activities under their own management perhaps reached its height in the Seattle general strike of 1919, when the various striking trades provided the necessary services for an entire city.

Though the cell-units of mass strikes may be individual work groups, labor conflicts by no means remain limited to them, but rather tend to spread in wider and wider circles. Indeed, in many cases we have seen solidarity spread across even the deepest divisions within the working class. The range of this process can be seen by selecting a few examples from the many we have described above. Practically the whole body of railroad workers in America joined in the sympathetic strike with the Pullman workers, who were not even railroad workers, as did workers of a great variety of trades in Chicago and elsewhere. Scores of traditionally hostile nationality groups separated by religion, language, history, and the deliberate divide-and-rule policies of the employers joined together in the steel strike and the Lawrence textile strike of 1919. Black and white workers in such Southern cities as St. Louis in 1877 and New Orleans in 1892 joined together in general strikes supporting each other's demands.

Numerous general strikes throughout the periods covered in this book reveal the willingness of workers in unrelated trades and industries to support each other. The railroad strike of 1877 and the Toledo Auto-Lite strike of 1934 involved the unemployed and impoverished joining together in the streets with those on strike. The Homestead strike showed mutual support between skilled and unskilled workers. In the General Motors sitdown of 1936-1937, employed women participated extensively in the strike, and nonemployed wives, whose social participation had previously been limited to home and family, emerged to play an active role in the struggle. The tendency of mass strikes—never fully realized—is toward joint action of all working people.

If the mass strike is a process marked by workers' challenge to existing authority, direction of their own activity, and spreading solidarity, what is its source? If workers possessed society's means of production and managed them themselves, there would be no basis for strikes against management. But since they do not, they have to work for those who do. The result is that all workers share a subordination to the control of employers, who have the power to make decisions that shape their daily lives.

While the particular issues that trigger workers' resistance to this domination may vary, their underlying source—control of production and the product by others—is the same. This is why the most intense battles may be fought over the most trivial issues, such as a fraction of a cent in wages.

In such struggles "the issue is not the issue." The real issue is an attempt by workers to wrest at least a part of the power over their lives away from their employers and exercise it themselves. This is frequently recognized explicitly by management. As an employer in Milwaukee said during the 1886 May Day strikes for the eight-hour day, it was a question of "my right to run my works and your right to sell me your time and labor."[18] Or as Alfred Sloan, president of General Motors, wrote at the height of the Flint sitdown strike, the "real issue" was, "Will a labor organization run the plants of General Motors … or will the Management continue to do so?"[19]

This process is not merely a struggle for power between two groups, however. For out of the very necessities of that struggle develop the two other aspects of mass strikes we have emphasized above: the tendencies toward self-management and toward solidarity—qualities that, if they were extended, could transform society. Most people in their work life and community life are frequently forced to be passive—submitting to control from above. They are also largely atomized—separated from each other. What we see in mass strikes is the beginning of a transformation of people and their relationships from passivity and isolation to collective action.

The tendency toward self-management in working-class history is rooted in the simple truth that unless people direct their own activities, somebody else will direct them—in ways that prevent them from pursuing their own ends. Self-management is the only alternative to management by somebody else. At one level, this tendency arises out of the immediate needs of the struggle—keeping the workplace closed, feeding strikers, and the like. At a more profound level, all the actions of a mass strike are responses to the fact that when a small minority manage society, they will generally do so in a way that conflicts with the needs of the majority. Mass strikes are thus implicitly an attack on elite domination of society.

Of course, self-management is not the only tendency within mass strikes. It is always possible that the authority wrested from those who hold it will be taken up by some new power. We can see this, for example, in the establishment of industrial unionism in the 1930s, when the unions subsequently took over much of management's responsibility for labor discipline. When this occurs, however, conflict may reemerge between the agency attempting to assert the new authority and the subjects of that authority—as in the case of the wildcat strikes that followed the CIO's suppression of the sitdowns.

Solidarity likewise is a response both to the immediate needs of the struggle and the fundamental problems of society. In the course of social struggles, solidarity arises directly out of the realization that the struggles will be lost without it. But fundamentally it is a response to the inability of individual solutions to solve people's problems. As the powerlessness of ordinary individuals makes their position look less and less tenable, the psychology of "looking out for number one" becomes futile. The need to support others who in turn will support you becomes evident, and a spirit of all-for-one and one-for-all spreads in a bond that is at once an intellectual recognition of reality and an emotional feeling of unity. That bond is summed up in the hallowed labor movement adage, "An injury to one is an injury to all."

The reason this sense of solidarity crystallizes so suddenly is the feeling that "I will only make sacrifices for you when I can sense that you will grasp the need to make sacrifices for me." Such mutuality develops in a thousand miniature experiments taking place in the background of a mass strike. As an Akron rubber worker quoted above put it, "during the sitdowns last spring I found out that the guy who works next to me is the same as I am, even if I was born in West Virginia and he is from Poland. His grievances are the same. Why shouldn't we stick?"[20]

The end product of this process is the sense of being part of a class. This is in some ways comparable to the sense of being part of a nation, but its source and result are different from those of nationalism. The common situation of workers is that individually they are powerless, but together they embody the entire productive force of society; their solidarity is the discovery of this. It reflects the fact that in modern society individuals can gain control of the social forces that determine their lives only by cooperating. Thus, "individualism" keeps the individual weak, while solidarity increases an individual's control over her or his life. Once the consciousness of this need for solidarity develops, it becomes impossible to say whether the motive for an act such as joining a "sympathetic strike" is altruistic or selfish, because the interest of the individual and the collective interest are no longer in conflict: they have come to be the same.

This unity of individual and collective interest and the feelings of unity it generates are the necessary basis of a society based on cooperation rather than competition. From one perspective, therefore, the mass strike can be seen as a process in which workers are transformed from people competing for jobs or advancement to people cooperating in pursuit of common interests. Combined with a replacement of managers by self-management, this represents in embryo a society of free human beings working together to meet their own needs by meeting each other's needs. From this perspective the mass strike is a revolutionary process whose outer expression lies in contesting the power of existing authorities, and whose inner expression is the transformation of those who do society's work from passive and isolated individuals to a collective of self-directing cooperators acting on their own behalf.

There are evident objections to this concept of the mass strike. The most obvious is the claim that those who have taken part in the actions described in this book simply have not aimed for any such social transformation, but rather sought much smaller and more specific changes in wages, hours, and working conditions. While it is true that strikes do in fact have such specific goals, this does not prove they have no other implications. The fact that the Boston Tea Party protested the English tea tax did not thereby rob it of meaning in the struggle for national independence. As sociologist Robert E. Park argues, "While a strike may be regarded as a single collective act in which minor clashes and individual cases of violence are incidents, every individual strike may be regarded as a single episode in a larger revolutionary movement, a movement of which the participants are perhaps only dimly conscious."[21] Or, in the words of *Business Week*, such industrial disputes are not "a series of isolated battles for isolated gains. Rather, they are part of a long-term, irrepressible struggle for power."[22]

A second objection is based on an excessively sharp distinction between political and economic struggles. The former are seen as challenges to the state and therefore potentially revolutionary. The latter, on the other hand, are regarded merely as attempts to win better conditions within the existing framework of society. The weakness of independent working-class political action in America, combined with the extraordinary struggles of American workers at the point of production, can then be interpreted as satisfaction with the existing system combined with a desire to make maximum gains within it.

But in periods of mass strike, this distinction between economic and political struggles breaks down. Strikes aim not just to win concessions but to increase the power of workers within the economy; this is a quintessentially political objective, for the economy itself is a system of political power—indeed, in our society, a central one. Further, in periods of mass strike, worker action often aims to affect the law and the state. Finally, even purely "economic" strikes, as we have seen, frequently arouse the direct political and military opposition of the state, making the conflict political even in the narrowest sense.

Of course, not all strikes challenge the organization of corporate power. Classic trade-union bargaining strikes take existing power relations as a given and play only on the marginal disadvantage a strike causes the employer in the marketplace. It is precisely to the extent that strike actions go beyond this framework that they challenge the existing organization of power.

Another, related criticism is the assertion that strikers aim to increase their power only in the narrow sense of their bargaining power in the market. This is a common view of economists and some labor leaders, who see workers essentially as people freely selling a commodity—their labor—in the market. If the price of labor is too low, the labor-sellers withdraw their labor from the market. Since this is ineffective if done by individual labor-sellers, they join together in trade unions and withdraw their labor together—that is, strike—until their commodity's price is raised.

The emphasis placed by unions on the conditions of supply and demand in the market, bargaining strategy, and the organization of the labor market flows from this perspective. Union officials' conception of "what is possible" usually flows from their conception of what is possible in the existing market, a view that is applicable enough to collective bargaining strikes in periods of stability, but that renders incomprehensible the kind of social struggles reviewed in this book.

In periods of mass strike, workers think, speak, and act not as vendors in a market, but as oppressed and exploited human beings in revolt. Their agenda is based on what they need, not on "what the market will bear." Their strikes are timed not to the balance of supply and demand, but to the felt intolerability of their present condition and their awareness of their shared determination to change it. Their relation to employers and to each other is not expressed in terms of buyers and sellers, but in terms of their anger at their oppressors and their solidarity with each other.

The Course of Mass Strikes

If the inner dynamic of mass strikes shows common patterns, the particular forms they take are always different. To discover why a period of mass strike developed in the particular way it did requires looking at its particular circumstances—the approach we have followed in the bulk of this book. But we can identify a number of factors that affect the general course of mass strikes and make a number of comparisons among them.

The course of each mass strike is determined in part by the existing structure of production. Before the widespread development of industry and employees, there could be no mass strikes. In the nineteenth century, by far the most important sector of capitalism was the railroads, and so railroad strikes formed the core of the mass strikes of 1877 and 1894. Because railroads were so dominant and reached every industrial center, railroad strikes tended to spread rapidly to national proportions and to workers in all industries.

In the twentieth century, no single industry has played this role. In 1919, the basic industries of steel and coal, along with other mass employers of the unskilled, formed the mass-strike storm center. By the 1930s, the automobile was the new heart of the economy, and truck drivers, auto and auto-parts workers, and rubber workers were particularly prominent in the strikes of 1934 to 1937.

Business cycles also affect the occurrence of mass strikes. Periods of depression generate widespread social misery and bitterness among workers; not only are millions unemployed, but wages are cut and managers try to reduce labor costs through speed-up. The large number of unemployed at such times as 1877 and 1934 may provide both a source of strikebreakers and a mass urban crowd charged with anger ready to join street battles in support of strikers. Strikes during depressions are often extremely bitter, but they are difficult to win because strikebreakers may be readily available and employers have little margin of profit from which to grant wage increases or improvements in working conditions. During periods of business recovery, conversely, workers may take advantage of their improved bargaining position to conduct a great many strikes. These tend, however, to aim primarily at making up ground lost during the previous downturn. Finally, periods of rapid inflation, such as after World Wars I and II and during the Vietnam War, cause real wages to drop for virtually all workers at a time of relatively full employment, thus generating discontent at a time when strikes can generally be won.

The conventional wisdom that intensive labor conflict is exclusively a product of depression, or of the business upswing, or of any other particular part of the business cycle does not hold up on examination. Yet at another level, there can be no question that mass strikes are part of the periodic crises—whether economic, political, or military—that have been a feature of industrial capitalism from its beginnings. The mass strikes of 1877, 1886, 1894, and the 1930s were phenomena of worldwide depression. Those of 1919 and 1946 were part of the reorganization that followed two of industrial capitalism's greatest crises, World Wars I and II. The Vietnam War era mass strike accompanied the crisis of "stagflation" that marked the end of the post-World War II era of steady economic growth in the United States and throughout much of the world.

Such crises augment workers' struggles even when (as in World Wars I and II) they raise workers' wages. This is in large part because they undermine the rhythms of daily life, the patterns of adaptation to which people have become accustomed and to which they tend to cling even when they perpetuate oppression. People will generally try to adapt to even the most unpleasant situation if it seems stable and they feel unable to change it—otherwise, they would be in a state of continuous revolt. Only when something disrupts the normal life pattern and makes it impossible to go on living in the old way, or provides a new sense of potential power, will large numbers of people cease to act in accustomed ways.[23] Once objective forces have broken these familiar patterns, people begin acting in new ways. The fact that mass strikes are a response to crises in the system of industrial capitalism gives them a further significance: it means that mass strikes are essentially mass responses to the failures and irrationalities of that system.

At a time of growing discontent, in which invisible, low-level conflicts at the workplace level generate a potential basis for solidarity, the action of one group of workers often serves as the triggering example to large numbers of others. The strike and defeat of the militia in Martinsburg, West Virginia, started a chain reaction in the Great Upheaval of 1877; victory over the nation's most notorious industrial magnate in the first Gould strike was a major factor in precipitating the struggles of 1886; the Great Northern strike laid the basis for the Pullman strike and the mass strike of 1894; the successful sitdowns of the rubber workers triggered the sitdown wave of the 1930s; and the illegal strike of New York postal workers ignited the nationwide postal wildcat of 1970 and provided a model for many subsequent wildcats. Each exemplary action demonstrated the power workers held because they could stop production, often backed by their willingness and capacity to withstand violence by company or state forces, thus infusing other workers with self-confidence and an appreciation of their own power.

It is not only workers' victories that lay the basis for mass strikes, however. In many cases, it is defeat or impending defeat that drives home the need for a wider solidarity and stronger tactics. The dramatic defeat of the Homestead strike of 1892 at the hands of the Carnegie Steel Company and the state militia had a great impact on workers throughout the country, laying the groundwork for the sense of class war and the intense solidarity revealed in the 1894 Pullman strike. Similarly, the San Francisco general strike of 1934 resulted from the impending defeat of the longshoremen by the National Guard. And the solidarity that marked the 1936-1937 General Motors strike grew largely from the experience of defeats in the preceding years in isolated plants in Toledo, Cleveland, and elsewhere. Thus within mass strikes we can see an evolution based on lessons learned from the successes and failures of the recent past.

The visible events that compose mass strikes are in large part community or national polarizations. As the impact of a strike on daily life grows greater, it tends to dissolve the infinite variety of subcommunities into two opposed camps: those who identify with the strikers and those who identify with the employers. This polarization can be seen most dramatically in general strikes, such as those in Seattle in 1919 and San Francisco in 1934, where much of the population divided into two organized blocs, with the social fabric that usually held them together largely dissolved.

Violence or armed state intervention often plays a critical role in precipitating this polarization, an important reason why those in positions of authority often prefer to avoid their use. Once blood is drawn or troops intervene, social struggles are dramatized as fundamental struggles over power, to which members of each side respond by coming to the aid of their fellows. It is through such events that the hidden development of class solidarity becomes manifest.

The same process of polarization occurs nationally, although it is often less visible due to the vastness and diversity of the country, and less tangible because it takes place largely in the realm of public opinion rather than direct action. It can be seen most vividly in the Pullman strike of 1894; but in all the periods we have studied, national sentiment became polarized on class lines as a result of dramatic strikes and confrontations. The development of public opinion on the employers' side is easy to trace. It is revealed in newspapers, statements by public figures, and the action of government officials, stressing law, order, authority, and property rights. The change in workers' attitudes, on the other hand, is extremely hard to investigate, except as it is revealed in mass actions. However, a few observations can be made on the development of workers' consciousness during periods of mass strike.

At most times, most American workers have not had a strong sense of being part of a class that is separate from the rest of society. As Charles R. Walker put it, "In everyday life ... [the working class] tends with slenderer means to approximate the social fashions and cultural content handed to it."[24] Workers' style of living is often as close as they can bring it to the classes above them. This is in contrast, for example, to England, where the awareness of being part of a separate class was long expressed in a wide range of cultural forms— pubs, co-ops, benefit societies, entertainment, folklore, neighborhoods, families, and the like—regardless of the current level of industrial conflict. In the United States, such separate subcultures tend to divide much more on racial, ethnic, generational, and other non-class lines. This does not mean that workers have not felt exploited and kicked around; that corporate managers are powerful while they are powerless; and that others are rich while they are barely able to get by. But class consciousness involves more than an individual sense of oppression. It requires the sense that one's oppression is a function of one's being part of an oppressed group, whose position can be challenged only by the collective action of the group. It is this consciousness that arises in the course of mass strikes, revealed in workers' attitudes as well as in concrete acts of solidarity. As Walker notes, members of the working class "are united by a common insecurity and despite variations a common way of making a living—by wages and not profits. They are united as well by the union against them—in time of crisis—of all other forces in society. At such times, the working class for brief periods develops ideas of its *own* interest apart from the middle class, and the faint beginnings of an original culture. It produces leaders, thinks up fresh forms of organization and strategy, and above all scans skeptically its own relation to the rest of society."[25]

This transformation can at times be seen in individual lives. In times of stability, American workers generally look to individual advancement for themselves or their children as the means to escape working-class status; in periods of mass strike, millions of them risk their jobs, their meager savings, and whatever security they have built up through respectability, trade unionism, or relations with their employers to engage in collective action.

But the most important change in consciousness in periods of mass strike is the growth of people's understanding that they can initiate and control action and make the decisions about their lives.[26] We can see this awareness growing in every mass strike action, superseding the feeling of impotence that marks life in ordinary times.

Occasionally, this consciousness has approached a belief that workers can and should take over the direction of production and society. The participants in the Seattle general strike explicitly saw their own activities in management during the strike as a preparation for the time that workers would run society. As *The Seattle Union Record* reported:

> If by revolution is meant that a Great Change is coming over the face of the world, which will transform our method of carrying on industry, and will go deep into the very sources of our lives, to bring joy and freedom in place of heaviness and fear—then we do believe in such a Great Change and that our General Strike was one very definite step towards it.
>
> We look about us today and see a world of industrial unrest, of owners set over against workers, of strikes and lock-outs, of mutual suspicions. We see a world of strife and insecurity, of unemployment, and hungry children. It is not a pleasant world to look upon.

Surely no one desires that it shall continue in this most painful unrest....

We see but one way out. In place of two classes, competing for the fruits of industry, there must be, eventually ONLY ONE CLASS sharing fairly the good things of the world. And this can only be done by THE WORKERS LEARNING TO MANAGE....

When we saw, in our General Strike:

The Milk Wagon Drivers consulting late into the night over the task of supplying milk for the city's babies;

The Provision Trades working twenty-four hours out of the twenty-four on the question of feeding 30,000 workers;

The Barbers planning a chain of co-operative barber shops;

The Steamfitters opening a profitless grocery store;

The Labor Guards facing, under severe provocation, the task of maintaining order by a new and kinder method;

When we saw union after union submitting its cherished desires to the will of the General Strike Committee:

THEN WE REJOICED.

For we knew that it was worth the four or five day's pay apiece to get this education in the problems of management. Whatever strength we found in ourselves, and whatever weakness, we knew we were learning the thing which it is NECESSARY for us to know....

Some day, when the workers have learned to manage, they will BEGIN MANAGING....

And we, the workers of Seattle, have seen, in the midst of our General Strike, vaguely and across the storm, a glimpse of what the fellowship of that new day shall be.[27]

The outlaw coal strikers of 1919 similarly saw their actions as a first step toward taking over "the mines for the miners," and attempted to spread the aim of a workers' take-over of production to other groups. More typically, however, workers have aimed for some kind of counter-power over management.

One other change in consciousness—indeed in life—is notable in mass strikes. This is a break with the day-to-day boredom, monotony, subservience, and limitation of individual possibilities that most working people experience in their daily lives. This is revealed in the frequent statements by mass strike participants to the effect that "suddenly I felt like a human being, not a machine." It comes out in the gaiety and the festival atmosphere that mark so many of the mass actions we have described, even when they were tinged with anger and bitterness as well. And it can be observed in the explosion of spontaneous creativity—in tactics, in songs, in organization—that we have seen. It is this that most of all foreshadows a real change in ordinary life, in which human activity flows from individual and group creativity, rather than from a minority who direct the social activity of others in their own interest.

The Containment of Mass Strikes

Although in this book we have focused on the actions of the workers, this is of course only half the story. The other half is the action of those who oppose them.

It is a truism that ruling groups try to control challenges from those subordinate to them by a combination of repression and concessions. The detailed history of employer and government labor policy during mass strikes can in most cases be reduced to various combinations of these two tactics. As management theorist Peter Drucker wrote: "A strike is essentially a revolt.... Historically, revolts have been ended in one of two ways: by force of arms or by giving the rebels what they wanted and thus taking the steam out of the revolution."[28]

Ruling groups usually call on force and violence only reluctantly, for doing so can be a great liability. It can shatter their image of benevolence and fairness, revealing them instead as oppressors ready to kill to retain their privileges. It reveals that their authority is breaking down, that they no longer receive automatic obedience by consent but must obtain it by force. In turn, violence pushes its victims into more extreme forms of opposition. Nonetheless, employers and the state have again and again had to resort to force to maintain their position in the face of workers' action. An entire history could be written of the apparatus constructed for this purpose, from the armories built in American cities in the wake of the Great Upheaval of 1877, to the Pennsylvania Coal and Iron Police, to the industrial munitions uncovered by the La Follette Committee in the 1930s, to the military surveillance of potential sources of civil disturbances—demonstrations, strikes, and riots—revealed by the Senate's Church Committee investigations in 1971.

A general pattern marks the mobilization of the forces of repression in the periods we have studied. Generally speaking, employers wield enormous power over the local politicians in strike areas and with their assistance can put together a force of company guards, sheriff's deputies (often paid for by the employer), local police, vigilantes, and the like. They try to break up the picket lines and generally harass and intimidate the strikers. If this is insufficient to break a strike, the next step is to call in the National Guard. Often previous confrontations provide pretexts for this step; if not, employers can easily provoke or fabricate them. Once the National Guard enters the scene and forces open access to workplaces, a strike can generally be broken unless workers respond with mass action on a large scale.

On numerous occasions in U.S. labor history, state governors have sent in the National Guard to assert the power of "law and order" and assist political allies. Even ostensibly pro-labor governors elected by labor votes have called out the guard against strikers. A vivid example is Governor Floyd B. Olson of Minnesota, elected by a Farmer-Labor Party representing unions and radical farmers' organizations. Olson had personally contributed $500 to the Teamsters strike fund and stated, "I am not a liberal ... I am a radical." Yet he sent in the National Guard to arrest the Minneapolis Teamsters strike leaders and capture strike headquarters in 1934. The reason for this seeming anomaly is that the government, despite its supposed neutrality in labor matters, is legally bound to protect private property rights and the orderly processes of society, and any politician who does not will stand condemned for failing to fulfill her or his job and nurturing anarchy.[29]

The formal division between state and federal government allows the federal government in most cases to avoid the onus of repression, thus maintaining its appearance of neutrality between labor and capital. This appearance is illusory, however. The various National Guards are trained, equipped, and supported by the U.S. Army, and when the National Guard is unable to do the job, the U.S. Army has generally been available to help out. We have seen federal troops directly suppressing strikes in the Great Upheaval of 1877, the Pullman Strike of 1894 (without the request and over the objections of the governor), and in the postal strike of 1970. We have seen them poised to intervene in the textile strike of 1934 and the railroad strike of 1946, as well as in various plant seizures during and after World War II. Such events are an index of the extent to which the normal authority of dominant elites has broken down, driving them to resort to naked force.

The granting of concessions has perhaps been as important as repression in containing mass strikes. No doubt the greatest number of strikes are ended simply by wage increases and related concessions, giving the appearance of a victory for the workers while leaving the power of their employers intact. Very often the government steps in at a point of deadlock, bringing conciliators, mediation, arbitration, fact-finding boards, and the like to propose or impose a settlement of this kind. Unlike armed intervention, this presents the state as neutral or even pro-labor, since it generally recommends at least some concessions from the employers. But it also throws the authority of the government behind a return to work on terms that do not threaten the power or prosperity of the employers.

No doubt the greatest concession made to American workers in the twentieth century was the recognition of unions and the acceptance of collective bargaining. This "class compromise" gave unions the legal right to represent and bargain on behalf of their members, but it also made them responsible for strictly limiting the means their members could use and the objectives they could pursue.

American employers were far more reluctant to recognize unions than to grant wage increases, for they saw unions as a threat to their own powers. The government, on the other hand, has frequently supported collective bargaining, recognizing (as the much-cited report of the English Royal Commission on Labor argued as early as 1894) that the evidence "points to the conclusion that on the whole and notwithstanding occasional conflicts on a very large scale, the increased strength of [labor] organization may tend toward the maintenance of harmonious relations between employers and employees."[30] Collective bargaining was endorsed by all twentieth-century presidents[31] and finally required by the Wagner Act in 1935. Union representation left the subordinate position of workers intact, but provided a mechanism for eliminating those grievances that could be rectified without undermining the profit-making of the employer.

Unions represent the principal type of organization through which American workers have attempted to pursue their collective interests. Throughout this book we have seen unions serve as the vehicle for workers' action. But ironically we have also seen them blocking and undermining mass strikes. As J. Raymond Walsh, professor of economics at Harvard and former director of research and education for the CIO, explained:

> [T]he records demonstrate that most unions make every effort to settle disputes without recourse to the strike. Many unions guard against hasty strike judgments by taking from their locals all authority in such matters, and concentrating it in the hands of national officers. Frequently the national officials, removed from the heat of the dispute [and the miseries that engender it, we might add], are much more likely to be reasonable and willing to mediate than are local officials, or an irritated rank-and-file....
>
> National officers ... are much easier to deal with than union committees from the shop. Far from fomenting trouble, they spend most of their time settling disputes before the strike stage is reached.[32]

What explains this apparently contradictory role of unions and their leaders? One aspect of the explanation lies in the fact that unions—like states, political parties, churches, and other organizations—can become bureaucratized. Trade unions often started when the informal work groups described above developed into permanent organizations. Over the course of time their character changed, however, and they generally became quite separate from the workplace, often controlled from above by professional officials kept in office by their own political machines.[33] This division between the union as an institution and its members can regularly be seen in the "discipline" imposed by union officials on workers who defy company or union authority, as in wildcat strikes. In times of mass strike, the conflict between the trade unions and rank-and-file members often intensifies.

This is not primarily a question of individuals "selling out," but rather of their identifying with organizational interests of the union that are distinct from those of its ordinary members. As industrial relations analyst E.A. Ross put it, trade unions must be considered as organizations with aims quite separate from their own members.

But Ross went too far when he added, "The formal rationale of the union is to augment the economic welfare of its members; but a more vital institutional objective—survival and growth of the organization—will take precedence whenever it comes into conflict with the formal purpose."[34] Rather, unions are arenas in which the objectives of government, employers, union officials, and rank-and-file members all contend. Mechanisms of democratic accountability, along with workers' cultures and traditions, at times can override such institutional imperatives. We have seen many cases in which rank-and-file pressure—or outright union insurgency—has resulted in a closer alignment of unions with their members' will.

A key to understanding the role of trade unions in periods of mass strike is the labor contract. For most of the twentieth century, this has essentially been an exchange of certain concessions from management for a union pledge to prevent strikes during the term of the contract. Ninety percent of union contracts included no-strike clauses by 1947. (Labor contracts have been the objective of virtually all modern American unions, though many unions in the nineteenth century and the IWW in the early part of the twentieth did not sign contracts running fixed periods. Labor organizations that do not make such contracts are not necessarily subject to the dynamics we discuss here.) As long as such a contract does not exist, a union may support and encourage the most militant action on the part of workers, including spontaneous strikes, violence, and occupations.

Once employers accept a contract, however, the stability of the union and the jobs of its officials will depend on its enforcing the contract—that is, preventing strikes. The union's central office "detaches itself from the masses it regiments, removing itself from the fickle eddy of moods and currents that are typical of the great tumultuous masses. The union thus acquires the ability to sign agreements and take on responsibilities, obliging the entrepreneur to accept a certain legality in his relations with the workers. This legality is conditional on the trust the entrepreneur has in ... [the union's] ability to ensure that the working masses respect their contractual obligations."[35]

Thus we have seen unions lead determined struggles with illegal means and full encouragement of mass initiative, only to turn around after winning recognition and apply the full panoply of employers' strikebreaking tactics to put down workers' strikes—including red-baiting, physical attacks, use of strikebreakers, loss of employment, and blacklisting. This is not necessarily the result of personal corruption. Indeed, it flows from a core function of unionism—setting the terms on which workers will submit to the employers' authority. This function can be carried out only if the workers do in fact submit.

This development in the role of unions helps clarify their contribution to the two elements of labor struggles that carry the seeds of social transformation: self-directed action and solidarity. In the prerecognition period, unions generally offer themselves as the vehicle of workers' self-initiative; where there is serious worker discontent but the existing unions fail to help workers express it, new leaders or unions may offer themselves for this role. (Thus, in the 1930s, workers turned to the CIO in response to the inadequacies of the AFL.) Unions may attempt to build support by championing workers' acts of defiance against the employer and may not discourage spontaneous strikes except on the basis of bad timing.

Once a contract is signed, however, the statements of union leaders—even radical ones—often ring with the need for discipline and order, proclaiming that the responsibility of the workers is no longer to act, but to obey union orders. When a conflict arises in the workplace, union leaders are likely to tell workers not to take impulsive action, but to let the union authorities take care of it through the grievance machinery. Above all, the workers are not to strike—that is a violation of the contract that jeopardizes the union's whole relation to the employer and thereby its existence.

The sanctity accorded to prohibitions on striking during the life of a contract varies among union officials and especially among different levels of union leadership. Union leaders who continue to hold regular jobs in the workplace, reflecting their own position not as officials but as workers, often encourage their co-workers to use their power directly; this is one of the reasons that the lowest-ranking union officials are frequently involved in wildcat strikes not authorized by the union. Occasionally a higher-level official will risk the same course or will at least refuse to help victimize others who do: Kansas United Mine Workers leader Alexander Howat, confronted with wildcat strikes, "would maintain since he had not ordered the strikers out, he could not order them back."[36]

Even union leaders personally averse to conflict with employers must sometimes appear to fight them to retain the support of the rank and file. They may do this by means of collective bargaining strikes when contracts expire. In these strikes union officials may try to limit workers' initiative by keeping them under strict discipline, but pent-up feelings sometimes break out in mass action initiated by the workers themselves, workers may refuse to accept the limited objectives proposed by the unions, or workers may refuse their terms of settlement.

The same development applies to solidarity. In the prerecognition period, unions often try to show that workers' problems can be solved only through collective action. They try to build up the sense of solidarity both among those who work together directly and throughout an industry. When a strike breaks out, unless they consider it poorly timed, they try to spread it, at least to all of those who would be covered by the same contract. Once a contract is achieved, however, this process is often reversed. If a strike breaks out, everything possible is done to isolate it and prevent its spread. Any direct coordination by the workers outside union channels is either taken over or fought by all means available. Solidarity with workers in other trades, industries, and unions is undermined most of all. Solidarity is undermined not only by conscious action, but by the institutional context of union contracts under which only those in a particular union advance together. The unions' divisive role becomes most clear in the bitterness with which union leaders oppose sympathetic strikes and general strikes, asserting that they violate the sanctity of the contract (and, since the 1940s, federal labor law as well).

Finally, trade unions often help circumscribe the aspects of life with which workers are supposed to concern themselves. First, most union contracts explicitly recognize the right of management to make the basic decisions affecting the company. This perpetuates the unpleasant and demeaning character of work by preventing workers from attempting to organize the work to better suit their own convenience. It also discourages them from taking any responsibility for what is produced, how well it is made, or whether the production process poisons the environment. Thus workers are prevented from trying to make their work serve each other's needs rather than those of their employers. Second, the union framework limits workers to questions that affect their particular sector, rather than the more general questions of social organization and policy that affect all workers in common. The first blocks development toward workers' management of production, the second toward their management of society.

Of course, these characteristics of trade unionism have not always been clear either to the workers who supported it or to the employers who fought it. Generally speaking, both parties saw in trade unionism a steadily encroaching control by the workers, leading to a power at least equal to that of the employers. As Judge Gary of U.S. Steel, long champion of the open shop, put it, "the contemplated progress of trade unions, if successful, would be to secure the control of the shops, then of the general management of business, then of capital, and finally of government."[37]

But in fact trade unions often turned out to be a means for taking unformed aspirations toward such control and channeling them into demands that were "realistic"—demands that employers could meet without giving up their power or going out of business. With rare exceptions, trade unions have opposed as irresponsible and unrealistic workers' demands that went beyond this line.

Since 1877, trade union leaders have generally recognized the mass strike process and consciously opposed it, even when trying to use certain of its manifestations. This is vividly revealed in Terrence Powderly's attempt to break up the 1886 general strike out of fear of another 1877; in Samuel Gompers' and the AFL's killing off of the Pullman strike; and in the CIO's attempt to break up the sitdown movement in the 1930s.

Trade unions and collective bargaining became legally mandated and fully institutionalized in the United States only at the end of the 1930s. In the periods of mass strike that followed, the basic elements of the mass strike process were not eliminated, but were greatly modified by the institutionalization of class conflict. Mass action expressed itself largely through pressure on unions or through wildcat strikes that usually came into direct conflict with union leaders. Sympathetic strikes and the spreading of strikes "by contagion" became rarer because both were likely to come into conflict with union contracts.

As we will see in the next chapter, unions and institutionalized collective bargaining declined radically following the Vietnam War era. The role they might play in possible future mass strikes remains to be determined.

•

What about the radical parties and organizations whose self-proclaimed goal was not just marginal improvements in workers' conditions but the creation of a different kind of society? We have run across them from time to time in the course of this book—Communists, Socialists, Trotskyists, Musteites, Socialist Labor, and other parties, as well as their members in the AFL, CIO, and dualist trade unions. Yet they have had only a modest role in instigating the mass struggles we have described. They have often been preoccupied with building their own organization, whether party or union, and have often regarded mass movements as important only insofar as they added to the membership or support for such organizations. They have not infrequently discouraged mass actions or been oblivious to their more radical potentialities. For example, the Communist and Socialist union leaders involved in the Flint sitdowns of 1936 and 1937 made a point of emphasizing that the sitdowners did not even discuss the idea of reopening the plants—then or eventually—under their own management. When radical leaders have succeeded in gaining organizational control over unions, the unions have usually operated within the framework of orderly collective bargaining like any others. In those cases where their members have played a radical role in mass movements, they have generally done so in response to the conditions they shared with other participants, not as a result of their organizational connections. The most radical upheavals have generally been as much a surprise to the radicals as to everyone else.

•

The ideology of the existing society exercises a powerful hold on workers' consciousness. The longing to escape from subordination to the boss is often expressed in the dream of going into business for yourself, even though the odds against success are overwhelming. The civics book cliché that the American government represents the ordinary people and is therefore legitimate survives even in those who find the government directly opposing their own needs in the interests of their employers. The desire to own a house, a car, or perhaps an independent business supports a belief in private property that makes expropriation of the great corporations seem to many a personal threat. The idea that everybody is really out for themselves, that it can be no other way, and that therefore the solution to one's problems must come from beating the others rather than cooperating with them is inculcated over and over by the very structure of life in a competitive society.

Divisions within the working class keep workers from realizing the power they have together by turning them against each other—instead of against their employers. This has often been fostered by the employers, who deliberately imported mutually hostile nationalities; used immigrants, women, blacks, and students as strikebreakers; and played skilled and unskilled, blue- and white-collar workers against each other. But these divisions have often been perpetuated by workers themselves. In part this has been the result of traditional prejudice, suspicion, ignorance, and racism. But to a great extent it has resulted from a deliberate strategy of maintaining a favored position at the expense of other workers. This can be seen most vividly when craft unions—often controlled by particular ethnic groups, and almost invariably by white men—exclude outsiders from their trade. But it is true of all unions insofar as they use their bargaining power primarily to improve their position vis-à-vis other workers. And it is true of all who hold privileged positions within the working class: skilled, male, white, native-born, and white-collar workers. The more these groups have turned their power against other workers, the weaker the working class has been as a whole. As the sociologists Seymour Martin Lipset and Reinhard Bendix wrote in *Social Mobility in Industrial Society:* "A real social and economic cleavage is created by widespread discrimination against ... minority groups and this diminishes the chance for the development of solidarity along class lines.... This continued splintering of the working class is a major element in the preservation of the stability of the American social structure."[38]

The mass strike process we have described in this chapter is the process of overcoming these weaknesses. In mass strikes, large numbers of workers learn that they are powerless only insofar as they are divided, and that together they represent the entire productive force of society.

While many mass strikes have been defeated, mass strikes have not been a failure. As a railroad engineer observed after the suppression of the Pullman strike, "If there had never been a strike or a labor organization I am satisfied that every railway employee in the country would be working for one-half what he has been working for of late. Strikes are not generally successful, but they entail a heavy loss on the company and it is to avoid that loss that the company ever meets us at all."[39]

The same is true of the various "reforms," such as the Wagner Act, grievance procedures, seniority systems, and the like: they are largely the result of the threat of disruption and revolution implicit in the mass strike. Mass strikes have shifted the equilibrium between classes, winning for workers rights and entitlements they were previously denied. They have shown friend and foe alike the power workers possess when they withdraw their cooperation from social institutions. And they have repeatedly reinvigorated the core belief of democracy—that ordinary people can and should participate in the decisions that affect their lives.

June 25, 1994: Illinois and city of Decatur police spray pepper gas on locked out workers at A.E. Staley Manufacturing and their supporters.
(Photo by and courtesy of Jim West.)

Chapter 9

American Labor on the Eve of the Millennium

Periods of mass strike don't last forever. If they don't lead to fundamental social change, they are likely to be followed by a truce between workers and employers, by a gradual erosion of workers' gains, or by cascading defeats. Gradually or rapidly, workers' assertiveness, autonomy, and solidarity diminish. Some turn to more individual solutions to their problems: "getting along by going along" and "looking out for number one." Others may pursue their interests as members of occupational, racial, ethnic, national, gender, or other groups, even at the expense of those with whom they previously sought to advance together. Under these circumstances, working people's common interests, past achievements, and potential power can fade to nearly forgotten dreams.

The quarter-century that followed the end of the Vietnam War surely resembles less a period of mass strike than the periods of working-class retrenchment and disorganization that have often come between periods of mass strike throughout U.S. history. In 1995, large strikes in the United States hit a fifty-year low. The U.S. government recorded only thirty-two strikes involving 1,000 or more workers—one-eighth of the number two decades before—many of them ending in devastating defeats. The proportion of workers belonging to unions fell to 15.5 percent—the lowest level since 1936.[1]

But individual and narrow group strategies rarely succeed for long. The basic structures that render workers powerless as individuals but powerful collectively remain. Even in times of economic growth, workers who are weak and unorganized are rarely offered a share of the gains. In hard times, the burden of involuntary sacrifice is placed on those who can't, or don't, resist.

Surely this has been the case for the past quarter-century. American workers have seen a 15 percent reduction in real wages; the rise of the twelve-hour day and the seven-day week; loss of health, pension, and social safety net protections; downsizing, outsourcing, and the erosion of job security.[2] Young people have been hardest hit: there has been a nearly 30 percent reduction in the real incomes of young families.[3]

From the failure of old strategies comes the search for new ones. The recovery of working people's lost history can make a contribution to that search, but finding out what works under new conditions requires experimentation. In periods of defeat, demoralization, and suffering, some people try new approaches, while others watch and wait. The experiments often end in defeat, but they also serve as the basis for learning, drawing conclusions, and formulating new strategies. In them the seeds of movements yet to come can sometimes be discerned.

This chapter examines the course of workers' struggles in America since the end of the Vietnam War era. It is the story of how employers have tried to render workers powerless, strip them of their capacity to cooperate in their own interest, and treat them not as human beings but simply as a quantity of labor to be bought and sold in the market. It shows the failure of individual efforts, narrow interest-group efforts, and established labor movement strategies to protect workers against the employers' assault. But it also describes a wide range of efforts to develop new strategies for workers. In many of these struggles we find—emerging on a small scale under new conditions—the elements of challenge to established authorities, self-directed action, and spreading solidarity that are found on a larger scale in periods of mass strike.

This chapter starts with the social and economic transformations that helped undermine workers' power and set the framework for the employers' offensive of the past twenty-five years. Then it examines the new and updated weapons workers have developed to try to deal with the adverse economic conditions that followed the end of the post-war economic boom. It recounts how these tactics and strategies were used in three of the major efforts to resist the employer offensive. It traces efforts by groups once under-represented in the labor movement, including women, racial and ethnic minorities, and immigrants, to develop new approaches to organizing. It looks at the new leadership that has emerged in the AFL-CIO. After examining a series of struggles in and around Decatur, Illinois—which together resembled a mass strike in miniature—the chapter describes the Teamsters' successful strike against United Parcel Service, widely perceived as a historic turning point for the U.S. labor movement. The chapter concludes with a look at the choices workers face at the end of the twentieth century.

The Attack on Working People

The quarter-century that followed World War II has often been called the "Golden Age of Capitalism." Governments used economic regulation and Keynesian economic techniques of government fiscal and monetary policy to stimulate economic growth and even out the business cycle. The global economy sustained an unprecedented annual growth rate of 5 percent from 1947 to 1973. The United States dominated much of the world militarily, politically, and economically. Workers shared in prosperity: U.S. workers' incomes doubled in a generation. Much of business accepted organized labor and saw orderly collective bargaining and rising incomes for workers as constructive elements of the economic system. Employers accepted, in short, an institutionalized class compromise. As Henry Ford II put it in 1946, "We of the Ford Motor Company have no desire to 'break the unions,' or to turn back the clock." Instead, Ford said, "We must look to an improved and increasingly responsible [union] leadership for help in solving the human equation in mass production."[4]

The end of the "Golden Age" was signaled in 1973 when the United States entered its deepest recession since the Great Depression. By the start of 1975, nearly a quarter of all United Auto Workers members at Ford, General Motors, and Chrysler were on indefinite layoff.[5] The mid-1970s saw a sharp decline in the wildcat strikes, contract rejections, on-the-job resistance, and mass popular insurgency that had marked the Vietnam War era.[6] As one study notes, "After about 1974, workers believed less and less that militant action could improve wages and working conditions. In part, higher unemployment levels forced workers to think in terms of job security instead of wage increases."[7] Companies hard hit by the recession began asking unions for concessions, which were often granted on the grounds that they were necessary for company survival. Many workers accepted almost any concessions rather than striking.

The 1973 recession turned out to be only the start of a historic crisis of the global economy. Global economic growth fell to half its former rate. Profit rates in the seven richest industrialized countries fell from 17 percent in 1965 to 11 percent in 1980; in manufacturing, profit rates fell from 25 percent to 12 percent.[8] In the United States, the years from 1973 to 1997 represented by some measures the longest period of weak economic growth since the Civil War.[9]

At first established remedies were tried: President Richard Nixon declared himself a Keynesian and imposed wage and price controls. But the combination of recession and inflation, which came to be known as "stagflation," confounded dominant economic theories and signaled the failure of the Keynesian techniques that had been used to address previous recessions.

Corporations experienced the economic crisis that began in the early 1970s as an intensification of international competition and a fall in their profits. As Jacques de Larosiere, chairman of the International Monetary Fund, noted in 1984, there was a clear pattern of "substantial and progressive long-term decline in rates of return to capital."[10] Corporations increasingly saw Keynesian economic regulation and class compromise as barriers to increasing their profits.

During the mid-1970s, corporate and political leaders veered among very different strategies for addressing the crisis, ranging from new forms of global cooperation (advocated by the Trilateral Commission) to restored nationalist economic and military mobilization (advocated by the Committee on the Present Danger). Gradually a new corporate agenda emerged that aimed to replace nationally regulated capitalism with a new "global free-market capitalism."

At the core of the new agenda was economic globalization. While in a sense the economy had been global for 500 years, in the 1970s corporations developed an unprecedented ability to move capital around the world with little regard for national boundaries. Goods and services were increasingly produced by a "global assembly line" in which different phases of production occurred in a series of locations in different countries. Corporations promoted government policies designed to reduce barriers to capital mobility worldwide. This included the reduction of protectionist measures and the creation and/or expansion of global institutions such as the World Trade Organization, the World Bank, and the International Monetary Fund and regional ones such as NAFTA (the North American Free Trade Agreement) and the European Union to create a global governance structure to protect and further their interests.[11] Globalization allowed business to pit workers, communities, and whole countries against each other worldwide, establishing what has been called a "global hiring hall." Globalization was in some ways comparable to the shift from local to national corporations and markets in nineteenth-century America—and had similarly drastic effects on unions and workers.

Globalization was accompanied by a new agenda for government. Instead of encouraging government to manage social conflict through interventionist economic and social policies, the new corporate agenda promoted deregulation, privatization of government functions, acceptance of high unemployment, gutting of the welfare state, and government encouragement for wage reductions and corporate attacks on labor.

Finally, corporations reorganized themselves. From the "merger movement" at the start of the twentieth century, American corporations had aimed to integrate the entire process of production and distribution from raw materials to the consumer into one centralized enterprise. For most of the century, a handful of such integrated enterprises dominated each major industry. In the face of increased globalization, corporations reorganized into what Bennett Harrison has described as an "emerging paradigm of networked production." They pursued "lean production" by downsizing in-house operations to "core competencies," farming out other work to "rings" of outside suppliers. Corporations constructed "strategic alliances among one another, both within and, especially, across national borders." Harrison describes this "emerging paradigm of networked production" as concentration of control combined with decentralization of production.[12] "Lean production, downsizing, outsourcing, and the growing importance of spatially extensive production networks governed by powerful core firms and their strategic allies, here and abroad, are all part of businesses' search for 'flexibility,' in order to better cope with heightened global competition."[13] Privatization led to a similar transformation in the public sector, with many government functions parceled out among a ring of private (often non-union) subcontractors.

Overall, the new corporate agenda constituted an end to the class compromise that characterized the period 1947-1972. As United Auto Workers president Douglas Fraser put it in 1978:

> The leaders of industry, commerce and finance in the United States have broken and discarded the fragile, unwritten compact previously existing during a past period of growth and progress.... [That compact] survived in part because of an unspoken foundation: that when things got bad enough for a segment of society, the business elite "gave" a little bit—enabling government or interest groups to better conditions for that segment....
>
> But today, I am convinced there has been a shift on the part of the business community toward confrontation, rather than cooperation.... I believe leaders of the business community, with few exceptions, have chosen to wage a one-sided class war on this country.[14]

Management abandoned the idea that stable employment created a stable market for their products and that stable, industry-wide collective bargaining prevented destructive forms of labor conflict and industry competition. Virtually all elements of the new corporate agenda helped capital cut real wages, reduce workforces, and speed up production, thereby helping to restore profitability. Some companies raised profits through direct attacks on workers' wages and benefits. Others benefited from a changing balance of forces—for example, from increased unemployment and the threat (or reality) of corporations moving operations to low-cost areas abroad.

Much of the new corporate agenda was already being implemented at the end of the Carter Administration. But its full implementation was achieved by Ronald Reagan's political alliance between big business and diverse "new right" groups working to reestablish hierarchies and cultural conformities eroded in the Vietnam War era. These groups represented a reaction against feminism, against gay liberation, against autonomous youth culture, against the advances of blacks and other minorities, against labor militancy, against the questioning of militarism and nationalism, and more generally against the acceptance of social diversity. Their principal goal was to resist the redistribution of power by scapegoating and repressing those they found socially or psychologically threatening. These groups provided the mass electoral and activist base for economic and social policies that benefited only the wealthiest individuals and most powerful corporations.

On taking office in 1981, the Reagan Administration deliberately deepened the already serious recession, cut the fraying social safety net, and began pulling the teeth out of agencies that provided some protection of workers' rights, such as the National Labor Relations Board and the Occupational Safety and Health Administration. These measures made workers more vulnerable to the threat of impoverishment and workplace injury and weakened unions' bargaining power.

Soon after Reagan's inauguration, the air traffic controllers' union, PATCO, struck. Reagan announced that if the controllers didn't return to work within forty-eight hours, the government would fire all of them. When the strike continued, the government permanently terminated the striking controllers and replaced them with supervisors, military controllers, and new hires.

The firing and replacement of an entire workforce had not been seen since the Great Depression. If permitted it would mean a drastic shift in the balance of power between unions and employers. There were widespread calls for job actions in support of PATCO, but AFL-CIO president Lane Kirkland sent a letter to affiliates attacking the idea: "I personally do not think that the trade union movement should undertake anything that would represent punishing, injuring or inconveniencing the public at large for the sins or the transgressions of the Reagan administration." Machinist president William Winpisinger, whose members could have closed down the airline industry overnight, wrote in *The Boston Globe*, "Our attorneys warn us that if I, as International president, should sanction, encourage or approve a sympathy strike under these conditions, I would risk the IAM's entire financial reserves."[15] The fired PATCO workers were barred from employment as flight controllers for more than a decade.

The early 1980s saw management demands for concessions in nearly every industry. In deference to existing labor law and public opinion, corporations did not demand the outright termination of union representation, but in other respects they followed the pattern of earlier "open shop" movements. In essence, they demanded the power to establish the conditions of labor unilaterally and as they pleased, with unions merely ratifying what management had already decided.

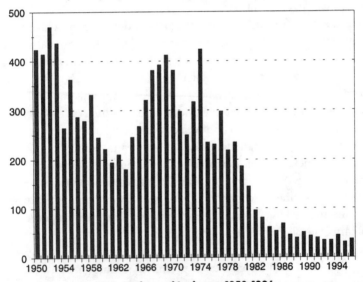

U.S. Strikes and Lockouts, 1950-1996

Source: United States Department of Labor, Bureau of Labor Statistics, "Work stoppages involving 1,000 workers or more, 1947-96" (http://www.bls.gov). Note: BLS measures strikes and lockouts involving more than 1,000 workers and lasting more than one shift.

Disastrous strikes and lockouts at Greyhound, Phelps-Dodge, Eastern Airlines, and many other companies convinced both union officials and rank-and-file workers that conventional strikes had lost much of their effectiveness. If corporations could replace striking workers with permanent replacements, move operations to other workplaces and even other countries, and continue making profits in their other operations while starving one isolated group of workers into submission, conventional strikes provided little bargaining power. Large-scale mobilization with mass picketing, sympathetic strikes, disregard of injunctions, and international labor support might or might not have shifted this balance of power, but in any case it was rarely attempted. Given the intense repression it would have induced, it would have demanded heavy sacrifices from rank-and-file workers and serious risks for unions and their leaders. Strike activity fell continuously from 1980 to 1995.

Beyond demanding concessions, management pushed for a fundamental shift in union goals. They proposed that unions should abandon any effort to remove labor costs as a factor in competition—for example, through industry-wide contracts and "pattern bargaining" that established the same labor conditions for all companies in an industry. Instead, unions should aim to make American corporations as competitive as possible against their foreign counterparts; employees should try to make their employers as competitive as possible against other corporations; and workers should strive to make their own workplace more productive than other workplaces in the same corporation. Management and politicians argued that only through such measures could people save their jobs in an increasingly competitive global economy.

Rather than engage in apparently futile resistance to concessions, many unions embraced the idea of helping employers become more competitive as a strategy to save jobs in their own workplace, company, and country. This went beyond particular concessions to the abandonment of pattern bargaining and unified industry and company wage rates, so that workers in the same union and sometimes even in the same company were in effect bidding against each other for work. It also involved active participation in "quality circles,"

"employee involvement," and "quality of worklife" programs designed to stimulate workers' cooperation with management in the
workplace. The logic of saving jobs through cheaper labor found expression in *The AFL-CIO News*, which maintained that moderation in
wage increases, rising productivity, and favorable currency exchange
rates made U.S. manufacturing workers a "best buy" compared to
workers in other industrial countries.[16]

Many union officials blamed the bad labor climate primarily on the
Reagan Administration and the Republican ascendancy, and portrayed the election of Democrats as the key to the reversal of labor's
fortunes. In the early 1980s, the AFL-CIO provided the Democratic
National Committee more than a third of its operating budget.[17]

New Tactics for Labor

In the face of employer attack, the proportion of workers in unions
fell from 27 percent in 1978 to 15 percent in 1996.[18] Many changes contributed to declining union membership. The traditional industrial,
cultural, and demographic base of the labor movement in white ethnic urban industrial communities was eroded by suburbanization
and deindustrialization. Many middle-income people—most of them
white—moved from cities to suburbs; so did most large modern
workplaces. People of color—African Americans, Asian Americans,
and Latinos—were concentrated in inner cities. Whole metropolitan
regions became divided into zones of different classes and ethnic
groups. In the Silicon Valley, for example, the homes, labs, and offices
of engineers and scientists gravitated to the northwest near Stanford
University, while unskilled, largely immigrant production workers
were concentrated around San Jose.[19] The working class was divided
geographically, racially, and economically into those with low-paid,
insecure jobs concentrated in centers of poverty in inner cities or other
ghettos (predominantly immigrants and people of color) and those
with substantially better-paid and more secure jobs (predominantly
white and suburban).

The decline of U.S. economic dominance, the rise of international
competition, accelerating capital mobility, and slow economic growth

eroded unions' bargaining power. The restriction of workers' legal right to organize and strike, the growth of non-union industries, declining public support for unions, and a broad cultural emphasis on individualism and consumerism rather than community and participation contributed to organized labor's decline as well.

But the long-term decline of organized labor was also due in substantial part to internal characteristics of the labor movement itself. These were not primarily characteristics of individual leaders; indeed, many of the problems went back for a century or more to the era of Samuel Gompers. Top-down control created a gulf between most union leaders and the rank and file. The assumption that it was the members' job to pay dues and the leaders' job to take care of union business led to apathy rather than active involvement; many unions had increasing difficulty even getting quorums for meetings. The tradition of national union autonomy blocked solidarity among workers even in the same workplaces, companies, industries, and communities. This tradition often made the AFL-CIO appear less the representative of the American working class than a vehicle for protecting the special interests of individual unions (or their leadership). Organized labor, dependent on government protection and an alliance with a business-dominated Democratic Party, was rarely willing to challenge legal limitations on worker action and solidarity. The expectation of cooperative relations with management, in which the role of the union was to administer an established contractual compromise, left unions disarmed when employers "declared class war."

These long-standing problems were compounded as the leadership of organized labor and the institution as a whole lost the vigor to defend their individual and institutional interests, let alone those of their members or the working class as a whole. Most existing unions showed little facility for reaching out to a changing workforce increasingly composed of African Americans, immigrants, and women, or for working on a global scale. The move toward cooperation with management on management's terms only reinforced the impression that unions provided workers nothing worth fighting for.

A minority of labor activists, local union leaders, and national union officials were unwilling to embrace the new forms of labor-management cooperation and began seeking alternatives. Recognizing that conventional strikes, in which workers simply quit working and waited for management to concede, were leading only to disaster, some sought supplemental arenas of action within the workplace itself or in wider communities. Many in the labor movement felt that the abandonment of the PATCO workers by the rest of the labor movement was a catastrophe, and some developed new forms of solidarity that crossed existing union boundaries. In response to globalization, some labor activists began to move beyond national horizons to develop a labor strategy for the global economy. As hired guards, detectives, police, the National Guard, injunctions, and court orders were used regularly against strikers, some began utilizing the techniques of non-violent civil disobedience. Many of these "new" tactics represented rediscoveries of techniques used in the past but largely forgotten in the era of class compromise.

The "Inside Game"

Employers are always dependent on workers' skills, knowledge, and cooperation, and workers have often used this fact to gain some informal power on the job.[20] The Industrial Workers of the World—the Wobblies—advocated "the conscious withdrawal of efficiency" or "striking on the job," a tactic that they were often accused of carrying to the point of "sabotage." Slowdowns and work-to-rules were standard tactics of the Congress of Industrial Organization campaigns of the 1930s. These tactics were revived as conventional strikes grew less and less effective.

In 1981, as Reagan was attacking the air traffic controllers, Moog Automotive in St. Louis, Missouri, demanded major concessions from its UAW workers, a diverse group that was about half black and half white, half male and half female. Management brought in a union-busting law firm and, according to information leaked to the union, pre-screened 400 potential strikebreakers. Jerry Tucker, then a staff member of UAW Region 5 in St. Louis, recalls:

> The tendency amongst some of the bargaining committee was to say, "Well, the hell with them. We'll just muscle them." But this was

a plant that had no long-term orientation for strikes and struggle. It simply would have destroyed them. There were already strikes going on in the community where 10,000 workers would show up to take the jobs of three or four hundred workers who were out on strike. This is 1981, and in each and every one of the cases, those strikes had been broken.[21]

Instead of striking, Tucker and the local union leadership proposed that union members vote down the proposed contract but stay in the plant and conduct a job action designed to "cause the company to rethink its position." The union recruited local leaders, both official and informal, to form a "Solidarity Committee" outside of the official union structure to wage the in-plant campaign; by constant recruiting it grew from a small initial nucleus to 100 of the 500 union members in the company. The strategy, according to Tucker, operated at two levels: "Individuals were going to have to depreciate productivity, and then there were going to be concerted and collective activities to do the same." He told workers that "each individual was going to have to find ways to re-evaluate their work procedures so as to get the company's attention."

Weekly meetings of the Solidarity Committee, supplemented by departmental meetings, shared information on the state of the struggle and planned the coming phase of action. Workers began following every possible rule, performing every procedure according to the book, and taking their time about it as well—in a process the workers came to call "running the plant backwards." "When a machine operator put a machine down, then the maintenance crew would come in and make sure it stayed down," Tucker explained. Workers wore union buttons and T-shirts, distributed leaflets in the plant, and sang union songs during breaks and lunchtime. The union anticipated the company would respond with firings and asked each worker to contribute $5 per week to a "solidarity program." When the company fired seven workers, this fund gave them support and the UAW provided regular strike benefits.

The union called meetings during the work day that stopped production, and other meetings occurred impromptu. The foundry workers, described by Tucker as "a bunch of big, mean, dirty-looking

guys," went to demand a meeting with their foreman. When the foreman ordered them back to work, their spokesperson, known as Pee
Wee, said, "No, we're going to have a meeting with you." "No you're
not," the foreman said. "Who's going to stop us?" Pee Wee asked.
The foreman sat down and listened to the foundry crew's concerns.
Skilled trades workers similarly confronted the vice-president of en-
gineering in his office.

After nearly six months, the company's attorney called Tucker and
said, "You've won. The company wants it over." Moog accepted the
union's original bargaining position and full amnesty for workers.

The in-plant strategy rapidly spread from Moog to UAW plants
from St. Louis to Texas, with many local variations. Workers at Bell
Helicopter in Ft. Worth, Texas, for example, adopted the slogan
"Worker in trouble—all workers assemble" and distributed metal
sports whistles to all workers in the plant. When two workers were
"taken upstairs" for refusing overtime, whistles started blowing and
soon 500 workers were crowding around the offices, leading management to call in the Ft. Worth police.

The inside strategy spread nationwide and was adopted by workers in many different unions. Its use was not limited to single plants
or even single companies. A campaign by cement workers, for instance, involved more than 100 locations with half-a-dozen or more
employers. When the Industrial Union Department of the AFL-CIO
published a manual on workplace actions called *The Inside Game*, demand was so strong that 100,000 copies were eventually distributed.[22]

Despite their effectiveness, inside strategies raised serious issues for
conventional trade unionism. For one thing, they tended to create
structures that bypassed existing leadership and lines of union
authority. Jeff Stansbury, a reporter for the UAW's *Solidarity* magazine, wrote: "You need to set up something like the solidarity committee, because in most cases you cannot rely on the existing
leadership. You cannot even necessarily rely on the activists of a local,
because those activists tend to have been formed under more rigid or
predictable circumstances than occur in a slowdown."[23] But empowering workers in the workplace in this way creates a source of power
that can potentially be used outside of or even against official union

channels. Further, the "inside game" can be used not only to force a
company to sign a contract, but also as an alternative to wildcat
strikes while a contract is in force, causing further problems for unions that see enforcement of contracts on both employers and workers as central to their function. While inside strategies were
increasingly adopted as an alternative to hopeless strikes, the extent
to which workers were genuinely encouraged to take their own initiative varied greatly from struggle to struggle.

Community-Labor Coalitions

For much of its history, the labor movement has been rooted in communities as well as workplaces. But the AFL-CIO in the era of George
Meany was, in the memorable image of labor historian David
Montgomery, like a great snapping turtle, "hiding within its shell to
shield the working class from contamination" and "snapping out" at
those outside forces that ventured too close.[24] Starting in the late
1970s, unions at the local level began reaching out for allies and
participating in a wide range of labor-community coalitions. While
no one has tallied them, such alliances must number in the thousands.[25]

Many of these alliances started out as vehicles for strike support;
indeed, major strikes without community-labor support efforts became the exception rather than the rule. Perhaps typical was the strike
against the International Paper Company centered in Jay, Maine. In
Jay, a weekly union-community meeting regularly attracted more
than 1,000 people. Caravans of strikers fanned out across New England, building support for a "corporate campaign" against companies
with ties to International Paper. In Boston, the caravaners created a
network of support groups that included local progressive unions,
church groups, university students and employees, and even Central
American solidarity organizations. Some of these developed into permanent strike support groups, ready to support workers' struggles as
they arose.

Local unions increasingly participated in issue coalitions that used
public education, lobbying, and direct action confrontations to push

concerns ranging from plant-closing legislation to expanded medical programs, housing, voter registration, and electoral reform. In New Haven, for example, a Community Labor Alliance, which grew out of a support campaign for striking Yale workers, pressed for increased contributions from Yale University to the city; use of city pension funds to finance housing; withdrawal of university investments in South Africa; and development of a local school lunch program to provide both nutrition and employment. Many local and state coalitions developed throughout the country to push for legislation regulating plant closings.

Local unions also became involved with community-based economic development. Several dozen coalitions developed to resist plant closings and deindustrialization by promoting worker buyouts, local economic development authorities, and other means of saving and creating jobs. The Naugatuck Valley Project in western Connecticut, for example, an organization composed of more than sixty local unions, church groups, and community groups, helped workers buy a local plant, found alternatives to the closing of other local companies, started an employee-owned home health aide company, and organized tenants to create permanently affordable housing. A similar coalition, the Tri-State Conference on Steel, campaigned to save steel plants through worker buyouts, developed plans for regional reindustrialization in the "rust belt," and promoted the creation of a public economic development authority, the Steel Valley Authority, as an alternative to private development.

New forms of labor-community cooperation also emerged in the electoral arena. A pioneering effort to put such efforts on a permanent footing was Connecticut's Legislative Electoral Action Program.[26] LEAP is a coalition initiated by UAW Region 9A and the Connecticut Citizens Action Group, a statewide community organizing and lobbying organization representing low-income and moderate-income people. LEAP's member organizations came to include the International Association of Machinists, Service Employees International Union, District 1199 (New England Health Care Workers Union), the Connecticut Federation of Teachers, and environmental, women's, gay and lesbian, African-American, Puerto Rican, and other organizations. LEAP recruited long-term activists to run for state legislature and provided them with training and volunteers. Those elected with its support formed a Progressive Caucus in the Connecticut legislature. A "Northeast Coalition Project" helped set up similar coalitions in New Hampshire, Maine, Massachusetts, New York, and elsewhere in the Northeast. A similar organization, the Minnesota Alliance for Progressive Action, grew out of a coalition of unions, peace groups, and religious groups campaigning to convert military industry to civilian production. The Rainbow Coalition led by Rev. Jesse Jackson, while shunned by most national labor leaders, received considerable labor support at a local level, especially in African-American communities.

An important vehicle for generating community-labor cooperation has been Jobs with Justice. Jobs with Justice was started in 1987 by a group of national unions within the Industrial Union Department of the AFL-CIO to mobilize support for workers' rights struggles that went beyond individual unions. The effort was built around a card individuals signed pledging that "during the next year, *I'll be there* at least five times for someone else's fight as well as my own. If enough of us are there, we'll all start winning." Within a few years, Jobs with Justice developed an identity of its own, organizing rallies, supporting picket lines, and providing material aid to labor and other struggles in hundreds of communities, many of them areas where unions were weak.[27] In some communities it has initiated Workers' Rights Boards composed of prominent citizens who evaluate and hold public hearings on alleged denials of workers' rights.

Local coalitions also became vehicles for several massive national coalition efforts. The unexpectedly successful campaign to block the appointment of Judge Robert Bork to the Supreme Court brought together "Jewish attorneys and law teachers and NAACP community activists, white male labor leaders and feminists, libertarians and politically liberal baby boomers, consumer advocates, environmentalists, and small-business leaders."[28] The struggle against NAFTA brought together not only local labor, environmental, farm, religious, human rights, and many other activists, but linked them with activists in Mexico and Canada.[29]

Corporate Campaigns

For much of its history, the labor movement used sympathetic strikes and boycotts to pressure employers. These techniques brought the power of dispersed supporters to supplement the power of those workers involved directly. But the no-strike clauses in union contracts and the restrictions on secondary strikes and boycotts in the Taft-Harley Act severely impeded such expressions of solidarity. Since the late 1970s, unions have developed "corporate campaigns" as a way to pressure companies without violating contracts or the Taft-Hartley Act.

The first corporate campaign to receive wide national attention was developed in 1976 by Ray Rogers and the Amalgamated Clothing and Textile Workers Union to force the giant textile firm J.P. Stevens to negotiate a contract with workers who had organized a union in its plants in North Carolina. Since fewer than a tenth of J.P. Stevens' plants nationwide were unionized, the company could easily beat a strike by moving work to its non-union plants elsewhere. The union had organized a consumer boycott, but only about one-third of the company's products could be directly boycotted by consumers.

Rogers reasoned that a corporation was essentially "a coalition of individual and institutional interests that can be challenged, attacked, divided and conquered."[30] The campaign's "power analysis" identified the interlocks between J.P. Stevens' board of directors and other businesses, particularly the banks and insurance companies that provided its financing. Most of the workers were black women, and alliances with civil rights and women's groups were actively and successfully developed. Then publicity, demonstrations, and letter-writing campaigns focused on demanding that banks and insurance companies withdraw their support from J.P. Stevens. Supporters ran slates against incumbent officers at corporate annual meetings. They began laying the groundwork for pulling the billions of dollars in union pension funds and members' insurance policies out of companies that supported J.P. Stevens.

In 1978, J.P. Stevens' board chair and another top official were forced off the board of Manufacturers' Hanover Trust Company. Then the chief executive of Avon resigned from the J.P. Stevens board. Finally, the chief executives of New York Life and J.P. Stevens resigned simultaneously from each other's boards, twenty-four hours after the head of New York Life proclaimed that such resignations would never happen.

Five years after the campaign began, J.P. Stevens agreed to accept unionization. Labor journalist A.H. Raskin wrote in *The New York Times*, "Pressure on giant banks and insurance companies and other Wall Street pillars, all aimed at isolating Stevens from the financial community, helped generate a momentum toward settlement that could not be achieved through the 1976-1980 worldwide boycott of Stevens products or through more conventional uses of union muscle such as strikes and mass picketing."[31]

Corporate campaigns became a common feature of labor struggles over the subsequent decade-and-a-half. In the era of the "disintegrated corporation" and networked production systems, corporate campaigns made it possible to target a corporation's entire network. Many corporate campaigns focused not only on labor issues but on environmental, civil rights, and other abuses committed by targeted corporations. Some were little more than anticorporate publicity campaigns; others were serious attempts to raise the costs of company behavior.

Global Solidarity

As capital has gone global, so has labor solidarity. One of the first U.S. labor battles in which international support was critical involved workers at the West Virginia facility of the Ravenswood Aluminum Corporation.[32] In what *Business Week* described as "an unprecedented global campaign that's likely to be emulated by other labor groups," the United Steel Workers of America "enlisted foreign unions" to force the employer's hand.[33]

In 1990, Ravenswood, formerly part of Kaiser Aluminum, was purchased by a group of three investors, one of whom was Swiss-based

investor Marc Rich, a fugitive from the United States, where he was
wanted for tax evasion and fraud. Less than a year after buying the
company, the new management locked out Ravenswood's 1,700
workers and hired replacement workers.

Local 5668 of the United Steel Workers launched an aggressive and
ultimately successful nineteen-month campaign to defeat the lockout
and win an acceptable contract. The campaign included strong rank-
and-file participation to spread word of the strike around the country
and to target end users—companies such as Coca-Cola and Stroh's
Brewing Company that used Ravenswood aluminum in their cans.

Strong international pressure focused on Rich and his associates
may have tipped the balance in favor of the workers. Under the direction of Joe Uehlein, special projects director for the AFL-CIO's Industrial Union Department, a sophisticated campaign was developed to
research Rich's financial holdings and embarrass him throughout the
world. Uehlein credits strong support from USWA president George
Becker, from the International Trade Secretariats, which links unions
in the same industries internationally, and from Swiss, Dutch, and
Eastern European unions. The USWA hired a full-time European co-
ordinator for the campaign. According to *Business Week*, the final victory came when "East European unions disrupted Rich's expansion
efforts in Czechoslovakia, Romania, and Russia." Soon after, "a top
Rich employee who owns most of Ravenswood's stock kicked out the
aluminum producer's chairman and replaced him with another Rich
associate. The company then agreed to restart contract talks with the
union."[34]

International support played a role in a growing proportion of labor struggles in the 1990s.

Non-Violent Civil Disobedience

Throughout its history, the core tactics of the labor movement have
been largely non-violent. Strikes, demonstrations, and picket lines
have involved a withdrawal of cooperation—disobedience to established authority—and an appeal for support from the wider community. Despite this, workers' actions have been met with violent

repression thousands of times and violence in response to repression has been common.[35]

Over the course of the twentieth century, social movements from India to Poland to the Philippines have developed forms of disciplined non-violence that have provided a kind of political jujitsu for dealing with repressive violence. Rather than either submitting to repression or responding violently, these techniques resist established authority—for example by blocking roads, occupying buildings, or demonstrating in violation of injunctions—without doing physical harm to company guards, police, soldiers, or other human beings who attempt to restore "law and order." Such disciplined non-violent resistance became an important part of American political practice with the civil rights struggles of the 1950s and 1960s.

In 1968, predominantly black sanitation workers in Memphis struck for union recognition. This labor struggle soon became the focus of local civil rights groups, which conducted marches and rallies to demand the workers' rights. It was in the midst of supporting this strike that Rev. Martin Luther King, Jr., was assassinated.

Since that time, disciplined non-violent civil disobedience has increasingly been adopted in major labor struggles. Indeed, nearly all the struggles recounted in the rest of this chapter have used it. Non-violent civil disobedience has helped neutralize repressive violence and the fear it is intended to instill, called public attention to the justice of workers' demands, and made clear the willingness to accept personal sacrifice in the interest of broader human purposes that underlies the solidarity of workers.

•

None of these tactics guaranteed success. Some managers became so frustrated with organized "inside game" workplace strategies that they locked out entire workforces and hired replacement workers to defeat them. Many strikes, such as the one by International Paper Company workers in Jay, Maine, were defeated despite exemplary community support. Many corporate campaigns have been clear failures, and few since the J.P. Stevens campaign have been clear successes.[36] International support by itself has rarely if ever won a strike. Many labor struggles in the 1980s and 1990s have been effectively broken despite civil disobedience on a substantial scale. But these methods did provide workers pinned down by the employers' offensive ways to begin recovering the initiative.

Resisting Concessions

The tactics outlined above, along with more conventional ones, were used repeatedly in the struggles against concessions during the 1980s and 1990s. Three of the most important—and most revealing—occurred at the Austin, Minnesota, plant of the Hormel meatpacking company, the Watsonville Canning company in southern California, and the Pittston Coal Company in Virginia. All three revealed a base of potential solidarity for embattled workers that was rarely appealed to in other conflicts of the period.

Austin P-9

At the start of the 1980s, the meatpacking industry was almost completely unionized with a master agreement providing a $10.69 wage rate. However, in the mid-1980s, the major packing companies initiated an extreme version of the offensive against labor taking place throughout American industry. Wilson filed for bankruptcy and cut wages from the negotiated $10.69 to $6.50. Con-Agra bought Armour, closed thirteen plants, then reopened them with non-union workers earning only $6 per hour. Swift slashed wages as well.[37]

In spring 1984, the United Food and Commercial Workers appeared ready to take a stand against further concessions at Hormel. UFCW National Packinghouse Division director Lewie Anderson ordered that no locals consent to concessions. But shortly thereafter, UFCW agreed to reopen the contract at Hormel's Ottumwa, Iowa, plant. Ottumwa workers voted overwhelmingly to refuse to reopen the contract. Then Hormel laid off 444 workers and announced it was considering closing the plant unless concessions were granted. The local voted again against reopening the contract. Hormel laid off another 114 workers. In a third vote, workers accepted concessions cutting wages from $10.69 to $8.75. Then the laid off workers were re-called.[38]

Hormel next demanded the same cuts from the rest of its UFCW locals. Local P-9 at Hormel's Austin, Minnesota, plant rejected concessions by a vote of 92 percent to 8 percent[39] and other locals in the chain followed suit. The UFCW then called a meeting of Hormel local union officials, who agreed to the concessions their members had just voted to reject, bringing the wage rate at Hormel plants to $9.

Meanwhile, Oscar Mayer cut wages to $8.25. Hormel responded by cutting wages at Austin 23 percent, to the same level as Oscar Mayer, based on contract language pegging wages to industry rates. Wages fell so low that some full-time workers became eligible for food stamps.

Throughout this series of cuts, Local P-9 in Austin became increasingly disenchanted with the leadership of the UFCW. In December 1983, it elected Jim Guyette president on a platform of opposition to further concessions. Local P-9 began looking for alternative ways to resist Hormel's offensive.

In September 1984, wives of P-9 workers began meeting in an Austin park and standing with signs at the plant gates once a week for all three shifts. By October, 400 women were coming to the meetings in the park. They called themselves the United Support Group, and soon began meeting in the Austin Labor Center. They organized a food shelf and a clothing exchange. Peter Rachleff, a labor historian who helped organize support for the strike, wrote, "The United Support Group transformed the Austin Labor Center—once the location of a local union that could not draw a quorum to its monthly meetings—into a beehive of activity. In so doing, they transformed Local P-9 from a trade union into a social movement."[40]

Local P-9 also began working with Ray Rogers and his consulting firm, Corporate Campaigns, Inc. Rogers proposed that P-9 mobilize its members and supporters to put pressure on First Bank Systems (FBS), Hormel's banker and the largest outside shareholder of Hormel stock. The local established a communications committee and began reaching out to union, church, and community groups across the

Midwest. Nightly meetings, dances, and other activities developed at the Labor Center.

But conflict with the UFCW also escalated. The union's president, William Wynn, warned Rogers it would be "regrettable" if P-9 launched a campaign without approval from the national union.[41] But in January 1985, P-9 members voted to assess themselves $3 per week to hire Corporate Campaigns, Inc. Hundreds began picketing Hormel offices and plants and First Bank branches. Hormel and First Bank complained to the National Labor Relations Board (NLRB), which held that the campaign was an illegal secondary boycott violating the Taft-Hartley Act. This put a serious crimp in Rogers' strategy of focusing pressure on First Bank. In August 1985, Austin workers voted to strike by a 93 percent margin. They also initiated a boycott against Hormel. The UFCW officially sanctioned the strike.

The P-9 strike rapidly became a symbol of resistance to concessions and the focus for support efforts nationwide. Speakers and caravans from Austin traveled around the country. Union stewards at the General Electric plant in Lynn, Massachusetts, passed out a leaflet that articulates why the P-9 struggle struck such a responsive chord: "Working men and women in Minnesota have scratched a line in the cold hard ground and declared that they will give up no more of their pride, wages, or benefits.... Their victory will be hailed as the turning point against concessions bargaining, or their loss will be another crushed union. What stands between their victory or loss is the resolve of all of us."[42]

Support came not only from unions but also from farmers, peace and justice activists, poor people's organizations, and environmental groups. Members of the peace group Women Against Military Madness conducted workshops in civil disobedience in Austin. Hundreds of workers and supporters subsequently participated in civil disobedience.

Governor Rudy Perpich sent 300 National Guard members into Austin to protect the strikebreakers who entered the plant across union picket lines. In early April, 6,000 labor activists from around the country came to Austin to attempt to shut the plant down with mass pickets and obstruction. An impromptu rally was met with tear gas, police attacks, and arrests on serious felony charges (all eventually dropped). Jesse Jackson flew into Austin and said, "What Selma, Alabama, was to the struggle for civil rights in the 1960s, Austin, Minnesota, is to the struggle for economic rights in the 1980s."[43]

According to Rachleff, "Rallies, parades, dances, picnics, food caravans, Christmas parties, picketing, and plant gate demonstrations attracted the greatest outpouring of labor solidarity [in the United States] since the 1930s.... More than 3,000 local unions sent material assistance. Tens of thousands of rank-and-filers and local union officers visited Austin and offered help of one kind or another."[44]

But the strike, originally sanctioned by the UFCW, met increasing resistance from union officials. At the annual convention of the Minnesota State Federation of Labor, the federation's president ordered P-9's information table shut down on the grounds that P-9 literature advocated a secondary boycott of First Bank and was thus illegal. Just before Thanksgiving in 1985, UFCW president William Wynn wrote to AFL-CIO officers and affiliates condemning the Adopt-a-Family program P-9 had established. When a Minneapolis-St. Paul International Association of Machinists Lodge voted to send $10,000 to adopt several families, IAM president William Winpisinger intervened to block the payment. (In response, the local convened an "emergency" meeting, paid out a $35 per diem to those present, adjourned the meeting, and signed the $10,000-plus in checks over to P-9.)[45] As official trade union support was increasingly blocked, forty-two independent "P-9 Support Committees" were organized around the country.[46]

In March 1986, Wynn ordered P-9 to return to work unconditionally. Eight hundred P-9 members met and voted overwhelmingly to ignore the order. Three weeks later, supporters poured into Austin and rallied at the plant gates in violation of an injunction. Seventeen were arrested on "felony riot" charges. Guyette and Rogers were charged with "aiding and abetting a riot" for having "mailed posters and leaflets" for the rally.[47]

The UFCW put the local into trusteeship on the grounds that it had disobeyed the UFCW order to call off the strike. Backed by a court order, the UFCW sent in its regional director to take control of P-9's office, bank account, and postbox. He ordered members to abandon all boycott activities and accept a new contract.

The UFCW-imposed contract allowed individuals to be fired for advocating a boycott of Hormel products or handbilling any business buying from or selling to Hormel. Under the contract dozens of workers were fired or refused recall rights for such crimes as having "Boycott Hormel" bumper stickers on their cars. One worker was eliminated from the rehire list for having a driver's license ID photo taken with a "Boycott Hormel" sticker on his forehead. When P-9 members continued the boycott, the UFCW sent out a mailing to local unions across the country urging them to *buy* Hormel products "made by union brothers and sisters."[48]

Watsonville

In 1985, the Watsonville Canning company demanded a wide range of concessions, including a wage cut from $6.66 to $4.25 per hour.[49] The 1,000 employees, members of Teamsters Local 91, who were mostly Latino women, struck. The strike was marked by strong roots in the Mexican-American community and its culture. When opponents of the strike tried to provoke a riot, for example, the strikers responded with a traditional Mexican pilgrimage on their knees to the local Catholic church, where they prayed for justice. The workers stayed on the picket line for eighteen months without a single defection.

Wells Fargo Bank provided Watsonville Canning $23 million in loans during the strike. The strikers' committee organized an informational picket at the local Wells Fargo branch, but canceled it when Teamsters officials objected. When the central role of the bank became ever clearer, the strikers voted to publicly protest the bank's support for the company and to ask the Teamsters to withdraw $800 million in funds from the bank. As the strikers began making preparations for a campaign against Wells Fargo, the bank foreclosed on the $23 million in unpaid loans it had made to Watsonville Canning, forcing the company out of business.

Teamster officials negotiated a contract with the new operator of the company, but workers, dissatisfied that many would be denied medical benefits under the new contract, voted to postpone ratification. The Teamsters announced that the strike was over, cut off strike benefits, locked the strikers out of the union hall, and threatened to put the local in trusteeship. Six women then began a hunger strike in front of the cannery; hundreds of strikers and supporters surrounded the plant. That night negotiations resumed, and two days later workers voted overwhelmingly to accept a new contract with medical benefits for all workers.

Pittston

In November 1988, the Pittston Coal Group, Virginia's largest coal operator and the second-largest coal exporter in the country, demanded a long list of concessions, including cuts in health and pensions, work-rule changes, and the right to open new non-union mines. The company demanded Sunday work and abandonment of the eight-hour day. When miners objected, Pittston Coal Group president Michael Odum said, "The world works seven days a week," and asserted that miners were only "using church as an excuse" to avoid Sunday work.[50]

United Mine Workers of America president Richard Trumka called the company's proposals "an economic death warrant"[51] for Appalachian communities and decided to stake the future of the union on resisting them. The union combined a strike, mass non-violent civil disobedience, mobilization of solidarity nationally and internationally, a corporate campaign, and a workplace occupation into a winning strategy.

After working for more than a year without a contract, 1,700 UMWA workers struck at Pittston on April 5, 1989. No union members crossed the lines. Pittston was not able to offer permanent replacement jobs to strikebreakers because the National Labor Relations Board found the company had engaged in unfair labor practices.

The UMWA brought in experienced peace activists to conduct non-violence training. Then strikers and their families, often dressed in the camouflage outfits that became the unofficial uniform of the strike, began blocking mines, roads, and coal trucks. More than 1,000 strikers and supporters were arrested the last week of April. A number of women organized a group called The Daughters of Mother Jones and occupied the company's regional headquarters overnight. Jesse Jackson told a rally of 12,000, "The tradition of John L. Lewis and the tradition of Martin Luther King, Jr., have come together in your actions."[52]

Even before the strike, Pittston had imported strikebreakers and Vance Security guards to protect them. Virginia's governor called out several hundred state police to protect strikebreakers and arrest strikers. Injunctions forbade most strike activities. At one point, driving too slowly was interpreted as a violation of a federal injunction. Federal marshals accompanied the state police who arrested the drivers, some of whom were sentenced to as much as 90 days for this traffic misdemeanor. Fines against the union exceeded $60 million.[53]

Officials of the mineworkers presented the strike as a struggle against the courts and federal labor laws. UMWA vice-president Cecil Roberts told a rally: "This is class war. The working class versus the corporate rich and their allies in state and federal government."[54] When Judge Don McGlothin, Jr., issued fines of more than $30 million against the union, miners organized a write-in campaign and elected a strike leader to replace McGlothin's father in the state legislature.

To protest fines, injunctions, and other government union-busting efforts, 46,000 miners in eleven states joined wildcat sympathetic strikes. The UMWA briefly sanctioned such strikes as contractually permitted "Memorial Days," but thereafter discouraged them. Hundreds of miners and sympathizers also picketed and closed down several coal-fired factories and non-union mines.

In summer 1989, the New Jersey Industrial Union Council voted to ask the AFL-CIO to call a "one day union work stoppage" in support of Pittston and other strikers.[55] But the AFL-CIO circulated an advisory letter to state federations and central labor councils discouraging sympathetic strikes:

> [T]raditional responses such as food banks and coverage of the strike story in labor newspapers are certainly appropriate. This strike presents a specific issue where the strike has spread to other than Pittston mines. In some cases AFL-CIO affiliates are signatory to labor agreements at those facilities [to] which they remain legally bound.
>
> As an AFL-CIO state or local labor council you are advised to support the UMW in those areas of activity which do not conflict with the legal obligations imposed by the court on the UMW or by existing labor agreements with AFL-CIO affiliates.[56]

Rank-and-file support for the Pittston strikers went considerably beyond food banks and newspaper articles. An estimated 30,000 supporters came to "Camp Solidarity" between June and September 1989, including not only labor but religious and peace activists. "If you'd told me a year ago all this would happen, that I'd meet people from nearly every state in the union, from Denmark and Pakistan, from Italy and Germany, come here to help us, I'd have almost said you were a liar," said a miner who had worked thirty-two years at Pittston. A roof bolter from an Exxon mine in southern Illinois who came to Camp Solidarity explained, "I don't want this at home. We've got to stop it here." The president of a Pittston local said:

> We've got people suffering badly here. So let's go ahead and fight the fight here. There's no use in letting some other groups somewhere else suffer. Let's just have it all out right here while we're at it. Maybe this will show these large companies that we're going to stick together.

One of the camp directors commented: "We've come to the point where we don't even call it a strike anymore. It's a people's movement. We're telling our people, 'Hey, if this thing ends tomorrow, we've got people out there who need our help.'"[57]

A corporate campaign put further pressure on Pittston. In Boston, a support committee targeted William Craig, a vice-president of Shawmut Bank, and picketed the bank. Trumka and fifty strikers spoke before the Boston City Council, which voted to withdraw city funds from Shawmut. Ultimately Craig was forced to resign as vice-president of the bank.

International support also played a role. A delegation from the International Confederation of Free Trade Unions, the largest global trade union confederation, visited the coalfields and protested the repression being imposed on the miners. At a time when the Reagan Administration was trumpeting its support of Polish democratization with the slogan "Solidarity with Solidarity," the delegation included a representative of the Polish Solidarity union who said he was "shocked to see what is happening in the great democracy."[58] The ICFTU delegation met with Pittston's chief executive officer and helped persuade Labor Secretary Elizabeth Dole to visit the strike. Dole then appointed a supermediator to encourage a settlement.

On September 17, ninety-eight miners and a clergyman (all owners of at least one share of Pittston stock) filtered around state police and arrived at Moss No. 3, Pittston's key coal treatment plant. UMWA leader Eddie Burke recalled:

> There were two Vance Security guards there. I told them, "We are an unarmed, nonviolent inspection team of stockholders coming to inspect our investment. You will not be harmed." The two Vance men left hurriedly. There were no weapons drawn.

The miners called the occupation "Operation Flintstone" in memory of the 1936-1937 Flint sitdown strikes.

A court ordered the occupiers to vacate, but they refused to do so. The next day, a crowd of 2,000 lined the road in front of the plant to protect the occupiers. Soon 5,000 supporters surrounded the plant. The state police withdrew to a distance, while workers directed traffic. The occupiers remained for four days, waited until a few hours after the court's September 20 evacuation deadline had passed, then marched triumphantly out of the plant.[59]

The strike-plagued company lost $25 million on its coal operations in the fourth quarter of 1989.[60] In October, Pittston returned to the bargaining table for the first time since July.[61] Negotiators reached a settlement December 31, 1989, which included few of the concessions

Pittston had demanded and required the company to meet the contract pattern established in the rest of the mining industry. *U.S. News and World Report* said miners "appeared to score a major victory" in "new job security provisions" limiting subcontracting to non-union firms. "Pittston's attempts to shed some of the burden of financing health care benefits" proved "largely fruitless."[62]

•

These struggles illustrate the revamped tactics the labor movement developed in the 1980s, from community support to mass nonviolent civil disobedience, and from corporate campaigns to international labor solidarity. They show national union leaderships in roles varying from militant strike leadership to outright strikebreaking. They demonstrate the powerful institutional constraints that labor law and union contracts put on the action of workers and unions. They reveal often unexpected reserves of commitment and solidarity among workers directly subject to employer attack and among a wide swath of supporters.

Organizing the New Workforce

Traditionally, the majority of American union members have been blue-collar white males. Over the past quarter-century, this group became a smaller and smaller minority in the workforce, while other groups—sometimes dubbed "the new workforce"—grew as a percentage of organized and unorganized workers..

The proportion of workers who were women started to grow dramatically as married women and women with children worked more and more outside the home. This shift in part reflected changing values regarding women's roles, but in larger part it was a result of the income squeeze that affected families starting in the 1970s. Despite gaining greater access to the workplace, women remained concentrated in a few clerical and other white-collar occupations and received far less pay and job security than men. In 1996, women comprised 39 percent of the membership of AFL-CIO affiliated unions, compared with 22 percent in 1972.[63]

The great migration of African Americans from the rural South to urban areas throughout the nation was completed in the 1960s. While a small black middle class won access to decent jobs, schooling, and homes, most African Americans have remained concentrated in industrial and low-paid service occupations in central cities and, as these declined, became subject to extremely high levels of unemployment.

Changes in U.S. immigration law in 1965 permitted a resurgence of immigration to the highest levels since the early 1920s. While immigrants were of diverse educational and class backgrounds, the largest numbers came from Asia, Latin America, and the Caribbean, and under America's peculiar caste system most were defined as people of color. Like previous generations of immigrants, they formed ethnic communities and found work in the poorest-paid occupations and industries. In some American cities, more than 100 languages were spoken in public schools.

As women spent an increasing proportion of their lives in the workforce, blacks left the rural South, and immigration rebounded, these groups became a growing proportion of the American workforce. With a shift in employment from goods-producing toward service-producing industries and from stable, full-time jobs to contingent ones, the traditional industrial strongholds of the labor movement were decimated. The established labor movement was largely cut off from these growing segments of the workforce—one of the principal reasons for its decline. Over the course of the 1980s and 1990s, however, immigrant, minority, and women workers have begun to develop new approaches to organizing themselves, on their own and in cooperation with established unions.

9 to 5

One-third of employed women are office workers, yet only a tiny minority of them are unionized. In the early 1970s, working women's organizations sprang up in a number of cities, and in 1977 several of them joined together to found 9 to 5: The National Association of Working Women. Rooted in the emerging women's liberation movement, 9 to 5 was a membership organization designed to improve wages, rights, and respect for office workers. It combined women's issues such as discrimination, pay equity, sexual harassment, and respect with union issues such as higher pay, job posting, and increased benefits.[64]

The organization developed an "Office Workers' Bill of Rights." It publicized the issues of low pay, poor benefits, and discriminatory treatment and then conducted street actions in front of large companies with such attractions as the "Heartless Employer Award" on Valentine's Day or "Scrooge of the Year" at Christmas. Combining such campaigns with suits for affirmative action violations won promotions and back-pay awards, job posting and grievance procedures, raises, and child-care programs.

In addition, 9 to 5 focused on building a working women's culture different from that of traditional unionism. It raised issues like sexual harassment, pay equity, day care, family leave, and contingent work that particularly affected women workers—issues that have gradually become part of the agenda of the wider labor movement. The organization also worked with the Service Employees International Union to form a union for office workers, SEIU Local 925. While it has experienced the same difficulties as other unions in organizing new workers, Local 925 has made a significant impact in developing new models for organizing women workers.

Yale University Clerical and Technical Workers

While Yale University's blue-collar workers had been organized since the 1930s, its 2,650 "clerical and technical" workers—80 percent of them women—were the target of five unsuccessful organizing drives by five different unions between 1950 and 1982.[65] In 1980, Local 35 of the Hotel and Restaurant Employees Union, which represented Yale's predominantly male blue-collar workers, decided to launch its own campaign to organize the white-collar clerical and technical workers. The local twice raised its dues to support an organizing drive and loaned its business manager, John Wilhelm, to serve as chief organizer for the new white-collar local, Local 34.

For its first year, Local 34 issued no literature and didn't push workers to sign union cards. Instead, it concentrated on building an organizing committee. Many of the initial organizing committee members were referred by members of Local 35. The union's strategy, according to Wilhelm, was to develop a rank-and-file organizing committee that "knows what it's talking about" and is able to gain employees' trust. Then workers organized "around the notion that the union is a tool for them to use to deal with whatever they want to, as opposed to insurance policy unionism, where you say, 'Well, if you join the union, you'll get fifty cents an hour more,' or 'If you join the union, we'll have good health and welfare.'"[66] Over the course of several years, Local 34 recruited 450 members to the organizing committee.[67] A steering committee of 150 met weekly; a "rank-and-file staff" of about sixty people worked even more intensively. Any union member could serve on any of the committees, as long as he or she put in the necessary time.[68] When workers came up against hostile supervisors, they organized petition drives or held small demonstrations in the supervisors' offices.

In May 1983, workers won a union representation election by less than 51 percent. The union then held hundreds of small-group meetings and two surveys of all clerical and technical workers to identify issues for negotiation. A 500-member contract committee developed initial contract proposals. Yale hired an anti-union law firm, one of whose partners had once said that it subscribed to "the bomb-them-into-submission school of labor relations."[69]

The union appealed for support from students, faculty, and the wider New Haven community. It focused on the issue of pay equity, analyzing Yale's salary figures to show that "female [clerical and technical workers] earn less than males, even though the women have worked at Yale longer" and that "black employees earn less than white employees, even though blacks have worked at Yale longer."[70] The local organized a one-day strike, dubbed "59-Cent Day," to draw attention to the fact that, on average, an American working woman earned only 59 cents for every dollar earned by a man.[71] The union's contract campaign was thereby framed as an issue of social justice and of equality for African Americans and particularly for women.

In September 1984, two-thirds of Yale's clerical and technical workers left their jobs. Ninety-five percent of Yale's maintenance and service workers honored their picket lines. Dining rooms were closed, garbage was uncollected, and sympathetic teachers and students moved hundreds of classes off campus. While the strike disrupted university life, it was not able to close down the campus, so outside support was crucial. The local labor movement, the New Haven Black Ministerial Alliance, and the Board of Aldermen gave support to the strike. So did national leaders, such as AFL-CIO president Lane Kirkland, Jesse Jackson, and Eleanor Smeal. More than 600 people were arrested in two acts of mass non-violent civil disobedience.[72] Despite threats of retribution from the university administration, many students, faculty, and other union supporters participated in a three-day "moratorium"—withdrawing from classes, meetings, and all other university activities while participating in marches, teach-ins, and other strike support activities.

The strike was marked by tactical creativity and the invention of hundreds of slogans, chants, and songs. To the tune of "Solidarity Forever," the workers sang:

> Your experiments depend on us, we tally up the stats;
> We work with agar-agar, pour the chemicals in vats.
> But until we get a contract, we won't feed your stupid rats,
> And the union makes us strong.[73]

After seven weeks, some union leaders proposed the tactic of "taking the strike inside" during the university holidays. The idea was hotly debated by the rank and file, which then voted to accept it, while voting also to reject Yale's "final offer" by a ten-to-one margin. Just as workers prepared to return to picket lines after six weeks on the job, Yale began making concessions in its negotiations with the union bargaining committee. On January 19, 1985, Yale agreed to a contract with its clerical and technical workers for the first time, providing a 20 percent salary increase over three years, improved pensions and job security, and a plan to correct years of inequity in job classifications.[74]

In the wake of the settlement, Local 34 reaffirmed its commitment to honor picket lines of the blue-collar workers in Local 35 should they have to strike. The local also became a major supporter of the campaign to force Yale to divest its funds from companies that invested in apartheid South Africa.

Workers' Centers

While unions are normally based in the workplace, the past two decades have seen experiments with worker organization based in the community that includes workers from different employers and industries. These organizations, often known as workers' centers, have developed particularly in immigrant communities and communities of color. These groups often have their own cultural traditions, face particular problems of discrimination, move frequently from job to job, are concentrated in industries with little union presence, and are often ignored or worse by established unions.

In 1978, Chinese restaurant workers in New York organized as members of the Hotel and Restaurant Employees Union, struck, and won the first union contract for Chinese restaurant workers in the city. They soon became dissatisfied with their contract and their union, however, and in 1980 formed the Chinese Staff and Workers' Association. CSWA organized independent unions at other restaurants; it organized Chinese garment industry workers to fight the frequent non-payment of wages and to put pressure on their union, the International Ladies Garment Workers Union, to enforce contracts and fight concessions; and it organized protests at construction sites to demand jobs for Chinese construction workers. Bringing together labor and community issues, it helped block construction projects that would gentrify large parts of Chinatown and drive out the restaurants where many of its members worked.[75]

In 1982, Asian Americans in the San Francisco area formed Asian Immigrant Women Advocates. AIWA provides Korean, Chinese, Vietnamese, and Filipina working women with English classes and workshops on contract rights, labor regulations, health and safety rules, and wage and hour laws. It has assisted immigrant women to express their concerns to their employer, union, politicians, and the public. While formally non-partisan, in practice it has helped develop Asian women's leadership for San Francisco unions, especially in the hotel industry, and has built a bridge between them and the Asian community.[76] A campaign initiated in 1992 to win $15,000 in wages owed to San Francisco seamstresses became a national campaign against Jessica McClintock Inc., involving picketing in eleven cities and endorsements from more than 400 organizations.[77]

In 1993, a Latino Workers Center was started in New York. It organized English classes and courses on labor rights and began working with small groups of workers from restaurants, garment factories, groceries, construction companies, office-cleaning companies, and home health care agencies. The center helped workers organize around withheld wages and sub-minimum wages. It organized protests against abusive employers and filed charges against them with the Department of Labor. It organized presentations in churches, leafleted near workplaces, tabled at community events, and initiated radio and television interviews to educate the Latino community about worker rights, anti-immigrant legislation, and the need for organizing. It organized a campaign against and boycott of three restaurants that owed workers back-pay, culminating in a "Via Crucis Por La Justicia" (Stations of the Cross March for Justice), stopping in front of each restaurant for a protest rally. The campaign forced partial concessions from the restaurants and directed the community's attention to .the possibilities of organizing to solve workplace problems.[78]

African-American workers in the South have created workers' centers that address labor issues and other concerns of the black community. The Carolina Alliance for Fair Employment in South Carolina, for example, has organized around issues ranging from the economic conversion of a recently closed local military base to environmental issues, and from contingent work to stopping development at a historic African-American cemetery. In 1994, the CAFE chapter on Hilton Head Island campaigned to have hotels pass on to banquet workers gratuities they collected on the workers' behalf. By 1996, CAFE had helped 140 workers at the Daufuskie Island Club and Resort on Hilton Head Island win union recognition and a 13 percent wage increase; it also helped bring NLRB charges against the employer when workers were subsequently fired.[79]

The replacement of regular employees with temporary or part-time, so-called contingent workers—usually with no union representation, job security, or benefits—has been a prime outcome of the new corporate agenda. Yet such workers have found it exceptionally difficult to organize. In Massachusetts, where contingent workers total about 25 percent of the workforce, a coalition of unions and community groups began a Campaign on Contingent Work. In 1996, the campaign opened a workers' center known as the TEMP—Temporary Employees Meeting Place—to bring together contingent workers for organizing meetings and educational workshops. The campaign pledged to support union organization where possible, but also to use direct action, workplace organizing, corporate campaigns, popular education, and media advocacy to challenge job degradation. The campaign developed a Bill of Rights for contingent workers and a Corporate Code of Conduct for employers who hire them. It also drafted and filed legislation that would require pay equity, pro-rated benefits, unemployment compensation, and maternity leave rights for contingent workers. When Woolworth's in Boston replaced more than thirty full-time workers, some of them with more than twenty-five years' seniority, with part-time workers, the Campaign on Contingent Work helped the workers picket Woolworth's, publicize the grievance, and even win support from the union that represented Woolworth's workers in Germany.[80]

Justice for Janitors

In 1984, the Service Employees International Union launched a national campaign to organize janitors and other building service employees. Most janitors were black and immigrant workers who worked for large building service corporations that were hired as subcontractors by building managers, who in turn were hired by building owners. Clearly new organizing techniques were needed to address such "networked production."

The Justice for Janitors campaign in Los Angeles began in 1987 with a focus on Century City, a high-class business district with a predominantly Latino and Latina cleaning staff. First, SEIU Local 399 began to rebuild the union in already unionized buildings by electing and training new stewards and other leaders. Next, union workers began making house calls and promoting the union in places where janitors socialized. Then the campaign organized "functional unions"—committees that acted like unions even though they lacked recognition—in non-union workplaces.

The campaign next decided to focus on International Service Systems, the world's largest cleaning contractor, a global corporation with its international headquarters in Denmark. Rather than use the NLRB election process, Justice for Janitors exerted direct pressure on ISS to recognize the union. Janitors organized daily meetings in their workplaces. They wore bandannas on their heads as signs of their support for the union; pulled short work stoppages, then more extended ones, in six different buildings, finally shutting down each building for a two-week period; and began marching through Century City's lobbies and outdoor walkways and disrupting happy hour at the district's swank saloons. A wide range of community supporters formed Solidarity with Justice for Janitors, raised money to support strikers, and encouraged political leaders to put pressure on building owners and managers.

When strikers and 300 supporters marched peacefully into Century City, they were attacked by more than 100 police officers:

> For two hours the Los Angeles Police Department sealed off Century City so that they could beat and arrest scores of striking janitors and their supporters. While horrified office workers and residents looked on, the police repeatedly flailed the front line of the Justice for Janitors march with riot batons, before launching a flanking attack that swept an entire section of the crowd into an underground parking structure. Those trapped inside were mercilessly pummeled: when they tried to flee, they were arrested for "failure to disperse."[81]

Ninety demonstrators were injured, nineteen seriously, including broken bones and a fractured skull. One pregnant woman suffered a miscarriage. The police riot was widely shown on television. Nine days later, ISS agreed to a contract with the union. Initially, the contract provided no wage increases, but when unionized ISS workers in New York City threatened a solidarity strike, ISS agreed to a wage increase as well.[82]

The Los Angeles victory inspired additional Justice for Janitors efforts around the country, including a dramatic blocking of bridges in Washington, D.C. But a bitter struggle soon broke out within Los Angeles SEIU Local 399. A rank-and-file caucus called the Multiracial Alliance charged:

> [F]or years, behind this facade of activism, bitter contradictions flourished between the union's administration and the membership. The truth is, the union was being governed in the style of the classic "old (white) boys" network. The only difference was that the old boys were self-described "progressives" who had fallen into anti-democratic practices, poor representation, and racism. The leadership excluded from decision-making those very workers who helped build the union.[83]

The Multiracial Alliance ran a slate of candidates and won 21 of 25 elected union leadership posts. When the new majority tried to make staff changes, the incumbent president asserted that only he had authority to do so. The SEIU soon placed the local in trusteeship, removed the elected Executive Board members, and appointed administrators to run the local.[84]

New Voice

The election of a Democratic president and Congress in 1992 provided no reversal for labor's declining fortunes. Hopes of addressing workers' deteriorating conditions via legislation crashed along with President Bill Clinton's compromised health care reform. When Clinton embraced the North American Free Trade Agreement, initiated by his predecessor George Bush, and pursued an even more vigorous support for corporate globalization than Bush and Reagan, the strategy of blaming Republicans for the labor movement's decline and looking to Democrats to reverse it lost credibility. More generally, the strategy of granting concessions and cooperating with employers against competing companies—and with "American" corporations against "foreign competition"—failed to save jobs or protect unions. "American" corporations continued to ship jobs abroad, and unions that had offered full cooperation to management were confronted with lockouts and demands for further concessions.

As a result, the 1990s saw moves toward change in what remained of national unions. Garment and textile unions merged to form a single union for the industry; the United Auto Workers, United Steel Workers, and International Association of Machinists prepared to do the same for metalworking. Some unions began experimenting with new ways of functioning day-to-day, adopting strategies such as the "organizing model," which aimed to use the techniques of a union organizing campaign to mobilize union members on the job. "Inside game" strategies of work-to-rule and slowdown became widely accepted as alternatives to strikes.

A significant break with the past came in the struggle over NAFTA. Large numbers of both union officials and rank-and-file members threw themselves into a campaign that a few years before would have drawn only a handful of dissidents. This struggle put them at odds with corporations, government, and most of the Democratic Party. At the same time it brought them into a broad alliance that included farm, environmental, anti-imperialist, religious, and many other groups, particularly at a local level. It legitimated a fundamental rethinking of the labor movement's relation to governments, global corporations, and foreign workers in the post-Cold War era. While nationalist, protectionist, and Mexico-bashing sentiments were expressed periodically, a new language of common interests with foreign workers also percolated through the labor movement. The loss of clout exemplified by labor's defeat on NAFTA also led to considerable soul-searching on the state of organized labor.

Early in 1995, leaders of the nation's largest unions, believing that inertia at the very top of the AFL-CIO was contributing to the decline of their own organizations, asked Lane Kirkland, for sixteen years the president of the AFL-CIO, to step down and let his second-in-command, Tom Donahue, take over. When Kirkland refused, several international officers asked Donahue to run against him, but Donahue declined. John Sweeney, head of the large and fast-growing Service Employees International Union, emerged as the insurgents' alternative. "I decided to run for president of the AFL-CIO because organized labor is the only voice of American workers and their families, and because the silence was deafening," Sweeney said.[85]

As Kirkland continued to hang on, the Sweeney campaign dubbed itself the "New Voice for American Workers" and developed a momentum of its own that went far beyond the initial palace power play. In addition to Sweeney, generally regarded as a dynamic but mainstream trade unionist, the New Voice ticket added Richard Trumka, president of the United Mine Workers, leader of the Pittston strike, and for many a symbol of militancy, and Linda Chavez-Thompson, vice-president of the American Federation of State, County, and Municipal Employees Union, representing women and people of color, groups notoriously under-represented in the AFL-CIO's top echelon.

New Voice articulated a trenchant critique of two decades of labor movement failure. Sweeney described the AFL-CIO as a "Washington-based institution concerned primarily with refining policy positions" instead of a "worker-based movement against greed, multinational corporations, race-baiting, and labor-baiting politicians."[86] He charged that the American labor movement is "irrelevant to the vast majority of unorganized workers in our country" and added that he had deep suspicions that "we are becoming irrelevant to our own members."[87] Chavez-Thompson attacked "thirty or forty years of AFL-CIO isolation and inaction."

Further, the national union presidents who initiated New Voice turned to forces outside the palace. New Voice mobilized thousands of activists and progressives and promoted many of their ideas and programs. By the time Kirkland finally accepted his opponents' original demand and stepped down in favor of Donahue, it was too late—there was no going back for the forces the Sweeney campaign had mobilized. It is symbolic of the new forces at play that Sweeney's margin of victory at the AFL-CIO convention in October 1995 was provided by the reformers who had taken over the Teamsters; it is also indicative of the continuity in the AFL-CIO's power structure that the presidents of a few large unions called most of the convention's shots.

In its first year in office, the new AFL-CIO leadership took important steps toward revitalizing the labor movement. It brought in a younger and more activist staff team. It created new departments dealing with such previously neglected subjects as women workers and employee ownership; completely reorganized other departments, for example, changing the mission of the International Affairs Department from enforcing Cold War anti-communism to promoting international labor solidarity; organized a "Union Summer" internship program for young union and college activists; and changed its public focus from the institutional interests of unions to the needs of all American working people. The new AFL-CIO expanded its political efforts and organized a grassroots campaign around the slogan "America Needs a Raise," which forced a Republican Congress to raise the minimum wage. While not ending Republican control of Congress, this political pressure may have contributed to shifting a right-wing juggernaut back toward the center.

Limits remained on how far the new AFL-CIO leadership was willing to go to challenge employers, however. Sweeney used the first anniversary of his election to tell business leaders:

> We want to help American business compete in the world and create new wealth for your shareholders and your employees.... It is time for business and labor to see each other as natural allies, not natural enemies. American labor no longer takes the position that quality, productivity and profits are not our business. They are our business. They are our jobs. And, indeed, they are our livelihoods.[88]

Sweeney and other top leaders have been arrested for participating in civil disobedience at several strikes and they organized major strike benefit contributions for striking Teamsters at UPS, but in their first two years they did not try to mobilize large-scale support for embattled workers or to create an organizational infrastructure for doing so. In the bitter lockout of workers at the Detroit newspapers, they resisted months of calls for a support mobilization, then called one only after national unions had ordered their Detroit workers to accept an unconditional return to work.

The major emphasis of the new leadership was on expanding union organizing, especially among low-wage workers. It greatly increased the AFL-CIO's own organizing activity and challenged its member unions to do the same. It picked several key organizing targets, including Mexican strawberry pickers in California; Las Vegas hotel, health care, and construction workers; and former welfare recipients now working in workfare programs. It attempted to reduce competition among unions by offering matching grants for joint organizing campaigns.[89]

The problems facing such a program are daunting. Sweeney suggested "modest goals of some growth every year, whether it's 3 or 4 percent." However, unions *lost* 388,000 members in 1995 and 92,000 members in 1996.[90] The legal right to organize is virtually a dead letter. A study by Harvard Law School professor Paul Weiler found that 10,000 workers lose their jobs each year for trying to organize unions.[91] Whether more organizing efforts can succeed without other fundamental changes in union structure and strategy remains an open question.

The War Zone

Despite booming profits and falling unemployment, the 1990s saw a new wave of employer demands for concessions, often backed by lockouts and the hiring of permanent replacement workers. The improbable focus for resistance to this drive was Decatur, Illinois, an industrial town of 84,000 on the prairie where three major strikes overlapped. By late 1995, virtually a third of Decatur's industrial workforce was on strike or locked out: 1,800 at Caterpillar, 1,250 at Bridgestone/Firestone, and 760 at A.E. Staley Manufacturing.[92] These struggles began separately, but they became intertwined in a manner resembling a regional mass strike.

Caterpillar

Caterpillar, Inc., is the world's largest manufacturer of earthmoving equipment and a pioneer of globalization with plants from Scotland and Mexico to Indonesia. It has also become a focus of conflict world-wide, including a 103-day factory occupation in Scotland in 1987 and a six-day occupation in Canada in 1991.[93]

In the 1980s, Caterpillar initiated a cooperation program with the United Auto Workers. Its 1989 contract was good enough for an official of the UAW's agricultural implements department to comment, "The company is not disloyal to their employees."[94] But at the same time, Caterpillar began a restructuring program that reduced its total workforce by about 30 percent while building new, non-union plants. By 1991, only 25 percent of its total workforce were UAW members.[95]

In 1991, Caterpillar demanded concessions, including a two-tier pay scale for new hires and changes in health insurance plans. Caterpillar said it needed the concessions to remain "globally competitive."[96] Its chairman, Donald V. Fites, "said he needed greater flexibility to set wages, benefits and working conditions to protect Caterpillar's pre-eminent position in competition with companies in Japan and Europe."[97] The UAW demanded that the company meet the pattern already established at competitor John Deere. When Caterpillar refused, workers struck in November 1991.

Caterpillar strikers evoked strong sentiments of solidarity among other workers throughout the Midwest and beyond. Twenty thousand union members attended a support rally in Peoria on March 22, 1992. The UAW established an Adopt-a-Striker program that raised $1 million. A UAW local in St. Paul, Minnesota, established a pledge campaign to raise $50,000 a month. Caterpillar workers in South Africa held a one-hour sympathetic strike.[98]

The bargaining chair of the largest Caterpillar local told the press, "As long as we hold the line and don't take our experience in there, we're going to be all right."[99] But after five months of the strike, Caterpillar threatened to bring in replacement workers. Strikers feared the loss of their jobs and the UAW leadership ordered them back to work.[100] "The abrupt end of a five-month strike against Caterpillar Inc. showed that management can bring even a union so mighty and rich as the United Automobile Workers to its knees," *The New York Times* wrote. The headline noted that "Caterpillar's Trump Card" was the "Threat of Permanently Replacing Strikers."[101]

Fifteen thousand UAW members worked for the next two and a half years without a contract under terms imposed by the company. According to nearly 100 unfair-labor-practice complaints issued by the National Labor Relations Board, Caterpillar disciplined union activists and transferred them to less desirable jobs, even punishing workers for wearing union T-shirts, buttons, and armbands or for leaving such union material in their cars.[102] A local union vice-president was told by a supervisor, "You are a worthless piece of —— and need to go away. And I'm going to make it happen." Then the worker was fired. Three years later the NLRB ordered Caterpillar to reinstate him with full back pay and benefits; the company defied the order.[103]

Workers responded with anger. In the course of a few months, eight wildcat strikes occurred. On one occasion, workers struck after the company said they would be disciplined for chanting union slogans. On another, workers walked out when a steward with a heart condition was harassed by the company and then taken to the hospital with chest pains.

The UAW hired a public relations firm to give its campaign a new public face. On its recommendation, the union toned down its rhetoric and reduced its bargaining demands.[104] The UAW also initiated an in-plant campaign to pressure Caterpillar. While the in-plant campaign represented a move toward tactics previously eschewed, critics of the union leadership charged that the campaign was ineffective because it didn't empower workers in the plants to act on their own, but rather expected them to turn their efforts on and off at the command of top union officials.

In June 1994, the UAW ordered its members back out on strike. The company attempted to continue production with thousands of managers, office workers, new hires, contract workers, and a substantial number of union members who crossed the picket lines. The apparent success of Caterpillar's hardball tactics found many imitators. John Deere, for example, began demanding concessions from the union. As *Business Week* wrote, "the company hasn't been eager to compromise because rival Caterpillar Inc. has shown that the UAW is vulnerable."[105]

In December 1995, after seventeen months on strike, the UAW negotiated a new agreement with Caterpillar. Caterpillar workers voted it down by nearly 80 percent. The UAW then "recessed" the strike and ordered union members back to work anyway. The rejected contract "dismantles representation in the plant," said the president of the Decatur local. Union representatives were severely restricted and the company claimed the right to unilaterally reject without appeal grievances it regarded as repetitive or frivolous. The contract established twelve-hour alternating work schedules that would be "voluntary, if possible"; allowed the expansion of the part-time and temporary workforce; and gave Caterpillar a wide range of other concessions. *The Wall Street Journal* concluded: "Management is in control."

Workers returning to Caterpillar referred to the conditions they faced as "Stalag Caterpillar." By the start of 1997, the UAW reported that 138 union members had been disciplined for such offenses as wearing a T-shirt that said "Families in Solidarity, UAW." In the Decatur plant, union members—but not strikebreakers and managers—were forced to wear safety glasses and earplugs at lunch.[106]

The UAW declared that "the fight for justice for Caterpillar workers is anything but over" and called the company "one of the worst corporate outlaws in America." They sent "Truth Squads" to leaflet at trade shows where the company displayed its wares "to let the nation know that it's not 'business as usual' at Caterpillar."

A year after the end of the seventeen-month strike, the NLRB ruled that Caterpillar's unfair labor practices (for which the board has filed over 250 separate complaints) caused and prolonged the strike. The NLRB also found that the company's "pattern of unlawful conduct convinces us that, without proper restraint, [Caterpillar] is likely to persist in its attempts to interfere with employees' statutory rights."[107]

Bridgestone/Firestone

In the early 1990s, Japanese-owned Bridgestone/Firestone was a model of labor-management cooperation. The union accepted company quality circles; in return, management accepted pattern bargaining and voluntarily let the United Rubber Workers organize its new plants. Then a new management team took over and began planning a change. In 1994, Bridgestone/Firestone refused to follow the contract pattern already accepted by Goodyear and Uniroyal Goodrich and proposed instead a new contract with twelve-hour work shifts, seven-day-a-week operations, health care cuts, a 30 percent wage cut for new hires, and other concessions. The company hired Vance Security guards and, as a memo later uncovered by the union revealed, prepared to import three million tires from Japan "as a strike countermeasure." In July 1994, 4,200 Bridgestone/Firestone URW members struck in six locations.[108]

In 1995, Bridgestone/Firestone hired 2,300 permanent replacement workers. In an attempt to save its members' jobs, the union agreed to end the strike unconditionally. But the company refused to reinstate nearly 700 of its union workers.

The union, which merged with the United Steel Workers in 1995, began a corporate campaign to publicize Bridgestone/Firestone's actions. In May 1996, hundreds of steelworkers waved black flags at the Indy 500 (in auto racing, the black flag is a sign of immediate disqualification for gross violation of rules). The union began a boycott of Bridgestone/Firestone with regular picketing of hundreds of its outlets. USWA president George Becker said, "We intend to make Bridgestone/Firestone a poster child for corporate greed and irresponsibility."[109] By September 1996, more than thirty local government bodies had voted to support the union's boycott.[110]

In July 1996, unions around the world organized "Days of Outrage" protests against Bridgestone/Firestone. In Argentina, a two-hour General Assembly of all workers at the gates of the Bridgestone/Firestone plant brought production to a halt while 2,000 workers heard American Bridgestone/Firestone workers describe the company's conduct. (The action also served as a warning to the company that its workers in Argentina were prepared to strike for their own demands.) Bridgestone workers also staged a series of one-hour work stoppages in São Paulo, then "worked like turtles"—the Brazilian phrase for a slowdown. Unions in Belgium, France, Italy, and Spain met with local Bridgestone managements and tabled demands for a settlement with the union in the United States. Bridgestone's European management reversed its previous position and met with a joint union delegation from Belgium, France, Italy, and Spain to discuss the U.S. dispute.

A leaflet signed by the Decatur local early in the strike asked people not to buy products "made by *the Japanese owned* Bridgestone/Firestone,"[111] and a picket sign referred to the company's policy as a "second Pearl Harbor." But the union shifted from Japan-bashing to seeking support of Japanese workers. U.S. Bridgestone/Firestone workers went to Japan and met with representatives of sixty Japanese union organizations including the largest Japanese national labor federation, RENGO. The gathering called for the immediate reinstatement of fired U.S. workers.[112] On the strike's second anniversary, Bridgestone/Firestone workers from the United States and 500 Japanese unionists marched through the streets of Tokyo.[113]

In November 1996, Bridgestone/Firestone reopened negotiations and four days later unexpectedly came to a settlement. Bridgestone/Firestone agreed to rehire all former strikers with seniority and provide partial back-pay and an immediate 40 cents-per-hour wage increase. The company won its demands for twelve-hour shifts and twenty-four-hour-a-day, seven-day-a-week operation, but abandoned most of the other concessions it had sought. (Returned strikers had already used a work-to-rule to force Bridgestone to abandon *rotating* twelve-hour shifts.) According to Kate Bronfenbrenner, research director of the Cornell School of Industrial and Labor Relations, "Bridgestone/Firestone understood that no matter what, the Steelworkers wouldn't go away until the workers got back in the plant. They would have a mosquito at the ear forever."[114]

Staley

In 1988, the A.E. Staley Manufacturing Company, a producer of corn-based sweeteners in Decatur, was acquired by the British conglomerate Tate & Lyle. The union charged that the ownership change led to "a big change in management's attitude toward safety," which led to the death of at least one worker. After a detailed investigation in 1991, the Occupational Safety and Health Administration fined Staley $1.6 million for 298 health and safety violations.[115] When the company demanded that written manuals be prepared detailing the job of each worker, workers concluded that Staley was looking to provoke a strike and replace them with strikebreakers. Members of the local prepared for a fight and voted almost unanimously to raise monthly union dues from $18 to $100.

In 1992, Staley gave a "best and final offer" filled with concessions, including the gutting of the seniority system and grievance process and twelve-hour shifts rotating every thirty days. The union voted the proposal down in September 1992 by 97 percent.[116] But workers, well aware of the threat of permanent replacement, did not go on strike. Instead, they turned to a corporate campaign, work-to-rule actions, community solidarity, and civil disobedience.

To help with their corporate campaign, the local brought in Ray Rogers of Corporate Campaigns, Inc. Activists organized boycotts of a bank chain on whose board two Staley executives served as directors and forced them to resign. Workers began to put pressure on State Farm Insurance Company, which owned a large share of Archer Daniels Midland, a competitor of Staley but also a large shareholder in Tate & Lyle.

The Deactur local also brought in Jerry Tucker as an adviser and organized a work-to-rule. Observers were struck by the impact of the in-plant strategy on the workers themselves. "They went unit by unit, department by department, and took the contract and discussed it line by line. They talked about it in groups, in the bars after work and in the plant."[117] Dan Rhodes, a feed dryer operator with twenty years experience at Staley, said:

For years you went out there and you did your job, see, and the companies really didn't have to do that much except for making sure you're there. They didn't have to make any decisions. I think the thing that scared the company the most was when they realized that to work to rule, we started using this [our heads] instead of this [our backs]. They looked over and said, "Hey, they're using their minds. We have lost control. If they start using their mind and target it towards us, we've lost control of that plant." And they'll spend millions of dollars [getting it back] ... [T]hat's what this is all about, control. And we took that power and control away from them.[118]

Workers estimated that the work-to-rule cut production by one-third to one-half. In June 1993, Staley locked out all 760 workers.

Staley workers responded by reaching out. In Decatur, they helped form a Campaign for Justice representing almost 4,000 striking or locked-out Caterpillar, Bridgestone/Firestone, and Staley workers that began meeting regularly in January 1994. When the city manager drew up an ordinance to restrict the right of citizens to parade, assemble, and rally, claiming it was to prevent rallies by the Ku Klux Klan, workers from the three unions filled the Civic Center where the city council was meeting. The ordinance failed.[119]

Decatur workers put out more than one million pieces of direct mail and raised more than $2 million. Many of them traveled the country as "road warriors," raising money and spreading the word about the "war zone" in Decatur.[120] Solidarity groups were formed in Illinois and throughout the country.

On June 25, 1994, workers blocked the entrance to the Staley plant. The police, whom the strikers had regarded as sympathetic up to that point, turned violent, using pepper gas to attack non-violent demonstrators. Five months later, 7,000 strikers and supporters from across the country gathered in Decatur for another demonstration. They carried signs reading "Corporate Greed is Tearing Decatur Apart" and "Labor Rights = Civil Rights." Father Martin Mangan of the St. James Catholic Church in Decatur christened a bridge "Workers' Memorial Viaduct" in honor of Jim Beals, who died in an accident at Staley in 1992.

In early 1995, a new labor-supported mayor and city council member were elected. Staley union president David Watts won in a primary for city council but was defeated in the general election. The week after the election, the assistant city manager fired four city workers, including an American Federation of State, County, and Municipal Employees local president who had been active in the Watts campaign. At a protest rally, Dave Watts said, "We're with you city workers 100 percent."[121]

Staley workers increasingly focused pressure on the company's major customers. This strategy involved seeking active support from the higher reaches of the labor movement. In January 1995, under pressure from their international union, the local ended its relationship with Ray Rogers and moved Jerry Tucker into the background. In February 1995, seventy workers from Staley, Caterpillar, and Bridgestone/Firestone went to lobby the AFL-CIO Executive Council at its annual meeting in exclusive Bal Harbour, Florida. Several Executive Council members pledged support, but the council turned down the delegation's proposal for a "solidarity bank" to support striking and locked-out workers around the country.[122]

Meanwhile, Staley workers were gradually being ground down. When Staley offered an even worse contract with twelve-hour shifts rotating from day to night every six days and with unlimited subcontracting, workers voted it down—but only by 57 percent.[123]

The locked-out Local 7837 members asked their national union and the AFL-CIO leadership to join in leading a national mobilization against Staley's major customers. Union pressure led the Miller Brewing Company to end its relationship with Staley. Then the focus moved to Pepsi, which bought about 30 percent of its corn sweeteners from Staley. The AFL-CIO Executive Council decided to support the Staley workers' campaign against Pepsi and to leaflet at Pepsi-sponsored events and at Taco Bell, KFC, and Pizza Hut—companies owned by Pepsi. By August 1995, Pepsi began informing protesting callers that it is "no longer buying from Staley's Decatur plant."[124]

Dan Lane, a nineteen-year employee of Staley, started a fast October 1, 1995. Lane said, "I'm no Gandhi or Dr. King, but I believe we're fighting for our lives here, just like they were. The fight is more than a labor dispute. It is a fight for human rights. It is about safety, workers being able to be with their families, and having job security."[125] Lane believed that given the large number of workers already on strike in Decatur, the emergence of several pending labor disputes, and the growth of outside support, workers should consider moving toward mass picketing and a citywide general strike, but this approach was not supported by local union leaders.

Lane ended his fast after sixty-five days when he received a pledge of support from newly elected AFL-CIO president John Sweeney. Staley workers believed this pledge included a commitment that the AFL-CIO would appoint a well-staffed task force to work on the campaign to stop Pepsi from renewing its contract with Staley, which was due to expire at the end of the year.[126] But according to an AFL-CIO official close to the proceedings, "There never was such a task force. It was a facade—a smoke-and-mirrors thing."[127] Lane never heard from Sweeney again.

On December 12, 1995, Jim Shinall, a former union officer who had long called for a settlement so that he and other older workers could retire, was elected president of the local by a vote of 249 to 201. (He announced that he would retire in April.)[128] On December 22, 1995, after thirty months of struggle, the Staley contract was ratified by 56 percent, 286 to 226. Little had changed from the original "best and final" offer rejected by 97 percent three years before, except that retirement provisions were sweetened to win votes of workers eager to get out. The contract gave the company unlimited subcontracting, twelve-hour rotating shifts every thirty days, mandatory overtime, no amnesty for workers fired for union activity, and immediate firing should workers "misspeak" to a strikebreaker.[129] Under contract, union jobs would be cut by two-thirds in 1997.[130]

The United Paperworkers International Union forced the vote even though the Local 7837 bargaining committee and executive board voted overwhelmingly not to take the package back to the membership, who had already rejected it twice. UPIU president Wayne Glenn informed Local 7837 president Dave Watts that he was exercising his power as the international head to overrule the local leadership.

Only one-fourth of locked-out Staley workers took back their jobs. More than 550 decided either to retire, take severance, or look for work elsewhere.

"We lost this battle," Dan Lane said, "but the war against American workers continues. The rest of corporate America was watching Decatur closely. Make no mistake, there'll be no peace for American workers. The question is, when are we going to unite, turn the AFL-CIO around, meet fire with fire, and fight until we win?"[131]

The UPS Strike

Despite the terrible defeats of the past quarter-century, workers still have power if they choose to use it. That power was rediscovered in the 1997 Teamsters strike at United Parcel Service.

UPS employs more than 340,000 workers in 200 countries. It delivers 80 percent of all packages shipped by ground in the United States and employs nearly 200,000 members of the Teamsters union. Its after-tax profits in 1996 exceeded $1 billion.[132]

UPS pioneered many of the techniques of labor control and speed-up that have spread through U.S. corporations since the 1970s. "Each task," according to *Fortune*, "from picking or delivering parcels on a route to sorting packages in a central hub, is carefully calibrated according to productivity standards."[133] One result of the ensuing pressure is that UPS has an OSHA recordable injury rate 2.5 times the industry average—itself far higher than in most other industries—according to the company's own health and safety manual.[134]

In 1982, the Teamsters accepted a two-tier wage system in which part-timers earned less than full-timers. In subsequent contracts, the Teamsters negotiated a series of raises for full-timers, but none for part-timers.[135] UPS took advantage of this pattern to expand its part-time workforce from 42 percent in 1986 to more than 60 percent by 1997. Part-timers were paid less than half the wages of full-time drivers.[136] Starting in 1993, 83 percent of new jobs created at UPS were part-time—or at least they were classified as part-time. In actuality, at least 10,000 UPS workers classified as part-time actually worked 35 or more hours a week.[137] Rachel Howard, a part-time worker in Burtonsville, Maryland, said, "There are many weeks that I have been at UPS that I have worked 60 and 65 hours a week but UPS calls me a part-timer and pays me part-time wages.... I am now in my eighth year and still waiting for a full-time job."[138]

Rank-and-file UPS workers, organized in the dissident groups UPSurge and Teamsters for a Democratic Union, had conducted a two-decade struggle against these conditions. These rank-and-file organizations engaged in job actions, contract rejections, and wildcat strikes, but met determined resistance from the leadership of the Teamsters union.[139] When the federal government forced a direct election of the Teamsters' president in 1991, Ron Carey—who had been a UPS driver for twelve years, head of the largest UPS local for twenty-four years, and a long-standing opponent of the national Teamsters leadership—was elected.[140]

In 1996, the Teamsters began preparing for a strike against UPS. The Teamsters made the centerpiece of their campaign a demand for 10,000 new full-time jobs for current part-timers. The demand received strong support not only from part-timers, but also from full-time workers who felt the growth of part-time work and a two-tiered wage system threatened their own position. Carey told members, "A contract that provides good jobs for working families certainly won't be won at the bargaining table. The only way you can win that is ... on the picket lines and in the community."[141]

On July 30, 1997, UPS made its "last, best, and final offer," which not only refused to create the full-time jobs the Teamsters demanded, but proposed a company takeover of the union's pension plan. The company entered the strike in strong financial condition and with a $4.5 billion line of credit.[142] The Teamsters had net assets of $17 million at the start of the year—barely enough to pay its 180,000 striking UPS members $55 weekly strike benefits for a week. The imbalance of resources "leaves the Teamsters chief running a tremendous risk," *Business Week* commented. "UPS clearly has the ability to outlast us," a Teamsters official acknowledged.[143] Nonetheless, the Teamsters walked off the job on August 4—starting the largest strike in the United States in twenty years.[144]

Fewer than 5 percent of Teamsters crossed picket lines.[145] During the strike, managers were able to move less than 5 percent of the company's normal 12 million packages a day.[146] UPS lost an estimated $30 million daily in profits.

The Teamsters' focus on the need for full-time jobs struck a responsive chord in an era in which as much as one-fourth of the workforce is now contingent. It made part-time work a symbol of the entire new system of work organization referred to as "lean production": downsizing, outsourcing, privatization, and use of part-time, temporary, and other contingent workers. A *USA Today*-CNN-Gallup poll indicated that 55 percent of those surveyed supported the Teamsters, compared with 27 percent backing UPS[147]—an extraordinary result in a strike that caused considerable inconvenience to the public. "American people can't live like that—four or five hours of work a day—I know I can't," observed an office worker from New Albany, Indiana.[148] The public's opinion helped make it less likely that President Clinton would bow to business pressure to intervene against the strike.

AFL-CIO president John Sweeney said, "UPS is leading the way in a dangerous trend which is threatening the living standards of all American working families ... [T]he Teamsters fight is our fight."[149] In a move with little precedent, Sweeney announced that AFL-CIO affiliates would lend the Teamsters $10 million a week, enough to provide $55 per week in strike benefits "for many, many weeks."[150] The AFL-CIO called a news conference with major women's groups to discuss how the shift to part-time jobs affected working women. Strikers planned solidarity rallies in thirty cities.[151] The 2,000 pilots at UPS, represented by the Independent Pilots Association, refused to cross the picket lines.[152] Reuters reported that "unions representing UPS workers in several European countries were planning job actions to drum up support."[153]

According to *The Wall Street Journal*, the UPS board of directors was preparing to meet and discuss "replacement-worker plans" and a team inside UPS was "developing plans" for replacement workers.[154] Instead, on August 18, after weathering the strike for fifteen days,

UPS unexpectedly accepted a settlement that included the bulk of the union's demands.

UPS agreed to create 10,000 new full-time jobs by combining existing part-time positions, as well as promoting a minimum of 10,000 part-timers to full-time jobs. UPS was prohibited from using subcontractors without agreement from local unions. Full-timers were granted a 15 percent raise over five years and, to reduce the wage differential, part-time workers were granted a 37 percent raise.[155] In exchange, the Teamsters made some fairly modest concessions, including acceptance of a five-year contract.

The Teamster victory was aided by factors not present in all such conflicts: the lowest unemployment rate in decades and a thoroughly unionized company with a near-monopoly and work that mostly can't be moved abroad. Nonetheless, the strike was widely perceived as a historic turning point for the labor movement. "I remember in the 1980s when the air traffic controllers union [PATCO] was wiped out," Ron Carey said. "For fifteen years after that, employers all across the country cut jobs, cut pensions, cut health coverage, and stepped on workers' rights. Working people were on the run, but not anymore. This strike marks a new era." The fight with UPS "shows what working people can accomplish when they all stick together."[156]

Rank-and-file UPS workers also expressed their satisfaction with the outcome. Gloria Harris, a thirty-nine-year old single mother in Chicago, said the strikers had felt inspired by a sense that they were standing up for other working people. "This sent a message to other companies that you can't keep pushing people so hard, and expect to get away with paying them part-time." She said that, except for those who crossed the picket lines, the strike brought people together in a way that company picnics and bowling leagues never could. "We now feel more like brothers and sisters than co-workers," she said, noting the diversity of the strikers, who, until the walkout, had often kept to their own racial or ethnic group. "We all learned something about color. It comes down to green."[157] Forty-nine-year old David Johnson of New York, who had worked for UPS since he was a teenager, noted, "I'm … looking out for the people who will come after me."[158] "It's a big win not only for the union but for labor," said Robert

Ridley, a forty-four-year old UPS driver in Austin, Texas. "This was labor against corporate America."[159]

Of Biblical Proportions

Globalization, corporate restructuring, employer intransigence, and other changes have weakened some of the methods workers have used to assert their power. Such changes have happened before and workers have developed new tools to deal with new situations. Globalization may undermine national labor movements, but it can be countered through global solidarity. The dis-integrated corporation may undermine conventional strike targeting, but it can be countered by corporate campaigns that target the entire corporate network or by strikes that target key links in the chain of suppliers. (Such "lean production" techniques as single sourcing and "just-in-time" parts delivery can make companies *more* vulnerable to strikes. When 3,000 workers at two brake plants in Dayton, Ohio, struck on March 5, 1996, twenty-five General Motors plants, with more than 175,000 workers, were shut down.[160]) Permanent replacement workers may be used to break strikes, but their use can be forestalled by inside strategies and by mass direct action. Such tools cannot use themselves, however. Only as workers come to believe it is necessary and possible to resist employers and other established authorities, take control of their own action, and advance together by supporting each other can the potential of these methods be realized.

In the last decades of the twentieth century, as is typical between periods of mass strike, powerlessness and defeats drove workers in two opposite directions: toward passive acquiescence and toward wider solidarity and more militant tactics. The general decline of the labor movement and of strikes and other visible forms of struggle illustrated the tendency toward passive acquiescence. Yet neither individualist efforts to curry favor with employers, nor union cooperation in increasing employer "competitiveness," nor nationalist or racist scapegoating provided solutions for the real problems working people faced.

The workers who participated in the thirty-month struggle at A.E. Staley Manufacturing in Decatur, Illinois, reflected deeply on the choices workers face at the end of the twentieth century. Art Dhermy, a veteran power systems operator at the company, said:

Right now, a "radical" is somebody that stands up and says enough's enough, we ain't taking no more. Instead of taking what they give you and run. Standing up for what you believe in, standing up for what your grandparents and parents have fought for fifty years to be able to give you an inheritance. Is that too radical? It's up to me now to stand up for my kids, and my grandkids. In fact, it's almost too late for my kids. It's time for me, really, to stand up for my grandkids, so they have somebody for them to look up to and say, "My grandfather saved this and gave this to me as an inheritance gift," like my grandfather did for me when he fought the coal mine wars here in central Illinois.... If we don't do it, where's it gonna stop? It's gonna stop when my grandkids are working for a dollar and a quarter an hour.[161]

"We have to get back to the concept of the IWW," said Royal Plankenhorn, a senior process operator for twenty years at Staley, "one big union."

Because we built these walls of internationals and locals and stuff, and it's worked against us. It's been, "Well, that's his fight. Don't bother me. He's the one going through that. I've got a job." We can't do that anymore. The fact is, we have to break down the walls that divide us because his battle is my battle, my battle is his battle, and your battle is my battle. We can't succeed any other way.[162]

According to Mike Griffin, another locked-out Staley worker:

This goes beyond Decatur, Illinois, and beyond our national borders. What you're looking at here is an all-out effort to destroy the labor movement. They're doing the same thing in France and Honduras and Canada and Haiti—I met with labor leaders from those countries two months ago in San Francisco. In order to generate this new world order you're looking at the IMF, the World Bank, the World Trade Organization, trying to create a worldwide two-class system. What is happening at Decatur is the cutting edge of a class struggle worldwide. They have to take out organized labor to get what they want.... We had better wake up as workers, union or non-union, in America or elsewhere around the world. They have to destroy those that have the means to fight back and organize.... It has biblical proportions.[163]

Thirty days into his fast, Staley worker Dan Lane told a story he had read in a novel:

It was way back during the Depression, in Akron, Ohio. It was a very brutal time. People were actually being thrown out into the street. They were freezing to death, or they were getting pneumonia and were dying as a result of it.

A family was being evicted from their home in Akron.

And now, here's the thing: People were aware of it, but people weren't organized, people didn't know how to react to it. The family was strung out all over the place, their goods and everything like that, and [the police] were still carrying them out, and here [the father] was sitting out there with his family, and he was just bawling like a baby. You know, everything he had ... and what was he going to do through the night?

An organizer of the unemployed walked up with a group, grabbed one of the chairs, and started walking back in to the house.

And he turns around, and he says to everybody, "Let's take it back." And there was no reaction. There was no reaction whatsoever. And just for a moment, this thought was running through his mind, which has always struck me. He says, "By God, they don't realize it. It's only *by them doing it*, will it ever get done."

People have to realize that. They can't continue to wait on the AFL-CIO, they can't wait on their international, they can't wait on everybody else. It has to be up to us, as individuals, to take and go that extra step, step out in front. Just like in the novel: Pick up that chair, and walk on in and past the cops, and not be so concerned about what is going to happen. Because you carrying that chair in there, you taking on that fight, is much greater than anything you're going to lose.[164]

•

In the past, working people have periodically responded to unacceptable conditions by adopting collective strategies and asserting themselves to gain more power over their lives and work. Whether or how workers move from individual to collective strategies depends on millions of personal experiences, social interactions, and decisions. It is possible that, in the era of globalization, this process is just history.

Don't count on it.

Teamsters celebrate their strike victory over United Parcel Service at a West 44th Street pub in New York City, August 19, 1997.
(Photo by Steve Berman, permission of *The New York Times*.)

For Further Reading and Viewing

A useful resource on workers' history is the two-volume American Social History Project series, *Who Built America?*—volume 1: *Who Built America?: Working People and the Nation's Economy, Culture, and Society: From Conquest and Colonization Through Reconstruction*, ed. Bruce Levine et al. (New York: Pantheon Books, 1990); volume 2: *Who Built America?: Working People and the Nation's Economy, Culture, and Society: From the Gilded Age to the Present*, ed. Joshua Freeman et al. (New York: Pantheon Books, 1992). • As part of a campaign to bring labor history into the school curriculum, the Westconn Area Local of the American Postal Workers Union has compiled and periodically updated an annotated bibliography of "the full spectrum of available labor studies and working class history including studies in women's topics and a full representation of the works available on Afro-American and minority working history." It includes more than 600 references, many with annotations by well-known labor historians. It is available from the local, which also makes available a listing of labor history videotapes ("Labor History/Studies Bibliography," American Postal Workers Union, Westconn Local, PO Box 3885, Danbury CT 06813). • The California Federation of Teachers makes available "Bringing Labor into the K-12 Curriculum: Resource Guide for Teachers" (California Federation of Teachers, One Kaiser Plaza, Suite 1440, Oakland CA 94612). • The Illinois Labor History Society publishes on-line "A Curriculum of United States Labor History for Teachers," edited by James D. Brown, Jr. (http://www.kentlaw.edu/ ilhs/curriculum.html). • The Organization of American Historians featured a special review of labor history literature in *OAH Magazine of History* 11: 2 (Winter 1997): "Special Issue on Labor History" (http://www.indiana.edu/~oah/magazine). • *Labor History* includes an annual bibliography of new publications in labor history. • For further video references, see Tom Zaniello, *Working Stiffs, Union Maids, Reds, and Riffraff: An Organized Guide to Films about Labor* (Ithaca: ILR Press-Cornell UP, 1996).

Notes to the Introduction

1. In 1989, the top 1 percent of U.S. families owned 38.9 percent of total net worth (the value of one's assets minus one's debts) and 48.1 percent of net financial assets. Lawrence Mishel, Jared Bernstein, and John Schmitt, *The State of Working America, 1996-1997* (Armonk: M.E. Sharpe, 1997), p. 278.

2. In 1983, the latest year for which data are available, 54 percent of American families had zero or negative net financial assets. Mishel et al., p. 280.

3. Of the 100 largest economies in the world, 51 today are corporations, not countries. Sarah Anderson and John Cavanagh, "The Top 200: The Rise of Global Corporate Power," Institute for Policy Studies, September 25, 1996.

4. Rosa Luxemburg, "Massenstreik, Partei und Gewerkshaften" ("The Mass Strike, the Political Party and the Trade Unions"), Hamburg, 1906, cited in J.P. Nettl, *Rosa Luxemburg*, vol. 2 (London: Oxford University Press, 1966), p. 500. *Strike!* is not intended to be a complete study of strikes, let alone a general history of the American working class in the industrial era. Many dimensions of working-class history—such as daily life in the workplace, community, and home; the dynamics of gender, race, and ethnicity; the sphere of politics; and the realm of culture and ideology—are touched on only as they affect the particular struggles presented.

5. George F. Addes and R.J. Thomas, in introduction to Henry Kraus, *The Many and the Few* (Los Angeles: Plantin Press, 1947).

Notes to the Prologue

1. Alexis de Tocqueville, *Democracy in America*, vol. 2 (New York: Vintage edition, 1959), p. 170.

2. *Ibid.*, p. 170.

3. *Ibid.*, p. 168.

4. *Ibid.*, p. 168.

5. *Ibid.*, p. 168.

6. *Ibid.*, pp. 168-69.

7. *Ibid.*, p. 169.

8. *Ibid.*, p. 171.

9. Ibid., p. 171.

10. Terence V. Powderly, *Thirty Years of Labor 1859-1889* (Columbus: Excelsior Publishing House, 1889), pp. 26-27.

11. Goldwin Smith, "The Labour War in the United States," *The Contemporary Review* 30 (September 1877): 537, cited in Robert V. Bruce, *1877: Year of Violence* (Indianapolis: Bobbs-Merrill, 1959), p. 26.

Notes to Chapter 1: The Great Upheaval

1. Minute Book Journal, p. 306, in B&O Archives; cited in Robert V. Bruce, *1877: Year of Violence* (Indianapolis: Bobbs-Merrill, 1959), p. 64. Bruce's book is not only a comprehensive study of the Great Upheaval of 1877, but also one of the few full-length studies of a period of American mass strike.

2. F. Vernon Aler, *Aler's History of Martinsburg and Berkeley County, West Virginia* (Hagerstown, Maryland: 1888), pp. 301-4, cited in Bruce, p. 76.

3. WPA, *Mathews Papers*, pp. 30-32, cited in Bruce, p. 77.

4. Aler, pp. 308-9, cited in Bruce, p. 77.

5. *Wheeling Register*, July 19, 1877, cited in Bruce, p. 78.

6. *Mathews Papers*, p. 34, cited in Bruce, p. 79.

7. *Wheeling Intelligencer*, July 18, 1877, cited in Bruce, p. 80.

8. *Baltimore Sun*, July 19, 1877, cited in Bruce, p. 83.

9. *Mathews Papers*, pp. 36-37, cited in Bruce, p. 80.

10. National Archives, Adjutant General's Office, Letters Received, 1877, No. 8035 (enclosure 80), cited in Bruce, pp. 81-82.

11. *Baltimore Sun*, July 18, 1877, cited in Bruce, p. 82.

12. *Wheeling Register*, July 18, 1877, cited in Bruce, p. 84.

13. *Martinsburg Independent*, July 21, 1877, cited in Bruce, pp. 84-85.

14. *Wheeling Register*, July 18, 1877, cited in Bruce, p. 85.

15. *Wheeling Register*, July 19, 1877, cited in Bruce, pp. 90-91.

16. Herbert G. Gutman, "Trouble on the Railroads in 1873-1874: Prelude to the 1877 Crisis?" *Labor History* 2: 2 (Spring 1961): 221.

17. *Ibid.*, p. 231.

18. *Ibid.*, p. 220.

19. *Ibid.*, p. 232.

20. *Ibid.*, p. 218.

21. *Ibid.*, p. 229.

22. *Ibid.*, p. 235.

23. Report of Riots Committee, p. 925, cited in Bruce, p. 50.

24. *Pittsburgh Post*, June 7, 1877, cited in Bruce, p. 51.

25. Report of Riots Committee, p. 671, cited in Bruce, p. 59.

26. *Ibid.*, pp. 673-74, cited in Bruce, p. 59.

27. *Pittsburgh Post*, June 7, 1877, cited in Bruce, p. 61.

28. *Pittsburgh Chronicle*, June 27, 1877, cited in Bruce, p. 62.

29. *Wheeling Intelligencer*, June 15, 1877, cited in Bruce, p. 65.

30. Clifton K. Yearley, Jr., "The Baltimore and Ohio Railroad Strike of 1877," *Maryland Historical Magazine* 51 (September 1956), cited in Bruce, p. 75.

31. Aler, pp. 301-4, cited in Bruce, p. 74.

32. *Cumberland Civilian*, July 22, 1877, cited in Bruce, p. 96.

33. *Wheeling Register*, July 21, 1877, cited in Bruce, p. 97.

34. *Wheeling Intelligencer*, July 23, 1877, cited in Bruce, p. 101.

35. *Philadelphia Inquirer*, July 23, 1877, cited in Bruce, p. 101.

36. *Baltimore Evening Bulletin*, July 21, 1877, cited in Bruce, p. 104.

37. *Baltimore Sun*, July 21, 1877, cited in Bruce, p. 108.

38. Bruce, pp. 15, 17. Richard B. Morris, ed., *Encyclopedia of American History* (New York: Harper and Brothers, 1953), p. 521.

39. Norman J. Ware, *The Labor Movement in the United States, 1860-1895: A Study in Democracy* (New York: Vintage Books, 1964), p. 45.

40. J.N.A. Griswold to R. Harris, July 7, 1877, cited in Bruce, p. 56.

41. *Pittsburgh Post*, July 19, 1877, cited in Bruce, p. 73.

42. Cited in Bruce, p. 119.

43. Bruce, pp. 122-23.

44. Report of Riots Committee, cited in Bruce, pp. 124-25.

45. *Railroad Dispatch*, July 20, 1877, cited in Bruce, p. 125.

46. *Ibid.*

47. Report of Riots Committee, cited in Bruce, p. 137.

48. Bruce, p. 143.

49. Bruce, pp. 143-44.

50. Report of Riots Committee, cited in Bruce, p. 140.

51. *Ibid.*

52. *Pittsburgh Leader*, cited in Bruce, pp. 135-36.

53. Bruce, p. 134.

54. Report of Riots Committee, cited in Bruce, p. 135.

55. Bruce, p. 141.

56. Bruce, pp. 141-22.

57. *Pittsburgh Commercial Gazette*, July 23, 1877, cited in Bruce, p. 147.

58. *Pittsburgh Commercial Gazette*, July 31, 1877, cited in Bruce, p. 147.

59. Report of Riots Committee, cited in Bruce, p. 155.

60. Bruce, pp. 166-67.

61. Carroll D. Wright, *The Battles of Labor* (Philadelphia, 1906), p. 122, cited in Bruce, p. 173.

62. Report of Riots Committee, p. 260, cited in Bruce, p. 176.

63. Bruce, pp. 175-76.

64. *Columbus Dispatch*, July 25, 1877, cited in Bruce, p. 207.

65. *Reading Eagle*, July 23, 1877, and *New York Times*, October 4, 1877, cited in Bruce, p. 189.

66. Bruce, pp. 192-93.

67. Bruce, p. 194.

68. *Ohio State Journal*, July 20, 1877, cited in Bruce, pp. 127-28.

69. Bruce, p. 182.

70. *Ohio State Journal*, July 24, 1877, cited in Bruce, p. 207.

71. Bruce, p. 250.

72. *Chicago Times*, July 25, 1877, cited in Bruce, p. 243.

73. Cited in Bruce, p. 156.

74. David T. Burbank, *Reign of the Rabble: The St. Louis General Strike of 1877* (New York: Augustus M. Kelley, 1966), p. 61.

75. *Ibid.*, p. 43.

76. *Ibid.* Coopers were paid on a piecework basis for the barrels they made.

77. Morris Hiliquit, *History of Socialism in the United States* (New York, 1910), p. 77, cited in Bruce, p. 260.

78. Burbank, p. 53.

79. *Ibid.*, p. 54.

80. *Ibid.*, p. 70.

81. *Ibid.*, p. 73.

82. *Daily Market Reporter*, cited in Burbank, p. 78.

83. Burbank, pp. 63-64.

84. *Ibid.*, p. 69.

85. *St. Louis Times*, July 25, 1877, cited in Bruce, p. 260.

86. Burbank, p. 112.

87. Bruce, p. 252.

88. AGO, Letters Received, 1844, Nos. 4413 and 4905 (enclosure 56), cited in Bruce, p. 286.

89. Major General Philip Sheridan, Annual Report of the Military Division of the Missouri for 1877, printed copy in Philip Sheridan Mss., Library of Congress, cited in Bruce, p. 88.

90. *Iron Molders' Journal* 13 (March 10, 1877): 275, cited in Bruce, p. 89.

91. R.B. Hayes Mss., cited in Bruce, p. 315.

92. *Labor Standard*, August 11, 1877, cited in Bruce, p. 229.

93. Bruce, p. 124.

94. *Columbus Dispatch*, July 20, 1877, cited in Bruce, pp. 128-9.

95. Irving Bernstein, *Turbulent Years: A History of the American Worker 1933-1941* (Boston: Houghton Mifflin, 1970), p. 217.

96. Rosa Luxemburg, "The Mass Strike, the Political Party and the Trade Unions," in *Rosa Luxemburg Speaks* (New York: Pathfinder Press, 1970), p. 182.

Notes to Chapter 2: May Day

1. Terence V. Powderly, *Thirty Years of Labor 1859-1889* (Columbus: Excelsior Publishing House, 1889), p. 539.

2. *Ibid.*, p. 538.

3. John R. Commons, *History of Labour in the United States*, vol. 2 (New York: Macmillan Co., 1918), pp. 373-74.

4. Harry Frumerman, "The Railroad Strikes of 1885-86," *Marxist Quarterly* 1 (October-December 1937): 394-6.

5. Norman J. Ware, *The Labor Movement in the United States, 1860-1895: A Study in Democracy* (New York: Vintage Books, 1964), p. 143.

6. Proceedings, 1885 General Assembly, pp. 84-91, quoted in Ware, p. 143.

7. Commons, vol. 2, p. 370.

8. John Swinton, *John Swinton's Paper*, April 12, 1885, cited in Ware, p. 66.

9. Ware, p. 66.

10. Powderly, p. 163.

11. Ware, p. xviii. To its shame, however, the Knights of Labor often supported anti-Chinese movements and activities.

12. Powderly, pp. 258-59.

13. *Ibid.*, p. 123.

14. *Ibid.*, p. 156.

15. *Ibid.*, p. 53.

16. Ware, pp. xv-xvi.

17. Powderly, p. 151.

18. Ware, p. 320.

19. Powderly, p. 275.

20. *John Swinton's Paper*, April 12, 1885, cited in Ware, p. 140.

21. Cited in Ware, p. 307.

22. Lucy E. Parsons, *Life of Albert R. Parsons with Brief History of the Labor Movement in America* (Chicago: Lucy E. Parsons, 1889), p. 22.

23. Henry David, *The History of the Haymarket Affair: A Study in the American Social-Revolutionary and Labor Movements* (New York: Collier Books, 1963), p. 21.

24. Ware, p. 302.

25. David, p. 21.

26. Report of the Commissioner of Labor, Third Annual Report, 1887, p. 12.

27. Commons, vol. 2, p. 366.

28. *John Swinton's Paper*, March 14, 1886, cited in Ware, p. 146.

29. Ruth Allen, *The Great Southwest Strike* (Austin: University of Texas, 1942).

30. *Ibid.*, p. 156.

31. *Ibid.*, pp. 132-33.

32. *New York Times*, March 20, 1886.

33. Allen, pp. 76-77.

34. *New York Times*, March 24, 1886.

35. *New York Times*, April 18, 1886.

36. Allen, pp. 77-78.

37. *New York Times*, April 3, 1886.

38. *New York Times*, April 10, 1886.

39. *Ibid.*

40. Proceedings, Federation of Organized Trades and Labor Unions, 1884, pp. 24-25, cited in Ware, p. 301.

41. Ware, p. 302.

42. Proceedings, Federation of Organized Trades and Labor Unions, 1885, cited in Powderly, pp. 499-500.

43. Powderly, p. 483.

44. Cited in David, p. 148.

45. *New York Times*, April 20, 1886.

46. Powderly, p. 495.

47. *Ibid.*

48. Cited in Powderly, p. 496.

49. David, p. 156.

50. Commons, vol. 2, p. 385. Powderly, p. 156.

51. Oscar Ameringer, *If You Don't Weaken* (New York: Henry Holt and Co., 1940), p. 44.

52. *Ibid.*, pp. 44-45.

53. Thomas W. Gavett, *Development of the Labor Movement in Milwaukee* (Milwaukee: University of Wisconsin Press, 1965), p. 58.

54. Wisconsin Bureau of Labor Statistics, Second Biennial Report, p. 319, cited in Gavett, p. 59.

55. *Ibid.*, p. 330, cited in Roger Simon, "The Bay View Incident and the People's Party in Milwaukee," unpublished paper, 1967, p. 6.

56. *Milwaukee Daily Journal*, May 5, 1886, cited in Simon, p. 9.

57. Cited in Gavett, p. 64.

58. *Milwaukee Daily Journal*, May 5, 1886, cited in Simon, p. 10.

59. Gavett, p. 64.

60. *Milwaukee Daily Journal*, May 5, 1886, cited in Simon, p. 11.

61. *New York Times*, May 2, 1886.

62. *John Swinton's Paper*, May 9, 1886.

63. *Ibid.*

64. *Ibid.*

65. *New York Times*, May 2, 1886.

66. *New York Times*, May 11, 1886.

67. *New York Times*, May 2, 1886.

68. *John Swinton's Paper*, May 9, 1886.

69. *Ibid.*

70. David, p. 159.

71. *Ibid.*, p. 161.

72. *New York Times*, May 1, 1886.

73. *Illinois State Register*, May 1, 1886, cited in David, p. 163.

74. *New York Times*, May 2, 1886.

75. David, p. 163.

76. *New York Times*, May 2, 1886.

77. *John Swinton's Paper*, May 9, 1886.

78. Cited in David, p. 179.

79. *New York Times*, cited in David, p. 183.

80. Cited in David, p. 194.

81. *John Swinton's Paper*, cited in David, p. 186.

82. Cited in David, p. 190.

83. Cited in David, p. 193.

84. Ameringer, p. 46.

85. Quoted in David, p. 412.

86. Clarence E. Bonnett, *History of Employers' Associations in the United States* (New York: Vantage Press, 1956), p. 282.

87. Commons, vol. 2, p. 414.

88. *Ibid.*

Notes to Chapter 3: The Ragged Edge of Anarchy

1. Frick to Carnegie, October 31, 1892, quoted in David Brody, *Steelworkers in America: The Non-Union Era* (New York: Harper and Row, 1969), p. 53.

2. Cited in Leon Wolff, *Lockout: The Story of the Homestead Strike of 1892: A Study of Violence, Unionism, and the Carnegie Steel Empire* (New York: Harper and Row, 1965), pp. 41-42.

3. Brody, p. 53.

4. U.S. House of Representatives, *Employment of Pinkerton Detectives*, 52nd Congress, 2d Sess., Report No. 2447 (Washington: Government Printing Office, 1893), p. 23, cited in Samuel Yellin, *American Labor Struggles* (New York: Harcourt, Brace and Co., 1936), p. 84.

5. Brody, p. 52.

6. *Ibid.*, p. 54.

7. Carnegie (May 1892), cited in Wolff, p. 80.

8. *Employment of Pinkerton Detectives*, p. 23, cited in Yellin, p. 80.

9. "The Fort That Frick Built," quoted in Wolff, p. 85.

10. Frick to Pinkerton (June 25, 1892), cited in Wolff, p. 86.

11. Wolff, p. 69.

12. *Ibid.*, p. 90.

13. *Ibid.*, p. 96.

14. *Ibid.*, p. 105.

15. *Ibid.*, p. 106.

16. *Ibid.*, p. 122.

17. *Ibid.*, p. 130.

18. *Ibid.*, p. 131.

19. *Ibid.*, p. 150.

20. *Ibid.*, p. 151.

21. *Ibid.*, p. 164.

22. AP dispatch, *Terre Haute Evening Gazette*, July 16, 1892, cited in Yellin, p. 93.

23. Judge Paxson, cited in Wolff, p. 213.

24. Wolff, p. 206.

25. *Ibid.*, p. 205.

26. Frick to Carnegie, cited in Wolff, p. 209.

27. *Ibid.*, November 21, 1892, in Wolff, p. 225.

28. Brody, p. 58.

29. *Ibid.*, p. 28.

30. *Ibid.*, pp. 48-49.

31. *Ibid.*, p. 42.

32. *Ibid.*, pp. 45-46.

33. Foster, cited in Henry David, "Upheaval at Homestead," in *America in Crisis*, Daniel Aaron, ed. (New York: Alfred A. Knopf, 1952), p. 167.

34. M.A. Hutton, *The Coeur d'Alenes, or A Tale of Modern Inquisition in Idaho*, p. 59, cited in Vernon H. Jensen, *Heritage of Conflict: Labor Relations in the Nonferrous Metals Industry up to 1930* (Ithaca: Cornell University Press, 1950), p. 29.

35. Jensen, p. 34.

36. Roger Wallace Shugg, "The New Orleans General Strike of 1892," *Louisiana Historical Quarterly* 21 (1937): 52.

37. *Ibid.*

38. *Ibid.*, p. 554.

39. *Ibid.*, p. 555.

40. House Journal (1889), Report of special committee to investigate public prisons, pp. 306-9, 322-25; cited in A.C. Hutson, Jr., "The Coal Miners' Insurrection of 1891 in Anderson County, Tennessee," *East Tennessee Historical Society's Proceedings* 7 (1935): 105.

41. *Birmingham Age-Herald*, August 8, 1889, cited in Woodward, p. 232.

42. *Nashville Daily American*, August 25, 1892, cited in Woodward, p. 233.

43. Special Report of the Commissioner of Labor, 1891, pp. 19-21, cited in Hutson, p. 108.

44. A.C. Hutson, Jr., "The Overthrow of the Convict Lease System," *The East Tennessee Historical Society's Proceedings* 8 (1936): 89.

45. Hon. Andrew Roy, *A History of the Coal Miners of the United States, from the Development of the Mines to the Close of the Anthracite Strike of 1902*, third ed. (Columbus: J.L. Trauger Printing Co., 1907), p. 302.

46. *New York Times*, April 22, 1894.

47. *New York Times*, April 13, 1894.

48. Roy, p. 303.

49. John R. Commons, *History of Labour in the United States*, vol. 2 (New York: Macmillan Co., 1918), p. 502.

50. Roy, p. 304.

51. *New York Times*, May 1, 1894.

52. *New York Times*, May 10, 1894.

53. *New York Times*, April 24, 1894.

54. *New York Times*, May 29, 1894.

55. W.T. Stead, "Incidents of Labour War in America," *The Contemporary Review* (July 1894): 67.

56. *New York Times*, May 1, 1894.

57. *New York Times*, April 30, 1894.

58. *New York Times*, May 5, 1894.

59. *New York Times*, May 10, 1894.

60. *New York Times*, June 2, 1894.

61. *New York Times*, May 26, 1894.

62. *New York Times*, May 25, 1894.

63. *Ibid.*

64. *New York Times*, May 26, 1894.

65. *New York Times*, May 25, 1894.

66. *New York Times*, May 24, 1894.

67. *Ibid.*

68. *New York Times*, May 25, 1894.

69. W. W. Taylor to John P. Attgeld, May 24,1894, in *Biennial Report of the Adjutant General of Illinois to the Governor and Commander-in-Chief 1893 and 1894* (Springfield: Ed. F. Hartman, 1895), p. vii (hereafter cited as "Report").

70. Report, p. viii.

71. *New York Times*, May 25, 1894.

72. *Ibid.*

73. *New York Times*, May 1, 1894.

74. *New York Times*, May 27, 1894.

75. *New York Times*, May 28, 1894.

76. *Ibid.*

77. *Ibid.*

78. *Ibid.*

79. *New York Times*, June 4, 1894.

80. *New York Times*, June 5, 1894.

81. *Ibid.*

82. *Ibid.*

83. *Ibid.*

84. *New York Times*, June 10, 1894.

85. *New York Times*, June 5, 1894.

86. *New York Times*, May 29, 1894.

87. *New York Times*, June 5, 1894.

88. *New York Times*, June 7, 1894.

89. *New York Times*, May 29, 1894.

90. *New York Times*, June 5, 1894.

91. *New York Times*, April 29, 1894.

92. *New York Times*, May 1, 1894.

93. *New York Times*, May 6, 1894.

94. *New York Times*, May 11, 1894.

95. *New York Times*, May 13, 1894.

96. *New York Times*, May 24, 1894.

97. *New York Times*, May 25, 1894.

98. *Ibid.*

99. *New York Times*, May 28, 1894.

100. *Ibid.*

101. *New York Times*, May 30, 1894.

102. *Ibid.*

103. *Ibid.*

104. *New York Times*, June 14, 1894.

105. Roy, p. 307.

106. *New York Times*, May 13, 1894.

107. *New York Times*, May 3, 1894.

108. *New York Times*, May 5, 1894.

109. Jensen, p. 45.

110. *Ibid.*, p. 46.

111. *Ibid.*, p. 49.

112. W.H. Carwardine, *The Pullman Strike* (Chicago: Charles H. Kerr and Co., 1894), p. 69, cited in Yellin, p. 104.

113. *Chicago Times*, June 13, 1894, p. 2, cited in Almont Lindsey, *The Pullman Strike* (Chicago: University of Chicago Press, 1964), p. 127.

114. U.S. Strike Commission Report, Senate Executive Document No. 7, 53d Congress, 3d Session (Washington: Government Printing Office, 1895), submitted to President Cleveland on November 14, 1894, p. 62.

115. Gerald G. Eggert, *Railroad Labor Disputes: The Beginnings of Federal Strike Policy* (Ann Arbor: University of Michigan Press, 1967), p. 147.

116. Ray Ginger, *The Bending Cross: A Biography of Eugene Victor Debs* (New Brunswick: Rutgers University Press, 1949), p. 97.

117. *Ibid.*, pp. 97-98.

118. *Ibid.*, p. 107.

119. *Ibid.*, p. 101.

120. *Ibid.*

121. *Chicago Times*, May 13, 1894, p. 20, cited in Lindsey, p. 126.

122. Ginger, pp. 117-18.

123. *Ibid.*, p. 118.

124. U.S. Strike Commission Report, p. 135.

125. *Ibid.*, p. 72.

126. *Ibid.*, p. 59.

127. *Ibid.*, p. 96.

128. *Ibid.*, p. 106.

129. *Ibid.*, p. 110.

130. *Ibid.*, p. 112.

131. *Ibid.*

132. Lindsey, pp. 134-35.

133. *New York Times*, June 29, 1894, cited in Lindsey, p. 203.

134. *Chicago Tribune*, July 3, 1894.

135. U.S. Strike Commission Report, p. 140.

136. *Ibid.*, p. 28; Lindsey, p. 240.

137. Eugene V. Debs, *Public Opinion*, July 5, 1894, cited in Yellin, pp. 115-16.

138. Yellin, p. 118.

139. Eugene V. Debs, *Writings and Speeches of Eugene Victor Debs* (New York: Hermitage Press, 1948), p. 45.

140. John Egan, *Inter Ocean*, July 3, 1894, p. 3, cited in Lindsey, p. 144.

141. Lindsey, p. 142.

142. Egan, cited in Lindsey, p. 144.

143. Olney to E. Walker, June 30, 1894, Appendix to the Report of the Attorney General, 1896, p. 60, cited in Lindsey, p. 150.

144. Grover Cleveland, *The Government in the Chicago Strike of 1894* (Princeton: Princeton University Press, 1913), p. 232.

145. Lindsay, p. 162.

146. John Swinton, *Striking for Life* (New York: Western W. Wilson, 1894), p. 92.

147. *Chicago Times*, July 3, 1894, p. 1, cited in Lindsey, p. 164.

148. Arnold to Olney, July 3, 1894, in *Chicago Strike Correspondence*, p. 66, cited in Eggert, pp. 170-71.

149. Olney, quoted in Eggert, p. 172.

150. U.S. Strike Commission Report, p. 39.

151. *New York Times*, July 5, 1894, cited in Lindsey, p. 175.

152. Eggert, p. 171.

153. U.S. Strike Commission Report, pp. 214-15.

154. *New York Times*, August 16, 1902, cited in Yellin, p. 122.

155. Nelson A. Miles, "The Lesson of the Recent Strikes," *North American Review* 159 (1894): 180-88, cited in Lindsey, p. 174.

156. Waite, *Inter Ocean*, July 7, 1894, cited in Lindsey, p. 168.

157. Lindsey, p. 250.

158. *Ibid.*

159. *Ibid.*, p. 260.

160. Eggert, p. 18.

161. Hugh D. Graham and Ted R. Gurr, *The History of Violence in America: A Report to the National Commission on the Causes and Prevention of Violence* (New York: Bantam Books, 1969), p. 298.

162. *Annual Report of the Secretary of War for the Year 1894*, vol. 1 (Washington: Government Printing Office, 1894), p. 109, cited in Lindsey, p. 214.

163. *Bradstreet's*, July 28, 1894, p. 467, cited in Yellin, p. 130.

164. U.S. Strike Commission Report, p. xlii.

165. Ginger, p. 122.

166. *Terre Haute Evening Gazette*, July 19, 1894, cited in Yellin, p. 123.

167. St. John, testimony in U.S. Strike Commission Report, p. 117.

168. Ginger, p. 143.

169. *New York Times*, July 12, 1894, cited in Lindsey, p. 225.

170. "Proceedings of Briggs Conference," p. 133, cited in Lindsey, p. 228.

171. *Chicago Tribune*, July 14, 1894, cited in Ginger, p. 150.

172. U.S. Strike Commission Report, p. xxviii.

173. "Proceedings of Briggs Conference," *American Federationist* 1 (1894).

174. U.S. Strike Commission Report, p. 190.

175. *Ibid.*, p. 192.

176. *Ibid.*, p. 194.

177. *Ibid.*, p. 199.

178. *Ibid.*, p. 556.

179. General Managers Association, *Minutes of Meetings* (Chicago, 1894), p. 94, cited in Eggert, p. 156.

180. U.S. Strike Commission Report, pp. 9, 11.

181. *Ibid.*, p. 169.

182. *Ibid.*, p. 76.

183. *Ibid.*, p. 146.

184. *Ibid.*, p. 50.

185. *Ibid.*, p. 161.

186. *Ibid.*, pp. 145-46.

187. *Ibid.*, p. 163.

Notes to Chapter 4: Nineteen Nineteen

1. "The Revolt of the Rank and File," *The Nation* 109: 2834 (October 25, 1919): 540.

2. Alexander M. Bing, *War-Time Strikes and Their Adjustment* (New York: E.P. Dutton and Co., 1921), p. 262.

3. *Ibid.*, pp. 168-69.

4. *Ibid.*, p. 7.

5. *Ibid.*, p. 9.

6. *Ibid.*, p. 293.

7. *Ibid.*, pp. 30, 136.

8. Commission of Inquiry, Interchurch World Movement, *Report on the Steel Strike of 1919* (New York: Harcourt, Brace and Howe, 1920), p. 152.

9. Sylvia Kopald, *Rebellion in Labor Unions* (New York: Boni and Liveright, 1924), p. 152.

10. Robert L. Friedheim, *The Seattle General Strike* (Seattle: University of Washington Press, 1964), p. 18.

11. *Ibid.*

12. William Short, *History of Activities of Seattle Labor Movement and Conspiracy of Employers to Destroy It and Attempted Suppression of Labor's Daily Newspaper, the Seattle Union Record* (Seattle: Seattle Union Record Publishing Co., 1919), pp. 1-2, cited in Friedheim, p. 24.

13. *Papers on Industrial Espionage* (Mss. in University of Washington Library, Seattle), report of Agent 106, June 11, 1919, cited in Friedheim, p. 29.

14. Anna Louise Strong, *I Change Worlds* (New York: Henry Holt and Co., 1935), p. 68.

15. *Seattle Times*, January 21, 1919, p. 1, cited in Friedheim, p. 75.

16. Strong, pp. 74-75.

17. *Ibid.*, pp. 72, 74.

18. *Seattle Times*, January 28, 1919, cited in Freidheim, p. 84.

19. History Committee of the Seattle General Strike Committee, *The Seattle General Strike* (Seattle: Seattle Union Record Publishing Co., 1920), p. 15.

20. Freidheim, p. 101.

21. William MacDonald, "The Seattle Strike and Afterwards" (written in Seattle, February 28, 1919), *The Nation*, March 29, 1919, cited in Wilfrid H. Crook, *Communism and the General Strike* (Hamden: Shoe String Press, Inc., 1960), p. 53.

22. History Committee, pp. 21-22.

23. *Ibid.*, p. 21.

24. *Ibid.*, p. 50.

25. *Ibid.*, pp. 4-6.

26. Ole Hanson, *Americanism versus Bolshevism* (Garden City: Doubleday, Page, 1920), p. 84, cited in Freidheim, p. 123.

27. Freidheim, p. 124.

28. History Committee, p. 46.

29. *New York Times*, February 9, 1919, cited in Crook, p. 51.

30. For a photocopy of the original, see State's Exhibit 40, transcript of *People v. Lloyd*, p. 467; Harvey O'Connor claimed authorship of "Russia Did It" in *Revolution in Seattle* (New York: Monthly Review Press, 1964), p. 143, cited in Freidheim, p. 101.

31. Reprinted in *Daily Bulletin*, February 8, 1919, p. 1, cited in Freidheim, p. 136.

32. Strong, pp. 81-82.

33. History Committee, p. 38.

34. *Ibid.*, p. 35.

35. *Ibid.*, p. 57.

36. *Ibid.*, p. 62.

37. John R. Commons, *History of Labour in the United States*, vol. 4 (New York: Macmillan Co., 1918), p. 438.

38. John A. Fitch, "Lawrence," *The Survey*, April 15, 1919, pp. 695-96.

39. *Ibid.*

40. *Ibid.*

41. *Ibid.*

42. Commons, vol. 4, p. 438.

43. Anne Withington, "The Telephone Strike," *The Survey*, April 26, 1919, p. 146.

44. *Wall Street Journal*, September 12, 1919, cited in Robert K. Murray, *Red Scare: A Study in National Hysteria, 1919-1920* (New York: McGraw-Hill Book Co., 1964), p. 129.

45. *Boston Evening Transcript*, September 12, 1919, cited in Murray, p. 129.

46. Arthur Warner, "The End of Boston's Police Strike," *The Nation* 109: 2842 (December 20, 1919): 790.

47. "The Week," *The Nation* 108: 2796 (February 1, 1919).

48. *The Survey* 42 (August 2, 1919): 674.

49. Graham Taylor, "An Epidemic of Strikes in Chicago," *The Survey* 42 (August 2, 1919): 645-46.

50. *Ibid.*

51. *Ibid.*

52. *Ibid.*

53. *Ibid.*

54. Cited in Brody, p. 181.

55. *Ibid.*, pp. 181-82.

56. *Ibid.*, p. 183.

57. AFL, *Weekly Newsletter*, January 15, 1922, cited in Brody, p. 199.

58. IWM *Report*, p. 160.

59. Theodore Draper, *The Roots of American Communism* (New York: Viking Press, 1963), p. 320.

60. IWM *Report*, p. 147.

61. *Ibid.*, p. 148.

62. *Ibid.*, p. 151.

63. Letter of manager of Edgar Thomson Works, quoted in "Inside History of Carnegie Steel Co.," by J. H. Bridge, p. 81, cited in IWM *Report*, p. 127.

64. Brody, p. 216.

65. *Ibid.*, p. 233.

66. IWM *Report*, p. 160.

67. *Ibid.*, p. 37.

68. *Ibid.*, p. 160.

69. *Ibid.*, p. 35.

70. William Z. Foster, *The Great Steel Strike and Its Lessons* (New York: B.W. Huebsch, Inc., 1920), p. 62.

71. IWM *Report*, p. 168.

72. Brody, p. 236.

73. IWM *Report*, p. 171.

74. Cited in Brody, p. 237.

75. IWM *Report*, p. 154.

76. Brody, p. 238.

77. IWM *Report*, p. 165.

78. Brody, p. 239.

79. Cited in IWM *Report*, p. 172.

80. Cited in Brody, p. 241.

81. Supplementary Reports of the Investigators to the Commission of Inquiry, Interchurch World Movement, *Public Opinion and the Steel Strike* (New York: Harcourt, Brace and Co., 1921), p. 173 (cited hereafter as IWM *Opinion*).

82. *Ibid.*, p. 178.

83. *Ibid.*, p. 177.

84. Foster, p. 133.

85. Brody, pp. 140-42.

86. Foster, p. 115.

87. IWM *Report*, p. 39.

88. *Ibid.*, p. 181.

89. Foster, p. 70.

90. *Strike Investigation*, vol. 2, 632-61, *Iron Age*, February 5, 1920, p. 415, cited in Brody, p. 257.

91. IWM *Report*, p. 181.

92. *Ibid.*, p. 320.

93. Foster, pp. 216-20.

94. IWM *Report*, pp. 39-40.

95. IWM *Opinion*, pp. 239, 241.

96. IWM *Report*, p. 119.

97. Mary Heaton Vorse, *Men and Steel* (London: Labour Publishing Co., 1922), p. 166.

98. IWM *Report*, pp. 131-32.

99. *Iron Age*, cited in Brody, pp. 242-43.

100. "The Revolution—1919," *The Nation*, October 4, 1919, p. 452.

101. Kopald, *Rebellion*, p. 128.

102. Commons, vol. 4, p. 453.

103. Kopald, *Rebellion*, p. 141.

104. *Ibid.*, p. 151.

105. *Ibid.*, p. 152.

106. Report of Jonas McBride, cited in Kopald, p. 154.

107. *Ibid.*

108. Cited in Kopald, pp. 74-75.

109. *Ibid.*, p. 73.

110. *Ibid.*

111. *Ibid.*, p. 62.

112. *Ibid.*, p. 84.

113. *Ibid.*, p. 87.

114. Sylvia Kopald, "Behind the Miners' Strike," *The Nation* 109: 2838 (November 22, 1919): 658.

115. McAlister Coleman, *Men and Coal* (New York: Farrar and Rinehart, 1947), p. 278.

116. *Cincinnati Enquirer*, November 12, 1919, p. 6, quoting Lewis; cited in Murray, p. 161.

117. *The Survey* 43: 8 (December 20, 1919): 254.

118. Commons, vol. 4, p. 477-9. On the Kansas coal miners strike, see James Gray Pope, "Labor's Constitution of Freedom," *The Yale Law Journal* 106: 4 (January 1997): pp. 1007-8, 1022-25.

119. Winthrop D. Lane, *Civil War in West Virginia* (New York: B.W. Huebsch, Inc., 1921), p. 106.

120. *Ibid.*

121. Commons, vol. 4, p. 480.

122. Lane, p. 106.

123. Commons, vol. 4, p. 483.

124. *Ibid.*, p. 483-84.

125. *Ibid.*, p. 485-86.

Notes to Chapter 5: Depression Decade

1. Louis Adamic, *My America, 1928-1938* (New York: Harper and Brothers, Publishers, 1938), p. 309.

2. Charles Walker, "Relief and Revolution," *The Forum* (September 1932): 156.

3. *Ibid.*, pp. 155-56.

4. Irving Bernstein, *The Lean Years: A History of the American Worker 1920-1933* (Baltimore: Penguin Books, 1960), p. 417.

5. *Ibid.*, pp. 423-24.

6. Adamic, p. 323.

7. Bernstein, *Lean Years*, p. 421.

8. Walker, p. 158.

9. Paul Mattick, "What Can the Unemployed Do," *Living Marxism* 3 (May 1938): 87 (author's italics).

10. Irving Bernstein, *Turbulent Years: A History of the American Worker 1933-1941* (Boston: Houghton Mifflin Co., 1970), p. 171.

11. Cited in Bernstein, *Turbulent Years*, p. 34.

12. "Songs from the Depression," New Lost City Ramblers. For a vivid picture of popular feelings during the Depression, especially in Appalachia, this record is well worth attention.

13. Samuel Yellin, *American Labor Struggles* (New York: Harcourt, Brace and Co., 1936), p. 328.

14. Bernstein, *Turbulent Years*, p. 266.

15. *Clarion*, May 18, 1934, cited in Wilfred H. Crook, *Communism and the General Strike* (Hamden, Connecticut: The Shoe String Press, 1960), p. 112.

16. Bernstein, *Turbulent Years*, p. 271.

17. *New York Times*, July 4, 1934, cited in Crook, p. 116.

18. *San Francisco Examiner*, July 5, 1934, cited in Crook, p. 117.

19. *Ibid.*

20. Cited in Crook, p. 112.

21. Bernstein, *Turbulent Years*, p. 280.

22. *Ibid.*, p. 282.

23. *Ibid.*, p. 283.

24. *San Francisco Examiner*, July 13, 1934, cited in Crook, p. 120.

25. *New York Times*, July 8, 1934, cited in Yellin, p. 344.

26. *New York Times*, July 16, 1934, cited in Crook, p. 138.

27. E. Burke, "Dailies Helped Break General Strike," *Editor and Publisher,* July 28, 1934, cited in Yellin, p. 348.

28. *Los Angeles Times*, cited in Yellin, p. 347.

29. Bernstein, *Turbulent Years*, p. 287.

30. *Ibid.*, p. 288.

31. *New York Times*, July 18, 1934, cited in Yellin, p. 350.

32. Bernstein, *Turbulent Years*, p. 293.

33. *Ibid.*, p. 295.

34. Adamic, p. 370.

35. George O. Bahrs, *The San Francisco Employers' Council* (Philadelphia: Wharton School of Finance and Commerce, 1948), p. 7.

36. Roy W. Howard of Scripps-Howard newspapers to Louis Howe in the White House, cited in Bernstein, *Turbulent Years*, p. 221.

37. Charles R. Walker, *American City: A Rank-and-File History* (New York: Farrar and Rinehart, 1937), pp. 97-98.

38. *Ibid.*, pp. 99-100.

39. *Ibid.*, pp. 102-3.

40. *Ibid.*, pp. 110-11.

41. *Ibid.*, p. 109.

42. *Ibid.*, p. 110.

43. *Ibid.*, p. 111.

44. *Ibid.*, p. 113.

45. *Ibid.*, p. 120.

46. Cited *ibid.*, pp. 168-69.

47. Cited *ibid.*, pp. 171-72.

48. *Ibid.*, p. 181.

49. *Ibid.*, pp. 208-9.

50. *Ibid.*, p. 211.

51. *Ibid.*, p. 208.

52. Herbert J. Lahne, *The Cotton Mill Worker* (New York: Farrar and Rine-hart, 1944), p. 216.

53. Bernstein, *Turbulent Years*, pp. 302-4.

54. *Ibid.*, p. 306.

55. Alexander Kendrick, "Alabama Goes on Strike," *The Nation*, August 29, 1934, p. 233.

56. *New York Times*, September 4, 1934.

57. *New York Times*, September 5 and 6, 1934.

58. *New York Times*, September 5, 1934.

59. *New York Times*, September 16, 1934.

60. *New York Times*, September 5, 1934.

61. *Ibid.*

62. Robert R.R. Brooks, "The United Textile Workers of America" (unpublished Ph.D. dissertation, Yale University, 1935), p. 376.

63. *New York Times*, September 10, 1934.

64. *New York Times*, September 6, 1934.

65. *Ibid.*

66. *Ibid.*

67. *Ibid.*

68. *Ibid.*

69. *New York Times*, September 7, 1934.

70. *Ibid.*

71. *New York Times*, September 10, 1934.

72. *New York Times*, September 12, 1934.

73. *New York Times*, September 13, 1934.

74. *New York Times*, September 14, 1934.

75. *Ibid.*

76. *New York Times*, September 12, 1934.

77. *New York Times*, September 16, 1934.

78. *New York Times*, September 18, 1934.

79. Brooks, p. 378; *New York Times*, September 19, 1934.

80. Bernstein, *Turbulent Years*, p. 314.

81. *Ibid.*

82. Brooks, p. 379,

83. Cited in Bernstein, *Turbulent Years*, p. 315.

84. Brooks, pp. 384-85.

85. Lahne, p. 231.
86. Saul Alinsky, *John L. Lewis: An Unauthorized Biography* (New York: G.P. Putnam's Sons, 1949), p. 72.
87. Bernstein, *Turbulent Years*, p. 99.
88. Ruth McKenney, cited in Bernstein, *Turbulent Years*, p. 98.
89. Ruth McKenney, *Industrial Valley* (New York: Harcourt, Brace and Co., 1939), p. 101.
90. *Ibid.*, pp. 134-35.
91. *Ibid.*, pp. 166-69, 178.
92. *Ibid.*, p. 188.
93. *Ibid.*, pp. 194-95.
94. Bernstein, *Turbulent Years*, p. 591.
95. McKenney, pp. 198-99.
96. Cited in McKenney, pp. 133-34.
97. Adamic, p. 405.
98. *Ibid.*, pp. 405-6.
99. *Ibid.*, p. 406.
100. *Ibid.*, p. 407.
101. *Ibid.*, p. 408.
102. *Ibid.*, pp. 408-9.
103. McKenney, cited in Bernstein, *Turbulent Years*, p. 99.
104. McKenney, pp. 261-62.
105. Bernstein, *Turbulent Years*, p. 593.
106. *Ibid.*, p. 595.
107. Adamic, p. 411.
108. Henry Kraus, *The Many and the Few* (Los Angeles: Plantin, 1947), p. 8.
109. *Ibid.*, p. 9.
110. Herbert Harris, *American Labor* (New Haven: Yale University Press, 1939), p. 272.
111. Sidney Fine, *Sit-Down: The General Motors Strike of 1936-1937* (Ann Arbor: University of Michigan Press, 1969), p. 55.
112. *Ibid.*, p. 56.
113. Harris, p. 271.
114. Fine, pp. 59, 57.
115. Harris, p. 281.
116. Kraus, p. 10.

117. Bernstein, *Turbulent Years*, pp. 182-83.

118. Kraus, p. 12.

119. Bernstein, *Turbulent Years*, pp. 184-85.

120. Cited in Fine, p. 31.

121. *Ibid*.

122. Kraus, p. 42.

123. *Ibid*.

124. *Ibid*., pp. 48-54.

125. Fine, p. 75.

126. J. Raymond Walsh, *C.I.O.: Industrial Unionism in Action* (New York: W.W. Norton, 1937).

127. Cited in Bernstein, *Turbulent Years*, p. 501.

128. Fine, p. 97.

129. Germer to Brophy, November 30, 1936, cited in Fine, p. 136.

130. Bernstein, *Turbulent Years*, p. 524.

131. *Ibid*.

132. Kraus, p. 87.

133. *Ibid*., p. 88.

134. *Ibid*., p. 89.

135. *Ibid*., p. 93.

136. *New York Times*, February 1 and 9, 1937, cited in Fine, p. 172.

137. Fine, p. 165.

138. Edward Levinson, "Labor on the March," *Harper's Magazine* 174 (May 1937), cited in Fine, p. 160. Cf. Edward Levinson, *Labor on the March* (Ithaca: ILR Press, 1995).

139. Cited in Fine, pp. 173-74.

140. Cited in Fine, p. 171.

141. Solomon Diamond, "The Psychology of the Sit-Down," *New Masses* 23 (May 4, 1937): 16, cited in Fine, p. 157.

142. Paul Gailico, "Sit-Down Strike," p. 159, cited in Fine, p. 171.

143. Genora Johnson, cited in Fine, p. 201.

144. Cited in Fine, p. 201.

145. *Ibid*.

146. Bernstein, *Turbulent Years*, p. 525.

147. Fine, p. 189.

148. *Ibid*., p. 188.

149. Kraus, p. 128.

150. Fine, p. 155.

151. *Ibid.*, p. 236.

152. Kraus, p. 211.

153. Fine, p. 281.

154. Kraus, p. 248.

155. Fine, p. 282.

156. *Ibid.*, pp. 306-7.

157. *Ibid.*, p. 307.

158. Kraus, p. 287.

159. Bernstein, *Turbulent Years*, p. 551.

160. Fine, p. 325.

161. *New York Times*, April 11, 1937.

162. Fine, p. 321.

163. *Ibid.*

164. Bernstein, *Turbulent Years*, p. 559.

165. *New York Times*, March 19, 1937.

166. *New York Times*, April 2, 1937.

167. *Ibid.*

168. Alfred H. Lockhart to Gernsley F. Gorton, March 7, 1937, William H. Phelps Papers, Michigan Historical Collection, cited in Fine, p. 328.

169. *New York Times*, April 11, 1937.

170. *New York Times*, April 4, 1937.

171. *New York Times*, April 7, 1937.

172. *Ibid.*

173. McKenney, p. 340.

174. *New York Times*, April 11, 1937.

175. Adamic, p. 415.

176. Harris, pp. 290-91.

177. *Ibid.*, p. 291.

178. *New York Times*, April 11, 1937.

179. *Ibid.*

180. Bernstein, *Turbulent Years*, p. 500.

181. *New York Times*, March 27, 1937.

182. *New York Times*, March 19, 1937.

183. *New York Times*, March 18, 1937.

184. *Ibid*.

185. *New York Times*, March 21, 1937.

186. *New York Times*, March 9, 1937.

187. *New York Times*, March 18, 1937.

188. *New York Times*, March 21, 1937.

189. *Ibid*.

190. *New York Times*, March 31, 1937.

191. *New York Times*, March 21, 1937.

192. *New York Times*, April 15, 1937.

193. Fine, p. 331.

194. Adamic, p. 408.

195. Bernstein, *Turbulent Years*, p. 468.

196. *New York Times*, March 18, 1937.

197. Bernstein, *Turbulent Years*, p. 468.

198. Adamic, pp. 431-33.

Notes to Chapter 6:
The War and Post-War Strike Wave

1. John T. Dunlop, "The Decontrol of Wages and Prices," in *Labor in Post-war America*, ed. Colston E. Warne (Brooklyn: Remsen Press, 1949), pp. 4-5.

2. Joel Seidman, *American Labor from Defense to Reconversion* (Chicago: University of Chicago Press, 1953), pp. 78, 79.

3. Philip Murray, cited in Art Preis, *Labor's Giant Step: Twenty Years of the CIO* (New York: Pioneer Publishers, 1964), p. 198.

4. "Bridges' Setback," *Business Week*, March 18, 1944, pp. 83-84.

5. Davis, cited in Preis, p. 155.

6. Seidman, pp. 91-92.

7. *Ibid.*, p. 62.

8. *Ibid.*, p. 94.

9. Republic Steel Corporation, *War Labor Report* 325 (July 16, 1942): 340-41, cited in Seidman, p. 101.

10. Cited in Preis, p. 155.

11. Seidman, p. 105.

12. Bureau of Labor Statistics, *Bulletin* 909 (1947): 1.

13. Davis, cited in Seidman, p. 134.

14. Bureau of Labor Statistics, *Bulletin* 878 (1946): 3.

15. *Ibid*.

16. Jerome F. Scott and George C. Homans, "Reflections on Wildcat Strikes," *American Sociology Review* (June 1947): 278.

17. *Ibid.*, p. 280.

18. *Ibid*.

19. *Ibid*.

20. *Monthly Labor Review* (April 1944): 783; (August 1944): 357; (November 1944): 1018.

21. Scott and Homans, p. 281.

22. *Ibid.*, p. 283.

23. *Ibid.*, p. 282.

24. *Wall Street Journal*, August 22, 1944; *Monthly Labor Review* (April 1944): 1218.

25. *Business Week*, November 25, 1944, p. 110.

26. *Business Week*, January 15, 1944, p. 88.

27. *Business Week*, March 18, 1944, pp. 88-89.

28. Preis, p. 236.

29. *Handbook of Labor Statistics*, Bureau of Labor Statistics, *Bulletin* 916 (1947): 137.

30. Bruce R. Morris, "Industrial Relations in the Automobile Industry," in Warne, p. 416.

31. *C.I.O. News*, April 2, 1945, cited in Preis, p. 257.

32. *New York Times*, July 30, 1944.

33. *Business Week*, December 16, 1944, p. 82.

34. Clark Kerr, "Employer Policies in Industrial Relations, 1945 to 1947," in Warne, p. 45.

35. Bureau of Labor Statistics, *Bulletin* 876 (1946): 8.

36. *Ibid.*, p. 17.

37. *Ibid.*, p. 1.

38. Seidman, p. 221.

39. Preis, pp. 262-63.

40. *Ibid*.

41. *Ibid.*, p. 262.

42. Bureau of Labor Statistics, *Bulletin* 918 (1947): 8.

43. Seidman, p. 235.

44. *Ibid.*

45. *Ibid.*, pp. 12-13.

46. *Ibid.*, p. 1.

47. Harry S. Truman, *Memoirs*, vol. 1 (Garden City: Doubleday, 1955), p. 498.

48. Richard B. Johnson, *Government Seizure in Labor Disputes* (Philadelphia: University of Pennsylvania Press, 1948), p. 106.

49. Truman, p. 504.

50. Morris, p. 416.

51. H.M. Douty, "Review of Basic American Labor Conditions," in Warne, p. 130.

52. Peter F. Drucker, "What to Do About Strikes," *Collier's*, January 18, 1947, p. 12.

53. Frank T. De Vyver, "Collective Bargaining in Steel," in Warne, p. 390.

54. Morris, p. 409.

55. Fred H. Joiner, "Developments in Union Agreement," in Warne, pp. 40-41.

56. *Ibid.*, p. 35.

57. De Vyver, p. 390.

Notes to Chapter 7:
The Unknown Labor Dimension
of the Vietnam War Era Revolt

1. *New York Times*, April 21, 1970.

2. In the 1967-1976 period, the average number of workers on strike rose 30 percent and the number of days lost to strikes rose 40 percent compared to the period 1948-1966. See Aaron Brenner, "Rank-and-File Teamster Movements in Comparative Perspective," in *Trade Union Politics: American Unions and Economic Change, 1960s-1990s*, ed. Glenn Perusek and Kent Worcester (Atlantic Highlands, New Jersey: Humanities Press, 1995), p. 112.

3. *Wall Street Journal*, April 20, 1970.

4. *New York Times*, June 1, 1970.

5. *Wall Street Journal*, June 26, 1970; and *New York Times*, June 15, 1970.

6. *Wall Street Journal*, August 6, 1970.

7. Bill Watson, "Counter-Planning on the Shop Floor," *Radical America* 5 (May-June 1971): 78.

8. *Ibid.*, pp. 79-80.

9. *Ibid.*

10. *Ibid.*, p. 82.

11. *Ibid.*, p. 84.

12. *Ibid.*, p. 85.

13. *Ibid.*, pp. 80-81, 82.

14. *Ibid.*, p. 85.

15. *Wall Street Journal*, November 24, 1970.

16. *Ibid.*

17. Martin Glaberman, "Marxism, the Working Class and the Trade Unions," *Studies on the Left* 4: 3 (Summer 1964): 68.

18. *Wall Street Journal*, November 24, 1970.

19. *Ibid.*

20. *New York Times*, March 31, 1971.

21. Jeremy Brecher and Tim Costello, *Common Sense for Hard Times* (Boston: South End Press, 1977), pp. 112-113.

22. President's Commission on Postal Organization, headed by Frederich R. Kappel, quoted in *Wall Street Journal*, March 19, 1970.

23. *Ibid.*

24. *Ibid.*

25. *Ibid.*

26. *Washington Post*, March 22, 1970.

27. *Ibid.*

28. *Ibid.*

29. *Ibid.*

30. *Ibid.*

31. *Root and Branch* 1 (June 1970): 3.

32. John Griner, quoted in *Washington Star*, in *Root and Branch* 1, p. 3.

33. Alan Whitney, radio interview, quoted in *Root and Branch* 1, p. 3.

34. *Wall Street Journal*, March 23, 1970.

35. *Wall Street Journal*, March 24, 1970.

36. *Wall Street Journal*, May 1, 1970.

37. *Wall Street Journal*, March 23, 1970.

38. *Ibid.*

39. *New York Times*, May 1, 1970.

40. *Wall Street Journal*, April 8, 1970.

41. *New York Times*, May 1, 1970.

42. *Ibid.*

43. *Washington Star*, May 6, 1970.

44. *Wall Street Journal*, January 27, 1970.

45. *Wall Street Journal*, April 8, 1970.

46. *Wall Street Journal*, April 10, 1970.

47. *Wall Street Journal*, April 8, 1970.

48. *Wall Street Journal*, April 10, 1970.

49. *Wall Street Journal*, April 13, 1970.

50. *New York Times*, April 30, 1970.

51. *New York Times*, May 1, 1970.

52. *New York Times Magazine*, June 21, 1970, p. 64.

53. *Ibid.*

54. Thomas O'Hanlon, "Anarchy Threatens the Kingdom of Coal," *Fortune*, January 1971, pp. 78, 82.

55. *Ibid.*, p. 78.

56. *Ibid.*

57. Paul Nyden, "In Memory of Joseph Yablonski, Coal Miners, 'Their' Union and Capital," unpublished manuscript, January 22, 1970, pp. 26-27.

58. *Wall Street Journal,* March 13, 1970.

59. *Wall Street Journal,* June 25, 1970.

60. *Wall Street Journal,* June 23, 1970.

61. *Wall Street Journal,* July 23, 1970.

62. *New York Times,* June 26, 1970.

63. *Wall Street Journal,* March 24, 1970.

64. *Ibid.*

65. Editorial, *New York Times,* July 21, 1970.

66. *Wall Street Journal*, November 20, 1970.

67. *Ibid.*

68. *Ibid.*

69. *Wall Street Journal,* October 29, 1970.

70. *Ibid.*

71. *Ibid.*

72. *Ibid.*

73. *Ibid.*

74. *Ibid.*

75. *Wall Street Journal,* October 5, 1970.

76. *Ibid.*

77. *New York Times,* July 18, 1971.

78. *Wall Street Journal,* November 20, 1970.

79. *Wall Street Journal,* October 5, 1970.

80. *Ibid.*; and Joel Stein, "Notes on the Official Strike in 1970," unpublished manuscript.

81. *New York Times,* March 1, 1970.

82. *New York Times,* June 22, 1971.

83. *New York Times,* March 3, 1971.

84. Testimony of Major General Wilston P. Wilson, Chief, National Guard Bureau, before the President's Commission on Campus Unrest, 116 Congress, Rec. E 7302 (daily ed., August 4, 1970), in "The National Guard and the Constitution," American Civil Liberties Union Legal Study, mimeographed, 1971, p. 1.

85. Testimony of United States Secretary of the Army before the Senate Armed Services Committee, 1969, p. 294.

86. For meat boycott, see Brecher and Costello, *Common Sense for Hard Times,* pp. 110-112.

87. *Ibid.*, pp. 112-113.

88. Glenn Perusek, "Leadership and Opposition in the United Automobile Workers," in Perusek and Worcester, ed., *Trade Union Politics,* p. 174.

89. *Ibid.*, p. 182.

Notes to Chapter 8:
The Significance of Mass Strikes

1. James Bryce, 1888, quoted in Henry David, *The History of the Haymarket Affair* (New York: Collier Books, 1963), p. 39.

2. Charles R. Walker, *American City: A Rank-and-File History* (New York: Farrar and Rinehart, 1937), p. xiii.

3. P. Taft and P. Ross, "American labor violence: its causes, character and outcome," in *Violence in America,* ed. H.D. Graham and T.R. Gurr (New York: Praeger, 1970), p. 281.

4. Marcus Raskin, *Being and Doing* (New York: Random House, 1971), p. xv.

5. Elton Mayo, *The Human Problems of an Industrial Civilization* (Cambridge: Harvard University Press, 1946), cited in Paul Romanto and Ria Stone, *American Worker* (Detroit: Facing Reality Publishing Co., 1947), p. 53.

6. Orvis Collins, Melville Dalton, and Donald Roy, "Restriction of Output and Social Cleavage in Industry" *Applied Anthropology* (Summer 1946): 4.

7. *Ibid.*

8. *Ibid.*, p. 8.

9. *Ibid.*, p. 7.

10. *Ibid.*, p. 9.

11. Donald Roy, "Making Out: A Counter-System of Workers Control of Work Situations and Relations," in *Industrial Man*, ed. Tom Burns (Baltimore: Penguin Books, 1969).

12. Clayton W. Fountain, *Union Guy* (New York: Viking Press, 1949), pp. 28-29.

13. The Commission of Inquiry, Interchurch World Movement, *Report on the Steel Strike of 1919* (New York: Harcourt Brace and Howe, 1920), p. 147.

14. Alvin W. Gouldner, *Wildcat Strike: A Study in Worker-Management Relationships* (New York: Harper and Row, Torchbooks edition, 1965), p. 66.

15. Hugh D. Graham and Ted R. Gurr, *The History of Violence in America: A Report to the National Commission on the Causes and Prevention of Violence* (New York: Bantam Books, 1969), p. 380.

16. *Ibid.*

17. Leon Wolff, *Lockout: The Story of the Homestead Strike of 1892: A Study of Violence, Unionism and the Carnegie Steel Empire* (New York: Harper and Row, 1965), p. 228.

18. *Milwaukee Daily Journal*, May 5, 1886, cited in Roger Simon, "The Bay View Incident and the People's Party in Milwaukee," unpublished paper, 1967, p. 9.

19. Alfred P. Sloan, Jr., January 5, 1937, Kraus Papers, Box 9, cited in Sidney Fine, *Sit-Down: The General Motors Strike of 1936-1937* (Ann Arbor: University of Michigan Press, 1969), p. 182.

20. Louis Adamic, *My America, 1928-1938* (New York: Harper and Brothers Publishers, 1938), p. 409.

21. Robert E. Park, in introduction to E.T. Hiller, *The Strike* (Chicago: University of Chicago Press, 1928), p. x.

22. *Business Week*, March 8, 1941, p. 52, cited in Joel Seidman, *American Labor from Defense to Reconstruction* (Chicago: University of Chicago Press, 1953), p. 46.

23. See Mac Brockway, "Keep on Trucking," in *Root and Branch: The Rise of the Workers Movements* (New York: Fawcett, 1975), pp. 39ff, for a discussion of this phenomenon.

24. Charles R. Walker, *American City: A Rank-and-File History* (New York: Farrar and Rinehart, 1937), p. 239.

25. *Ibid*.

26. Paul Mattick, Jr., in introduction to Anton Pannekoek, *Workers Councils* (Cambridge: Root and Branch Pamphlet 1, 1970), p. ii.

27. History Committee of the Seattle General Strike Committee, *The Seattle General Strike* (Seattle: The Seattle Union Record Publishing Co., 1920), pp. 7-8.

28. Peter Drucker, "What to Do About Strikes," *Collier's*, January 18, 1947, p. 12.

29. See, for example, Walker, pp. 73-6, 203.

30. "Final Report of the Royal Commission on Labor," *Parliament Papers*, 1894.

31. Graham and Gurr, p. 387.

32. J. Raymond Walsh, *C.I.O.: Industrial Unionism in Action* (New York: W.W. Norton, 1937), pp. 173-74.

33. For a summary of the process by which this developed and a discussion of union democracy, see Jeremy Brecher and Tim Costello, "The Sovereignty of the Workers," *Z Magazine*, February 1989.

34. E.A. Ross, "The Trade Unions as a Wage-Fixing Institution," *American Economic Review* (September 1947): 587.

35. Antonio Gramsci, "Unions and Councils—II," *L'Ordine Nuovo*, June 12, 1920, in *New Left Review* 51, p. 39.

36. U.S. Coal Commission, *Report of the United States Coal Commission* 1307 (1925), cited in James Gray Pope, "Labor's Constitution of Freedom," *Yale Law Journal* 106: 4 (January 1997): 969.

37. Judge Gary, *Steel Institute Yearbook* (1920), p. 19, cited in David Brody, *Steelworkers in America: The Non-Union Era* (New York: Harper Torchbooks, 1969), p. 275.

38. Seymour Martin Lipset and Reinhard Bendix, *Social Mobility in Industrial Society* (Berkeley: University of California Press, 1963), p. 106.

39. U.S. Strike Commission, p. 121.

Notes to Chapter 9:
Labor on the Eve of the Millennium

1. Steven Greenhouse, "Strikes Decrease to a 50-Year Low," *New York Times*, January 29, 1996. Current official U.S. statistics on strikes provide only one measure of working-class militance, since they no longer include small strikes, short strikes, wildcat strikes, or other kinds of job action. The number of large strikes rebounded slightly, to 37, in 1996 ("Work Week," *Wall Street Journal*, May 20, 1997).

2. Lawrence Mishel, Jared Bernstein, and John Schmitt, *The State of Working America, 1996-97* (Armonk: M.E. Sharpe, 1997), p. 140 (see table of Real Average Weekly Earnings for Production and Nonsupervisory Workers).

3. *Ibid.*, table, p. 48.

4. Quoted in Howell John Harris, *The Right to Manage: Industrial Relations Policies of American Business in the 1940s* (Madison: University of Wisconsin Press, 1982), p. 146.

5. Glenn Perusek, "Leadership and Opposition in the United Automobile Workers," in *Trade Union Politics: American Unions and Economic Change, 1960s-1990s*, ed. Glenn Perusek and Kent Worcester (Atlantic Highlands, New Jersey: Humanities Press, 1995), p. 174.

6. See Chapter 7.

7. Glenn Perusek and Kent Worcester, "Introduction: Patterns of Class Conflict in the United States since the 1960s," in *Trade Union Politics*, p. 10. The impact on workers' action was rather similar to that of the sharp recession of the early 1920s.

8. Profit rates are defined here as net operating surplus divided by net capital stock at current prices. Andrew Glyn, Andrew Hughes, Alain Lipietz, and Agit Singh, "The Rise and Fall of the Golden Age," in *The End of the Golden Age*, ed. Stephen Marglin and Juliet Schor (New York: Oxford University Press, 1989), pp. 39-125, cited in Bennett Harrison, *Lean and Mean: The Changing Landscape of Corporate Power in the Age of Flexibility* (New York: Basic Books, 1994), pp. 125-26.

9. Louis Uchitelle, "That Was Then and This Is the 90's," *New York Times*, June 18, 1997.

10. Quoted in Howard Wachtel, *Money Mandarins: The Making of a New Supranational Economic Order* (New York: Pantheon Books, 1986), p. 137.

11. Harrison, *Lean and Mean*, p. 127.

12. *Ibid.*, pp. 9, 171.

13. *Ibid.*, p. 190.

14. Douglas Fraser, letter of resignation from the Labor-Management Advisory Committee, July 19, 1978, quoted in David Gordon, *Fat and Mean* (New York: Free Press, 1996), p. 205.

15. Perusek and Worcester, "Introduction," *Trade Union Politics*, p. 20, n. 24.

16. *Labor Notes*, January 1990, pp. 7-8. This was during a period when real wages in the United States were actually falling.

17. Perusek and Worcester, "Introduction," *Trade Union Politics*, p. 13.

18. Michael Goldfield, *The Decline of Organized Labor in the United States* (Chicago: University of Chicago Press, 1987), p. 10; *New York Times*, January 29, 1996.

19. Harrison, *Lean and Mean*, p. 115.

20. For a review of informal on-the-job resistance, see Jeremy Brecher and Tim Costello, *Common Sense for Hard Times* (Boston: South End Press, 1977).

21. This account of the Moog strike is based on Dan La Botz, *A Troublemaker's Handbook: How to Fight Back Where You Work—And Win!* (Detroit: Labor Notes, 1991), pp. 117-120.

22. Author interview with Joe Uehlein, July 1, 1997. For a discussion of the implications of "the inside game" strategy, see the correspondence between Stan Weir and Uehlein in the June, August, and October 1987 issues of *Labor Notes*.

23. La Botz, *A Troublemaker's Handbook*, p. 121.

24. Quoted in Jeremy Brecher and Tim Costello, ed., *Building Bridges: The Emerging Grassroots Coalition of Labor and Community* (New York: Monthly Review Press, 1990), pp. 199-200.

25. For a fuller account, see Brecher and Costello, *Building Bridges*.

26. See Bruce Shapiro, "Connecticut LEAP: A New Electoral Strategy," in Brecher and Costello, ed., *Building Bridges*, and David Reynolds, "Building a Party Within a Party: Connecticut's Legislative Electoral Action Program," in *Democracy Unbound: Progressive Challenges to the Two Party System* (Boston: South End Press, 1997), pp. 127-47.

27. Andrew Banks, "Jobs with Justice: Florida's Fight Against Worker Abuse," in Brecher and Costello, ed., *Building Bridges*, pp. 25ff.

28. Michael Peutschuck and Wendy Schaetzel, "Blocking Bork: Grassroots Aspects of a National Coalition," in Brecher and Costello, ed., *Building Bridges*, p. 175.

29. See Jeremy Brecher and Tim Costello, *Global Village or Global Pillage: Economic Reconstruction from the Bottom Up* (Boston: South End Press, 1994), pp. 97-102.

30. La Botz, *A Troublemaker's Handbook*, p. 128.

31. Quoted in La Botz, *A Troublemaker's Handbook*, p. 130.

32. See Brecher and Costello, *Global Village or Global Pillage*, pp. 157-58.

33. "How the USW Hit Marc Rich Where It Hurts," *Business Week*, May 11, 1992, p. 42.

34. *Ibid.*

35. Deliberate violence, such as bombings and assassinations, has been used occasionally by criminal elements in the labor movement but rarely by either rank-and-file workers or labor radicals. See Louis Adamic, *Dynamite: The Story of Class Violence in America* (New York: Harper and Row, 1934).

36. For an evaluation of the Jay strike and of corporate campaigns, see Jane Slaughter, "Corporate Campaigns: Labor Enlists Community Support," in Brecher and Costello, ed., *Building Bridges*, pp. 47ff.

37. Peter Rachleff, *Hard-Pressed in the Heartland: The Hormel Strike and the Future of the Labor Movement* (Boston: South End Press, 1993), p. 50. See also Hardy Green, *On Strike at Hormel: The Struggle for a Democratic Labor Movement* (Philadelphia: Temple University Press, 1990).

38. Rachleff, *Hard-Pressed in the Heartland*, p. 52.

39. *Ibid.*, p. 53.

40. *Ibid.*, p. 55.

41. *Ibid.*, p. 56.

42. *Ibid.*, p. 63.

43. *Ibid.*, p. 68.

44. *Ibid.*, pp. 61-62.

45. *Ibid.*, p. 71.

46. *Ibid.*, p. 72.

47. *Ibid.*, p. 84.

48. *Ibid.*, p. 85.

49. This account is drawn from *Labor Notes*, April 1989.

50. Jim Green, "Camp Solidarity: The United Minewokers, the Pittston Strike, and the New 'People's' Movement," in Brecher and Costello, ed., *Building Bridges*, p. 18.

51. *Labor Notes*, June 1989, p. 15.

52. *Ibid.*, p. 1.

53. *Labor Notes*, March 1990.

54. Green, "Camp Solidarity," in Brecher and Costello, ed., *Building Bridges*, p. 22.

55. *Labor Notes*, August 1989, p. 14.

56. Quoted in *Labor Notes*, September 1989, p. 15.

57. Green, "Camp Solidarity," in Brecher and Costello, ed., *Building Bridges*, p. 21.

58. *Ibid.*, p. 19.

59. *Ibid.*, p. 21.

60. *Labor Notes*, March 1990, p. 14.

61. *Labor Notes*, November 1989, p. 1.

62. *U.S. News and World Report*, January 15, 1990.

63. *The Labor Educator*, January/February 1997, p. 1.

64. Cindia Cameron, "Noon at 9 to 5: Reflections on a Decade of Organizing," in Brecher and Costello, ed., *Building Bridges*, pp. 177ff.

65. Toni Gilpin, Gary Isaac, Dan Letwin, and Jack McKivigan, *On Strike for Respect: The Yale Strike of 1984-85* (Chicago: Charles H. Kerr, 1988), pp. 14-19.

66. *Ibid.*, p. 22.

67. *Ibid.*, p. 25.

68. *Ibid.*

69. *Ibid.*, p. 37.

70. *Ibid.*, p. 45.

71. *Ibid.*, p. 46.

72. *Ibid.*, pp. 65-66.

73. *Ibid.*, p. 2.

74. *Ibid.*, p. 89.

75. John C. Antush, "Chinatown Lockout Defeated," *Against the Current*, July-August 1994.

76. Patricia Lee, "Sisters at the Border: Asian Immigrant Women and HERE Local 2," in Brecher and Costello, ed., *Building Bridges*, pp. 38ff.

77. Gary Delgado, "How the Empress Gets Her Clothes: Asian Immigrant Women Fight Fashion Designer Jessica McClintock," in *Beyond Identity Politics: Emerging Social Justice Movements in Communities of Color*, ed. John Anner (Boston: South End Press, 1996), pp. 81-94.

78. David Levin, "Latino Workers Center Experience," *Against the Current*, September/October 1994.

79. *Labor Notes*, September 1994; *Justice Speaks: Black Workers for Justice*, April 1997.

80. *Boston Globe*, June 25, 1997, and author interview with Tim Costello of the Campaign on Contingent Work, July 1997.

81. Mike Davis, "Police Riot in Century City," *LA Weekly*, June 22-28, 1990, quoted in La Botz, *A Troublemaker's Handbook*, p. 194.

82. On Justice for Janitors, see La Botz, *A Troublemaker's Handbook*, pp. 192-94.

83. *Multiracial Allliance, 1995*, quoted in Michael Eisenscher, *Critical Juncture: Unionism at the Crossroads* (Boston: Center for Labor Research, University of Massachusetts-Boston, 1996), p. 12.

84. *Ibid.*, pp. 12-13.

85. Bureau of National Affairs, *Daily Labor Report*, October 25, 1995.

86. *Ibid.*

87. Bureau of National Affairs, *Daily Labor Report*, Interview, September 1, 1995.

88. Steven Greenhouse, "Union Leader Urges Companies to Forge Alliance With Labor," *New York Times*, October 27, 1996.

89. *New York Times*, February 17, 1997.

90. *Ibid.*

91. Cited by John Sweeney, quoted in Greenhouse, *New York Times*, October 27, 1996.

92. Tom Frank and Dave Mulcahey, *Solidarity in the Heartland* (Westfield, New Jersey: Open Magazine Pamphlet Series, 1996), p. 3.

93. *Labor Notes*, May 1992, p. 11.

94. *Labor Notes*, January 1989, p. 4.

95. *Labor Notes*, February 1996, p. 3 (based on study by CS First Boston).

96. *Labor Notes*, May 1992.

97. *New York Times*, April 16, 1992, quoted in Chris Toulouse, "Political Economy After Reagan," in Perusek and Worcester, ed., *Trade Union Politics*, p. 22.

98. *Labor Notes*, May 1992, p. 11.

99. *Ibid.*, p. 11-12.

100. *Ibid.*, p. 11.

101. *New York Times*, April 16, 1992, quoted in Tolouse, "Political Economy After Reagan," in Persuek and Worcester, ed., *Trade Union Politics*, p. 22.

102. *Labor Notes*, June 1994, pp. 1-14.

103. UAW *Solidarity*, January-February 1997.

104. *Labor Notes*, June 1994, pp. 1-14.

105. *Business Week*, October 31, 1994, quoted in *Labor Notes*, December 1994, p. 1.

106. *Labor Notes*, February 1996, p. 3.

107. UAW *Solidarity*, January-February 1997.

108. *Labor Notes*, October 1994, p. 8.

109. *Labor Notes*, July 1996, p. 11.

110. ICEM *Info* 4 (1996): 5.

111. "The Japanese Owned Bridgestone/Firestone Strike Issues," leaflet signed "URW Local #713 members," Decatur, Illinois.

112. ICEM *Info* 3 (1996).

113. *Labor Notes*, December 1996, p. 14.

114. *Ibid.*

115. Frank and Mulcahey, *Solidarity in the Heartland*, pp. 8-9.

116. *Labor Notes*, August 1995, p. 16.

117. Steven Ashby, quoted in Frank and Mulcahey, *Solidarity in the Heartland*, p. 21.

118. Frank and Mulcahey, *Solidarity in the Heartland*, p. 15.

119. *Labor Notes*, October 1994, pp. 8-9.

120. Marc Cooper, "Harley-Riding, Picket-Walking Socialism Haunts Decatur," *The Nation*, April 8, 1996.

121. *Labor Notes*, May 1995, pp. 5-12.

122. *Labor Notes*, April 1995, p. 3.

123. *Labor Notes*, August 1995, p. 16.

124. *Ibid.*

125. *Labor Notes*, November 1995, p. 6.

126. *Labor Notes*, December 1995, p. 11.

127. Author interview, July 1997.

128. *Labor Notes*, February 1996, p. 11.

129. *Ibid.*, p. 1.

130. Cooper, p. 21.

131. *Labor Notes*, February 1996, p. 11.

132. International Brotherhood of Teamsters News Release, "UPS Shift to 60% Part-Time Workforce Harms Communities, New Studies Show," June 26, 1997 (http://www.teamster.org).

133. Kenneth Labich, "Big Changes at Big Brown," *Fortune*, January 18, 1988, pp. 56-64, cited in Dan La Botz, *Rank-and-File Rebellion: Teamsters for a Democratic Union* (New York: Verso, 1990), p. 218.

134. UPS Comprehensive Safety and Health Manual, "OSHA Recordable Injury Rate," based on December 1995 OSHA data. Supplied by Carolyn Robinson, Secretary-Treasurer, IBT Local 315, Union Chair of the

National IBT-UPS Safety and Health Negotiating Committee, September 1997.

135. *San Francisco Chronicle*, April 15, 1997.

136. "This Package is a Heavy One for the Teamsters," *Business Week*, August 25, 1997.

137. International Brotherhood of Teamsters News Release, "UPS Shift to 60% Part-Time Workforce Harms Communities, New Studies Show," June 26, 1997 (http://www.teamster.org).

138. Reuters, "U.S. Unions Unite Behind UPS Strikers," August 13, 1997.

139. For a detailed account, see La Botz, *Rank-and-File Rebellion*.

140. "This Package is a Heavy One for the Teamsters," *Business Week*, August 25, 1997. See also Jeremy Brecher, "Teamsters Reform: A New Unionism?" *Z Magazine*, February 1992.

141. Reuters, "UPS, Teamsters Extend Talks," August 15, 1997.

142. Reuters, "U.S. Unions Unite Behind UPS Strikers," August 13, 1997.

143. "This Package is a Heavy One for the Teamsters," *Business Week*, August 25, 1997.

144. The strike was the largest in the United States since a three-day Teamsters freight strike of 400,000 in 1976. Reuters, "UPS, Union Reach Tentative Deal to End Strike," August 19, 1997.

145. "UPS Strikers Haul Freight For Delivery Competitors," *Wall Street Journal*, August 18, 1997.

146. "This Package is a Heavy One for the Teamsters," *Business Week*, August 25, 1997.

147. Associated Press, "Striking Teamsters Winning Battle for America's Hearts, Minds," August 15, 1997.

148. *Ibid.*

149. International Confederation of Free Trade Unions OnLine, "UPS: An International Issue," August 13, 1997 (http://www.poptel.org.uk/cgi-bin/bb2web/GEO2:ICTFU-ONLINE?msg=317).

150. "Unions Plan Loan to Teamsters; UPS Warns of Layoffs," *New York Times*, August 13, 1997.

151. Reuters, "UPS, Teamsters Extend Talks," August 15, 1997.

152. Reuters, "UPS Strike Will Hit Economy, Affect Millions," August 4, 1997.

153. Reuters, "UPS, Teamsters Extend Talks," August 15, 1997.

154. "UPS Strikers Haul Freight For Delivery Competitors," *Wall Street Journal*, August 18, 1997.

155. Dirk Johnson, "Rank and File's Verdict: A Walkout Well Waged," *New York Times*, August 20, 1997.

156. *Ibid.*

157. *Ibid.*

158. *Ibid.*

159. *Ibid.*

160. See Staughton Lynd, "The Dayton Strike," *New Politics* (Summer 1996): 55-60.

161. Frank and Mulcahey, *Solidarity in the Heartland*, pp. 26-27.

162. *Ibid.*, p. 23

163. *Ibid.*, p. 25.

164. Quoted in *Impact* 4: 6 (September 1996). Dan Lane notes that he read this story in Ruth McKenney, *Industrial Valley* (New York: Harcourt Brace, 1939).

Index

About South End Press

South End Press is a nonprofit, collectively run book publisher with more than 200 titles in print. Since our founding in 1977, we have tried to meet the needs of readers who are exploring, or are already committed to, the politics of radical social change. Our goal is to publish books that encourage critical thinking and constructive action on the key political, cultural, social, economic, and ecological issues shaping life in the United States and in the world. In this way, we hope to give expression to a wide diversity of democratic social movements and to provide an alternative to the products of corporate publishing.

Through the Institute for Social and Cultural Change, South End Press works with other political media projects—Z *Magazine*, Speak Out, and Alternative Radio—to expand access to information and critical analysis. For a free catalog, please write to: South End Press, 116 Saint Botolph Street, Boston, MA 02115-4818; call 1-800-533-8478; or visit our web site at http://www.lbbs.org/sep.

Other Titles of Interest from South End Press